# Postmodern *After*-Images

# Postmodern
# *After*-Images
## A Reader in Film, Television and Video

Edited by

## Peter Brooker and Will Brooker

A member of the Hodder Headline Group
LONDON • NEW YORK • SYDNEY • AUCKLAND

First published in Great Britain in 1997 by
Arnold, a member of the Hodder Headline Group,
338 Euston Road, London NW1 3BH
175 Fifth Avenue, New York, NY 10010

Distributed exclusively in the USA by
St Martin's Press, Inc.
175 Fifth Avenue, New York, NY 10010

*British Library Cataloguing in Publication Data*
A catalogue record for this book is available from the British Library

*Library of Congress Cataloging-in-Publication Data*
Postmodern after-images: a reader in film, television, and video /
    edited by Peter Brooker and Will Brooker.
        p.   cm.
        Includes bibliographical references and index.
        ISBN 0-340-67692-2 (hb). — ISBN 0-340-67691-4 (pb)
        1. Motion pictures—Philosophy.   2. Motion pictures—Social
aspects.   3. Television—Philosophy.   4. Television broadcasting—
Social aspects.   5. Postmodernism—Social aspects.   I. Brooker.
Peter.   II. Brooker, Will. 1970–
PN1995,P6825   1997                                                  96-48152
791.43'01—dc21                                                        CIP

ISBN 0 340 67692 2 (hb)
ISBN 0 340 67691 4 (pb)

Typeset in 10/11pt Palatino by Saxon Graphics Ltd, Derby
Printed and bound in Great Britain by
J W Arrowsmith Ltd, Bristol

*To Joe,*
*a James Joyce amongst jangly guitarists*

# Contents

**Video: commerce and collage**   **225**

# Acknowledgements

Grateful acknowledgement is made to the following authors and publishers for permission to reproduce material in this book previously published eleswhere. Every effort has been made to trace copyright holders. If any have been inadvertently overlooked the publisher will be pleased to make the necessary arrangements at the first opportunity.

Fredric Jameson, 'The nostalgia mode', from 'Postmodernism and consumer society,' in E. Ann Kaplan, ed., *Postmodernism and its discontents*, Verso, 1988.

Linda Hutcheon, 'Postmodern film?', from *The politics of postmodernism*, Routledge, 1989.

Barbara Creed, 'From here to modernity', from *Screen*, 1987, Oxford University Press and the author.

David Harvey, 'Time and space in the postmodern cinema', from *The condition of postmodernity*, Basil Blackwell, 1989.

Scott Bukatman, "Who programs you"? The science fiction of the spectacle', from A. Kuhn, ed., *Alien zone*, Verso, 1990.

Vivian Sobchack, 'Postmodern modes of ethnicity', from L.D. Friedman, ed., *Unspeakable images. Ethnicity and the American cinema*, © 1991 by the Board of Trustees of the University of Illinois. Used with the permission of the author and the University of Illinois Press.

Kobena Mercer, 'Recoding narratives of race and nation', from *Black film, British cinema*, The Institute of Contemporary Arts, London, 1988. (A later version of this article also appeared in *Welcome to the jungle*, Routledge, 1995.)

Marshall McLuhan, from Marshall McLuhan and Quentin Fiore, *The medium is the massage*, produced by Jerome Agel, copyright © 1967 by Jerome Agel (2 Peter Cooper Road, New York, New York 10010, USA).

Umberto Eco, 'A guide to the Neo-Television of the 1980s', Paul Willeman and *Framework*, 1984.

Jean Baudrillard, 'The end of the panopticon', from *Simulacra and simulation*, trans. Sheila Faria Glaser, Ann Arbor The University of Michigan, 1994.

Jean Baudrillard, 'The reality gulf', from *The Guardian*, 11 January 1991.

Christopher Norris, 'Postscript', from *Uncritical theory: postmodernism, intellectuals and the Gulf War*, Lawrence & Wishart, 1992.

Douglas Kellner, '*Beavis and Butt-Head*. No future for postmodern youth', from *Media culture*, Routledge, 1995.

Marie Gillespie, 'Ambivalent positionings: the Gulf War', from *Television, ethnicity and cultural change*, Routledge, 1995, and the author.

Jim Collins, 'Television and postmodernism', from R.C. Allen, ed., *Channels of discourse, reassembled: Television and contemporary criticism*, copyright © 1992 by the University of North Carolina Press. Used by permission of the publisher.

Lynne Joyrich, 'Critical and textual hypermasculinity', from P. Mellencamp, ed., *Logics of Television*, Indiana University Press, 1990.

Peter Wollen, 'Ways of thinking about music video (and Postmodernism), from C. MacCabe, ed., *Futures for English*, Macmillan, 1988.

E. Ann Kaplan, 'Feminism/Oedipus/postmodernism', from E. Ann Kaplan, ed., *Postmodernism and its discontents*, Verso, 1988, and the author.

E. Ann Kaplan, from *Rocking around the clock. Music television, postmodernism and consumer culture*, Routledge,1987, and the author.

Fredric Jameson, 'Surrealism without the unconscious' and 'Nostalgia for the present' from *Postmodernism, or, the cultural logic of late capitalism*, copyright 1991, Duke University Press, Durham, NC. Reprinted with permission of the publisher and author.

Patricia Mellencamp, 'Uncanny Feminism', from *Indiscretions. Avant-garde film, video and feminism*, Indiana University Press, 1990.

Pratibha Parmar, 'That moment of emergence', from M. Gever, P. Parmar and J. Greyson, eds, *Queer looks. Perspectives on lesbian and gay film and video*, Routledge, 1993.

An earlier version of Peter and Will Brooker's 'Pulpmodernism: Tarantino's affirmative action' appeared in Deborah Cartmell, I. Q. Hunter et al., eds, *Pulping fictions*, Pluto, 1996.

Will Brooker's article 'New Hope: the postmodern project of *Star Wars*' was written for the present volume.

# Introduction

*Peter Brooker and Will Brooker*

## Postmodernisms

From the start 'postmodernism' has been an elastic and somewhat nomadic term. It has ranged across the arts and culture, on the one hand spotlighting particular texts, artists, buildings and environments as conspicuously postmodern, while on the other hand claiming to describe the whole contemporary period of advanced consumer society by naming either its dominant socio-economic trends or its prevailing sensibility. Its most obvious examples have been found in a playful and allusive architecture and literature, or more precisely, 'meta-literature', since one of the most consistent signs of the postmodern has been its ironic self-referentiality. At the same time, postmodernism has been closely associated with, even indebted to, the new visual media and information technologies.

The consequent ubiquity of visual images throughout public culture, in conjunction with an apparently unstoppable process of commodification, prompted Guy Debord, the spokesperson for the anarchistic French Situationists, to speak in the late 1960s of a 'society of the spectacle', and Marshall McLuhan, who had more of an eye to the dramatic evolution and psychic impact of the new technologies, to anticipate a 'global village' of instant communication and cross-cultural community. These prognoses were accentuated in the following decades particularly in the writings of Jean Baudrillard, though increasingly in a tone that was more resigned than protesting or celebratory. Baudrillard famously sees a universe of detached, floating signifiers, free of content and reference. By this reckoning, we inhabit a contemporary society of the image, indeed of the self-generating image, or simulacrum – the copy without an original. Ours is a culture of unrelenting style and surface for which television's flattened screen provides the perfect medium and metaphor. Further developments, in the 1980s and 1990s, from the Walkman to the Internet and embryonic forms of 'virtual reality', would seem only to confirm Baudrillard's description of a symptomatic 'ecstasy of communication' and 'promiscuity' of information, as media and computer industries continue to expand and new technologies to invade domestic and personal space. The body in postmodern times is transformed, augmented spectacularly by implants, or in routine ways by the microchip and computer as it was in an earlier age by the driving wheel and telephone. The result, so it is said, is a loss of boundaries and borders and thus the erosion of common grounds for discrimination and critical distance. Everywhere there is difference which makes no difference. 'Too great a proximity of everything', says Baudrillard, creates a form of schizophrenia (1992, p. 154), a diagnosis adopted by Fredric Jameson who sees in postmodernism a pervasive 'schizophrenia in the form of a rubble of distinct and unrelated signifiers' (1991, p. 26).

Along these lines, unprecedented access to images and information produces its mirror image, a loss of historical sense, the end of artistic originality and the unified subject, or individualism, seen now to be the illusion of an earlier cultural moment. This is the postmodernism of depthless pastiche, made familiar especially by Fredric Jameson, and explored conspicuously elsewhere in the narratives of cyberpunk fiction and film. Here we enter a world of new time–space relations and new permutations on the relation of the human and the machine. In this future-present, information has become the new object of power and vicarious stimulation the order of the day. The individual, in this account, is enveloped in a chaos of 'stylistic diversity and heterogeneity', in Jameson's words, and this is a mere step or reflex away from the global supermarket where goods and styles circulate without hindrance. The global village turns out to be a world market-place, permanently open for business. As Lyotard describes the resulting 'degree zero of contemporary general culture': 'one listens to reggae, watches a western, eats McDonald's food for lunch and local cuisine for dinner, wears Paris perfume in Tokyo and "retro" clothes in Hong Kong; knowledge is a matter of TV games', (1979, p. 76).

It is easy to extrapolate a postmodernism of 'easy come, easy go' from such statements. And, for all its ambiguity, we cannot fail to recognise many of the features of this postmodernism in our lives and the fictions of contemporary culture. Perhaps too, we sense the difficulty of telling our lives and fictions apart. Lyotard, himself, it should be noted, does not endorse this condition (the 'realism of the "anything goes"', he comments, 'is in fact that of money', p. 76). His argument is rather that the 'grand narratives' of intellectual and political thought guiding an earlier modern order are discredited in the present era where we are engaged in the 'language games' of various micro-narratives. This also brings its ambiguities and differences. We might, for instance, find this scenario of the end of 'grand narratives' confirmed in the lack of convincing social and political prospect in national and international life, or choose to resist this analysis in a defence of modernity, or in the interests of a re-grounded long-term social and ethical vision. Alternatively, we might find here a theoretical rationale for a new style of non- or anti-realist narrative, modelled on the flow and bricolage of networked communication systems, or for a style of grass-roots, single-issue or alliance politics.

Such are the positions and continuing debates in postmodernism. For some, indeed, these debates have come to signal a passage, in the late 1980s and 1990s, beyond the postmodern. In the composition of the present volume, we mean to convey a sense of this transition by providing both key, remember, is not the omniscience of individual postmodernist texts, though such programmes and texts do obviously exist, but their co-presence with other modes and the co-existence and mobility of different audiences. If we concede, with Jameson, that postmodernism is a cultural dominant, a context and set of conditions rather than a mere style, then it is clear that it may include modernist, realist and documentary modes within its orbit, and also that, at the very least, the governing assumptions of these modes will be challenged as they pass under its gaze.

It would be false to read off any direct or automatic ideological relation to consumer or late capitalist society from this cultural dominant, however. Postmodernism emerges, once more, whether as broad context or individual text, with mixed potential, its particular accent or effect a matter of purpose, agency and appropriation. Most often, these issues have been focused upon questions of individual and social identity or subjectivity. Does postmodern textual diversity or 'hyperconsciousness' free the individual subject from fixed norms, or confound that subject's self-empowerment in a blanket of difference which in the end converts to sameness? Feminism has long been alert to this problem, in film and media studies as elsewhere. Within cultural studies, TV and the media generally have been understood primarily in terms of their textuality and the subject positions of viewers, a model indebted primarily in the 1970s and the 1980s, through the influence of Stuart Hall in particular, to Antonio Gramsci's concept of hegemony. More recently, attention has turned towards questions of ethnicity in association with other determinations upon the formation of sexual and cultural identity. This comprises one of the most productive areas of dialogue within 'late' postmodernism. Kobena Mercer and Vivian Sobchack take up these issues in their essays on film, as indicated above. As Marie Gillespie confirms of British cultural studies in her study of ethnicity and television, 'debates about "Black Britishness" have been among the most important in cultural studies in the late 1980s and 1990s and indeed, in many ways constitute the most theoretically advanced area within the field in relation to postmodern debates about cultural identity' (1995, p. 6). The work of Stuart Hall and Paul Gilroy has been especially influential here, and Gillespie brings their thinking on the construction and reconstruction of ethnicities within cross-national diasporic formations to her ethnographic study of the 're-creative consumption' of television among Punjabi-British youth in West London in the period 1988–91. Her argument is that a concept such as the 'reinvention of ethnicity' needs to be understood in terms of lived practice, as identities are 'negotiated in everyday discourse' via television (p. 8). We introduce this style of work in the extract from her discussion of the response of young people to the Gulf War news reports.

The questions of appropriation and agency these examples raise, within either the more textualist or ethnographic tradition of cultural studies, suggest there is a further aspect to TV's postmodern plurality which is neither a matter of aesthetic–ideological form nor of cultural identity alone, but involves the relations of an evolving technical apparatus and changed socio-economic order. Marie Gillespie's point is that even as the textualist-ideological model has extended in later work to considerations of ethnic and cultural identity, it has failed to take sufficient account of negotiated meanings as they are lived by actual audiences. But, arguably, neither form of work takes sufficient account of more material developments in media technology, organisation and control. In the 1960s, McLuhan had drawn attention to the influence of the communications apparatus. Print, radio, TV and other technologies he saw as the benign extension of human faculties, enabling the participants of the 'global village' to share the benefits of accelerated transmission and open access to information. Many saw this spectacular scenario as a naive and unhistorical form of technological determinism. But however we interpret its effects, the sheer fact and influence of technological development in media communications is undeniable. The cinema-going experience was altered significantly by the adoption of CinemaScope as *the* film format from the late 1950s and will be altered again by more recent innovations in wide-screen formats, such as IMAX. Meanwhile, our everyday experience of television over recent years has been marked by an unprecedented technological development – chiefly in the introduction of multi-channelled and satellite and cable TV systems, and most recently of digitalised transmission. Such developments alter the conditions in which we watch both film and TV – whether in a wide-screen art-house or multiplex cinema, in a drive-in, in the classroom, in pubs and bars or on different sets at home. Domestic viewing habits themselves have also changed rapidly since the mid 1950s, from the ritualised homage paid to the set in the front room at times of collective family viewing to the flexibility of 'a new regime of watching' as John Hartley describes it, in which people dip 'in and out of TV; in an alternating current of concentration and distraction' (1992, p. 213).

The VCR, as we suggest below, further changed TV's content and viewing habits, bringing in variable scheduling and new viewing constituencies, from teenagers to foreign language audiences, who might effectively use the TV set simply as a monitor. Stereo-television, as Hartley points out, suggests another new and perfectly feasible development in technology and use. Integrated systems, in which the TV's internal sound and visual functions might be separated to free the monitor for other functions, would be built into a total hi-fi system, along with phono, cassette player, FM/AM radio and compact disc functions, each accompanied by their own remote control – in itself, certain proof that the postmodern has entered the home: 'the visible sign', as Hartley says, 'of people's control over not just their own equipment but over the act of looking too' (p. 215).

In another respect, the proliferation of hidden cameras in shopping centres, on motorways, at school gates and cashpoints, even inside telephone boxes, has introduced a new regime of looking, where power lies with a select and invisible few – caretakers, security guards and the police, for example. Closed-circuit television has made us all, *pace* Baudrillard below, the potential objects of a contemporary panopticon, unsure whether we are being watched at any given moment. This phenomenon has met with little resistance, perhaps because of a common sense of its proven success, as in the UK, the use of video to identify the murderers of the two-year-old Jamie Bulger, or the conviction through video evidence of those guilty of violent 'road rage' offences. Nevertheless, this new form of television is already producing artefacts from a culture of surveillance, whether in video art which incorporates police footage or in the 'anti-identification'-style hooded parkas designed for urban youth. Also, important questions of morality, civil rights and censorship have been raised by such video compilations as *Police – Stop!* and *Caught in the Act!*, whose highlights include car crashes and sex in a lift, and by the growing underground mail-order market for video clips of open-air sex and street violence. The world of J.G. Ballard's *Crash* (1964), so admired by Jean Baudrillard, has become the reality of a video world, at the very moment that, all too appropriately, it is filmed in an award-winning but controversial adaptation by David Cronenberg.

This uneasy combination of new technologies, a newly released human 'potential for perversity' and a consequent crisis of values is enacted at the same time in relation to material on the Internet. So-called 'parental control filters' like *Surfwatch* and *Net Nanny* currently enable parents to restrict their children's access, and the more explicit sites have been subject, since the passing of the Communications Decency Act (1996) in the US to censorship of any reference to 'sexual or excretory activities and organs'. The legislation came too late, however, to affect the Internet site for Paul Verhoeven's *Showgirls*, which invited audiences to come backstage to 'talk' to its cast of strippers, and has not yet reached the home pages for fans of Winona Ryder, Drew Barrymore and *The X-Files'* Gillian Anderson, where fantasies and semi-nude images freely circulate.

As such examples suggest, the Internet has altered and augmented the experience of TV and cinema-going, enabling a semi-interactive re-working or re-experiencing of texts, either through 'official' or fan-based sites. The most sophisticated to date, fittingly, is *Toy Story*, which offers state-of-the-art graphics, animated characters, and sound and video clips. Four major soap operas currently run on the Net; the most popular, *East Village*, attracts major advertisers and 35 000 viewers daily, all of whom can talk to their favourite character, subscribe to their 'clique' and access their favourite music tracks. Clearly, the activity of 'consuming' this most standard of TV cultures is undergoing radical changes, if only for a select audience at present.

This variety of venues, along with the altered circumstances of viewing, or being viewed, and the augmented 'sites' of information and exchange, should alert us more to the forms and effects of the technological *apparatus* and in turn alter accounts of how we, or others, 'read' film and TV *texts*. Like other features of postmodern global communications and postmodern society at large, new technologies, like new environments, acquire social meaning from patterns of consumption and use. Both textualist and ethnographic studies seek, in their own terms, to address the creation of such meanings. Yet media texts and the situated social relations in which their meanings are mobilised and negotiated are shadowed by a further local, national, cross-national and global network – the system which arguably seeks to govern the terms of dialogue and identity-formation and to connect people via the interlocking grids of monopoly and multinational control and ownership.

If it is a mistake simply to *identify* postmodernism with late American or Western capitalism, or to see it as consistently reproducing capitalism in the realm of culture, postmodernism as text, context and experience is nevertheless at the very least 'contemporary' with this socio-economic order.

This is what McLuhan failed to consider, and is now what most vexes and divides commentators on the postmodern. The ambiguities of a textual or cultural postmodernism carry through to the nightmare of a totalized system of anonymous control or the utopia of popular multicultural democracy. Neither scenario, we might think, is complex enough to match the circumstances of globalisation or their relation to local or individual use. Apart from anything else, however, these broader implications reveal that a narrowly textualist model, or an interest in media texts and their reception which treats this relation as if it were a disembodied and unlocated transaction, are in themselves inadequate. The postmodern has brought us, amidst the contradictions of late capitalism, to a world of complexly situated discourse, marked by class, gender and ethnicity in a conflictual or consensual relation to the homogenising tendencies of global media products: to dialogic interaction with media messages and to multinational media networks, that is to say, as well as to pastiche and intertextuality.

## Video

One of the developments affecting TV which has been jointly cultural and technological has, of course, been video. The majority of programmes now use video rather than film for live footage and studio work. Also, the widespread use of VCRs gives unprecedented access to the viewing of films and makes it possible for viewers to re-schedule TV programmes at their own convenience. The postmodern combinations across modes and types already implicit in an evening's mixed programming can be infinitely multiplied. We can, in the 1990s, view or review *The Big Sleep*, made in 1946, in the same evening, if we wish, as Eisenstein's *Strike* (1925) and *Judge Dredd* (1995). We can watch previous and present sporting events, comedy shows, soap operas, or what we will, scheduling our own film or TV festival. Beyond TV's and mainstream cinema's own outputs, there are also easily available films made for first-time video rather than cinema release, including soft porn or so-called 'adult' films. That this side of the video industry operates at the bottom end of the market shows how the use of new technology can trouble distinctions between quality and low culture, with all the questions of value and controversy over effects that this trails, but how, once more, questions of artistic or moral value are so evidently entangled in the extending postmodern market-place with arguments about economic value. At the same time, video has an independent life and potential other than as a poor relation or parasite upon TV and film. Technically, its key difference lies in its reproducibility. Video, as we well know but tend to take for granted, can be erased and re-used. Its quality, distribution and reproducibility are therefore markedly different from film and make it open to practically unlimited popular use, whether by viewers or video-makers. In this volume, both Wollen and Jameson recognise video's unique features and synchronicity with descriptions of postmodernism. For Jameson, indeed for all the claims made for film or the media generally as the dominant art forms of the century, video is the more convincing candidate, the 'supreme, and privileged symptomatic, index of the zeitgeist' (1991, p. 69).

Jameson's distinction between the commercial and artistic use of video is a further instance of the relation of the economic and cultural which characterises postmodernism. We might think these uses of video are fairly obviously opposed. If the techniques employed in making art and selling motor-cars are similar, their purposes surely distinguish them in decisive ways, or so we might assume. The world of video and of music videos, in particular, teaches us another lesson, however, as the commentators here point out. Music video has emerged as a recognisable sub-genre with its own unique use of narrative or narrative fragments supporting or more loosely accompanying a lyric. In MTV, of course, it also has its own dedicated TV channel. At one level, music videos are close cousins to the TV commercial, but their song-lyric and performance aspect introduce an aesthetic dimension which arguably raises them above purely commercial interests. For the artist they are vehicles for individual creative expression, while for viewers, likewise engaged in the active production of meanings, they can serve as a means for constructing, deconstructing and reconstructing a taste in music, fashion and thus their own gendered and generational identities. Music video therefore raises the question of exploitation and/or invention, manipulation and/or autonomy, at issue in postmodernism generally. Dick Hebdige and, in the present collection, E. Ann Kaplan offer an early response to this. Kaplan's essay on MTV includes part of her longer discussion of Madonna, whom many commentators – and viewers – return to still in the 1990s. If video is the index of the *Zeitgeist*, Madonna must surely be the index of the index, the metasign of postmodern performance. Yet since this *is* postmodernism, who or what the sign of 'Madonna' signifies is many-sided, mobile and elusive.

The concern with social and cultural meanings in these essays is, for the most part, textually based. This, too, as in the case of studies on TV, implies the making of variant meanings by heterogeneous audiences. Once more, where earlier media studies hypothesised a homogenous audience or saw this as differentiated primarily in terms of social class, more recent work, influenced by post-structuralist and non-Marxist social theory which see the media and society in general as decentred and understand cultural and economic power as exercised in dispersed and multiple ways, suggest that audiences are patterned or grouped in shifting alliances or are the constructions of the institutions which require them. In the arguments for a critical postmodernism, alert to the social and political agendas of the 1990s, the determinants of class, gender, generation, sexuality and ethnicity are viewed alike as affecting the production of meaning, the expression of taste and the composition of social identities. As with televison, this awareness has directed the empirical study of actual audiences and users. For example, in one such study, by Ann Gray, women are shown to have a restricted use of VCR systems within the family home, but as exercising greater choice, productive of different kinds of meaning, when alone or watching with other women (1996).

Clearly, however, work of this kind is still concerned with viewers when, *unlike* TV or film, many video-viewers will also be video-makers. Another perspective would therefore lead to the discussion of home video and access TV, to programmes on British TV such as 'Video Nation', 'Your Shout' or Jeremy Beadle's 'Hot Shots', a programme made up of viewers' imitations and parodies of Hollywood films and adverts. In the USA, the Guerillo TV channel is entirely devoted to viewer videos. Also, there is the widespread 'independent' uses of video by political or pressure groups, local community organisations, or individuals using video to record their own lives or communicate news in 'video letters' to separated family members and friends. With new cameras and equipment it is possible also to make 'scratch videos', combining self-shot and pre-recorded sequences from videotape TV, cassette or CD, and, potentially, to combine these with computer graphics. As yet these independent or commercial and non-commercial 'popular' forms are little studied, and sometimes only rarely practised. Here, we draw attention to the inflection given to the tradition of independent avant-garde video by a feminist postmodernism in the essay by Patricia Mellencamp on Cecilia Condit, and to the difference made by a consciously adopted ethnic and lesbian identity in the essay by the video film-maker, Pratibha Parmar.

These different essays offer positive understandings of video. In one scenario, it appears as the medium which potentially bridges distinctions between the avant-garde and the popular, offering the possibility of pluralistic and transgressive meanings from a marginalised or oppositional position, especially for young people and women. As a hands-on technology, what is more, video is set against the commercial system of Hollywood cinema, and offers not only artists but 'ordinary people' an alternative to the relative passivity of the TV spectator and systems of multinational ownership. Art, whether avant-garde or popular, or a postmodern combination of the two, potentially triumphs over commerce; the local and specific countermands the anonymously global. Like any new technology, however (the Internet most topically), video has an *ambiguous* potential, either for democratic participation or for centralised and exclusive control. In itself, it has no more an automatic aesthetic or economic form or effect than do TV or cinema. It presents us with the interests of advertising and business on the one hand, and the interests of different subordinated groups or alliances and independent, counter-cultural artists on the other. At its most interesting, at the point where the postmodern and its 'after' are emerging, this binary distinction can be unsettled by work which is avant-garde or critical, which is open to theory, cognisant of a burgeoning world of mass media images, and yet seeks to challenge the mainstream or directly intervene in a mainstream TV network. Such is the interest of Mellencamp's video criticism and of Pratibha Parmar's video work.

One last general word is relevant in conclusion. The study of media, as we have indicated, has derived from two main traditions. These have been concerned as a matter of emphasis with, in turn, the relations of the text and reading or reception, sometimes empirically pursued, and with the processes of production. The first has drawn upon theories of discourse, psychoanalysis, ideology and power, whereas the second has been more concerned with institutions and political economy. As such, this describes the difference between cultural and media studies, or text-based studies associated with literary and film criticism on the one hand, and sociology on the other.

The editors of a recent media studies reader (Marris and Thornham, 1996) suggest that the composition of their volume and their own approach has been much influenced by Stuart Hall's work, and in particular his essay 'Encoding decoding' which employed the notion of hegemony, referred to above. Media and cultural studies would appear to have arrived here at a fruitful working relationship. That the editors term their introduction 'Some introductions' suggests the further influence of post-structuralist critique of notions of a single or consensual truth. Yet the contents of the volume, as the editors point out, concentrates on work in television and broadcasting and excludes film. This, they say, is covered elsewhere, in other readers in cultural studies.

So the division persists. Some would see this state of affairs as itself typically postmodernist: disciplines are blurred, but at the same time there is a fragmentation and divergence of specialisms without the coherence or unity of purpose characterising an earlier 'modernist' model. We are pleased that in this reader the inclusion of work on film as well as on TV and video contradicts one division, at least, between areas of study and cultural paradigms. We have wanted also to introduce changes in these fields of work in the belief that this is the very nature of the challenge which 'postmodernism' presents. The 'classic' essays of the 1980s are telling and pertinent still, but do not, and cannot, represent the last word on postmodern media, since this cultural phase in not simply over and a thing of the past, but in transition. 'Postmodernism' is best understood, we believe, as a term for precisely this movement of art, ideas, cultural forms and society. The later arguments which address the themes of ethnicity and feminism and the changing 'structures of feeling' of new generational groups confirm this view. They show, too, in some ways contrary to earlier assumptions, that postmodernism is not without emerging models of critical understanding. Patricia Mellencamp writes of how 'video embodies the historical avant-garde's critique of the constraints and values of institutions, in particular commercial television' (1990, p. xvi ). 'Critique' has been associated of course with the earlier modernist paradigm. To invoke it in this later period does not mean such writers, or film- or video-makers, mean to return to modernist values or methods, since this is a period of commercial TV and mass culture. As Mellencamp writes,

> I chose *avant-garde*, in the end, because of the oppositional stance to institutions, and *postmodern* because of the recycling, quotation, and references of images and sounds (including rock 'n' roll) and the always /already positioning of film and video within mass culture. ( p. xvii)

Earlier strategies are 'reinvented', as she says, in a creative and critical dialogue with the past. We have wanted to stress this aspect of dialogue and to include examples of more recent work where readers/critics are seeking a re-grounded critical practice, one that draws upon, but re-configures, earlier practices and imperatives and so re-inflects postmodernism for contemporary times. The essays by Sobchack, Mercer and ourselves on film, by Collins, Joyrich, Kellner and Gillespie on TV, and by Mellencamp and Parmar on video are of this type. Perhaps they give us some idea of what 'comes after' in the study as well as the practice of postmodern media.

## References

Baudrillard J. 1992: The ecstasy of communication. In Jencks C., (ed.), *The post-modern reader*. London: Academy Editions, 151–7.

Collins J. 1993: Genericity in the nineties. In Collins J., Radner H. and Preacher Collins, A. (eds), *Film theory goes to the movies*. London: Routledge, 242–63.

Diawara M. 1992: *African cinema. Politics and culture*. Bloomington IN: Indiana University Press.

Gillespie M. 1995: *Television, ethnicity and cultural change*. London: Routledge.

Gray A. 1996: Behind closed doors. Video recorders in the home. In Marris P. and Thornham S. (eds), *Media studies. A reader*. Edinburgh: Edinburgh University Press, 327–36.

Hartley J. 1992: *Tele-ology. Studies in television*. London: Routledge.

hooks b. 1993: Postmodern blackness. In Natoli J. and Hutcheon L. (eds), *A postmodern reader*. Albany, NY: State University of New York Press, 510–18.

Jameson F. 1984: Postmodernism, or, the cultural logic of late capitalism. *New Left Review* **146** (July–August), 53–92.

Jameson F. 1990: *Signatures of the visible*. London and New York: Routledge.

Jameson F. 1991: *Postmodernism, or, the cultural logic of late capitalism*. London: Verso.

Jameson F. 1992: *The geopolitical aesthetic. Cinema and space in the world system*. Bloomington, IN: Indiana University Press; London: BFI.

Lyotard J.F. 1979, trans. 1984: *The postmodern condition. A report on knowledge*. Manchester: Manchester University Press.

Marris P. and Thornham S. (eds), 1996: *Media studies. A reader*, Edinburgh: Edinburgh University Press.

Mellencamp P. 1990: *Indiscretions. Avant-garde film, video and feminism*. Bloomington, IN: Indiania University Press.

Taylor C. 1988: Black cinema in the post-aesthetic era. In Pines J. and Willemen P. (eds), *Questions of third cinema*. London: BFI, 90–110,

Yearwood G.L. (ed.) (1982): *Black cinema aesthetics. Issues in independent black film making*. Athens, OH: Ohio University Center for Afro-American Studies.

Young R. 1990: *White mythologies, writing history and the west*. London: Routledge.

West C. 1988: Interview with Cornel West. In Ross A. (ed.), *Universal abandon*. Edinburgh: Edinburgh Univeristy Press, 269–86.

## Further reading

Best S. and Kellner D. 1991: *Postmodern culture. Critical interrogations*. London: Macmillan.

Brooker P. (ed.) 1992: *Modernism/postmodernism*. London: Longman.

Connor S. 1989: *Postmodernist culture*. Oxford: Blackwell.

Docherty T. 1993: *Postmodernism. A reader*. Hemel Hempstead: Prentice Hall/ Harvester.

Ellis J. 1982, rev. 1992: *Visible fictions. Cinema, television, video*. London: Routledge.

Featherstone M. 1991: *Consumer culture and postmodernism*. London and Beverley Hills, CA: Sage.

Foster H. (ed.) 1983: *Postmodern culture*. London: Pluto Press.

Hall S. Hobson D., Lowe A. and Willis P. (eds), 1980: *Culture, media and language*. London: Hutchinson.

Haywood P. and Wollen T. (eds), 1993: *Future visions. New technologies of the screen*. London: BFI.

Hebdige D. 1988: *Hiding in the light*. London: Routledge.

Hutcheon L. 1989: *The politics of postmodernism.* London: Routledge.

Kellner D. 1995: *Media culture.* London: Routledge.

Lash S. and Friedman J. 1992: *Postmodernism and identity.* Oxford: Blackwell

Morley D. and Chen K-H. (eds), 1995: *Stuart Hall. Critical dialogues in cultural studies,* esp. Introduction and Part V. London: Routledge.

Nicholson L. J. (ed.), 1990: *Feminism/postmodernism.* London: Routledge

Poster M. 1995: *The second media age.* Oxford: Polity.

Poster M. 1995: Postmodern virtualities. In Robertson G., Curtis B., et al. (eds), *PostNatural.* London: Routledge.

Strinati D. 1995: *Introduction to theories of popular culture.* London: Routledge.

# Film

## Section I
## Nostalgia and the unknown

The three essays below address the major postmodern theme of the loss of historicity and confirm how, as suggested above, postmodernism, on this as on other topics, is less an object or homogenised event than a set of debates. The two extracts from Jameson illustrate his argument on the loss of historical sense, or rather the substitution for history of an 'idea' of the past, and the evidence for this in 'nostalgia films'. Jameson identifies at least three different types of this common *mode rétro*. Thus, *American Graffiti* or *Chinatown*, for instance, reproduce the atmosphere of the 1950s and 1930s, echoing past styles and popular icons in a 'simulation' only of that earlier period, while *Star Wars* triggers a nostalgia for the movie-going experience of Saturday morning pictures, and *Body Heat* both echoes other films and evokes an 'eternal 1930s . . . beyond history' which blots out any contemporary reference to the 1980s.

In the later extract, Jameson argues of *Blue Velvet* and *Something Wild* that their iconic representations of the 1950s and 1960s are selective and clichéd – stereotypes dressed in the received ideas of those periods. If our relationship to the past is limited to visits to the 'imaginary museum', *Something Wild* returns history to us in the form of a corny waxworks where we find 'the fascinating woman' and 'the leader of the motorcycle gang'. Here, 'evil', embedded in a 1950s style of rebellion, becomes 'playing at being evil' while in *Blue Velvet*'s confrontation between a simulated 1950s small town America and a simulated 'Sixties', 'evil has finally become an image' (pp. 30, 33 below).

Jameson reads these films as allegories of the difficulty of naming the present, of knowing and mapping our postmodern condition – arguments which connect with his discussion elsewhere of film narratives of the 1970s and early 1980s (*Parallax View, All the President's Men, Blow Out* and *Videodrome*) where paranoia and conspiracy theory provide one way, at least, of knowing what is otherwise unknowable, of naming the anonymous yet unprecedentedly invasive system of institutional structures and communication networks (1992, Part One, pp. 9–84).

Discussion of postmodern cinema has frequently returned to Jameson's analysis and to the forms and implications of a self-referential recycling of cinematic styles within and across genres. Linda Hutcheon prefers to think of postmodern narratives as employing less the pastiche Jameson discovers than parody. *Contra* Jameson, she argues that films such as *Body Heat* and *Star Wars* do indeed engage with history and that, rather than a 'nostalgic escapism', they represent the past as we experience it – as contingent, inter-textual and ironically mediated. For her, postmodern film is 'obsessed with history and how we can know the past today', yet revisits that past with a 'double voiced irony' (pp. 39, 40 below) which situates the subject in a position of simultaneous distance and engagement, inside and outside the weave of texts.

Barbara Creed is more directly concerned with the relationship of post-modernism to feminism, a topic much explored since, most often in film studies in discussions of genre, gendered meanings and spectatorships. Jameson is 'in-different' to feminism, Creed feels, and ignores the possibility of differently gendered expressions of nostalgia as well as the implications in his chosen texts of a lost or reasserted partriarchal mastery. She looks else-where, therefore, to Craig Owens' much cited early essay, 'The Discourse of Others' and to Alice Jardine's study *Gynesis* (see References to her essay). Owens, Creed concludes, conflates the postmodern critique of representa-tion and the feminist critique of patriarchy, oversimplifying Lyotard's 'grand narratives' first to 'master narratives' and then to 'narratives of mastery'. Jardine's theory of gynesis – the 'putting into discourse of woman' – Creed finds more productive and she especially employs this in a reading of the hybrid sci-fi horror genre. Gynesis places the feminine within the 'spaces' in the master narrative, the points of lost control. In her analysis of the *Alien* films and their generic counterparts, Creed reads 'woman' – the female body, and especially the process of reproduction – as representing the spaces of the unknown and monstrous. Key moments of 'horror' in *Alien*, *The Fly* and *Videodrome*, therefore, she sees as involving the transformation of the male body into this 'monstrous feminine' – giving birth, metamor-phosing, growing a vagina-like wound.

For Jardine, 'gynesis' is practised by both female and male artists, yet Creed suspects that the latter may be yet another 'ruse of reason'. In conclu-sion, she also warns against any easy affinity between postmodernism and feminism or any totalising explanation – a final and profound difference from Jameson who believes that we stand in need of precisely this.

## Reference

Jameson F. 1992: *The geopolitical aesthetic. Cinema and space in the world system.* Bloomington, IN: Indiana University Press; London: BFI.

# 1

# The nostalgia mode and nostalgia for the present

*Fredric Jameson*

[1]From 'Postmodernism and Consumer Society', in E. Ann Kaplan (ed.) *Postmodernism and its discontents* (Verso 1988).
[2]From *Postmodernism, or, the cultural logic of late capitalism*, F. Jameson. (Verso 1991 and Duke University Press, 1991).

. . . [I]n a world in which stylistic innovation is no longer possible, all that is left is to imitate dead styles, to speak through the masks and with the voices of the styles in the imaginary museum. But this means that contemporary or postmodernist art is going to be about art itself in a new kind of way; even more, it means that one of its essential messages will involve the necessary failure of art and the aesthetic, the failure of the new, the imprisonment in the past.

## The nostalgia mode[1]

As this may seem very abstract, I want to give a few examples, one of which is so omnipresent that we rarely link it with the kinds of developments in high art discussed here. This particular practice of pastiche is not high-cultural but very much within mass culture, and it is generally known as the 'nostalgia film' (what the French neatly call *la mode rétro* – retrospective styling). We must conceive of this category in the broadest way: narrowly, no doubt, it consists merely of films about the past and about specific generational moments of that past. Thus, one of the inaugural films in this new 'genre' (if that's what it is) was Lucas's *American Graffiti*, which in 1973 set out to recapture all the atmosphere and stylistic peculiarities of the 1950s United States, the United States of the Eisenhower era. Polanski's great film *Chinatown* does something similar for the 1930s, as does Bertolucci's *The Conformist* for the Italian and European context of the same period, the fascist era in Italy; and so forth. We could go on listing these films for some time: why call them pastiche? Are they not rather work in the more traditional genre known as the historical film – work which can more simply be theorized by extrapolating that other well-known form which is the historical novel?

I have my reasons for thinking that we need new categories for such films. But let me first add some anomalies: supposing I suggested that *Star*

*Wars* is also a nostalgia film. What could that mean? I presume we can agree that this is not a historical film about our own intergalactic past. Let me put it somewhat differently: one of the most important cultural experiences of the generations that grew up from the 1930s to the 1950s was the Saturday afternoon serial of the Buck Rogers type – alien villains, true American heroes, heroines in distress, the death ray or the doomsday box, and the cliffhanger at the end whose miraculous resolution was to be witnessed next Saturday afternoon. *Star Wars* reinvents this experience in the form of a pastiche: that is, there is no longer any point to a parody of such serials since they are long extinct. *Star Wars*, far from being a pointless satire of such now dead forms, satisfies a deep (might I even say repressed?) longing to experience them again: it is a complex object in which on some first level children and adolescents can take the adventures straight, while the adult public is able to gratify a deeper and more properly nostalgic desire to return to that older period and to live its strange old aesthetic artifacts through once again. This film is thus *metonymically* a historical or nostalgia film: unlike *American Graffiti*, it does not reinvent a picture of the past in its lived totality; rather, by reinventing the feel and shape of characteristic art objects of an older period (the serials), it seeks to reawaken a sense of the past associated with those objects. *Raiders of the Lost Ark*, meanwhile, occupies an intermediary position here: on some level it is *about* the 1930s and 1940s, but in reality it too conveys that period metonymically through its own characteristic adventure stories (which are no longer ours).

Now let me discuss another interesting anomaly which may take us further towards understanding nostalgia film in particular and pastiche generally. This one involves a recent film called *Body Heat*, which, as has abundantly been pointed out by the critics, is a kind of distant remake of *The Postman Always Rings Twice* or *Double Indemnity*. (The allusive and elusive plagiarism of older plots is, of course, also a feature of pastiche.) Now *Body Heat* is technically not a nostalgia film, since it takes place in a contemporary setting, in a little Florida village near Miami. On the other hand, this technical contemporancity is most ambiguous indeed: the credits – always our first cue – are lettered and scripted in a 1930s Art-Deco style which cannot but trigger nostalgic reactions (first to *Chinatown*, no doubt, and then beyond it to some more historical referent). Then the very style of the hero himself is ambiguous: William Hurt is a new star but has nothing of the distinctive style of the preceding generation of male superstars like Steve McQueen or even Jack Nicholson, or rather, his persona here is a kind of mix of their characteristics with an older role of the type generally associated with Clark Gable. So here too there is a faintly archaic feel to all this. The spectator begins to wonder why this story, which could have been situated anywhere, is set in a small Florida town, in spite of its contemporary reference. One begins to realize after a while that the small town setting has a crucial strategic function: it allows the film to do without most of the signals and references which we might associate with the contemporary world, with consumer society – the appliances and artifacts, the high rises, the object world of late capitalism. Technically, then, its objects (its cars, for instance) are 1980s products, but everything in the film conspires to blur that immediate contemporary reference and to make it possible to receive this too as nostalgia work – as a narrative set in some indefinable nostalgic past, an eternal 1930s, say, beyond history. It seems to me exceedingly symptomatic to find the very style of nostalgia films invading and colonizing even those movies today which have contemporary settings: as though, for some reason, we were unable today to focus our own present, as though we have become incapable of achieving aesthetic representations of our own current experience. But if that is so, then it is a terrible indictment of consumer capitalism itself – or, at the very least, an alarming and pathological symptom of a society that has become incapable of dealing with time and history . . . we seem condemned to seek the historical past through our own pop images and stereotypes about that past, which itself remains forever out of reach.

## Nostalgia for the present[2]

. . . [I]f the historical novel 'corresponded' to the emergence of historicity, of a sense of history in its strong modern post-eighteenth-century sense, science fiction equally corresponds to the waning or the blockage of that historicity, and, particularly in our own time (in the postmodern era), to its crisis and paralysis, its enfeeblement and repression. Only by means of a violent formal and narrative dislocation could a narrative apparatus come into being capable of restoring life and feeling to this only intermittently functioning organ that is our capacity to organize and live time historically. Nor should it be thought overhastily that the two forms are symmetrical on the grounds that the historical novel stages the past and science fiction the future.

Historicity is, in fact, neither a representation of the past nor a representation of the future (although its various forms use such representations): it can first and foremost be defined as a perception of the present as history; that is, as a relationship to the present which somehow defamiliarizes it and allows us that distance from immediacy which is at length characterized as a historical perspective. It is appropriate, in other words, also to insist on the historicality of the operation itself, which is our way of conceiving of historicity in this particular society and mode of production; appropriate also to observe that what is at stake is essentially a process of reification whereby we draw back from our immersion in the here and now (not yet identified as a 'present') and grasp it as a kind of thing – not merely a 'present' but a present that can be dated and called the eighties or the fifties. Our presupposition has been that today this is more difficult to achieve than at the time of Sir Walter Scott, when a contemplation of the past seemed able to renew our sense of our own reading present as the sequel, if not particularly the culmination, of that genetic series.

[Philip K. Dick's] *Time Out of Joint*, however, offers a very different machine for producing historicity than Sir Walter Scott's apparatus:[1] what one might in the strong sense call a trope of the future anterior – the estrangement and renewal as history of our own reading present, the fifties, by way of the apprehension of that present as the past of a specific future. The future itself – Dick's 1997 – is not, however, centrally significant as a representation or an anticipation; it is the narrative means to a very different end, namely the brutal transformation of a realistic representation of the present, of Eisenhower America and the 1950s small town, into a memory and a reconstruction. Reification is here indeed built into the novel itself and, as it were, defused and recuperated as a form of praxis: the fifties is a thing, but a thing that we can build, just as the science fiction writer builds his own small-scale model. At that point, then, reification ceases to be a baleful and alienating process, a noxious side-effect of our mode of production, if not, indeed, its fundamental, dynamic, and is rather transferred to the side of human energies and human possibilities. (The reappropriation has, of course, a good deal to do with the specificity of Dick's own themes and ideology – in particular, the nostalgia about the past and the 'petit bourgeois' valorization of small craftsmanship, as well as small business and collecting.)

This novel has necessarily become for us a historical one: for its present – the 1950s – has become our past in a rather different sense than that proposed by the text itself. The latter still 'works': we can still feel and appreciate the transformation and reification of its readers' present into a historical period; we can even, by analogy, extrapolate something similar for our own moment in time. Whether such a process today can be realized concretely, in a cultural artifact, is, however, a rather different question. The accumulation of books like *Future Shock*, the incorporation of habits of 'futurology' into our everyday life, the modification of our perception of things to include their 'tendency' and of our reading of time to approximate a scanning of complex probabilities – this new relationship to our own present both includes elements formerly incorporated in the experience of the 'future' and blocks or forestalls any global vision of the latter as a radically transformed and different system. If catastrophic 'near-future' visions of, say, overpopulation, famine, and anarchic violence are no longer as effective as they were a few years ago, the weakening of those effects and of the narrative forms that were designed to produce them is not necessarily due only to overfamiliarity and overexposure; or rather, this last is perhaps also to be seen as a modification in our relationship to those imaginary near futures, which no longer strike us with the horror of otherness and radical difference. Here a certain Nietzscheanism operates to defuse anxiety and even fear: the conviction, however, gradually learned and acquired, that there is only the present and that it is always 'ours', is a kind of wisdom that cuts both ways. For it was always clear that the terror of such near futures – like the analogous terror of an older naturalism – was class based and deeply rooted in class comfort and privilege. The older naturalism let us briefly experience the life and the life world of the various under-classes, only to return with relief to our own living rooms and armchairs: the good resolutions it may also have encouraged were always, then, a form of philanthropy. In the same way, yesterday's terror of the overcrowded conurbations of the immediate future could just as easily be read as a pretext for complacency with our own historical present, in fear is that of proletarianization, of slipping down the ladder, of losing a comfort and a set of privileges which we tend increasingly to think of in spatial terms: privacy, empty rooms, silence, walling other people out, protection against crowds and other bodies. Nietzschean wisdom, then, tells us to let go of that kind of fear and reminds us that whatever social and spatial form our future misery may take, it will not be alien because it will by definition be ours. *Dasein ist je mein eigenes* – defamiliarization, the shock of otherness, is a mere aesthetic effect and a lie.

Perhaps, however, what is implied is simply an ultimate historicist breakdown in which we can no longer imagine the future at all, under any form – Utopian or catastrophic. Under those circumstances, where a formerly futurological science fiction (such as so-called cyberpunk today) turns into mere 'realism' and an outright representation of the present, the possibility Dick offered us – an experience of our present as past and as history – is slowly excluded. Yet everything in our culture suggests that we have not, for all that, ceased to be preoccupied by history; indeed, at the very moment in which we complain, as here, of the eclipse of historicity, we also universally diagnose contemporary culture as irredeemably historicist, in the bad sense of an omnipresent and indiscriminate appetite for dead styles and fashions; indeed, for all of historical thinking – which we may not even call *generational* any longer, so rapid has its momentum become – has also become universal and includes at least the will and intent to return upon our present circumstances in order to think of them – as the nineties, say – and to draw the appropriate marketing and forecasting conclusions. Why is this not historicity with a vengeance? and what is the difference between this now generalized approach to the present and Dick's rather cumbersome and primitive laboratory approach to a 'concept' of his own fifties?

In my opinion, it is the structure of the two operations which is instructively different: the one mobilizing a vision of the future in order to determine its return to a now historical present; the other mobilizing, but in some new allegorical way, a vision of the past, or of a certain moment of the past. Several recent films (I will here mention *Something Wild* and *Blue Velvet*) encourage us to see the newer process in terms of an allegorical encounter; yet even this formal possibility will not be properly grasped unless we set in place its preconditions in the development of nostalgia film generally. For it is by way of so-called nostalgia films that some properly allegorical processing of the past becomes possible: it is because the formal apparatus of nostalgia films has trained us to consume the past in the form of glossy images that new and more complex 'postnostalgia' statements and forms become possible. I have elsewhere tried to identify the privileged raw material or historical content of this particular operation of reification and of the transformation into the image in the crucial antithesis between the twenties and the thirties, and in the historicist revival of the very stylistic expression of that antithesis in art deco. The symbolic working out of that tension – as it were, between Aristocracy and Worker – evidently involves something like the symbolic reinvention or production of a new Bourgeoisie, a new form of identity. Yet like photorealism, the products themselves are bland in their very visual elegance, while the plot structures of such films suffer from a schematization (or typification) which seems to be inherent in the project. While we may anticipate more of these, therefore, and while the taste for them corresponds to more durable features and needs in our present economicopsychic constitution (image fixation *cum* historicist cravings), it was perhaps only to be expected that some new and more complicated and interesting formal sequel would rapidly develop.

What was more unexpected – but very 'dialectical' indeed, in a virtually textbook way – was the emergence of this new form from a kind of cross, if not synthesis, between the two filmic modes we had until now been imagining as antithetical: namely, the high elegance of nostalgia films, on the one hand, and the grade-B simulations of iconoclastic punk film, on the other. We failed to see that both were significantly mortgaged to music, because the musical signifiers were rather different in the two cases – the sequences of high-class dance music, on the one hand, the contemporary proliferation of rock groups, on the other. Meanwhile, any 'dialectical' textbook of the type already referred to might have alerted us to the probability that an ideologeme of 'elegance' depends in some measure on an opposite of some kind, an opposite and a negation which seems in our time to have shed its class content (still feebly alive when the 'beats' were felt to entertain a twin opposition to bourgeois respectability and high modernist aestheticism), and to have gradually migrated into that new complex of meanings that bears the name *punk*.

The new films, therefore, will first and foremost be allegories of that, of their own coming into being as a synthesis of nostalgia-deco and punk: they will in one way or another tell their own stories as the need and search for this 'marriage' (the wonderful thing about aesthetics – unlike politics, alas – being that the 'search' automatically becomes the thing itself: to set it up is by definition to realize it). Yet this resolution of an aesthetic contradiction is not gratuitous, because the formal contradiction itself has a socially and historically symbolic significance of its own.

But now the stories of these two films need to be briefly outlined. In *Something Wild* a young 'organization man' is abducted by a crazy girl, who initiates him into cutting corners and cheating on credit cards, until her husband, an ex-convict, shows up and, bent on vengeance, pursues the couple. In *Blue Velvet*, on the other hand, a young high-school graduate discovers a severed ear, which puts him on the trail of a torch singer mysteriously victimized by a local drug dealer, from whom he is able to save her.

Such films indeed invite us to return somehow to history: the central scene of *Something Wild* – or at least the one on which the plot structure pivots decisively – is a class reunion, the kind of event which specifically demands historical judgments of its participants: narratives of historical trajectories, as well as evaluations of moments of the pat nostalgically re-evoked but necessarily rejected or reaffirmed. This is the wedge, or opening, through which a hitherto aimless but lively filmic narrative suddenly falls into the deeper past (or that deeper past into it); for the ten-year reunion in reality takes us back twenty more, to a time when the 'villain' unexpectedly emerges, over your shoulder, marked as 'familiar' in all his unfamiliarity to the spectator (he is the heroine's husband, Ray, and worse). 'Ray' is, of course, in one way yet another reworking of that boring and exhausted paradigm, the gothic, where – on the individualized level – a sheltered woman of some kind is terrorized and victimized by an 'evil' male. I think it would be a great mistake to read such literature as a kind of protofeminist denunciation of patriarchy and, in particular, a protopolitical protest against rape. Certainly the gothic mobilizes anxieties about rape, but its structure gives us the clue to a more central feature of its content which I have tried to underscore by means of the word *sheltered*.

Gothics are indeed ultimately a class fantasy (or nightmare) in which the dialectic of privilege and shelter is exercised: your privileges seal you off from other people, but by the same token they constitute a protective wall through which you cannot see, and behind which therefore all kinds of envious forces may be imagined in the process of assembling, plotting, preparing to give assault; it is, if you like, the shower-curtain syndrome (alluding to Hitchcock's *Psycho*). That its classical form turns on the privileged content of the situation of middle-class women – the isolation, but also the domestic idleness, imposed on them by newer forms of middle-class marriage – adds such texts, as symptoms, to the history of women's situations but does not lend them any particular political significance (unless that significance consists merely in a coming to self-consciousness of the disadvantages of privilege in the first place). But the form can also, under certain circumstances, be reorganized around young men, to whom some similarly protective distance is imputed: intellectuals, for example, or 'sheltered' young briefcase-carrying bureaucrats, as in *Something Wild* itself. (That this gender substitution risks awakening all kinds of supplementary sexual overtones is here self-consciously dramatized in the extraordinary tableau moment in which the stabbing, seen from behind – and from the woman's visual perspective – looks like a passionate embrace between the two men.) The more formal leap, however, will come when for the individual 'victim' – male or female – is substituted the collectivity itself, the U.S. public, which now lives out the anxieties of its economic privileges and its sheltered 'exceptionalism' in a pseudo-political version of the gothic – under the threats of stereotypical madmen and 'terrorists' (mostly Arabs or Iranians for some reason). These collective fantasies are less to be explained by some increasing 'feminization' of the American public self than by its guilt and the dynamics of comfort already referred to. And like the private version of the traditional gothic romance, they depend for their effects on the revitalization of *ethics* as a set of mental categories, and on the reinflation and artificial reinvigoration of that tired and antiquated binary opposition between virtue and vice, which the eighteenth century cleansed of its theological remnants and thoroughly sexualized before passing it on down to us.

The modern gothic, in other words – whether in its rape-victim or its political-paranoid forms – depends absolutely in its central operation on the construction of *evil* (forms of the good are notoriously more difficult to construct, and generally draw their light from the darker concept, as though the sun drew its reflected radiance from the moon). Evil is here, however, the emptiest form of sheer Otherness (into which any type of social content can be poured at will). I have so often been taken to task for my arguments against ethics (in politics as well as in aesthetics) that it seems worth observing in passing that Otherness is a very dangerous category, one we are well off without; but fortunately, in literature and culture, it has also become a very tedious one. Ridley Scott's *Alien* may still get away with it (but then, for science fiction, all of Lem's work – in particular the recent *Fiasco* – can be read as an argument against the use of such a category even there); but surely Ray of *Something Wild* and Frank Booth of *Blue Velvet* don't scare anybody any longer; nor ought we really to require our flesh to creep before reaching a sober and political decision as to the people and forces who are collectively 'evil' in our contemporary world.

On the other hand, it is only fair to say that Ray is not staged demonically, as a representation of evil as such, but rather as the representation of someone *playing at being evil*, which is a rather different matter. Nothing about Ray, indeed, is particularly authentic; his malevolence is as false as his smile; but his clothes and hairstyle give a further clue and point us in a different direction from the ethical one. For not only does Ray offer a simulation of evil, he also offers a simulation of the *fifties*, and that seems to me a far more significant matter. I speak of the oppositional fifties, to be sure: the fifties of Elvis rather than the fifties of Ike, but I'm not sure we can really tell the difference any more, as we peer across our historical gap and try to focus the landscape of the past through nostalgia-tinted spectacles.

At this point, however, the gothic trappings of *Something Wild* fall away and it becomes clear that we have to do here with an essentially allegorical narrative in which the 1980s meet the 1950s. What kind of accounts actuality has to settle with this particular historicist ghost (and whether it manages to do so) is for the moment less crucial than how the encounter was arranged in the first place: by the intermediary and the good offices of the 1960s, of course – inadvertent good offices to be sure, since Audrey/Lulu has very little reason to desire the connection, or even to be reminded of her own past, or Ray's (he has just come out of prison).

Everything turns, therefore, or so one would think, on this distinction between the sixties and the fifties: the first desirable (like a fascinating woman), the second fearful and ominous, untrustworthy (like the leader of a motorcycle gang). As the title suggests, it is the nature of 'something wild' which is at stake, the inquiry into it focused by Audrey's first glimpse of Charley's nonconformist character (he skips out on his lunch bill). Indeed, the nonpaying of bills seems to function as the principal index for Charley's 'hipness' or 'squareness' – it being understood that neither of these categories (nor those of conformity/nonconformity used above) corresponds to the logic of this film, which can be seen as an attempt very precisely to construct new categories with which to replace those older, historically dated and period-bound (uncontemporary, unpostmodern) ones. We may describe this particular 'test' as involving white-collar crime, as opposed to the 'real,' or lower-class, crime – grand theft and mayhem – practiced by Ray himself. Only it is a petit-bourgeois white-collar crime (even Charley's illicit use of company credit cards is scarcely commensurable with the genuine criminality his corporation can be expected, virtually by definition, to imply). Nor are such class markers present in the film itself, which can in another sense be seen very precisely as an effort to repress the language and categories of class and class differentiation and to substitute for them other kinds of semic oppositions still to be invented.

Those necessarily emerge in the framework of the Lulu character, within the sixties allegory (which is something like the 'black box' of this particular semic transformation). The fifties stands for genuine rebellion, with genuine violence and genuine consequences, but also for the *romantic representations* of such rebellion, in the films of Brando and James Dean. Ray thus functions both as a kind of gothic villain, within this particular narrative, and also, on the allegorical level, as the sheer *idea* of the romantic hero – the tragic protagonist of another kind of film, that can no longer be made. Lulu is not herself an alternate possibility, unlike the heroine of *Desperately Seeking Susan*. The framework here remains exclusively male, as the lamentable ending – her chastening, or taming – testifies, along with the significance of clothing, which we will look at in a moment. Everything depends, therefore, on the new kind of *hero* Lulu somehow allows or enables Charley to become, by virtue of her own semic composition (since she is a good deal more than a mere woman's body or fetish).

What is interesting about that composition is that it first of all gives us the sixties seen, as it were, through the fifties (or the eighties?): alcohol rather than drugs. The schizophrenic, drug-cultural side of the sixties is here systematically excluded along with its politics. What is dangerous, in other words, is not Lulu at her most frenzied but rather Ray; not the sixties and its countercultures and 'life-styles' but the fifties and its revolts. Yet the continuity between the fifties and the sixties lay in what was being revolted *against*, in what life-style the 'new' life-styles were alternatives *to*. It is, however, difficult to find any content in Lulu's stimulating behavior, which seems organized around sheer caprice; that is to say, around the supreme value of remaining unpredictable and immune to reification and categorization. Shades of André Gide, in *Lafcadio's Adventures*, or of all those Sartrean characters desperately attempting to evade that ultimate objectification by another's Look (it is impossible, and they end up simply being labeled 'capricious'). The costume changes lend this otherwise purely formal unpredictability a certain visual content; they translate it into the language of image culture and afford a purely specular pleasure in Lulu's metamorphoses (which are not really psychic).

Yet viewers and protagonist still have to feel that they are on their way somewhere (at least until the appearance of Ray gives the film a different kind of direction): as thrilling and improvised as it seems, therefore, Lulu's abduction of Charley from New York has at least an empty form that will be instructive, for it is the archetypal descent into Middle America, into the 'real' United States, either of lynching and bigotry or of true, wholesome family life and American ideals; one doesn't quite know which. Nonetheless, like those Russian populist intellectuals in the nineteenth century setting forth on foot to discover 'the people', something like this journey is or was the *scène à faire* for any American allegory worthy of its vocation: what this one reveals, however, is that there is no longer anything to discover at the end of the line.

For Lulu/Audrey's family – reduced in this case to a mother – is no longer the bourgeoisie of sinister memory: neither the sexual repression and respectability of the fifties nor the Johnsonia authoritarianism of the sixties. This mother plays the harpsichord, 'understands' her daughter, and is fully as much an oddball as everybody else. No Oedipal revolts are possible any longer in this American small town, and with them all the tension goes out of the social and cultural dynamics of the period. Yet if there are no longer any 'middle classes' to be found in the heartland, there is something else that may serve as something for a substitute for them, at least in the dynamic of narrative structure itself: for what we find at Lulu's class reunion (besides Ray and her own past) is Charley's business colleague, that is to say, a yuppie bureaucrat, along with his pregnant wife. These are unquestionably the baleful parents we sought, but of some distant and not quite imaginable future, not of the older, traditional American past: they occupy the semic slot of the 'squares', but without any social basis or content any longer (they can scarcely be read as embodiments of the Protestant ethic, for example, or of puritanism or white racism or patriarchy). But they at least help us to identify the deeper ideological purpose of this film, which is to differentiate Charley from his fellow yuppies by making him over into a hero or protagonist of a different generic type than Ray. Unpredictability, as we have shown, in a matter of *fashion* (clothing, hairstyle, and general body language): Charley himself must therefore pass through this particular matrix, and his metamorphosis is concretely realized, appropriately enough, when he sheds his suit for a more relaxed and tourist-type disguise (T-shirt, shorts, dark glasses, etc.). At the end of the film, of course, he also sheds his corporate job; but it would probably be asking too much to wonder what he does or can become in its stead, except in the 'relationship' itself, where he becomes the master and the senior partner. The semic organization of all this might be laid out as follows (and symmetry preserved by seeing the pregnant and disapproving yuppie wife as the concrete manifestation of the neutral term):

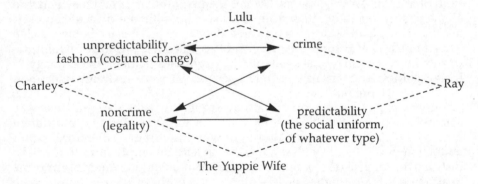

The Yuppie Wife

We have not yet mentioned the handcuffs, which can serve as the transition to a similar type of narrative allegory, one whose combinations and atmosphere are very different from this one. *Blue Velvet*, indeed, tries to place sadomasochism squarely on the mass-cultural map with an earnestness altogether lacking in the Demme movie (whose handcuff love scene is as sexy as it is 'frivolous'. S&M thus becomes the latest and the last in the long line of those taboo forms of content which, beginning with Nabokov's nymphets in the 1950s, rise one after the other to the surface of public art in that successive and even progressive widening of transgressions which we once called the counterculture, or the sixties. In *Blue Velvet*, however, it is explicitly related to drugs, and therefore to crime – although not exactly organized crime, rather to a collectivity of misfits and oddballs – the transgressive nature of this complex of things being tediously reinforced by repetitive obscenity (on the part of the Dennis Hopper character).

Yet if history is discreetly evoked and invoked in *Something Wild*, it is rather its opposite – Nature – which is given us as the overall frame and inhuman, transhuman perspective in which to contemplate the events of *Blue Velvet*. The father's stroke, which opens the film like an incomprehensible catastrophe – an act of God which is peculiarly an act of scandalous violence within this peaceful American small town – is itself positioned by David Lynch (director of *Eraserhead* and *Dune*) within the more science fictional horizon of the Darwinian violence of all nature. From the shot of the father lying paralyzed, the camera withdraws into the bushes surrounding the house, enlarging its microscopic focus as it does so, until we confront a horrible churning which we take first and generically, in good horror-film format, to be the hidden presence of the maniac, until it proves to be the mandibles of an insatiable insect. The later insistence on robins with worms twisting desperately in their beaks also reinforces this cosmic sense of the dizzying and nauseating violence of all nature – as though within this ferocity without boundaries, this ceaseless bloodshed of the universe as far as the eye can see or thought can reach, a single peaceful oasis had been conquered by the progress of humanity and whatever divine providence guided it; namely – unique in the animal kingdom as well as in the horrors of human history as well – the North American small town. Into this precious and fragile conquest of civilized decorum wrenched from a menacing outside world, then, comes violence – in the form of a severed ear; in the form of an underground drug culture and of a sado-masochism about which it is finally not yet really clear whether it is a pleasure or a duty, a matter of sexual gratification or just another way of expressing yourself.

History therefore enters *Blue Velvet* in the form of ideology, if not of myth: the Garden and the Fall, American exceptionalism, a small town far more lovingly preserved in its details like a simulacrum or Disneyland under glass somewhere than anything the protagonists of *Something Wild* were able to locate on their travels, complete with high-school leads on the order of the most authentic fifties movies. Even a fifties-style pop psychoanalysis can be invoked around this fairy tale, since besides a mythic and sociobiological perspective of the violence of nature, the film's events are also framed by the crisis in the paternal function – the stroke that suspends paternal power and authority in the opening sequence, the recovery of the father and his return from the hospital in the idyllic final scene. That the other father is a police detective lends a certain plausibility to this kind of interpretation, which is also strengthened by the abduction and torture of the third, absent, father, of whom we only see the ear. Nonetheless the message is not particularly patriarchal-authoritarian, particularly since the young hero manages to assume the paternal function very handily: rather, this particular call for a return to the fifties coats the pill by insistence on the unobtrusive benevolence of all these fathers – and, contrariwise, on the unalloyed nastiness of their opposite number.

For this gothic subverts itself fully as much as *Something Wild*, but in a rather different way. There, it was the simulated nature of Ray's evil that was underscored for us even while he remained a real threat: revolt, statutory illegality, physical violence, and ex-convicts are all genuine and serious matters. What *Blue Velvet* gives us to understand about the sixties, in contrast, is that despite the grotesque and horrendous tableaux of maimed bodies, this kind of evil is more distasteful than it is fearful, more disgusting than threatening: here evil has finally become an image, and the simulated replay of the fifties has generalized itself into a whole simulacrum in its own right. Now the boy without fear of the fairy tale can set out to undo this world of baleful enchantment, free its princess (while marrying another), and kill the magician. The lesson implied by all this – which is rather different from the lesson it transmits – is that it is better to fight drugs by portraying them as vicious and silly, than by awakening the full tonal range of ethical judgments and indignations and thereby endowing them with the otherwise glamorous prestige of genuine Evil, of the Transgressive in its most august religious majesty. Indeed, this particular parable of the end of the sixties is also, on another metacritical level, a parable of the end of theories of transgression as well, which so fascinated that whole period and its intellectuals. The S&M materials, then – even though contemporary with a whole new postmodern punk scene – are finally called on to undo themselves and to abolish the very logic on which their attraction/repulsion was based in the first place.

Thus these films can be read as dual symptoms: they show a collective unconscious in the process of trying to identify its own present at the same time that they illuminate the failure of this attempt, which seems to reduce itself to the recombination of various stereotypes of the past. Perhaps, indeed, what follows upon a strongly generational self-consciousness, such as what the 'people of the sixties' felt, is often a peculiar aimlessness. What if the crucial identifying feature of the next 'decade' is, for example, a lack of just such strong self-consciousness, which is to say a constitutive lack of identity in the first place? This is what many of us felt about the seventies, whose specificity seemed most of the time to consist in having no specificity, particularly after the uniqueness of the preceding period. Things began to pick up again in the eighties, and in a variety of ways. But the identity process is not a cyclical one, and this is essentially the dilemma. Of the eighties, as against the seventies, one could say that there were new political straws in the wind, that things were moving again, that some impossible 'return of the sixties' seemed to be in the air and in the ground. But the eighties, politically and otherwise, have not really resembled the sixties, especially, particularly if one tried to define them as a return or a reversion. Even that enabling costume-party self-deception of which Marx spoke – the wearing of the costumes of the great moments of the past – is no longer on the cards in an ahistorical period of history. The generational *combinatoire* thus seems to have broken down at the moment it confronted serious historicity, and the rather different self-concept of 'postmodernism' has taken its place.

Dick used science fiction to see his present as (past) history; the classical nostalgia film, while evading its present altogether, registered its historicist deficiency by losing itself in mesmerized fascination in lavish images of specific generational pasts. The two 1986 movies, while scarcely pioneering a wholly new form (or mode of historicity), nonetheless seem, in their allegorical complexity, to mark the end of that and the now open space for something else.

## Editors' note

1. Jameson writes of how Philip K. Dick's novel *Time Out of Joint* (1959):

evokes the fifties: President Eisenhower's stroke; Main Street, U.S.A.; Marilyn Monroe; a world of neighbors and PTAs; small retail chain stores (the produce trucked in from the outside); favorite television programs; mild flirtations with the housewife next door; game shows and contests; sputniks distantly revolving overhead, mere blinking lights in the firmament, hard to distinguish from airliners or flying saucers.

At the same time there is a twist, Jameson notes, which turns the novel into science fiction:

> for it transpires, from an increasing accumulation of tiny but aberrant details, that the environment of the novel, in which we watch the characters act and move, is not really the fifties after all (I do not know that Dick ever uses this particular word). It is a Potemkin village of a historical kind: a reproduction of the 1950s – including induced and introjected memories and character structures in its human population – constructed (for reasons that need not detain us here) in 1997, in the midst of an interstellar atomic civil war.

# 2

# Postmodern film?

## Linda Hutcheon

From *The politics of postmodernism* (Routledge 1989)

In his article, 'Metacinema: a modern necessity,' William Siska characterizes 'modernist' cinema in terms of a new kind of self-reflexivity, one that challenges the traditional Hollywood variety of movies about movie-making that retain the orthodox realist notion of the transparency of narrative structures and representations: *Sunset Boulevard, Day for Night, Singin' in the Rain* (Siska 1979: 285). The 'modernist' contesting of this, he argues, takes the form of an insistence on formal intransitivity by such techniques as the rupturing of the chain of causation upon which character and plot motivation depend, spatial or temporal fragmentation, or the introduction of 'alien forms and information' (286). Examples would include *W. R., Persona*, and *8½*. But what happens when the 'alien' form introduced is parody? And what if it is that very self-conscious introduction of the 'alien' that is itself being parodied? What happens when we get Woody Allen's *Stardust Memories* parodying and challenging, however respectfully, Fellini's modernist *8½*?

What happens, perhaps, is something we should label as postmodern, something that has the same relation to its modernist past as can be seen in postmodern architecture today: both a respectful – if problematized – awareness of cultural continuity and a need to adapt to changing formal demands and social conditions through an ironic contesting of the authority of that same continuity. The postmodernist is in this sense less radical than the modernist; it is more willfully compromised, more ideologically ambivalent or contradictory. It at once exploits and subverts that which went before, that is, both the modernist and the traditionally realist.

Parody, of course, is omnipresent in contemporary film and it is not always challenging in mode. Parody can work to signal continuity with (though today it is usually with some ironic difference from) a tradition of film-making: *Witness* rewrites *High Noon*'s characterization structure (law officer male/pacifist woman) and even echoes individual shots (villains on the high road), but adds the distancing irony of the increased (not, as might be expected, decreased) ruralization of the modern world, at least in terms of the Amish community. Similarly, *Crossroads* reworks *Leadbelly*'s thematic and formal structure in fictionalized terms, with differences that foreground the relation of race to the blues. While both music films operate within the same historical framework (Allan Lomax and Folkway recordings figure prominently in both plots), the new climactic contest scene has significant ironic differences: it pits the electric guitar versus the acoustic (in the original it was six- versus twelve-string) and adds a heavy dose of Faustian challenge.

Another way of talking about the political paradoxes of parody would be to see it as self-consciously intransitive representation (film recalls film) which also milks the power of transitivity to create the spectator's identification. In other words, it simultaneously destabilizes and inscribes the dominant ideology through its (almost overly obvious) interpellation of the spectator as subject in and of ideology (Althusser 1971; Belsey 1980: 56–84). In other chapters, too, I have argued that the question of ideology's relation to subjectivity is central to postmodernism. The challenges to the humanist concept of a coherent, continuous, autonomous individual (who paradoxically also shares in some generalized universal human essence) have come from all sides today: from poststructuralist philosophical and literary theory, Marxist political philosophy, Freudian/Lacanian psychoanalysis, sociology, and many other domains. We have also seen that photography and fiction – two art forms with a certain relevance for film – have shared in this questioning of the nature and formation of subjectivity. Where modernism investigated the grounding of experience in the self, its focus was on the self seeking integration amid fragmentation. In other words, its (for many, defining) focus on subjectivity was still within the dominant humanist framework, though the obsessive search for wholeness itself suggests the beginnings of what would be a more radical postmodern questioning, a challenging brought about by the doubleness of postmodern discourse. In other words, postmodernism works both to underline and to undermine the notion of the coherent, self-sufficient subject as the source of meaning or action.

Think of films like Woody Allen's *Zelig*, with its many parodic intertexts, including actual historical film footage and the conventions of documentary as well as other specific films from *Citizen Kane* to *Reds*. Parody points at once to and beyond cinematic textuality to the ideological formation of the subject by our various cultural representations. *Zelig* is centrally concerned with the history and politics of the prewar years for which the chameleon Zelig becomes the ironic symbol. Real historical personages (Susan Sontag, Saul Bellow) 'document' and 'authenticate' Zelig in this symbolic role: his freakishness becomes his typicality. But what does it mean to be a symbol of something when that something only wants to be other than what it is? The implied historical intertexts give us the answer to this contradiction: as a Jew, Zelig has a special (and historically ironic) interest in fitting in, in being other than what he is – as we know from subsequent history. In other words, this is more than just the typical Allen assimilation anxiety: the history of the Holocaust cannot be forgotten by the contemporary viewer of this film. Nor can the history of the representation of the subject in cinema. The story of a self that changes constantly, that is unstable, decentered, and discontinuous, is a parody both of the traditional filmic subject of realist cinema and also of the modernist searching for integration and wholeness of personality. Here the only wholeness attained is that of the media monster the public makes of the protean protagonist. *Zelig* is 'about' the formation of subjectivity, both the subjectivity of the spectator and that created by the spectator – the Star.

This critique from within the institution and history of film production is part of what is postmodern about Allen's work: its insider – outsider doubled position. Through parody, it uses and abuses dominant conventions in order to emphasize both the process of subject-formation and the temptations of easy accommodation to the power of interpellation. It questions the nature of the 'real' and its relation to the 'reel' through its parody and metacinematic play. This questioning becomes even more overt in *The Purple Rose of Cairo*, where real and reel life mingle with self-conscious irony. This kind of postmodern film never loses sight of the appeal of that humanist-modernist wholeness; indeed, it exploits it. But the exploitation is done in the name of contesting the values and beliefs upon which that wholeness is constructed – with the emphasis on the act of construction – through representations.

. . . Films made from postmodern novels seems to be particularly open to the referential complexities of parody. While all filming of novelistic narrative involves the clash of two very different representational systems, in the postmodern form there are added levels of intricacy. John Fowles's *The French Lieutenant's Woman*, with its intense self-reflexivity of narration and its dense parodic intertextuality (of both specific Victorian novels and generic conventions), had to be cinematically transcoded in order to change its insistently novelistic focus into a filmic one.

Another example would be Manuel Puig's novel, *Kiss of the Spider Woman*, where the ironies of Molina's parodic verbal representations of films had to be visually inscribed for the spectator, while remaining narrated for Molina's cell companion, Valentin. The number of narrated films in the novel had to be drastically reduced in the film without losing the function and significance of the representational process itself. In addition, as we have already seen, the irony of the novel's extended paratextual parody in the form of long footnotes full of authenticating psychoanalytic sources of information (which explain nothing of the subjectivity they presume to illuminate) has to be played out solely through character interaction.

In these and other films, parody is not a form of self-regarding narcissism or in-joke elitist allusions by film-school trained directors. The complex transcoding in Carlos Saura's *Carmen* of French high art (Bizet's opera and Mérrimée's literary text) into the conventions of Spanish flamenco offers a good example of the kind of political critique of which parodic representation is indeed capable. Flamenco is historically not the music and dance of high art; it is the regional and popular art of the poor and the socially marginalized. Saura's film is about the relation of the present to the past traditions of both Spanish folk art and European high-art culture (with its fascination for the stereotypically exotic).

Like *The French Lieutenant's Woman*, however, this is a very postmodern film in its dialogic doublings. It is textually aware of – and challenges – the boundaries between genres and ultimately between art and life. The wall-size studio window onto the outside world is curtained, and the performance goes on *behind* those curtains. Somewhat reminiscent of the one in Fellini's *The Orchestra Rehearsal*, the performance is both a documentary on a form of music and a rehearsal of a fiction. Added to this is the plot structure's reflexivity, wherein the dancers begin to enact – in their private lives – the jealousy and passion of the fiction. The fact that as viewers we often cannot tell whether we are watching the fiction or the dancers' 'real'-life action underlines the doubling boundary play of the film. The self-reflexivity of *Carmen* also raises another issue of ideological import: this is a film about the production of art, about art as representation derived from the words and music of others, but as filtered through the imagination of the artist figure, the male Pygmalion who wills reality – a woman and a dancer – to take the form of art and become his Carmen. The overt process of subject-formation here underlines the cognate relationship between subject and subjection.

The dominant view of postmodern parody as trivial and trivializing that we saw earlier is also to be found in the field of film criticism. Jameson (1983, 1984) argues that parody in films like *Body Heat* or *Star Wars* is a sign of nostalgic escapism, 'the imprisonment of the past' through pastiche that prevents confronting the present. However, at the same time, we have seen that Jameson laments a loss of a sense of history in today's art. He sees parodic art as simply narcissistic, as 'a terrible indictment of consumer capitalism itself – or at the very least, an alarming and pathological symptom of a society that has become incapable of dealing with time and history' (Jameson 1983: 117). However, *Zelig, Carmen, The French Lieutenant's Woman*, and other postmodern films do indeed deal with history and they do so in ironic, but not at all un-serious, ways. The problem for Jameson may simply be that they do not deal with Marxist History: in these films there is little of the positive utopian notion of History and no unproblematic faith in the accessibility of the 'real referent' of historical discourse.

What they suggest instead is that there is no directly and naturally accessible past 'real' for us today: we can only know – and construct – the past through its traces, its representations. As we have repeatedly seen, whether these be documents, eye-witness accounts, documentary film footage, or other works of art, they are still representations and they are our only means of access to the past. Jameson laments the loss of a sense of his particular definition of history, then, while dismissing as nostalgia the only kind of history we may be able to acknowledge: a contingent and inescapably intertextual history. To write this off as pastiche and nostalgia and then to lament that our contemporary social system has 'begun to lose its capacity to retain its own past, has begun to live in a perpetual present' (Jameson 1983: 125) seems of questionable validity. Postmodernist film (and fiction) is, if anything, obsessed with history and with how we can know the past today. How can this be an 'enfeeblement of historicity' (Jameson 1986: 303)?

Writing as I do in an Anglo-American context, I think that Jameson's blanket condemnation of Hollywood for its wholesale implication in capitalism (made from within an academy that is just as implicated) is what is behind his distrust of irony and ambiguity, a distrust that blinds him to the possibilities of the potentially positive oppositional and contestatory nature of parody. Postmodern film does not deny that it is implicated in capitalist modes of production, because it knows it cannot. Instead it exploits its 'insider' position in order to begin a subversion from within, to talk to consumers in a capitalist society in a way that will get us where we live, so to speak. The difference between postmodern parody and nostalgia – which once again I do not deny is part of our culture today – lies in the role of this double-voiced irony. Compare the ponderousness of *Dune* (which takes itself most seriously) with *Star Wars'* irony and play with cultural conventions of narrative and visual representation or with *Tampopo's* cultural inversion of both the traditional western (e.g. *Shane* with its lone hero helping needy widow) and the Italian 'spaghetti western' into what might literally be called a 'noodle eastern.' What postmodern parody does is to evoke what reception theorists call the horizon of expectation of the spectator, a horizon formed by recognizable conventions of genre, style, or form of representation. This is then destabilized and dismantled step by step. It is not accidental, of course, that irony has often been the rhetorical vehicle of satire. Even a relatively 'light' parody such as De Palma's *Phantom of the Paradise* offers irony working with satire, ranging in target from the sexism of Hugh Hefner-like harems (Swan's – with ironic echoes perhaps of *Du côté de chez Swann*) to the interpellation of the Star by the public and its taste for extremes. The vehicle of this satire is multiple parody: of *The Bird Man of Alcatraz* (transported to Sing Sing – a more appropriate site for a singer-composer), *Psycho* (the knife replaced by a plunger; the female victim by a male), *The Picture of Dorian Gray* (the painting updated to video tape). Despite the obvious fun, this is also a film about the politics of representation, specifically the representation of the original and originating subject as artist: its dangers, its victims, its consequences. The major intertexts are *Faust* and the earlier film, *The Phantom of the Opera*, here transcoded into rock music terms. This particular parodied text and only this can explain such otherwise unmotivated details as the organ overtones to the protagonist's opening piano playing. The *Faust* parody is overt as well, since the phantom writes a rock cantata based on it. And of course his pact with the demonic Swan is signed in blood.

Multiple and obvious parody like this can paradoxically bring out the politics of representation by baring and thus challenging convention, just as the Russian formalists had suggested it could. Metacinematic devices work in much the same way. The mixing of the fictive and the historical in Coppola's *Cotton Club* warns the spectator to beware of institutionalized boundaries, to refuse to let life and art get either too separated or totally merged, so that when the club's stage acts echo and foreshadow the action of the main plot, we do not miss the implications. For instance, the dance of the light-skinned Lila Rose and the darker Sandman Williams prefigures on stage their tortured relationship for she, but only she, can pass in a white world. Genre boundaries are structurally analogous to social borders (here racially defined) and both are called to account.

This parodic genre-crossing between the discourses of fiction and history may well reflect a general and increasing interest in non-fictional forms since the 1960s. In film, popular works such as *The Return of Martin Guerre* and (somewhat more problematically) *Amadeus* would support such an interpretation of the orientation of much current culture. But a film like Maximilian Schell's *Marlene* can also parody the documentary genre in a postmodern cinematic way. It opens asking 'Who is Dietrich?' and the question is

revealed as unanswerable. The postmodernist investigation of subject-formation combines here with one of the forms that the postmodern challenge to
historical knowledge has taken: the one that operates in the realm of private
history, that is, biography. Novels like Banville's *Kepler* or Wiebe's *The
Temptations of Big Bear* or Kennedy's *Legs* all work to present a portrait of an
individual and yet to subvert any stability in or certainty of ever knowing –
or representing – that subject. This is what *Marlene* is also about. The much
photographed Dietrich remains off-stage, never represented visually. She is
only a querulous voice, a cantankerous absent presence.

Schell turns this to postmodern advantage by making this into a film
about trying to make a documentary about a willfully absent subject, one
who refuses to be subjected to the discourses and representations of others
any longer. Dietrich has her own version of her life, one which, as the
metacinematic frame makes clear, is itself a fictionalized one. She claims at
one point that she wants a documentary without criticism: what Schell
should do is show archival pictures of, for instance, the boat on which she
arrived in America. Schell then immediately offers us these very pictures
and the effect is both humorous and revelatory: the archive may be real
but it tells us little about the subject. The portrait of Dietrich that emerges
here is of a woman of contradictions, business-like yet sentimental, self-
denigrating yet proud, rejecting almost all her work as rubbish yet moved
to enthusiasm by watching Schell in *Judgment at Nuremburg*. The suggestion is that all subjectivity would be as radically split as this if we were to
examine it this closely, that the humanist ideal representation of a whole,
integrated individual is a fiction – a fiction that not even the subject (or her
biographer) can ever successfully construct. Schell's despair is as much at
this as at Dietrich's stubborn inaccessibility to his camera. He can edit her
films all he likes (and we watch him do so), but she remains elusive and for
ever contradictory.

*Marlene* is the kind of film I would label as postmodern: parodic, metacinematic, questioning. Its constantly contradictory doubled discourse calls to
our attention the issue of the ideological construction – through representation – of subjectivity and of the way we know history, both personal and
public. Very few films have managed to raise these particular issues as
obsessively as has Peter Greenaway's *A Zed and Two Noughts*. Everything in
this movie is doubled, from the characters to the parodies. The master intertext is the ('photographic') realist representation of Vermeer's paintings (the
lighting techniques of which are echoed directly in the filming). But even
this overt intertext becomes problematic. Within the film's narrative there is
a surgeon named Van Meegeren. This is also the name of Vermeer's principal forger, the man who successfully convinced Goebbels (and the rest of
the world) that there existed more than the once accepted twenty-six
authenticated Vermeer paintings. As in Ackroyd's *Chatterton*, the real and
the fictive or the authentic and the fake cannot be separated. And, by means
of one character's personal sense of loss, the entire history of the human
species is placed in the context of evolution and devolution: Charles Darwin
becomes both a biological historian and an ingenious storyteller.

*A Zed and Two Noughts* seems to me to be a borderline case, however, a *cas
limite* of the postmodern film. Its challenges to the spectator's expectations

are more radical than those of any of the other films I have mentioned. While its contradictions are not really resolved, they are certainly stylized in the extreme. Postmodern film, as I see it, would be more compromised than this. Its tensions would be more deliberately left unresolved, its contradictions more deliberately left manifest. This constant double encoding – inscribing and subverting prevailing conventions – is what causes some critics to reject such films utterly, while others acclaim them enthusiastically. This discrepancy may be caused by the fact that if only one side – either – of the postmodern contradiction is seen (or valued), then the ambivalent doubleness of the parodic encoding can easily be resolved into a single decoding. Postmodern film is that which paradoxically wants to challenge the outer borders of cinema and wants to ask questions (though rarely offer answers) about ideology's role in subject-formation and in historical knowledge. Perhaps parody is a particularly apt representational strategy for postmodernism, a strategy once described (Said 1983: 135) as the use of parallel script rather than original inscription. Were we to heed the implications of such a model, we might have to reconsider the operations by which we both create and give meaning to our culture through representation. And that is not bad for a so-called nostalgic escapist tendency.

## References

Althusser, L. 1971: *Lenin and philosophy and other essays*, trans. Ben Brewster. London: New Left Books.

Belsey, C. 1980: *Critical practice*. London: Routledge.

Jameson, F. 1983: Postmodernism and consumer society. In Foster, H. (ed.), *Postmodern culture*. London: Pluto, 111–25.

Jameson, F. 1984: Postmodernism, or, the cultural logic of late capitalism. *New Left Review* **146**, 53–92.

Jameson, F. 1986: On magic realism in film. *Critical Inquiry* **12**:(2), 310–25.

Said, E. 1983: *The world, the text, and the critic*. Cambridge, MA: Harvard University Press.

Siska W. C. 1979: Metacinema. A modern necessity. *Literature/Film Quarterly* **7**:(1), 285–9.

# 3

# From here to modernity

*Barbara Creed*

From *Screen* 28: 2, 47–67 (Oxford University Press 1987)

What is at stake in the debate surrounding a possible intersection between feminist theory and postmodern theory? The future of feminist theory itself: its directions, theoretical bases, alignments? Is feminism a symptom or result of the postmodern condition or is feminism linked more directly to this crisis in theory? Alice Jardine and Craig Owens have explored the connections between feminism and postmodernism. A comparison of their work should prove helpful to the newcomer – myself included – who is attempting to negotiate what Owens rightly describes as a 'treacherous course' between the two (1983, p. 59).

In 'The Discourse of Others: Feminism and Postmodernism,' Owens argues that there is an 'apparent crossing of the feminist critique of patriarchy and the postmodernist critique of representation' (59). Owens points out that his intention is not to propose a relationship of either 'antagonism or opposition' between the two (although at times he seems to do just this) but rather to explore this possible intersection in order 'to introduce the issue of sexual difference into the modernism/postmodernism debate,' an issue of which this debate 'has until now been scandalously in-different' (59) – a debatable point.

According to Owens there are many areas where feminism is not only compatible with, but also an instance of postmodern thought (62): both feminism and postmodernism endorse Lyotard's argument that there is a crisis in the legitimizing function of narrative, that the *grands récits* or Great Narratives of the West have lost credibility; both present a critique of representation, that 'system of power that authorizes certain representations while blocking, prohibiting or invalidating others' (59); both agree that the 'representational systems of the West admit only one vision – that of the constitutive male subject' (58); both present a critique of binarism, that is, thinking by means of oppositions; both insist on the importance of difference and incommensurability (61–62); both seek to heal the breach between theory and practice and support an artistic strategy of simultaneous activity on multiple fronts (63); both critique the privileging of vision as the superior sense and as the guarantor of truth. The difference, it appears, is that where postmodernism, defined as a cultural theory, sees itself as engaging in a debate with modernism, feminism identifies patriarchal ideology as its 'other.' For instance, in relation to the issue of vision, feminism 'links the privileging of vision with sexual privilege' (70), particularly in relation to the psychoanalytic theory of castration, whereas postmodernism situates the problem as one of 'modern aesthetics.' . . .

In her book, *Gynesis: Configurations of Woman and Modernity* (1985), Alice Jardine further explores this common ground. She concentrates her discussion of feminism and postmodernism on the relationship between contemporary French thought (the writings largely of male writers: Lacan, Derrida, Deleuze, Duras, Goux, Blanchot, Tournier), the process of 'gynesis' which she argues is central to these writings, and feminism. It is important to realize that Jardine is using the term 'modernity' in a specialized sense: although she writes that she is not certain if the word 'should or can be defined' as she uses it, she does actually offer a definition over the course of the book. First, however, she indicates what modernity does not mean: '. . . modernity should not be confused (as it most often is in the United States) with "modernism" – the generic label commonly attached to the general literary movement of the first half of the twentieth century' (23). Jardine uses the term 'modernity,' which is used in France to refer to what is known 'more problematically in the United States [as] "post-modernism"' (22). (Because of Jardine's specialized use of the term, I shall also adopt her practice when referring to her work.)

The major question Jardine explores in *Gynesis* is this: '. . . are feminism and modernity oxymoronic in their terms and terminology? If so, how and why? If not, what new ruse of reason has made them appear – especially in France – to be so?' (22). The 'new ruse of reason' which Jardine isolates for analysis is a process that she defines as 'gynesis.' Gynesis, which Jardine argues has always been discernible in the religious and literary texts of the West, is a process of requestioning and rethinking – a process brought about by the collapse of the master narratives of the West and a reexamination of the main topics of philosophy: Man, Truth, History.

. . . Thus, gynesis represents a valorization of the feminine or woman as intrinsic to the development of new postmodern modes of speaking and writing. However, it is important to stress, as Jardine does, that the process of gynesis is not necessarily about women or feminism. She points to the fact that the majority of writers in France, who are working in this area, deal almost exclusively with the fictional writings of men. For 'feminine writing' does not necessarily signify writing by a woman. Throughout *Gynesis*, Jardine refers to the general agreement amongst contemporary writers that in order to write the male poet must 'become a woman.' She cites the work of Deleuze and Guattari in which they:

> . . . refer to Virginia Woolf as having incorporated the process of what they call 'becoming woman' (le devenir femme) in her writing – but 'not to the same extent' as Henry James, D. H. Lawrence, or Henry Miller. (62)

Jardine argues that modernity signifies a '*re*definition of the world' brought about by the 'complex destructuring, disintegration, of the founding structures in the West.' Modernity represents an attempt to take those terms which are 'not attributable to *Man:* the spaces of the *en-soi*, Other, without history – the feminine' and to give these spaces a *'new language'* (72–73) . . . .

## The 'nostalgia' film

I would like to relate this discussion to Fredric Jameson's argument about postmodernism and the nostalgia film. Jameson discusses this phenomenon without any reference to feminism or questions of sexual difference, apparently 'in-different' to these issues in a context where, I would have thought, they were crucial. Jameson argues that the changes currently taking place in post-industrial (1984, p. 66) society have been registered in the postmodern fascination for the nostalgia film. He sees a 'desperate attempt to appropriate a missing past' in films such as *American Graffiti, Rumble Fish, Chinatown, The Conformist, Body Heat*. He refers to 'the colonization' of our immediate past and argues that the preference for films which rely on quotation (of past versions, other remakes, the original novel, etc.) represents an attempt to construct '. . . "intertextuality" as a deliberate, built-in feature of the aesthetic effect, and as the operator of a new connotation of "pastness" and pseudo-historical depth, in which the history of aesthetic styles displaces "real" history.' Jameson sees this 'mesmerizing new aesthetic mode . . . as an elaborated symptom of the waning of our historicity, of our lived possibility of experiencing history in some active way . . .' (1984, pp. 67–68).

In an earlier article, Jameson discussed another category of films (*Star Wars, Raiders of the Lost Ark*) which, while not strictly historical, recreate cultural experiences in the form of pastiche as well as reawakening a sense of the past in the viewer. Jameson argues that for those who grew up in the '30s to the '50s one of the major cultural forms was the adventure serial, awash with 'alien villains, true American heroes, heroines in distress.' He argues that a film like *Star Wars*:

> . . . reinvents this experience in the form of a pastiche: that is, there is no longer any point to a parody of such serials since they are long extinct. Star Wars, far from being a pointless satire of such now dead forms, satisfies a deep (might I even say repressed?) longing to experience them again: it is a complex object in which on some first level children and adolescents can take the adventures straight, while the adult public is able to gratify a deeper and more properly nostalgic desire to return to that older period and to live its strange old aesthetic artifacts through once again. This film is thus metonymically a historical or nostalgia film . . . . (1983, p. 116)

What is most interesting about Jameson's otherwise incisive observations is that he does not analyze this longing for the 'past.' Exactly what is it that modern audiences wish to feel nostalgic about? Does this nostalgia take a different form for men and women? Since Jameson refers to two different forms of the nostalgia film – the period recreation and the adventure film – I shall discuss this question in relation to each.

The intensely polarized gender roles of the adventure serial, with its true heroes and distressed heroines, invoke a desire to relive a 'time' when gender roles were more clearly defined, stable predictable. I am not arguing that this 'time' was the '30s or the '50s; it may be that audiences of those decades were also watching the serials in order to satisfy their desire to relive an imaginary order – an order where gender identity was secure and appeared to validate the social contract established by the myth of romantic love. Given the current crisis in gender roles, often cited as an instance of postmodernism and certainly represented in the cinema, and audience incredulity in the face of cinematic derring-do, films like *Raiders of the Lost Ark* are required both to romanticize and parody the roles of hero and heroine. (I would also include *Crocodile Dundee* in this category.)

The problem with Jameson's argument is that he situates that 'older period' literally in the past; he does not consider the possibility that all generations may have similar longings (although often tempered with cynicism), and that the cinema, along with other forms of popular culture, addresses these longings in different ways and through different filmic modes across the decades. It is difficult to see how Jameson could embark on such an analysis without considering the theoretical work already undertaken by feminism in this area in relation to questions of desire and the construction of sexual difference in the cinema.

Jameson's discussion of the history/nostalgia film also suffers from a similar lack. Given Lyotard's comments about the attempts of the patriarchal order to disguise the fact that 'there is no signifier,' isn't it possible that the 'missing past' which lies at the heart of these films is that which once validated the paternal signifier? Significantly, at least three of the films quoted by Jameson, *Chinatown*, *The Conformist* and *Body Heat*, belong to the category of *film noir*, a genre which deliberately plays with the notion of the *femme fatale*, the phallic mother whose image constantly threatens to undermine the phallocentric order and turn son against father. In each of these remakes the male protagonist fails in his self-appointed task, largely because the patriarchal symbolic, the Law, has also failed – reduced already to the status of just one 'class' among many, to cite Lyotard again. In *Chinatown* (the title itself is used as a metaphor for corruption at all levels of city government), all characters – including the hero – have a 'past.' The possibility of incest, symbolically alluded to in the '40s *noir* film, has become a reality in *Chinatown*; it signifies the complete failure of the symbolic order. In *The Conformist* the four symbolic fathers (Italo, Quadri, Mussolini and the hero's own 'mad' father) all signify the end of an order and a failure of 'truth' suggested by the myth of Plato's cave[1]; while *Body Heat* alludes continuously, through its references to earlier *films noirs*, to the failure of the paternal figure and the power of the phallic mother.

In her discussion of the differences between French and North American versions of gynesis, Jardine argues that contemporary texts by male writers in North America have not been influenced by gynesis as an 'abstract, conceptual process.' 'Gynesis – the putting into discourse of "woman" or the "feminine" as problematic – seems to exist here only at the level of *representation*. It has, in a sense, been externalized rather than internalized, and thematized rather than practiced . . .'(236). In a footnote, she adds: 'In some ways, the American version of gynesis is more prevalent in "popular culture" than it is in "high theory" especially in film.' We can see this process at work in Jameson's postmodern filmography.

## Gynesis, postmodernism and the sci-fi horror film

Jardine maintains that within gynesis the 'feminine' signifies, not woman herself, but those 'spaces' which could be said to conceptualize the master narrative's own 'non-knowledge,' that area over which the narrative has lost control. This is the unknown, the terrifying, the monstrous – everything which is not held in place by concepts such as Man, Truth, Meaning. Interestingly, she does not claim that this situation is new; in fact, she stresses the importance of remembering:

> That of all the words used to designate this space (now unbound) – nature, Other, matter, unconscious, madness, hylé, force – have throughout the tenure of Western philosophy carried feminine connotations (whatever their grammatical gender) . . . Those connotations go back, at the very least, to Plato's chora. Julia Kristeva has pointed out that space in general has always connoted the female: 'Father's Time, mother's species,' as Joyce put it; and, indeed, when evoking the name and destiny of women, one thinks more of the space generating and forming the human species than of time, becoming, or history. (88–89)

The sci-fi horror film's current interest in the maternal body and processes of birth points to changes taking place on several fronts. Among the most important of these are the developments taking place in reproductive technology which have put into crisis questions of the subject, the body and the unconscious. Lyotard draws attention to this. In a discussion on architecture and the postmodern, he speaks of the fact that the mother's body, the infant's first home, is under threat; given the possibility of birth taking place in an artificial womb, we may well in our lifetimes witness the 'disappearance of that first dwelling.'

> My question is the following: the body is to my mind an essential site of resistance, because with the body there is love, a certain presence of the past, a capacity to reflect, singularity – if this body is attacked, by techno-science, then that site of resistance can be attacked. What is the unconscious of a child engendered in vitro? What is its relationship with the mother and with the father? (1986, p. 31)

The sci-fi horror film, I would argue, is using the body of woman not only to explore these possibilities in a literal sense but also as a metaphor for the uncertainty of the future – the new, unknown, potentially creative and potentially destructive future. The threat offered by the 'alien' creature, particularly the alien that impregnates woman, is also one of an uncertain future. The theme of birth and the possibility of new modes of conception and procreation is, of course, not new to science fiction. Over the decades the sci-fi horror film has dealt with scientific alternatives to human conception (the Frankenstein films); other modes of sexual reproduction (*Invasion of the Body Snatchers*); parthenogenetic modes of conception (*The Thing*); cloning (*The Boys from Brazil*); the transformation of robots into human beings (*DARYL*); and the impregnation of women by aliens (*I Married a Monster from Outer Space, Village of the Damned, Xtro, Inseminoid*). There is even a soft-porn film based on the latter – a deliberate parody of *Xtro* called *Wham Bang! Thank You Mr Spaceman*.

In more recent years, as experiments with reproductive technology have begun to make enormous headway, the sci-fi horror film has become increasingly preoccupied with alternative forms of the conception-gestation-birth process. One of the most interesting and significant developments in the genre has been a concentration on imagery connected with the female reproductive cycle. The latter is most thoroughly explored in films such as *Xtro, Dune, Blue Velvet, Inseminoid*, the John Carpenter remake of *The Thing, Alien* and *Aliens*. A study of these films, particularly the last three, reveals a fascination with the maternal body – its inner and outer appearance, its functions, its awesome powers. In many of these texts, it is not the body of the human/earth woman which is being explored but rather the 'bodies' of female alien creatures whose reproductive systems both resemble the human and are coded as a source of abject horror and overpowering awe. In the final scenes of *Aliens* we confront the Mother Alien – a monstrous, deadly procreative machine, prepared to protect her young at all costs – primitive, amoral, female. In the two *Alien* films, this coding is taken to extremes – virtually all aspects of the *mise-en-scène* are designed to signify the female: womb-like interiors, fallopian-tube corridors, small claustrophobic spaces.

*Xtro* pushed the birth-potential of woman's body to extremes; woman is impregnated by an alien, and a short time later gives birth to a fully-grown man. Here, the body becomes a site of the 'unknown' – physically capable of mating with 'other,' able to expand like a balloon, without physical limits. In *Inseminoid*, woman is impregnated by an alien, later giving birth to two monstrous half-human twins who, it is indicated, will eventually return to Earth and wreak havoc on the planet. In the remake of *The Fly*, the heroine wakes up from a nightmare in which she sees herself giving birth to a giant maggot. In *The Brood*, woman gives birth to a monstrous brood of dwarf children in a symbolic materialization of her inner rage. Her womb is a large sac attached to the side of her stomach. In the final scenes, when her husband secretly watches a birth, he is repelled and disgusted, particularly when she bites through the umbilical cord and looks up at him, her face smeared with blood. In *Aliens* human bodies become nests for alien embryos; when the alien infant is ready to hatch it gnaws its way through the stomach. The human body, both male and female, has become a cocoon for a hostile life form. Why this preoccupation with the maternal body, processes of birth; monstrous offspring, the alien nature of woman, her maternal powers – and most recently the representation of the male body as 'womb'? I would argue it is because the body, particularly woman's body, through the process of gynesis, has come to signify the spaces of the unknown, the terrifying, the monstrous. This would register Lyotard's concern about the body losing its capacity to function as 'an essential site of resistance' – clearly a postmodern anxiety.

I think we can also see this process of gynesis at work in the cinema's increasing preoccupation with the theme of 'becoming woman' – literally. If a collapse of the symbolic function gives rise to what Jardine describes as 'an inability of words to give form to the world' then this may well lead to a struggle to control that which has discredited the paternal function – the 'space which has begun to threaten all forms of authorship (paternity).' The new theoretical discourses (feminism? postmodernism?) which have begun to take the place of the master discourses, seeing themselves as no longer in 'a system of loans and debts to former master truths' have, according to Jardine, begun to conceptualize a new space, that of woman (100).

The theme of 'becoming woman' is explored symbolically in the horror film (*Psycho*, *Dressed to Kill*) and literally in those sci-fi films in which man either gives birth to 'another' (*Alien* and *Aliens*) or in which he gives birth to himself (*Altered States*, *The Terminator*) or to himself as another life form (*The Thing*, *The Fly*). I am not suggesting that this is a new theme; it is dealt with in all the mad-scientist films in which man attempts to create his own life forms in the laboratory – the scientist as Mother/God. However, in the contemporary text, there has been an intensification in the exploration of 'becoming woman.' Most critical articles written on cross-dressing in the cinema rarely consider the possibility that man, at an unconscious level, may well desire to 'become woman' (*Tootsie*, *Some Like It Hot*). In France this possibility is treated with seriousness – a male poet must become a woman in order to write. Deleuze and Guattari, of course, have written at length about the whole world 'becoming woman,' although this again has little to do with actual women.

In her article on postmodern theory, 'The Terror of Pleasure' (1986), Tania Modleski analyses *Videodrome* in these terms; the hero having been subjected to 'massive doses of a video signal' not only discovers he can no longer distinguish reality from fantasy but also that his body, completely unable to resist attack, has become a video terminal. Modleski draws attention to the fact that the wound which opens up in his stomach, into which the video cassette is inserted, is 'gaping' and 'vagina-like.' He has become – to cite Baudrillard – 'a pure screen, a switching center for all the networks of influence' (1983, p. 133)

Modleski – and Pete Boss (1986) in the 'Body Horror' issue of *Screen* – sees films such as these, in which there is a breakdown in distinctions between subject and object, as postmodern. The individual is a prey to everything, unable to produce the limits of his own body or being. In defining the postmodern, Boss argues that the 'categories of Otherness which traditionally functioned in the horror film are no longer adequate' (1986, p. 2) a distinction which I think – in the light of Jardine's work – needs further qualification. Traditional concepts of Otherness may currently be rejected (or embraced?), yet they may well emerge in a new form. It is relevant to note that the male protagonist of *Videodrome* also inserts his gun into the vagina-like wound in his stomach – his gun as symbolic phallus, like the cassette, signifies a different narrative, one in which he is man violating himself-as-woman. Significantly, his desire to experiment with videodrome was aroused by the masochistic desires of his female lover. He eventually takes her desires as his own. Clearly, one way of analyzing the process in which man becomes woman is to regard it, from a male perspective, as the ultimate scenario of powerlessness, the ultimate violation of the body. In *Alien* the scenes in which man 'conceives' and gives birth through his stomach are represented as major scenarios of horror: the oral 'impregnation' of the man, the details of the birth scene, his pain, the savage tearing apart of his stomach, the horrified faces of the crew – all of these are shown in graphic detail.

In Cronenberg's *The Fly*, a witty pastiche of the horror genre, 'becoming woman' is represented as a true metamorphosis comparable to the one in Kafka's novel. When a woman appears on the scene, the male scientist suddenly realizes why his experiments are not working – he is ignorant of the flesh, the body. Woman signifies carnal pleasure: man is intellectual, remote from the body. She awakens his libido, he is able to progress with his research. Not until he begins the metamorphosis does he experience bodily pleasures to the full. Through the metaphor of the body, the film draws parallels between the woman and the fly – reinforced by the nightmare in which she gives birth to a gigantic maggot. The film plays continually with audience expectations of 'bad taste' and always manages to go one step further. In the final scene the connections are developed through the *mise-en-scène*. The metamorphosis is complete and the giant insect advances menacingly towards the 'castrated' male victim (he has lost several limbs), recalling a similar scene from *The Incredible Shrinking Man* in which the hero falls victim to a giant black spider – compared through cross-cutting with his wife. Through the early stages of the metamorphosis, the fly is referred to as the 'Brundle-fly' – it is a cross between man and fly. Not until the metamorphosis is complete does man fully signify the female – a monstrous fetishized insect. Interestingly, Jardine in her discussion of the process of becoming woman in the texts of French male writers, particularly Deleuze and Guattari, refers to a metamorphosis.

> For what is involved here is le devenir femme de tout le monde, the becoming woman of everyone, everything, the whole world. With D&G, 'to become woman' is less a metaphor for describing a certain social or textual process than a true metamorphosis – one thinks of Kafka's Gregor Samsa waking up as a bug. (214–215)

## Feminism and gynesis: The search for the mother

> The interrogative return to the sources of our knowledge in the West has involved an obligatory return to the mother's body – a female body, no matter how unrecognizable; no matter how hysterical, textual, inanimate, or actual – *Gynesis*, p. 237.

Throughout her book Jardine distinguishes between texts of gynesis written by men and texts by women, although she primarily addresses herself to the former. In her final chapters, she draws attention to the fact that most of the significant women writers and theorists in France are also involved in the re-working of 'male' and 'female' in a process of gynesis. She raises, but does not answer, the question of whether or not they are writing 'woman' differently. Whatever the answer to this question, one thing is certain – in the writings of French women theorists we can clearly discern what might be described as 'a quest for the mother.' This search is evident in Kristeva's work on the 'semiotic chora,' Irigaray's concept of woman and 'two-lipped discourse' and Cixous's theory of 'feminine writing.' Such a search is an ancient theme – the mother Demeter's search for her daughter Persephone. This narrative has also been explored in the cinema (*Marnie, Mildred Pierce, Imitation of Life, Now Voyager*) but not until recently, with the release of

*Aliens*, has the mother-daughter quest been represented from a perspective other than that of the paternal signifier.

Like Demeter, Ripley (Sigourney Weaver), the heroine of *Aliens*, enters the underworld in order to search for Newt, her missing 'surrogate' daughter who has been snatched away by the Queen of Hell – the Mother Alien. The quest splits the feminine into 'bad' (Alien) and 'good' (Ripley) mothers: in the final combat, Ripley confronts the monstrous mother whom she must destroy if she is to save her 'daughter' and herself. None of the three stands in a biological relation with either of the others; the configurations of the mother–daughter constellations are multiple, and contradictorily, symbolic. It is the lethal Mother Alien who bears children (Ripley has none of her own) yet threatens Newt. Occupying the place conventionally assigned to the hero, Ripley must eventually confront the Queen Alien – a contemporary version of the Sphinx.

Mother Alien, half-human and half-creature, embodies the narrative enigma. She is revealed as the source of the terror and the key to the film's mystery. Where are the aliens coming from? What are their origins? Can the source be destroyed? Can their birth processes be stopped? Like Oedipus, Ripley must encounter the Sphinx but not on the road to Thebes. The confrontation takes place in the Mother's incubation chamber, where Ripley watches in horror as countless eggs drop from the Alien's enormous ovipositor. In the combat that follows, Ripley launches a series of grenades into the Mother's egg sac, tearing it apart from within. Finally, her vast incubator in a state of total destruction, the floor littered with broken eggs, the enraged Mother pursues Ripley and Newt. The 'scene of creation' has been destroyed. On her journey of self-discovery, Ripley has encountered the generative aspect of femininity and demolished it. She has annihilated the biological definition of motherhood (woman-as-breeding-machine). Has Ripley, the woman-hero, been enlisted to destroy 'herself' in the interests of a new society where birth is under the control of science and technology? If we draw the parallel between the two monstrous creatures still closer, we could argue that the Alien, like the Sphinx, is the origin of the plague (birth as an uncontrolled, amoral activity) which is destroying the city. After Oedipus destroyed the Sphinx he then became the source of the plague: does this mean that Ripley, and whatever signifies her 'plague,' will also threaten the city when she returns to Earth?

Because Ripley is uncertain of her final destination (is she a 'new' woman? a mother? both?), positioned as subject (woman-as-hero) encountering herself as 'other' (the generative female), signifying the conventional characteristics of both woman ('intuitive,' 'emotional,' 'mothering') and man ('brave,' 'intelligent,' 'savior'), she emerges as what Vladimir Propp has described as a 'hybrid' figure. [2]Ripley is a heroine whose representation derives from a period of profound social and cultural change; she embodies both male and female gender characteristics with ease and intelligence. Her representation does not involve simple role reversal, a factor made clear by the contrasted figure of the tough woman trooper, Vasquez (Jenette Goldstein) who is more heroic than most of the men. *Aliens* is extremely self-conscious about its play with gender roles – and funny: in the final scenes the only 'man' at Ripley's side is the android Bishop, who has been severed at the waist by the Mother Alien. He is literally 'half-a-man.'

It is refreshing to note the increasing tendency in contemporary texts to play with the notion of manhood. Figures such as Sylvester Stallone and Arnold Schwarzenegger (once described by an Australian critic as 'a condom stuffed with walnuts') could only be described as 'performing the masculine.' Both actors often resemble an anthropomorphized phallus, a phallus with muscles, if you like. (Parodies of a lost ideal or menacing images of an android future?) They are simulacra of an exaggerated masculinity, the original completely lost to sight, a casualty of the failure of the paternal signifier and the current crisis in master narratives.

Here it is relevant to note that the process of 'becoming woman' does have a related, although not identical counterpart in the increasing emphasis on the androgynous figure in popular culture (Boy George, Laurie Anderson) and the woman/man in the cinema (*Victor/Victoria, Second Serve*). Once again this is not new – cults of the androgyne have occurred throughout history. In sixteenth century Venice, the authorities became so concerned with the fashion in women's clothing and hairstyle that they passed a law forbidding gender confusion of this kind with the threat of excommunication (Brown, 1986, p. 204). Lyotard argues that the creation of a social-psychological androgyne is one of the major goals of a society organized around the continual circulation of exchange objects. But this postmodern fascination with the androgyne and the 'neuter' subject may indicate a desire *not* to address problems associated with the specificities of the oppressive gender roles of patriarchal society, particularly those constructed for women. The postmodern fascination with the 'new,' with breaking down boundaries, could well prove inimical to the development of theory if the 'old' is denied proper analysis and understanding.

## Conclusions

In her final chapters, Jardine argues that it would be 'a fatal mistake' for feminism to ignore or dismiss modernity as just 'one more "male concept," participated in and theorized and fictionalized by men, for men' (257). Not only would such a stance increase 'the dangers of anachronism' – the feminist repetition of the humanist errors of the modern period, recentering a Cartesian Woman Subject, with Woman's Truth and Woman's History – it would also close down the possibilities of 'developing radically new fields of conceptuality essential to feminist theory and practice today' (258). While I agree with Jardine that either tactic would indeed be a 'fatal mistake,' I am not convinced that for 'modernity and feminism to unite in their efforts' is necessarily the answer.

Jardine doesn't specify the terms of this alliance, but one can foresee major problems. First, any attempt to assimilate feminism to postmodernism may well result in a confusion over terms, as revealed in the way in which Lyotard's notion of the grand narrative has been misleadingly reduced to 'master' narrative; such confusion only serves to undermine the specificities of the positions of both feminism and postmodernism. Second, I have attempted to demonstrate, some theorists of the postmodern – such as Jameson – have been completely indifferent to feminism and its theorization of the current crisis; this has resulted, in some instances, in an inadequate analysis of the postmodern film. Third, writers such as Owens, in his attempt to 'introduce' feminism into the postmodern debate, do so in terms which situate feminism as if it were a 'guest,' the other brought in from the cold to join the 'host.' Owens never considers the possibility that feminist theory may not see itself as marginal to postmodernism and wish to join the club. Fourth, according to my reading of the changes presently occurring in the cinema, the crisis of the master narratives may not necessarily benefit women. Nor, even if there is a process of gynesis at work in the cinema, particularly in the sci-fi horror film, is it yet clear whether this also will be of benefit to women. At the moment it is too early to predict future directions. As Jardine states repeatedly throughout her study, questions concerning the relationship of women to the processes of modernity 'may be unanswerable for some time to come' (117): gynesis as written by men, could well prove to be a 'new ruse of reason.'

Finally, it may be possible that postmodern theory is more in debt to feminism than it is prepared to acknowledge. Jardine discusses the work of Rosa Braidotti, who argues that historical crisis in the West's systems of knowledge have occurred when women have played a more prominent – some would argue decisive – role in periods of change. Jardine refers to at least three epochs in which it is possible to specify such an historical 'coincidence': the transition between the Middle Ages and the Renaissance – the period of the famous *Querelle des femmes*; the time of the French Revolution and the Saint-Simoniens; and the present crisis ushered in by the events of post-1968 France which occurred simultaneously with the rise of the women's movement. Jardine suggests an hypothesis: 'might it not be that a series of if not causal at least etiological links could be established between those periods in the West when women were most vocally polemical and those so called "epistemological breaks"?' (93).

The title of this article was originally intended to designate the strategy of a feminism speaking from a position not identical to that which Jardine calls 'modernity' and others 'postmodernism.' I wanted to keep a tension, a space between the two. Having travelled a little way down the road, trying to negotiate Craig Owens's 'treacherous course,' I am glad I did not try to unite them. Any attempt to speak from a 'place' is immediately rendered problematic by the fact that one of the positions central to postmodernism is that there are no places left from which to speak – there are no 'Truths,' 'Beliefs,' or 'Positions.' Yet, this is in itself a position, and one now in danger of becoming a new orthodoxy. Even, perhaps, a master discourse? The paradox in which we feminists find ourselves is that while we regard patriarchal discourses as fictions, we nevertheless proceed as if our position, based on a belief in the oppression of women, were somewhat closer to the truth. Perhaps Lyotard is 'correct' (*sic*) to recommend at least the provisional abandonment of all 'Truths' in favor of the short narratives which the master discourses have attempted to suppress in order to validate their own positions. It would therefore be crucial that any theoretical discourse which emerges from the current crisis should not attempt to explain 'everything', to become a totalizing theory, be it feminism *or* postmodernism.

## Notes

1. See Irigaray (1985) for a fascinating reinterpretation of Plato's myth of the cave.
2. For a commentary on this, see de Lauretis (1984), pp. 113–16.

## References

Baudrillard J. 1983: The ecstasy of communication. In Foster (ed.), *The anti-aesthetic*. Port Townsend, WA: Bay Press.
Boss P. 1986: Vile bodies and bad medicine. *Screen*, 27: 1, 14–24.
Brown J. C. 1986: *Immodest acts. The life of a lesbian nun in Renaissance Italy*. Oxford: Oxford University Press.
De Lauretis T. 1984: *Alice doesn't. Feminism, semiotics, cinema*. Bloomington, IN: Indiana University Press.
Irigaray L. 1985: *Speculum of the other woman*, Ithaca; NY: Cornell University Press.
Jameson F. 1983: 'Postmodernism and consumer society.' In Foster (ed.), *The anti-aesthetic*. Port Townsend, WA: Bay Press.
Jameson F. 1984: 'Postmodernism, or, the cultural logic of late capitalism.' *New Left Review*, 146 (July-August), 53–92.
Jardine A. 1985: *Gynesis. Configurations of woman and modernity*. Ithaca and London: Cornell University Press.
Lyotard J-F. 1986: 'A response to Kenneth Frampton.' *Postmodernism*, ICA Documents 4, London.
Modleski T. 1986: 'The terror of pleasure: The contemporary horror film.' In Modleski T. (ed.), *Studies in entertainment. Critical approaches to mass culture*. Bloomington: T.N: Indiana University Press.
Owens C. 1983: The discourse of others. Feminists and postmodernism. In Foster H. (ed.), *The anti-aesthetic, essays on postmodern culture*. Port Townsend, WA: Bay Press.

# Film

## Section II
## Styles of pluralism

So much recent Anglo-American cinema employs a postmodern aesthetic that it might seem redundant to single out specific 'postmodern films' for analysis. 'Nostalgia' is all too apparent in sequels or oblique and self-conscious remakes, in 'heritage films' (*Remains of the Day, The Browning Version, Sense and Sensibility*), in takes on a standard genre (the road movie in *Thelma and Louise*, the prison drama in *The Shawshank Redemption*, the screwball comedy in *The Hudsucker Proxy*). Films as diverse as *Batman Forever, CutThroat Island*, Ian McKellen's *Richard III* and Kenneth Branagh's *Hamlet* 'pick and mix' historical signifiers and poach self-consciously from earlier cinema texts, while, at an extreme of narrowing intertextuality, *Judge Dredd* and *Independence Day* look to simulate the already eclectic and 'nostalgic' *Star Wars* of 1977.

A distinction can still be made, however, between films representative of a postmodern aesthetic and those which are, in Scott Bukatman's words, '*of* postmodernism, rather than simply . . . *about* it' (p. 86 below). David Cronenberg's *Videodrome* (1983) is surely one such example *of* postmodernism. Bukatman argues below that the film's subversion of narrative expectations and realist conventions echoes William Burroughs's 'cut-up' prose technique; its fragmented discourse coming to figure as content and to engage the reader/viewer in a process of active interpretation which resists 'the totalization of meaning' (see pp. 72–9, 86 and Jameson, 1991). Ambiguously positioned between visual representations of the protagonist's delirium and nightmarish depictions of a media-saturated future, the viewer is denied any assurance that the first is 'real' and the second 'fantasy'. The very experience of viewing *Videodrome*, then, subjects its audiences to the extreme of postmodern schizophrenia – a theme park ride through Baudrillard's world of simulation.

If recent cinema presents us with anything comparable it might lie in the conflation of the protagonist's dreams with an imagined dystopia in Terry Gilliam's *Twelve Monkeys* (1996). Like *Videodrome*'s Max Wren, James Cole in *Twelve Monkeys* is a pawn in the system, a victim whose death marks the end of the narrative. Yet even this sacrifice, in a seeming death of the subject, fails to provide a satisfying closure or to illuminate what has gone before. We are left with multiple, even contradictory discourses of truth and history, unsure – as in the further conspicuous example *of* the postmodern, *The Usual Suspects* (1995) – whether there is a core reality or of 'what really happened' under the layers of spectacle and fabrication.

Perhaps the closest cinema has come to Baudrillard's third phase of the autonomous image, however, masking not reality but its absence, is Disney's full-length computer-generated animation film, *Toy Story* (1996), a film shot, according to its promoters, 'entirely on location in cyberspace'. The use of traditional clay models for the film's characters, from which wire-frame graphics were then constructed, suggests that even here the referent still tugs at the floating signifier. Many critics were unnerved, all the same, by the film's apparently more optimistic take on a Baudrillardian scenario, preferring the more traditional Wallace and Gromit to Disney's all too clean and depthless artifice.

This by now familiar complaint against postmodern cinema's flatness, its obsession with style over content and its hollow amorality took a more serious and vehement turn in relation to the issue of screen violence, with, for a time, Quentin Tarantino's *oeuvre* – *Reservoir Dogs* (1992) and *Pulp Fiction* (1994), in particular – the main object of attention. We argue below that *Pulp Fiction*'s aesthetic of recycling – whether of film motifs and devices, obscure surfing tracks or the flagging careers of Hollywood actors – can be read as an affirmative 'bringing back to life', a 'making new', which extends to the film's cyclical and overlapping narratives. The way characters react to life's contingencies in *Pulp Fiction*'s postmodern milieux has a fundamentally moral aspect and a potentially liberating or restorative effect. A noticeable act of 'violence' in the film, for example – the plunging of a hypodermic into Mia's chest – doubles, symptomatically, as an act of resurrection, a calling back, which one can see echoed not only in the film's narrative and style but in the activity of reviewing and 'riffing' on favourite lines that characterises the fan reception of the film.

Perhaps postmodernism is especially productive of cult texts. Certainly Tarantino's work rapidly acquired this status, as did David Lynch's earlier *Eraserhead, Blue Velvet* and *Twin Peaks* (see Jameson, pp. 32–4, above; Collins, pp. 202–6 below; Denzin, 1991; Corrigan, 1991). A further example would be the *Star Wars* trilogy. So long trapped in academic discussion as a type of 'nostalgia film' for an ageing generation (see Jameson, p. 23 above), *Star Wars* too, as Will Brooker shows, can be read for a positive and progressive set of cultural meanings, now further enlivened and re-contextualised for both new and dedicated fans in the series' re-release and 'continuation' in the mid-1990s, even as its motifs and markers are diminished in the echoing mirrors of the almost entirely imitative *Judge Dredd*.

If the above are cult texts, however, they are outdone by the enduring and practically canonised *Blade Runner* (1981), on both counts the opposite of what postmodernism is supposed to do and be. Fifteen years after its first release, *Blade Runner* surely remains the *sine qua non* of postmodern cinema. In his essay on the film, David Harvey draws on Giuliana Bruno's analysis to describe the 'recycling, fusion of levels, discontinuous signifiers, explosion of boundaries and erosion' in the Los Angeles of 2019. Harvey notes the archetypal postmodern fragmentation and uncertainty of the film's *mise-en-scène* and sidesteps to draw similar conclusions from Wim Wenders's portrait of late 1980s Berlin in his *Wings of Desire* (1987). Wenders's city is equally fragmented and forlorn, peopled by lost souls whose many languages we eavesdrop upon. Like *Blade Runner*'s replicants, the citizens of *Wings of Desire* seek to fix their identities and histories through photographs and documents of the past, motivated by the need to construct a whole, completed subjectivity. Yet ultimately both films can offer hope only through romanticism and the union of the traditional heterosexual couple. As Harvey notes, the unconvincing nature of such solutions is signalled by Wender's last line 'fortsetzung folgt' – 'to be continued'. Endings can indeed be a problem for postmodern texts. Yet as *afficianados* of *Blade Runner* will be aware, one unconvincing ending can be re-worked into the greater ambiguity of a second, even if this means taking us, in a loop of postmodern time, forward yet back to the earlier preferred version of the 'director's cut'.

Harvey's juxtaposition of *Blade Runner* and *Wings of Desire* – specifically the parallels he draws between the replicant of 2019 and the human condition of the late 1980s – highlights as it questions *Blade Runner*'s central opposition between the human and the machine, or self and other. As Vivian Sobchack notes, the human–replicant relationship in *Blade Runner*'s 'polyglot megalopolis' has become the site for a displaced enactment of ethnic difference and discrimination evident, at its most blatant, in Bryant's contemptuous 'skinjobs', which Deckard's voice-over translates as 'niggers'. The distinction between the human and less than human is problematised within the film itself, however, by the frequent visual links and suggested affinities between Deckard and his adversaries, especially in the director's cut. Notions of difference are by no means subsumed in *Blade Runner*, then, despite their transposition. In common with other films cited by Sobchack, it foregrounds the provisionality of human and, by implication, white ethnic subjectivity. In Sobchack's further examples, *Zelig*, *Moscow on the Hudson* and *The Brother from Another Planet*, concepts of 'sameness' and 'otherness' are explored in a parodic mode which reveals the multiplicity of differences comprising contemporary 'Americanness' and the consequent fragility of ethnic identity. *Zelig*'s successful assimilation of Jewish, black, Chinese, and Greek cultural roles, and the impossible project in *Moscow on the Hudson* to erase all ethnic difference and so produce a 'standard American', are seen in a reading of postmodernism's 'double-codedness' both to assert and to undermine patterns of segregation and stable ethnic definition.

Films of this kind, Sobchack argues, open binary divisions into a dialogue between diverse cultural positions, undermining master narratives of homogeneity and celebrating difference. Elsewhere, difference and diversity have been explored in the double-coded recycling of genres, whether of sci-fi, *film noir* or the crime thriller, as so often above, or the Western, musical, animated cartoon or woman's film – or hybrid versions of these, working to ironise the conventional binaries of the human and alien, the lawman or detective and criminal, or, on occasion, stereotypical gender roles and the conventions of a normative sexuality, as, for example, in the postmodern, or 'post-classical' romantic comedies *Pretty Woman* (1990) and *Sleepless in Seattle* (1993) (see Garrett, 1995). As Kobena Mercer notes, too, the dialogic and deconstructive impulse in postmodernism has a particular relevance to the black experience of decentred and displaced subjectivity. Black film-making, Mercer argues, is therefore in a unique position to represent the 'crisis in cultural authority' and breakdown of hierarchies symptomatic of postmodern society. Like the video work of Pratibha Parmar in our final section, the film practice Mercer describes in *Handsworth Songs* and *Territories* incorporates a plurality of styles, appropriating TV news footage and found material in a discourse which mixes theory with the 'street' culture of rap and reggae. In a vivid phrase, indebted, as are other contributors, to the theories of Mikhail Bakhtin, Mercer speaks of 'carnivalising' the film text, creating a fragmentary collage which resists closure and emphasises a fluidity of position and expression. As such, Mercer argues, this film making enacts and 'celebrates the "in-between-ness" of the black British condition . . . as a position from which critical insight is made possible' (p. 142 below). These films deconstruct the myth of the 'black community' as a homogenous unity and stress instead a plurality of identities, not merely within the nation as a whole, as Sobchack's examples attempt, but within the subgroup 'black society'.

In these ways, the archetypal postmodern techniques of quotation and discontinuity, the erosion of boundaries, a resistance to linearity and the undermining of 'grand' narratives become tools for the political project which postmodern film (and postmodernist art in general) is so frequently said to lack. In an irony of postmodernism's own – and a sign in the present context of its delayed 'after-effect' – it is in association with marginal film practices and groups that this notoriously 'hollow' and 'superficial' aesthetic has been appropriated as a shaping influence upon projects for cultural change.

## References

Corrigan T. 1991: *A cinema without walls. Movies and culture after Vietnam*. London: Routledge.

Denzin N. 1991: *Images of postmodern society. Social theory and contemporary cinema*. London: Sage.

Garrett R. 1995: Retro romance and the female spectator. Seminar paper. London: Dept of Cultural Studies, University of East London.

Jameson F. 1991: *Postmodernism, or, the cultural logic of late capitalism*. London: Verso.

## Further reading

Baudrillard J. 1987: *The evil demon of images*. Sydney: The Power Institute.

Bruno G. 1990: Ramble city. Postmodernism and *Blade Runner*. In Kuhn A. (ed.), *Alien Zone*. London: Verso.

Collins J., Radner H. and Preacher Collins A. (eds) 1993: *Film theory goes to the movies*. London: Routledge.

Diawara M. (ed.) 1993: *Black cinema. History, authorship, spectatorship*. London: Routledge.

Donald J. (ed.) 1989: *Fantasy and the cinema*. London: BFI.

Dyer R. 1990: *Now you see it. Studies in lesbian and gay film*. London: Routledge.

Friedberg A. 1993: *Window shopping. Cinema and the postmodern*. Berkeley, CA: University of California Press.

Friedman L. D. (ed.) 1991: *Unspeakable images. Ethnicity and the American cinema.* Bloomington, IL: University of Illinois Press.

Kuhn A. (ed.) 1990: *Alien zone. Cultural theory and contemporary science fiction cinema.* London: Verso.

Massey D. 1994: Exclusively masculine modernism. *Blue Velvet* and *Blade Runner. Space, place and gender.* Cambridge: Polity.

Mercer K. 1995: *Welcome to the jungle. New positions in black cultural studies.* London: Routledge.

Mulvey L. 1989: *Visual pleasure and other narratives.* London: Macmillan.

Pribram E. D. (ed.) 1988: *Female spectators. Looking at film and television.* London: Verso.

Sharrett C. (ed.) 1993: *Crisis cinema. The apocalyptic idea in postmodern narrative film.* Washington DC: Maisoneuve Press.

Shohat E. and Stam R. 1994: *Unthinking Eurocentricism. Multiculturalism and the media.* London: Routledge.

Stacey J. 1994: *Star gazing. Hollywood cinema and female spectatorship.* London: Routledge.

See also the journals:

*Camera Obscura*, **27** (Sept. 1991) and **32** (Sept.-Jan., 1993–4).
*Screen*: 'Postmodern Screen', **28**(2) (1987).

# 4

# Time and space in the postmodern cinema

*David Harvey*

From *The condition of postmodernity* (Basil Blackwell 1989)

Postmodern cultural artefacts are, by virtue of the eclecticism of their conception and the anarchy of their subject matter, immensely varied. I think it
useful, however, to illustrate how the themes of time–space compression
that have been elaborated on here get represented in postmodern works.
For this purpose I choose to look at the cinema, in part because this is an art
form which (together with photography) arose in the context of the first
great burst of cultural modernism, but also because, of all the art forms, it
has perhaps the most robust capacity to handle intertwining themes of
space and time in instructive ways. The serial use of images, and the ability
to cut back and forth across space and time, free it from many of the normal
constraints, even though it is, in the final analysis, a spectacle projected
within an enclosed space on a depthless screen.

The two films I shall consider are *Blade Runner* and *Himmel über Berlin*
(called *Wings of Desire* in English). Ridley Scott's *Blade Runner* is a popular
science fiction movie, considered an excellent example of its genre by many,
and a film that still circulates in the late-night cinemas of large metropolitan
areas. It is a piece of pop art that nevertheless explores important themes. I
am particularly indebted to Giuliana Bruno's perceptive analysis of its postmodern aesthetics. Wim Wenders's *Wings of Desire*, on the other hand, is a
piece of 'highbrow' cinema, very favourably received by the critics (a 'bitter-
sweet masterpiece' one critic wrote), but hard to grasp at first viewing. It is
the kind of film that has to be worked at to be understood and appreciated.
However, it explores similar themes to those set out in *Blade Runner*, though
from a rather different perspective and in a very different style. Both films
exemplify many of the characteristics of postmodernism, and in addition
pay particular attention to the conceptualization and meanings of time and
space.

The story of *Blade Runner* concerns a small group of genetically produced human beings, called 'replicants', who return to face their makers.
The film is set in Los Angeles in the year 2019 and hinges around the
search of the 'blade runner' Deckard to uncover the presence of the replicants and to eliminate or 'retire' them (as the film has it) as a serious danger to the social order. The replicants have been created for the specific

purpose of working on highly skilled tasks in particularly difficult environments at the frontiers of space exploration. They are endowed with
strengths, intelligence, and powers that are at the limit of, or even beyond
that of, ordinary human beings. They are also endowed with feelings; only
in this way, it seems, can they adapt to the difficulty of their tasks in such a
way as to make judgements consistent with human requirements.
However, fearing that they might at some point pose a threat to the established order, their makers have given them a life-span of only four years.
If they escape control during these four years they have to be 'retired'. But
to retire them is both dangerous and difficult precisely because of their
superior endowments.

The replicants are, it should be noted, not mere imitations but totally
authentic reproductions, indistinguishable in almost all respects from
human beings. They are simulacra rather than robots. They have been
designed as the ultimate form of short-term, highly skilled and flexible
labour power (a perfect example of a worker endowed with all of the qualities necessary to adapt to conditions of flexible accumulation). But like all
workers faced with the threat of a shortened working life, the replicants do
not take kindly to the restrictions of their four-year life-span. Their purpose
in returning to their makers is to try to find ways to prolong their life, by
infiltrating to the heart of the productive apparatus that made them, and
there persuading or forcing their makers to re-programme their genetic
make-up. Their designer, Tyrell (head of a vast corporate empire of that
name), points out to Roy, the leader of the replicants, who ultimately penetrates into his inner sanctum, that the replicants have more than adequate
recompense for the brevity of their life-span – they live, after all, with the
most incredible intensity. 'Revel in it', says Tyrell, 'a flame that burns twice
as intensely lives half as long.' The replicants exist, in short, in that schizophrenic rush of time that Jameson, Deleuze and Guattari, and others see as
so central to postmodern living. They also move across a breadth of space
with a fluidity that gains them an immense fund of experience. Their persona matches in many respects the time and space of instantaneous global
communications.

In revolt against their conditions of 'slave labour' (as Roy, the leader of
the replicants, calls it) and seeking to prolong their life-spans, four replicants fight and kill their way back into Los Angeles, where the 'blade runner' Deckard, an expert in methods of detecting and retiring escaped
replicants, is summoned to deal with them. Though tired of all the killing
and violence, Deckard is forced out of retirement and given no option by
the authorities except to undertake the task, on pain of his own reduction in
status to that of 'little person'. Both Deckard and the replicants, therefore,
exist in a similar relation to the dominant social power in society. This relation defines a hidden bond of sympathy and understanding between the
hunted and the hunter. During the film, Deckard's life is twice saved by a
replicant, while he, in turn, saves the life of a fifth, a recently created and
even more sophisticated replicant called Rachel, with whom Deckard eventually falls in love.

The Los Angeles to which the replicants return is hardly a utopia. The
flexibility of the replicants' capacity to labour in outer space is, as we have

recently come to expect, matched in Los Angeles by a decrepit landscape of deindustrialization and post-industrial decay. Empty warehouses and abandoned industrial plant drip with leaking rain. Mist swirls, rubbish piles up, infrastructures are in a state of disintegration that makes the pot-holes and failing bridges of contemporary New York look mild by comparison. Punks and scavengers roam among the garbage, stealing whatever they can. J. F. Sebastian, one of the genetic designers who will eventually provide access to Tyrell for the replicants (and who himself suffers from a disease of premature aging called 'accelerated decrepitude') lives alone in such an empty space (actually a deserted version of the Bradbury building built in Los Angeles in 1893), surrounding himself with a fantastic array of mechanical and talking toys and dolls for company. But above the scenes of street-level and interior chaos and decay, there soars a high-tech world of zooming transporters, of advertising ('a chance to buy again in a golden land', proclaims one advertisement circulating in the sky of mist and pouring rain), of familiar images of corporate power (Pan Am, surprisingly still in business in 2019, Coca-Cola, Budweiser, etc.), and the massive pyramidal building of the Tyrell Corporation that dominates one part of the city. The Tyrell Corporation specializes in genetic engineering. 'Commerce', says Tyrell, 'more human than human, that's our business.' Opposed to these images of overwhelming corporate power, however, is another street-level scene of seething small-scale production. The city streets are full of all sorts of people – Chinese and Asiatics seem predominant, and it is the smiling face of a Japanese woman that advertises the Coca-Cola. A 'city-speak' language has emerged, a hybrid of Japanese, German, Spanish, English, etc. Not only has the 'third world' come to Los Angeles even more than at present, but signs of third world systems of labour organization and informal labour practices are everywhere. The scales for a genetically produced snake are produced in a tiny workshop, and human eyes are produced in another (both run by Orientals), indicating intricate relations of sub-contracting between highly disaggregated firms as well as with the Tyrell Corporation itself. The sense of the city at street level is chaotic in every respect. Architectural designs are a postmodern mish-mash – the Tyrell Corporation is housed in something that looks like a replica of an Egyptian pyramid, Greek and Roman columns mix in the streets with references to Mayan, Chinese, Oriental, Victorian and contemporary shopping mall architecture. Simulacra are everywhere. Genetically reproduced owls fly, and snakes slither across the shoulders of Zhora, a genetically reproduced replicant, as she performs in a cabaret that looks like a perfect 1920s imitation. The chaos of signs, of competing significations and messages, suggests a condition of fragmentation and uncertainty at street level that emphasizes many of these facets of postmodern aesthetics. The aesthetic of *Blade Runner*, says Bruno, is the result 'of recycling, fusion of levels, discontinuous signifiers, explosion of boundaries, and erosion'. Yet there is also an overwhelming sense of some hidden organizing power – the Tyrell Corporation, the authorities who commission Deckard to his task without offering any choice, the rapid descent of the powers of law and order when necessary to establish street control. The chaos is tolerated, precisely because it seems so unthreatening to overall control.

Images of creative destruction are everywhere. They are most powerfully present, of course, in the figure of the replicants themselves, created with marvellous powers only to be prematurely destroyed, and most certainly to be 'retired' should they actually engage their own feelings and try to develop their own capacities in their own way. The images of decay everywhere in the landscape reinforce exactly that same structure of feeling. The sense of shattering and fragmentation in social life is highlighted in an incredible sequence in which Deckard pursues one of the women replicants, Zhora, through the crowded, incoherent, and labyrinth-like spaces of the city. Finally tracking her down in an arcade full of stores exhibiting their commodities, he shoots her in the back as she goes crashing though layer after layer of glass doors and windows, dying as she sends shards of glass flying in a million and one directions in the final plunge through a huge window.

The search for the replicants depends upon a certain technique of interrogation, which rests on the fact that they have no real history; they have, after all, been genetically created as full adults and lack the experience of human socialization (a fact which also renders them potentially dangerous should they evade control). The key question that exposes one of the replicants, Leon, is 'Tell me about your feelings around your mother?' To which Leon replies, 'Let me tell you about my mother', and shoots his interrogator dead. Rachel, the most sophisticated of the replicants, tries to convince Deckard of her authenticity as a person (after she suspects that Deckard has seen through her other defences) by producing a photograph of a mother and a little girl which she claims is her. The point here, as Bruno perceptively observes, is that photographs are now construed as evidence of a real history, no matter what the truth of that history may have been. The image is, in short, proof of the reality, and images can be constructed and manipulated. Deckard discovers a whole range of photographs in Leon's possession, presumably meant to document that he has a history too. And Rachel, seeing Deckard's photographs of his family (and it is interesting that the only sense of history that we have for Deckard is provided by his photographs), tries to integrate with them. She puts her hair in the style of the photographs, plays the piano as if in a picture, and acts as if she knows what home means. It is this willingness to search for identity, home, and history (the match with Bachelard's views on the poetics of space is almost perfect here) that ultimately leads to her reprieve from 'retirement'. Deckard is certainly touched by it. But she can re-enter the symbolic realm of a truly human society only by acknowledging the overwhelming power of the Oedipal figure, the father. That is the only route she can take in order to be able to respond to the question, 'Tell me about your mother?' In submitting to Deckard (trusting him, deferring to him, and ultimately submitting to him physically), she learns the meaning of human love and the essence of ordinary sociality. In killing the replicant Leon as he is about to kill Deckard, she provides the ultimate evidence of the capacity to act as Deckard's woman. She escapes the schizoid world of replicant time and intensity to enter the symbolic world of Freud.

I do not think Bruno is correct, however, when he contrasts Roy's with Rachel's fate as hinging upon Rachel's willingness to submit to the symbolic order and Roy's refusal so to do. Roy is programmed to die shortly, and no reprieve or salvation is possible. His demand to overcome all the waste of his own condition simply cannot be met. His anger, as well as that of the other replicants, is huge. Gaining access to Tyrell, Roy first kisses him before tearing out Tyrell's eyes and killing his maker. Bruno quite reasonably interprets this as a reversal of the Oedipal myth and a clear sign that the replicants do not live within the frame of the Freudian symbolic order. This does not mean, however, that replicants have no human feelings. We have already seen something of Roy's capacity to feel, in his moving and deeply affectionate response to the death of the woman replicant Pris, shot down by Deckard in the midst of J. F. Sebastian's replicas. Roy's subsequent pursuit by Deckard, which quickly reverses into the hunted pursuing the hunter, culminates with Roy at the last minute rescuing Deckard from falling into the canyon of a street below. And it is almost exactly at that moment that Roy reaches his own programmed end.

But before he dies, Roy recounts something of the wondrous events he has participated in and the sights he has seen. He voices his anger at his condition of enslavement, and the waste that allows all his incredible intensity of experience to be 'washed away in time like tears in rain'. Deckard acknowledges the power of those aspirations. The replicants, he reflects, are just like most of us. They simply want to know 'where they have come from, where they are going to and how much time they've got'. And it is with Rachel, who has not been programmed to die in the four years, that Deckard escapes, after the four other replicants are dead, into a natural landscape of forests and mountains where the sun, never seen in Los Angeles, shines. The replicant has become the simulacrum to such perfection that she and the human can set off into their own futures, though with both of them 'wondering how much time we've got'.

*Blade Runner* is a science fiction parable in which postmodernist themes, set in a context of flexible accumulation and time–space compression, are explored with all the imaginary power that the cinema can command. The conflict is between people living on different time scales, and seeing and experiencing the world very differently as a result. The replicants have no real history, but can perhaps manufacture one; history for everyone has become reduced to the evidence of the photograph. Though the socialization is still important to personal history, that too, as Rachel shows, can be replicated. The depressing side of the film is precisely that, in the end, the difference between the replicant and the human becomes so unrecognizable that they can indeed fall in love (once both get on the same time scale). The power of the simulacrum is everywhere. The strongest social bond between Deckard and the replicants in revolt – the fact that they are both controlled and enslaved by a dominant corporate power – never generates the slightest hint that a coalition of the oppressed might be forged between them. While Tyrell's eyes are indeed torn out during his killing, this is an individual rather than I class act of rage. The finale of the film is a scene of sheer escapism (tolerated, it should be noted, by the authorities) that leaves unchanged the plight of replicants as well as the dismal conditions of the seething mass of humanity that inhabits the derelict streets of a decrepit, deindustrialized, and decaying postmodernist world.

In *Wings of Desire*, we similarly encounter two groups of actors living on different time scales. Angels live in enduring and eternal time, and humans live in their own social time, and, of course, they each see the world very differently. The film articulates that same sense of fragmentation that suffuses *Blade Runner*, while the question of the relations between time, space, history, and place is directly rather than indirectly posed. The problem of image, particularly that implied by the photograph, versus the telling of a story in real time, is central to the construction of the film.

The film begins with a fairy-tale-like narration of what it was like when children were children. It was a time, we are told, when children thought everything was full of life and life was as one, when they had no opinion on anything (including, presumably, having opinions, which would be totally acceptable to a postmodernist philosopher like Rorty), and when they were not even disturbed by photographs. Nevertheless, children ask important questions such as: 'Why am I me and not you?' 'Why am I here and not there?' and, 'When did time begin and where does space end?' These questions are repeated at several key points in the film, and frame the thematic material. Children, at various points in the film, look upwards or around them as if they are partially aware of the angels' presence in ways that the preoccupied and self-referential adults seem incapable of doing. The questions children ask are, of course, fundamental questions of identity, and the film explores two parallel tracks for defining answers.

The place is Berlin. In a sense it is a pity that Berlin disappears from the English title because the film is a wonderful and sensitive evocation of the sense of that place. We are quickly given to understand, however, that Berlin is one city among many in a global interactive space. Peter Falk, an instantly identifiable international media star (many will recognize him as the detective Columbo in a media series of that name, and that role is directly referenced several times) flies in by air. His thoughts go 'Tokyo, Kyoto, Paris, London, Trieste, . . . Berlin!' as he locates the place for which he is bound. Shots of airliners leaving or arriving punctuate the film at various key points. People think their thoughts in German, French, and English, with other languages occasionally used (language has not yet degenerated to the condition of 'city-speak' in *Blade Runner*). References to the international space of the media are everywhere. Berlin is, evidently, just one place of many, and it exists in a cosmopolitan world of internationalism. Yet Berlin is still the distinctive place to be explored. A moment before we listen in to Falk's thoughts, we overhear a young girl thinking about how to draw the space of home. The relation between space and place is early put straight onto the agenda.

The first part of the film examines Berlin through the monochromatic eyes of a pair of angels. Outside the human time of becoming, they exist in the realm of pure spirit, in infinite and eternal time. They can also move effortlessly and instantaneously in space. For them, time and space just are, an infinite present in an infinite space which reduces the whole world to a monochromatic state. Everything seems to float in the same undifferentiated present, much as contemporary social life floats in the undifferentiated and homogenizing stream of international money. The angels cannot, however, get inside the problem of human decision-making. They cannot resonate with 'here' and 'now' precisely because they live in a world of 'always' and 'forever'.

The picture of Berlin that emerges from their perspective is an extraordinary landscape of fragmented spaces and ephemeral incidents that has no binding logic. The opening shots take us from on high, down into the inner courtyards and divided spaces of nineteenth-century worker housing. From there we go into labyrinth-like interior spaces, listening in with the angels, to people's inner thoughts. Isolated spaces, isolated thoughts, and isolated individuals are all we can see. A youth in a room contemplates suicide over a lost love, while his father and mother think quite disparate thoughts about him. In the underground, on a bus, in cars, in an ambulance racing with a pregnant woman, on the street, on a bicycle, everything appears as fragmented and ephemeral, each incident recorded in the same monotone and monochrome as the other. Being outside human space and time, all the angels can do is to offer some spiritual comfort, try to soothe the fragmented and often shattered feelings of the individuals whose thoughts they monitor. They sometimes succeed, and just as often fail (the youth commits suicide, and the high school student taking to prostitution is inconsolable at the loss of her dead boy friend). As angels, one of them complains, we can never really participate, only pretend.

This extraordinary evocation of an urban landscape, of alienated individuals in fragmented spaces caught in an ephemera of unpatterned incidents, has a powerful aesthetic effect. The images are stark, cold, but endowed with all of the beauty of old-style still photography, though set in motion through the camera lens. It is a selective landscape that we see. The facts of production, and the necessary class relations that attach thereto, are noticeable by their absence. We are treated to a picture of the urban that is, in the fashion of postmodern sociology, entirely *déclassé*, much closer to Simmel (in his 'Metropolis and Mental Life' essay) than to Marx. Death, birth, anxiety, pleasure, loneliness are all aestheticized on the same plane, empty of any sense of class struggle or of ethical or moral commentary.

The identity of this place called Berlin is constituted through this alien but quite beautiful imagery. The distinctive organization of space and time is, moreover, seen as the framework within which individual identities are forged. The image of divided spaces is particularly powerful, and they are superimposed upon each other in the fashion of montage and collage. The Berlin Wall is one such divide, and it is again and again evoked as a symbol of overarching division. Is this where space now ends? 'It is impossible to get lost in Berlin', someone says, 'because you can always find the wall.' More fine-grained divisions exist, however. Germany, the driver of a car reflects as he tracks through street scenes that conjure up images of war-time destruction, has become fragmented to the point where every individual constitutes a mini-state, where each street has its barriers surrounded by a no man's land through which one can pass only if one has the right password. Even access from any one individual to another demands payment of a toll. Not only may this extreme condition of alienated and isolated individualism (of the sort that Simmel described) be considered a good thing (compared with the collective life of Nazism that had gone before) but individuals may seek it out. 'Get a good costume, that's half the battle', says Falk thinking about the part he is to play, and, in a wonderfully humorous scene he tries on hat after hat in order, he says, to be able to pass unrecognized among the crowd and achieve the anonymity he desires. The hats he puts on turn into virtual masks of characters, in much the same way that Cindy Sherman photographs mask the person. This hat makes him look like Humphrey Bogart, this one is for going to the races, that one for going to the opera, and another is for getting married in. The act of masking and disguising connects with spatial fragmentation and alienated individualism.

This landscape bears all the marks of high postmodernist art as Pfeil (1988, 384) for one has recently described it. 'One is confronted not with a unified text, much less by the presence of a distinct personality and sensibility, but by a discontinuous terrain of heterogeneous discourses uttered by anonymous, unplaceable tongues, a chaos different from that of the classic texts of high modernism precisely insofar as it is not recontained or recuperated within an overarching mythic framework.' The quality of utterance is 'deadpan, indifferent, depersonalized, effaced', so as to cancel out 'the possibility of traditional audience participation'. Only the angels have an overall view, and they, when they perch on high, hear only a babble of intersecting voices and whispers, and see nothing but a monochromatic world.

How can some sense of identity be forged and sustained in such a world? Two spaces assume a peculiar significance in this regard. The library – a repository of historical knowledge and collective memory – is a space into which many are evidently drawn (even angels seem to take their rest there). An old man enters the library. He is to play an extremely important, though ambiguous role. He sees himself as the story-teller, the muse, the potential guardian of collective memory and history, the representative of 'everyman'. But he is disturbed at the thought that the tight circle of listeners who used to gather round him has been broken up and dispersed, he knows not where, as readers who do not communicate with each other. Even language, the meanings of words and sentences, he complains, seem to slip and slide into incoherent fragments. Forced now to live 'from day to day', he uses the library to try and recuperate a proper sense of the history of this distinctive place called Berlin. He wants to do it not from the standpoint of leaders and kings, but as a hymn of peace. The books and photographs, however, conjure up images of the death and destruction wrought in World War II, a trauma to which the film again and again makes reference, as if this was indeed when this time began and when the spaces of the city were shattered. The old man, surrounded by model globes in the library, spins a wheel, thinking that the whole world is disappearing in the dusk. He leaves the library and walks in search of the Potsdamer Platz (one of those urban spaces that Sitte would surely have admired), the heart of old Berlin, with its Café Josti where he used to take coffee and a cigar and watch the crowd. Walking alongside the Berlin Wall, all he can find is an empty weed-strewn lot. Puzzled, he collapses into an abandoned armchair, insisting that his quest is neither hopeless nor unimportant. Even though he feels like a poet ignored and mocked on the edge of no man's land, he cannot give up, he says, because if mankind loses its story-teller then it loses its childhood. Even though the story may in parts be ugly – and he recalls how when flags appeared in the Potsdamer Platz the crowd turned unfriendly and the police brutish – it still has to be told. Besides, he feels personally protected, saved, he says, 'from present and future troubles by the tale'. His search to reconstruct and tell this tale of salvation and protection is a subtle sub-plot throughout the film that assumes its importance only at the very end.

But there is a second site where a fragile sense of identity prevails. The circus, a spectacle held together within the enclosed space of a tent, offers a venue of special interaction within which some kind of human relating can go on. It is within this space that the trapeze artist, Marion, acquires some sense of herself, a possibility of achieving and belonging. But the news that the circus is out of money and has to close shows immediately how ephemeral and contingent that identity is. The short-term contract prevails here too. Yet Marion, while plainly distressed at this news, insists she has a story, and that she is going to go on creating one, though not in the circus. She even imagines going into a photo-automat and emerging with a new identity (the power of the photo image, once more), taking up a job as waitress or whatever. Her own history, we are reminded as one of the angels watches her in her caravan, can in any case be collapsed (like that of Deckard) into family photographs pinned to the wall, so why not build a new history with the aid of photographs? These fantasies are suffused, however, with a powerful aura of desire to become a whole rather than a fragmented and alienated person. She longs to be complete, but recognizes that this can come to be only through a relation with another. After the tent is down and the circus is gone, she stands alone on the empty site, feeling herself a person without roots, without history, or without country. Yet that very emptiness seems to hold out the possibility of some radical transformation. 'I can become the world', she says, as she watches a jet airliner cruise across the sky.

One of the angels, Damiel, already chafing at his powerlessness to resonate with the here and now, is attracted by Marion's energy and beauty, particularly in the performance of her trapeze act. He becomes caught up in her inner longings to become rather than just to be. For the first time he gets a glimpse of what the world would look like in colour, and he is increasingly drawn to the idea of entering the flow of human time, leaving behind the time of the spirit and of eternity. Two catalytic moments trigger his decision. She dreams of him as the resplendent 'other', and he sees himself reflected in her dream. Invisible still, he follows Marion into a night club and, as she dances dreamily by herself, he touches her thoughts. She responds with a sense of rapturous well-being, as if, she says, a hand is softly tightening within her body. The second catalytic moment is with Peter Falk who, it later transpires, is an angel come to ground some time ago. He senses the presence of the invisible Damiel as he takes a cup of coffee at a street stall. 'I can't see you, but I know you're there', he says to a surprised Damiel, and then goes on to speak with warmth and humour of how good it is to live in the flow of human time, to feel material events, and take tangible account of the whole range of human sensations.

Damiel's decision to come inside is taken in the no man's land between two lines of the Berlin Wall, patrolled by soldiers. Fortunately, his fellow angel has the power to place him on the western side. There Damiel wakes up to a world of rich and vibrant colours. He has to navigate the city in real physical terms, and in so doing experiences the exhilaration that comes with creating a spatial story (in the manner of de Certeau) simply by traversing the city, which then no longer seems as fragmented but which assumes a more coherent structure. This human sense of space and motion contrasts with that of angels, earlier depicted as a hyper-space of speeding flashes, each image like a cubist painting, suggesting a totally different mode of spatial experience. Damiel shifts from one mode to the other as he enters the flow of time. But he needs money, now, to survive. He borrows enough from a passer-by to buy a cup of coffee and trades in a piece of ancient armour (which we subsequently learn is the initial endowment of all angels who come to earth) and emerges from the shop with a colourful set of clothes and a watch which he inspects with the greatest interest. He comes across the set where Peter Falk is filming, and here experiences a major check because the guard will not let him enter. Cursing the guard, he has to shout to Falk through a chain link fence. Falk, who guesses immediately who he is, asks him, 'How long?' Damiel replies, 'Minutes, hours, days, weeks, . . . TIME!' to which Falk immediately responds, with kind and gentle humour, 'Here, let me give you some dollars!' Damiel's entry into this human world is now firmly located within the co-ordinates of social space, social time, and the social power of money.

The coming together of Damiel and Marion is clearly meant as the climactic point of the film. The two circle each other in the same night-club she had been in before, watched tiredly by Damiel's earlier angel companion, before coming together in the bar close by. There they meet in an almost ritualistic way, she ready and determined to make her history, to supersede being with becoming, he determined to learn the meaning of the flow of human experience in space and time. In the lengthy monologue that follows, she insists on the seriousness of their common project even though the times themselves may not be serious. She insists on doing away with coincidence and contingency. The temporary contracts are over. She tries to define a way of coming together that has a universal meaning beyond this particular place and time. There may not be any destiny, she says, but there is certainly decision. And it is a decision in which all the people of the city, even of the world, can participate. She imagines a square full of people, and that she and Damiel are so full of that place that they can make a decision for all. It is a decision to forge a bond between a man and a woman around a common project of becoming, in which a woman can say 'my man' in such a way as to open up a whole world to fresh insight and interpretation. It means entering the labyrinth of happiness through the transformation of desire into love, so that she can finally be truly alone with herself, because to be truly alone presupposes a wholeness that can come only through a non-contingent relation to another. It seems she now has answers to the compelling questions: 'Why am I me and not you?' 'Why am I here and not there?' and 'Where did time begin and where does space end?' What is born of their coming together, reflects Damiel as he helps her to practise her trapeze act after their first night together, is not a child but an immortal image that all can share and live by.

It is hard to prevent this ending slipping into banality (presaged by the kitschy dream sequence in which the angel comes to Marion in resplendent silver costume). Are we to conclude, after all, that it is merely romantic love that makes the world go round? A charitable reading might be that we should not let our jaded experience of kitsch and pastiche stand in the way of liberating romantic desire and undertaking major projects. But the final shots are portentous indeed. The film switches back into the monochrome of enduring time. The old man, with whom we have lost all contact in the coloured sequences of the film, shuffles towards the Berlin Wall, saying, 'Who will look for me, their story-teller? They need me more than ever'. The camera suddenly zooms past him and up into the clouds, as if taking off in flight. 'We are on our way', says Marion. More is to follow, the final credit assures us.

I read this second part of the film as an attempt to resurrect something of the modernist spirit of human communication, togetherness, and becoming, out of the ashes of a monochromatic and dead-pan postmodernist land-scape of feeling. Wenders is plainly mobilizing all his artistic and creative powers in a project of redemption. He proposes, in effect, a romantic myth that can redeem us 'from the formless universe of contigency'. The fact that many angels, according to Falk, have chosen to come to earth, suggests that it is better always to be inside than outside the flow of human time, that becoming always has the potential to break with the stasis of being. Space and time are constituted in radically different ways in the two parts of the film, and the presence of colour, creativity, and, we should not forget, money as a form of social bonding, provides the necessary framework with-in which some sense of common purpose can be found.

Yet there are serious dilemmas to be resolved. Damiel has no history, and Marion is cut off from her roots, her history reduced to a set of photographs and a few other 'objects of memory' of the sort that now constitute the sense of history both in the home and in the museum. Is it possible to set about the project of becoming a-historically? The old man's persistent voice seems to question the viability of that. The sheer romanticism of the ending, he seems to say, has to be tempered by a real sense of history. Indeed, Marion's image of a whole 'Platz' of people participating in their decision, raises the spectre of when the Potsdamer Platz turned ugly as it filled with flags. Put more formally, there is a tension in the film between the power of spatial images (photographs, the film itself, the striving of Damiel and Marion at the end to make an image the world can live by) and the power of the story. The old man (described as Homer, the story-teller in the credits) is in many respects marginalized within the film, and complains explicitly at that very fact. Becoming, according to him, has to be more than creating just another set of depthless images. It has to be situated and understood histor-ically. But that presupposes that history can be captured without the use of images. The old man leafs through a book of photographs, wanders into the Potsdamer Platz trying to reconstitute its sense of place from memory, and remembers it when it turned ugly, not conducive to that epic of peace that he seeks. This dialogue between image and story provides an underlying dramatic tension in the film. Powerful images (of the sort that Wenders and his brilliant cameraman, Henri Alekan, know how to wield only too well) can both illuminate and obscure stories. In the film they overwhelm the ver-bal messages the old man tries to communicate. It is almost as if the film gets caught in the circularity (known in the postmodernist lexicon as 'intertextuality') of its own images. Within this tension lies the whole issue of how to handle the aesthetic qualities of space and time in a postmodern world of monochromatic fragmentation and ephemerality. 'Perhaps', says Marion, 'time itself is the sickness', leaving us to wonder, as in the final sequence of *Blade Runner*, 'how much time we've got'. But whatever that may mean to the participants, the monochromatic landscape of eternal time and infinite but fragmented space plainly will not do.

It is both intriguing and interesting that two films otherwise so disparate should depict such similar conditions. I do not believe the similarity is accidental or contingent. It supports the idea that the experience of time–space compression in recent years, under the pressures of the turn to more flexible modes of accumulation, has generated a crisis of representation in cultural forms, and that this is a subject of intense aesthetic concern, either *in toto* (as I think is the case in *Wings of Desire*) or in part (as would be true of everything from *Blade Runner* to Cindy Sherman's photographs and the novels of Italo Calvino or Pynchon). Such cultural practices are important. If there is a crisis of representation of space and time, then new ways of thinking and feeling have to be created. Part of any trajectory out of the condition of postmodernity has to embrace exactly such a process.

The distressing side of both films, in spite of the overt optimism of Wenders's ending, is the inability to go much further than romanticism (individualized and strongly aestheticized) as a solution to the conditions that both film makers so brilliantly portray. It seems as if the film makers are unable to break free from the power of the images they themselves create. Marion and Damiel seek an image to replace images, and seem to see that as an adequate conception of how to change the world. The turn in both cases to romanticism is, from this standpoint, dangerous precisely because it presages the continuation of a condition in which aesthetics predominates over ethics. The qualities of the romanticism on offer vary of course. The tired machismo of Deckard and the submission of Rachel are entirely different from the meeting of minds and of souls in the case of Marion and Damiel (both of whom are set to learn from each other). Yet even here there is a sense that *Blade Runner* speaks with a rather more authentic (though not necessarily praiseworthy) voice, because it is at least concerned with what nature of symbolic order we might be in (a question that Wenders evades). Wenders likewise evades the question of class relations and consciousness entirely by casting the social problem as the unmediated relationship between individuals and collectivity (the state). While signs of objective class relations abound in *Blade Runner*, the participants in the action evidently see no purpose in relating to them even if they are, like Deckard, vaguely aware of their existence. Brilliant portrayals though both films are of the conditions of postmodernity and in particular of the conflictual and confusing experience of space and time, neither has the power to overturn established ways of seeing or transcend the conflictual conditions of the moment. This must, in part, be attributed to the contradictions inherent in the cinematic form itself. Cinema is, after all, the supreme maker and manipulator of images for commercial purposes, and the very act of using it well always entails reducing the complex stories of daily life to a sequence of images upon a depthless screen. The idea of a revolutionary cinema has always run aground on the rocks of exactly this difficulty. Nevertheless, the *malaise* lies rather deeper than that. Postmodern art forms and cultural artefacts by their very nature must self-consciously embrace the problem of image creation, and necessarily turn inwards upon themselves as a result. It then becomes difficult to escape being what is being imaged within the art form itself. Wenders, I think, really struggles with that problem and the fact that he does not, in the end, succeed, is perhaps most clearly signalled in the final caption that 'more is to follow'. Within these limits, however, the mimetic qualities of cinema of this sort are extraordinarily revealing. Both *Wings of Desire* and *Blade Runner* hold up to us, as in a mirror, many of the essential features of the condition of postmodernity.

## References

Bruno G. 1987: Ramble city: postmodernism and *Blade Runner*. *October* **41**, 61–74.
Pfeil, F. 1988: Postmodernism as a 'structure of feeling'. In Nelson C. and Grossberg L. (eds), *Marxism and the interpretation of culture*. Urbana, IL: Routledge.

# 5

# Who programs you? The science fiction of the spectacle

*Scott Bukatman*

From A. Kuhn (ed.), *Alien zone* (Verso 1990)

We are living in the era of the blip, what Alvin Toffler has labelled *blip culture*.[1] Toffler has written of our bombardment by these 'short, modular blips of information',[2] but for others the blip is more pervasive and more crucial in its implications. Into the 1990s, the human subject has become a blip: ephemeral, electronically processed, unreal.[3] Numerous writers have noted this implosion, the passage of experiential reality into the grids, matrices and pulses of the electronic information age. Exploration outward has been superseded by the inward spiral of orbital circulation – in cybernetic terms, the feedback loop. The world has been reconstituted as a simulation within the mega-computer banks of the Information Society, and terminal identity exists as the mode of engagement with the imploded culture.

Jean Baudrillard writes of orbital circulation as the matrix of the implosive process,[4] which implies a constant *turning-in*, and Arthur Kroker adds the valuable metaphor of 'black hole', that massive gravitational anomaly which draws all into it, from which no information can reliably emerge. Below the event horizon lie only abstraction and hypothesis; direct experience is, by definition, impossible. Acknowledging the strength of McLuhan's axiom, 'the medium is the message' ('the key formula of the age of· simulation'),[5] Baudrillard notes that it is not only this implosion of the message in the medium which is at stake, but also the concurrent '*implosion of the medium and the real* in a sort of nebulous hyperreality . . .'.[6]

Television, still the axiomatic form of electronic simulation, due to its mass penetration and continually functioning national and global networks, is therefore not to be seen as presenting an image or mirror of reality (neutral or otherwise), but rather as a constituent portion of a new reality. Society, the arena of supposed 'real' existence, increasingly becomes 'the mirror of television'.[7] 'The result of this image bombardment', Toffler wrote in *Future Shock*, 'is the accelerated decay of old images, a faster intellectual through-put, and a new, profound sense of the impermanence of knowledge itself.'[8] In the science fiction horror film *Videodrome* (David Cronenberg, 1982), media prophet Brian O'Blivion informs us that 'Television is reality, and reality is less than television.' Soon, 'everyone will have special names . . . names designed to cause the cathode-ray tube to resonate'. A new subject is being constituted, one which begins its process of being through the act of viewership. 'The TV self is the electronic individual *par excellence* who gets everything there is to get from the simulacrum of the media', write Kroker and Cook.[9]

The technologies of the mass media have thus been crucial to the maintenance of instrumental reason as a form of rational (and hence natural, invisible and neutral) domination. 'Domination has its own aesthetics', wrote Marcuse, 'and democratic domination has its democratic aesthetics.'[10] The plurality of channel selections serves as a kind of guarantee of the freedom of the subject to choose, to position one's *self* within the culture, while the constant flow of images, sounds and narratives seemingly demonstrates a cultural abundance and promise. Yet the choice is illusory: to view is to surrender. Early on, Baudrillard wrote: 'It is useless to fantasize about state projection of police control through TV . . . TV, by virtue of its mere presence, is a social control in itself . . . .'[11]

Guy Debord's 1967 manifesto, *Society of the Spectacle*, begins by acknowledging the passage into a new mode of phenomenological and commercial existence. 'In societies where modern conditions of production prevail, all of life presents itself as an immense accumulation of *spectacles*. Everything that was directly lived has moved away into a representation.'[12] The citizen/viewer, no longer engaged in the act of producing reality, exists now in a state of pervasive separation – cut off from the producers of the surrounding media culture by a unilateral communication and detached from the mass of fellow citizen/viewers as the new community of television families and workplaces arise invisibly to take their place.

The spectacle controls by atomizing the population and reducing their capacity to function as an aggregate force, but also by displaying a surfeit of spectacular goods and lifestyles among which the viewer may electronically wander and experience a simulation of satisfaction. Within the conditions of late capitalism, 'the satisfaction of primary human needs is replaced by *an uninterrupted fabrication of pseudo-needs* which are reduced to the single pseudo-need of maintaining the reign of the autonomous economy' (thesis 51, my emphasis). 'The real consumer becomes a consumer of illusions' (thesis 47). Kroker and Cook describe the 1980s self as 'a blip with a lifestyle'.[13]

Science fiction (from the 1950s), like critical theory (from much earlier), has frequently portrayed the mass media as a pacifying force; an opiate. In Ray Bradbury's *Fahrenheit 451* (1953), for example, the wife of the book-burning fireman is addicted to both tranquillizers and television. This juncture of technology, control and addiction evokes the writings of William S. Burroughs, whose incantatory prose reveals a world – a galaxy – completely given over to the pervasiveness and vulnerability of addiction. Addiction is pervasive in that it transcends the use of narcotics: one can be addicted to money or to dope; there are orgasm addicts, control addicts and image addicts. Vulnerability exists because when the desperation of addiction is brought into being, the potential for manipulation escalates. 'The pusher always gets it all back. The addict needs more and more junk to maintain a human form . . . buy off the Monkey. Junk is the mold of monopoly and possession.' Burroughs then analogizes addiction and capitalist control: 'Junk is the ideal product . . . the ultimate merchandise. No sales talk necessary. The client will crawl through a sewer and beg to buy . . . the junk merchant does not sell his product to the consumer, he sells the consumer to his product.'[14]

The nexus commodity/addiction/control is replicated in Debord's post-Frankfurt School analysis. The spectacle is the ultimate commodity in that it makes all others possible: advertisements generate the conditions for consumption, and thus for production as well. The spectacle stimulates the desire to consume (the one permissible participation in the social process), a desire which is continually displaced onto the next product, and the next. It is infinitely self-generating. Ultimately, the spectacle takes on the totalizing function of any addictive substance; it differs from dope only in that its addictive properties remain hidden within the rational economic structures of capitalist society. Contrast the metaphors of Burroughs to these of Debord: 'The spectacle is the moment when the commodity has attained the *total occupation* of social life' (thesis 42). The spectacle is a permanent opium war which aims to make people identify goods with commodities and satisfaction with survival . . .' (thesis 44). '[T]he spectacle is the *main production* of present-day society' (thesis 15). 'The spectacle subjugates living men to the extent that the economy has totally subjugated them' (thesis 16).

The spectacle-addict recurs in science fiction, and the more sophisticated works begin with the premise of voluntarism. The addiction to the video-narcotic means that the control apparatus is already emplaced and invisibly operating to secure the false consciousness of cohesion, democratic order and freedom. Works such as *Fahrenheit 451* or Orwell's *1984* ignore the crucial postulate of Marcuse's democratic domination: an effective ideological state apparatus replaces the need for the overt exercise of power. As Burroughs observed, 'A *functioning* police state needs no police.'[15]

According to Marshall McLuhan, our (post)modern technological capabilities function as 'the extensions of man'.[16] 'During the mechanical ages we had extended our bodies in space', while today, 'we have extended our central nervous system in a global embrace, abolishing both time and space as far as our planet is concerned'.[17] The metaphor reassures by fostering an acceptance of media culture as a natural evolutionary state. To extend the nervous system outside the body further empowers the brain and further centralizes the individual.

Other theorists are less sanguine. Debord clearly posits unilateral forms of communication as an intrusive force: 'Lived reality is materially invaded by the contemplation of the spectacle' (thesis 8). Technologies might hold the possibility of revolutionizing society but, since 'freedom of the press is guaranteed only to those who own one',[18] the possibility also exists that it will serve to consolidate rather than disseminate power. Power is the operative lack in McLuhan's discourse, rendering his vision compelling but incomplete. Baudrillard's writings share McLuhan's fascination with technological change, but always accompanied by a massive awareness of power's reification. He differs from Debord in several ways which distance him from a traditional Marxist position. First, technology replaces economics as the structuring force of the discourse on power. Second, there is Baudrillard's rejection of 'use-value' in favour of a position which guarantees no rigid site of meaning.[19] Finally, he argues that power has been subsumed by technological forces to such a degree that it is no longer the province of the state, much less the citizen.[20] In Baudrillard's imploded universe, human power has itself become a simulation.[21] Power now resides in a technology which holds humanity in its thrall. The media are invading; there will be no survivors.

This shift accounts for the changing style of Baudrillard's prose from a rationally argued Debordian resentment at the reifying deployment of spectacular power, to a hyper-technologized, jargon-ridden language which refuses the possibility of a critical position. Baudrillard's text aspires to the condition of science fiction, and ultimately becomes performative of the process he once merely described.

The usurpation of power by the new technologies of information control leads Baudrillard to reject the neural metaphors of McLuhan. In its place, another biological trope is employed. What exists now is 'a *viral*, endemic, chronic, alarming presence of the medium . . . dissolution of TV into life, the dissolution of life into TV'.[22] The media are no longer the extensions of man, man instead extends the media in becoming a 'terminal of multiple networks'.[23]

Burroughs has frequently deployed virus as a metaphor for all the infiltrating forces of control to which people are subject. *Junky, Naked Lunch* and *Cities of the Red Night* all incorporate viral figures, but it is in the Nova trilogy,[24] and especially in *Nova Express*, that the control virus appears as an *image*: a media-form controlled by invading alien forces. Biology and the media are linked through the node of the image. Images are tangible and material, neither ephemeral nor temporary. A death-dwarf is a literal image-addict ('images – millions of images – That's what I eat . . .' [*Nova Express* (*NE*), p. 68]).

As Burroughs demonstrates, science fiction becomes the discourse best equipped to contend with this new state of things. Samuel Delany and Teresa de Lauretis both argue that the genre is defined by rhetorical heightening and a continual linguistic play resistant to any totalization of meaning.[25] Something further is added in what we may term the science fiction of the spectacle, a subgenre which includes works by Burroughs; J. G. Ballard; James Tiptree, Jr (Alice Sheldon); Philip Dick; David Cronenberg; Norman Spinrad and others. Representation and textuality become the explicit subjects of the text; discourse will comprise the content as well as determine textual form. The inherent rhetoricity of the genre is extended as the text turns in upon its own production and status. The science fiction of the spectacle often demands the recognition of its own imbrication in the implosion of the real. These discursive strategies are dominant in contemporary critical writing as well: Baudrillard's essays, for example, bear rhetorical resemblances to the fictions of Dick and William Gibson, resemblances which are hardly coincidental.

Burroughs has generated his mythology for the space age around the nexus of junk, virus, addiction, control and surrender: 'Hell consists of falling into enemy hands, into the hands of the virus power, and heaven consists of freeing oneself from the power, of achieving inner freedom, freedom from conditioning.'[26] In the Nova trilogy, 'image *is* virus', and 'junk is concentrated image'. Baudrillard nearly quotes Burroughs when he writes about 'this viral contamination of things by images'.[27] The Nova Police reports: 'This virus released upon the world would infect the entire population and turn them into our replicas' (*NE*, p. 48).

The virus is a powerful metaphor for the power of the media, and Burroughs's hyperbolic Manicheism does not completely disguise the accuracy of his analysis. Whether the viral form is an actual living protocell or simply a carrier of genetic information, it clearly possesses an exponentially increasing power to take over and control its host organism. The injection of information leads to control, mutation, and passive replication: the host cell 'believes' that it is following its own biologically determined imperative; it mistakes the new genetic material for its own. The image/virus is posited as invasive and irresistible; a parasite with only self-replication as its function.

Compare this to Debord's economic analysis, where the pervasiveness of the spectacle serves the similar function of creating a deceptive cohesion for the purpose of infinite self-regeneration. The hegemony of the subject is illusory; indeed, imagistic; while control over these images is elusive; in fact impossible. The recurrent image of the virus (the virus of the image), biologizes the rise of spectacle and the consequent waning of autonomous reason. The subject becomes a 'carrier' of spectacle, of image, of pseudo-reality. This is what Eric Mottram has called 'the virus transformation into undifferentiated man, the terminal image of man as patient-victim'.[28] Earth's fate is all too clear: 'The entire planet is being developed into *terminal identity* and complete surrender' (*NE*, p. 19). Terminal identity: an unmistakably doubled articulation in which we find both the end of the subject and a new subjectivity constructed at the computer station or television screen. Again the human is configured as a 'terminal of multiple networks'.

McLuhan wrote that *Nova Express* takes place 'in a universe which seems to be someone else's insides',[29] recognizing that Burroughs's work represents an inversion of his own. He further notes that: 'The human nervous system can be reprogrammed biologically as readily as any radio station can alter its fare.' In this statement, which anticipates *Videodrome*, there is an acknowledgement of political and social control which is rare in McLuhan, and which allows a perception of the unasked question which lurks behind a reading of his works: whose nervous system is this, anyway?

The similarities between Burroughs and film maker David Cronenberg are certainly extensive. The invasion and mutation of the body, the loss of control, and the transformation of the self into Other are as obsessively deployed in the works of the latter as in those of the former. Christopher Sharritt has written that the pervasive concern for both is 'the rise of the addictive personality cultivated by dominant culture and the changing structures of power . . . [Neither] finds a solution in organized revolt since the new technological environment absorbs and dilutes ideological principles and abstract values.'[30] Similarly, Baudrillard has written that

> All the movements which bet only on liberation, emancipation, the resurrection
> of the subject of history, of the group, of speech as a raising of consciousness . . .
> do not see that they are acting in accordance with the system, whose impera-
> tive today is the overproduction and regeneration of meaning and speech.[31]

Language is, in multiple senses, the definition and controller of the self, the site of identity; and Baudrillard's pessimism and rhetorical surrender are commensurate with Burroughs's tactics. Like Baudrillard, Burroughs assimilates the linguistic excess of science fiction, but goes further than Baudrillard towards the demolition of communication. The appropriation of other authors and other texts wrecks the hegemony of both writer and novel, while the technique of the cut-up, in its explicit evocation of surgical procedure which links textual and corporeal bodies, obliterates the linear coherence which generally defines the identity of the text. Relations among signifiers are lost, each now exists in glittering isolation: the rational *telos* of the narrator is replaced by a rhetorical intensification which foregrounds and reveals the random bombardments of the spectacular society. Mutation becomes an act of sabotage, and the cut-up becomes a crucial *immunization* against the invasive forces of the media-virus.

Cronenberg replaces this emphasis on the physicality of language with an attention to the image of the body. While he constructs an elaborate semiotics of the body in all his work, it is only in *Videodrome*, to date, that he fully addresses the construction of *the body of the text*: the cinematic signifier. In Cronenberg's films, the eruptive and incisive mutations which the body undergoes rival Burroughs's cut-ups for their violence, randomness, and capacity to produce chaos. The penile organ emerging from Marilyn Chambers's armpit in *Rabid* (1976), the extruded 'children' of *The Brood* (1979), and the genetic cut-up represented by the human/fly melange in *The Fly* (1986) all enact the breakdown of human hegemony through the deployment of new technologies. Burroughs wrote: 'The realization that something as familiar to you as the movement of your intestines the sound of your breathing the beating of your heart is also alien and hostile does make one feel a bit insecure at first.'[32]

These transformations cannot be completely subsumed within the mind/body dualism of Cartesianism, as one critic proposes to do.[33] Such humanistic balance fails to account for the evident and pervasive antihumanism of Cronenberg's production, as demonstrated by the recurrent fears of human contact, sexuality, or physicality in any form. David Cronenberg is the film maker of *panic sex* (Kroker's pungent phrase) with the body as the overdetermined site for the expression of profound social anxiety.[34] The subject of the Cronenberg film is hardly human action: it is instead, as Sharritt states, the structures of external power and control to which the individual (in body *and* soul) is subjected. The dissolution of identity into new forms is connected to the rise of new technologies, and this has become evident in three of his more recent films, *Scanners* (1980), *Videodrome* and *The Fly*, in which the apparent mind/body dichotomy is superseded by the trichotomy of mind/body/machine. Carrie Rickey is closer to the mark when she writes that Cronenberg is: 'a visionary architect of a chaotic biological tract where mind and body, ever fighting a Cartesian battle for integration, are so vulnerable as to be *easily annexed by technology*.'[35] The mind/body struggle is a blind for the larger Burroughsian issues of addiction, technological control, and the malleability of reality and identity.

*Videodrome* presents a destabilized reality in which image, reality, hallucination and psychosis become indissolubly melded: the most estranging portrayal of image addiction and viral invasion since Burroughs. 'Videodrome', a TV programme, itself broadcasts brutal torture and sadism in a grotesque display which exerts a strong influence upon its viewers. Cable-station operator Max

Renn desires 'Videodrome': as a businessman he needs it to rescue his foundering station; as an individual he finds himself drawn irresistibly to its horrors. Connected to Renn's quest for the source of 'Videodrome' is a profoundly ontological passage beyond spectacle to the ultimate dissolution of the boundaries which might serve to separate and guarantee definitions of 'spectacle', 'subject' and 'reality' itself.

At times *Videodrome* seems to be a film which hypostatizes Baudrillard's own polemic. Here, with remarkable syntactic similarity, Baudrillard and a character from Cronenberg's film are both intent upon the usurpation of the real by its own representation; upon the imbrication of the real, the technologized and the simulated. The language is hypertechnologized but anti-rational; moebius-like in its evocation of a dissolute, spectacular reality:

> *Jean Baudrillard*: 'We are here at the controls of a micro-satellite, in orbit, living no longer as an actor or dramaturge but as a terminal of multiple networks. Television is still the most direct prefiguration of this. But today it is the very space of habitation that is conceived as both receiver and distributor, as the space of both reception and operations, the control screen and terminal which as such may be endowed with telematic power . . . .'[36]

> *Professor O'Blivion*: 'The battle for the mind of North America will be fought in the video arena – the Videodrome. The television screen is the retina of the mind's eye. Therefore the television screen is part of the physical structure of the brain. Therefore whatever appears on the television screen emerges as raw experience for those who watch it. Therefore television is reality and reality is less than television.'

Both, in fact, seem to be following Debord's programme that 'When *analyzing* the spectacle one speaks, to some extent, the language of the spectacular itself in the sense that one moves through the methodological terrain of the very society which expresses itself in spectacle' (thesis 11) – precisely why science fiction has obtained such a lately privileged position. Baudrillard embraces a high-tech, alienating and alienated science fictional rhetoric to explore the very paradigm of high-tech alienation, while Cronenberg's horror films about the failure of interpersonal communications are an integral part of an industry which privileges the spectacular over the intimate, and pseudo-satisfaction over genuine comprehension. Both construct discourses of anti-rationalism to expose and ridicule any process or history of enlightenment occurring through the exercise of a 'pure' reason.

Television pervades *Videodrome*. O'Blivion is the founder of the Cathode Ray Mission, a kind of TV soup kitchen for the city's derelicts: 'Watching TV will patch them back into the world's mixing board.' Television is often a medium of direct address. Renn is awakened by a videotaped message. O'Blivion refuses to appear on television 'except *on* television', his image appears on a monitor placed beside the programme's host (in a gesture reminiscent of Debord's own pre-recorded lectures).[37] As Renn awaits his own talk show appearance, he chats with Nicki Brand, but an interposed monitor blocks our view. The image on the monitor is coextensive with its own background, however – Magritte-like – and consequently, the conversation is between a live Renn and a video Brand. Such examples offer a preliminary blurring of the distinction between real and televisual experiences.

This parody of McLuhan's global TV village serves as backdrop to the enigma of 'Videodrome', which is finally revealed to be a government project. The explanation for 'Videodrome' is at least as coherent as any from Burroughs: Spectacular Optical, a firm which specializes in defence contracts, has developed a signal which induces a tumour in the viewer. This tumour causes hallucinations which can be recorded, then revised, then fed back to the viewer: in effect, the individual is reprogrammed to serve the controller's ends. Burroughs offered a similar vision: 'you are a programmed tape recorder set to record and play back/who programs you/who decides what tapes play back in present time'.[38]

But as Barry Convex of Spectacular Optical asks Renn, 'Why would anyone watch a scum show like "Videodrome"?' 'Business reasons', is Renn's fast response, but his interest transcends the commercial. Coincident with his exposure to the 'Videodrome' signal is his attraction to Nicki Brand, an outspoken, alluring personality for C-RAM radio.[39] Transgression thus enters Renn's life in at least three ways: socially, via his soft-porn, hard-violence cable TV station; sexually, through his forays into sadomasochism with Brand; and the political and sexual transgressions of 'Videodrome' itself. The three levels are linked in a spiralling escalation which culminates in Renn's own hallucinated appearance on 'Videodrome', whipping, first Brand, then her image on a television monitor. Brand is the guide who leads Renn on towards his final destiny; after her death, her image remains to spur him on. Her masochism might indicate a quest for sensation: this media figure admits that: 'We live in overstimulated times. We crave stimulation for its own sake.' Brand wants to 'audition' for 'Videodrome': 'I was *made* for that show', she brags, but it might be more accurate to say that she was made *by* that show. Renn is told that 'They used her image to seduce you.'

The 'Videodrome' programme is explicitly linked by both Renn and Convex to male sexual response (something 'tough' rather than 'soft') and penetration (something that will 'break through'). Renn takes on the 'tough' sadistic role with Brand, and yet there is no doubt that it is she who controls the relationship, she who dominates.[40] Similarly, the power granted to the 'Videodrome' viewer to observe and relish its brutality masks the programme's actual function: to increase social control and establish a new means of dominance over the population. Renn is superficially the master of Brand and 'Videodrome', but ultimately master becomes slave. In a Baudrillardian revision of the Frankenstein myth, even Brian O'Blivion is condemned: the creator of 'Videodrome' is its first victim.

The Third World flavour of the *mise-en-scène* of the 'Videodrome' programme, found in its low-tech electrified clay walls and the neo-stormtrooper guise of the torturers, exists in distinct contrast to the 'Videodrome' technology, which is electronic and invisible, disseminated 'painlessly' through the mass media. 'In Central America', Renn tells Brand, 'making underground videos is a subversive act.' In North America too, it would seem, as the 'Videodrome' signal is subversive of experience, reality, and the very existence of the subject.

It is the voluntarism of the television experience which permits the incursion of controlling forces. A strictly political-economic reading of *Videodrome* would find little difficulty in situating the work within Debord's model, but *Videodrome* moves beyond the classically political through its relentless physicality. Following his exposure to the 'Videodrome' signal, Renn begins a series of hallucinations. Renn assaults Bridey, his assistant, and in a series of shot/reverse shot pairings, Bridey becomes Brand, then Bridey again. Disoriented, Max apologizes for hitting her. Bridey answers, 'Max . . . you didn't hit me.' As O'Blivion tells him: 'Your reality is already half-video hallucination.'

A videotaped message from O'Blivion suddenly becomes more interactive. 'Max', he says, all trace of electronic filtering gone, 'I'm so happy you came to me.' O'Blivion explains the history of the 'Videodrome' phenomenon while being readied for execution: the executioner is Nicki Brand. 'I want *you*, Max', she breathes. 'Come to me. Come to Nicki.' Her lips fill the screen, and the set begins to pulsate, to breathe. Veins ripple the hardwood cabinet; a videogame joystick waggles obscenely. All boundaries are removed as the diegetic frame of the TV screen vanishes from view: the lips now fill the movie screen in a vast closeup. Renn approaches the set as the screen bulges outward to meet his touch, literalizing the notion of the screen as breast. His face sinks in, his hands fondle the panels and knobs of the set as the lips continue their panting invitation.

Later, Renn's body literally opens up – his stomach develops a massive, vaginal slit – to accommodate a new videocassette 'programme'. Image addiction and image virus reduce the subject to the status of a videotape player/recorder; the human body mutates to become a part of the massive system of reproductive technology ('you are a programmed tape recorder'). The sexual implications of the imagery are thus significant and not at all gratuitous: video becomes visceral.[41]

Cronenberg moves the viewer in and out of Renn's hallucinations, creating a deep ambiguity regarding the status of the image. It is easy to accept his attack as real, although the transmigration of identities clearly marks Renn's demented subjectivity. Yet the attack was entirely hallucinated: the 'real' cinematic image is unreliable. In the extended hallucination of the eroticized, visceral television, the film maker gracefully dissolves the bonds which contain the spectacle. The TV screen is contained by its own frame, but Cronenberg's closeup permits the image to burst its boundaries and expand to the non-diegetic limits of the cinema screen. In a later hallucination, a video-Brand circles Renn with whip in hand, proferring it for him to wield. The image moves from video hallucination to cinematic reality within a single shot; the shift in visual register marks the spectacle's passage from visual phenomenon to new reality. Renn accepts the whip, but Brand is now no longer present in corporeal form; she only exists, shackled, on a TV screen. Renn attacks the bound(ed) image in another moment which recalls the visual punning of Magritte.

Cronenberg, then, does not reify the cinematic signifier as 'real', but continually mutates the real into the image, and the image into the hallucination. There is no difference in the cinematic techniques employed, no 'rational' textual system, which might distinguish reality from hallucination for the film viewer. Each moment is presented as 'real': that is, as corresponding to the conventions of realist film making. These unbounded hallucinations jeopardize the very status of the image: we must believe everything or nothing. Through these textual mutations, these estrangements of cinematic language, the science fiction of the spectacle destabilizes the field of representation by constructing a set of indefinite semantic constructs.[42]

Renn hallucinates his appearance on 'Videodrome', but is 'Videodrome' a programme composed entirely of recorded hallucinations? If so, then there is a progression from hallucination, through image, to reality: the scene is real because it is televised, it is televised because it is recorded, it is recorded because it is hallucinated. In its themes and structure, the film serves as a graphic example of Baudrillard's viral immixture of TV and life (which echoes Burroughs's injunction that 'image *is* virus'). Baudrillard adds that the media is a virus which 'controls the mutation of the real into the hyperreal'. The viral metaphor is strikingly apt when applied to *Videodrome* – the literalized invasion of the body by the image, and the production of tumours which produce images. Image is virus; virus virulently replicates itself; the subject is finished. We remain trapped within a universe which seems to be someone else's insides.

Body and image become one: a dissolution of real and representation, certainly, but also of the boundaries between internal and external, as the interiorized hallucination becomes the public spectacle of the 'Videodrome' programme. In the post-spectacle society all such boundaries dissolve: 'We will have to suffer this new state of things, this forced extroversion of all interiority, this forced injection of all exteriority . . . we are now in a new form of schizophrenia.' Our response changes: 'No more hysteria, no more projective paranoia, properly speaking, but this state of terror proper to the schizophrenic: too great a proximity of everything, the unclean promiscuity of everything which touches, invests and penetrates without resistance.'[43] The subject has 'no halo of private protection, *not even his own body*, to protect him anymore'.[44]

The slippage of reality which marks the textual operations of *Videodrome* can certainly be associated with the commensurate process in the writings of the saboteur Burroughs, who repeatedly declared that we must 'Storm the Reality Studio and retake the universe'.[45] Burroughs's cinematic metaphor reaches a kind of apotheosis in *Videodrome*, as the images flicker and fall, their authority ultimately denied, but there is no glimpse of a Reality Studio behind the levels of reality-production.

Reality-slippage, with its echoes from Plato's cave, is also the province of science fiction author Philip K. Dick, another obvious influence on Cronenberg. Dick's paranoid sensibility explores the alienation which results from seeing *through* the spectacle. The central characteristic of his protagonists involves their crises of subjectivity which begin when the real violently dissolves around them. Such a metaphysical dilemma does not represent a failure to map oneself onto the world, but is interwoven with ontological change and primarily with the rise of spectacle and the expansion of the technologies of reproduction.

Dick challenges the instrumental rationalism of spectacular society through estranging rhetorical structures which construct a maze of decentred ambivalence in which multiple characters interact in a futile quest to fix reality, and therefore themselves, in place. The reader is plunged into the neologistic excess which characterizes the science fiction text. These terms cannot be read through, for the unfamiliarity they engender is precisely their purpose. The discursive ambiguities of *Videodrome* surely derive from Dick's, and Burroughs's, spectacular/structural deformations.

Dick's novel *UBIK* (1969) is dominated by telepaths and half-lifers, dead people who retain some residual brain function and exist in a cryogenic partial existence. Joe Chip (a blip culture name if ever there was one) is subjected to reality erosion, as temporality itself seems to reverse its valence. Only UBIK, a product packaged in historically appropriate forms (aerosol, ointment, elixir), can briefly restore the familiarity of the present day, and so the narrative propels its characters on a quest for answers and for UBIK. *UBIK* first seems to stand as a Platonic meditation on the rift between appearance and reality. Objects are shadows of an ideal form. Chip's refrigerator devolves from computerized servant to freon-based cooling system to icebox: a reversed succession of manifestations of the Idea of a Refrigerator. Appearance, image and spectacle are homologous terms when placed in dichotomous opposition to 'the real'. If *UBIK* simply remained with this Platonic analysis, it would only be notable for its ultimate reification of a reality which underlies shifting levels of appearance. But *UBIK* undermines such idealism. A character's ability to alter the past implies the existence of myriad presents, none more real, finally, than any other.

The depressing truth is that Chip is trapped in half-life, his 'reality' subject to the whims of a deranged, but stronger, psyche. He might be privileged to look upon the final level, the Reality Studio where reality is staged: but reality is nothing more than the fantasies of a madman. A final shift moves the reader out from Chip's half-life experience to his employer's position in the 'real world'. The living human finds currency adorned with the image of Joe Chip, just as Chip had earlier found money bearing his employer's image. 'This was just the beginning.' Final reality is itself only a shadow; the reification of the real is replaced by a recursive structure of infinite regression. *UBIK* presents, not a dichotomy of appearance and reality, but an unresolved dialectic.

Further, *UBIK* gains its force and originality by examining the central importance of the *idea* of reality, while resisting its existence. UBIK is in demand because it fixes reality (in both senses of the word: it repairs the real and locks it in place). Appearance is not simply negated as a deception, but is posited as a necessary condition of existence.

Five years after *UBIK*'s publication, Dick reworked it as a screenplay for Jean-Pierre Gorin. In a manoeuvre recalling the cinematic mutations of Burroughs's screenplay-novel, *The Last Words of Dutch Schultz* (1975),[46] Dick wanted his work to end by regressing to black and white stock, silent footage, flickering effects, and by finally bubbling and burning to a halt. The screenplay retains some of this: a drive through a simulated landscape features the repeating backgrounds of inexpensive television cartoons; a character speaks with defective sound synchronization; another scene is 'very dim, as if "bulb" is weak in "projector"'.[47] Film becomes a physical substance which bears traces of reality, but which remains pure appearance. Dick's manipulations, like Cronenberg's, deny cinema's status as transparent conduit of truth.

*UBIK* performs an effective deconstruction through its very structures, but it is in that commodity of commodities, UBIK, that the work rejoins the analysis of the spectacle performed by Debord, Baudrillard, Burroughs and Cronenberg. UBIK is the product which permits the maintenance of appearance and, in the novel, each chapter begins with an advertisement for this mysterious and ubiquitous balm. In becoming a consumer, the subject overcomes perceived lack, fixes appearance, becomes an image. The commodity defined reification for Marx; labour's abstraction is contained in its inertia.[48] Commodities and spectacles reassure and threaten by confirming a relation to the world through a temporary pseudo-satisfaction lasting only until the can is empty or a new commercial is on. UBIK stands as the ultimate example: the ur-commodity. *UBIK* becomes *the* work of commodity fetishism, featuring a product whose function is *only* to sustain the illusion of coherence. 'I came to UBIK after trying weak, out-of-date reality supports', beams a happy and secure(d) housewife.

In the screenplay these commercials interrupt the action, but also serve as a superimposition, a layering of images which blocks appearance. 'We understand that despite [the image's] fidelity to graphic representationalism, it is incomplete' (p. 31). The spectacle is displayed in spectacular fashion, faithful to reality but, through its apparent incompletion, not interchangeable with it. 'Something has come between us and what we have been watching, something in a sense more real or anyhow real in a visibly different sense.' Diegetic reality shatters in a gesture which reflects on the experience of the real through the experience of the cinematic, as in *Videodrome*.

Reprogrammed by Bianca O'Blivion in *Videodrome*, Max Renn prepares to take the next step. 'You've become the video word made flesh', she tells him. 'Death to "Videodrome" – long live the new flesh.' The terror must be overcome, the attachment to the body surrendered. Renn makes his way to a rusted hulk – a 'condemned vessel' – in the harbour. The decaying walls match the colour of his jacket. Renn is another 'condemned vessel', trapped within the confines of the old flesh, an outmoded conception of the body and the self. Aboard the vessel, Max fires at his own temple and there the film concludes; ambiguously, unsatisfyingly. What is the new flesh?

One postulation might hold that Max has attained the paradoxical status of pure image – an image which no longer retains any connection with the 'real'. *Videodrome* comes strikingly close to moving through the four successive phases of the image characteristic of the era of simulation as described by Baudrillard.[49] First, the image functions as 'the reflection as a basic reality'. Clearly, until the hallucinations begin, the viewer trusts the cinematic image as the sign of truth. Doubts may be raised concerning the enigmatic image of the 'Videodrome' programme, its ostensible Third World aesthetic belied by its Pittsburgh transmission point. Here the image 'masks and perverts a basic reality'. In the third phase, the image 'masks the *absence* of a basic reality', which has, in fact, been the argument behind the works explored here. The film propels its audience along this trajectory, possibly achieving the status of Baudrillard's fourth phase, in which image 'bears no relation to any reality whatever: it is its own pure simulacrum'. Beyond representation itself, such an image could not be represented, and thus the film ends. *Videodrome*, then, enacts the death of the subject and the death of representation simultaneously, each the consequence of the other.

*Videodrome* presents a destabilized reality in which image, reality, hallucination and psychosis become indissolubly melded, and it is on this level that the film becomes a work *of* postmodernism, rather than simply a work *about* it. The subversion of conventional structures of filmic discourse here corresponds to the 'progressive' use of language in science fiction where a neologistic excess and literalization of language foreground the reading process in a discursive play which resists the totalization of meaning. The viewer of the film is analogous to the viewer of the TV show: trapped in a web of representations which infect and transform reality. Cronenberg evidences an extensive concern with this dissolution of boundaries in all of his films. Plague viruses and parasites demonstrate the vulnerability of the body to invasion from without; telepathy and physical projection break down the dichotomy between public and private; subjectivity and temporality collapse; man merges with machine; a teleporter is proclaimed to end all concepts of borders. A particular yearning cuts across Cronenberg's body of work (work of the body); a desire for dissolution which is always accompanied by a fear of the void.

The final stage of Baudrillard's four phases of the image, wherein the image no longer bears a relation to an unmediated reality, is the hallmark of the age of postmodernism. The potential trauma which might be expected to accompany this realization is frequently elided by a regression to simple nostalgia, as both Jean Baudrillard and Fredric Jameson have noted.[50] Arthur Kroker has further written that 'The postmodern scene is a panic site, just for the fun of it'; an era of crises for their own sake, where the injunction of crisis now ironically serves to cover over the abyss of non-meaning.[51] Conversely, the insistent figurations of Baudrillard, Burroughs, Cronenberg and Dick represent a stunning hypostatization of the concerns of postmodern culture, and constitute a discursive field which retains the power to unsettle, disorient and initiate the crucial action of questioning the status of the sign in sign culture: a spectacular immunization against the invasive powers of the image virus.

## Notes

1. Alvin Toffler, *The Third Wave* (New York, Bantam Books, 1981), p. 165.
2. Toffler, *The Third Wave*, p. 166.
3. Arthur Kroker and David Cook, *The Postmodern Scene. Excremental Culture and Hyper-Aesthetics* (New York, St Martin's Press, 1986), p. 279.
4. Jean Baudrillard, *In the Shadow of the Silent Majorities*, trans. Paul Foss, (New York, Semiotext(e), 1983), p. 21.
5. Baudrillard, *In the Shadow*, p. 101.
6. Baudrillard, *In the Shadow*, p. 101.
7. This variation on Oscar Wilde is to be found in Kroker and Cook, *The Postmodern Scene*, p. 268.
8. Alvin Toffler, *Future Shock* (New York, Bantam Books, 1971), p. 161.
9. Kroker and Cook, *The Postmodern Scene*, p. 274.
10. Herbert Marcuse, *One-Dimensional Man* (Boston, MA, Beacon Press, 1964), p. 65.

11. Jean Baudrillard, 'Requiem for the Media', in *For a Critique of the Political Economy of the Sign*, trans. Charles Levin (St Louis, MO, Telos Press, 1981), p. 172.
12. Guy Debord, *Society of the Spectacle* (Detroit, MI, Black & Red, 1983), thesis 1. Henceforth, thesis numbers follow quotations in the body of the text.
13. Kroker and Cook, *The Postmodern Scene*, p. 279.
14. William S. Burroughs, *Naked Lunch* (New York, Grove Press, 1959), pp. xxxviii and xxxix.
15. Burroughs, *Naked Lunch*, p. 36.
16. Marshall McLuhan, *Understanding Media* (New York, New American Library, 1964).
17. McLuhan, *Understanding Media*, p. 19.
18. A. J. Liebling, *The Press*, second revised edn (New York, Ballantine Books, 1975), p. 32.
19. Jean Baudrillard, *The Mirror of Production*, trans. Mark Poster (St Louis, MO, Telos Press, 1975).
20. Jean Baudrillard, *Forget Foucault*, trans. Nicole Dufresne (New York, Semiotext(e), 1987), p.11.
21. Baudrillard, *Forget Foucault*, p. 11.
22. Jean Baudrillard, 'The Precession of Simulacra', in *Simulations*, trans. Paul Foss, Paul Patton and Philip Beitchman (New York, Semiotext(e), 1983), pp. 54–5.
23. Jean Baudrillard, 'The Ecstasy of Communication', in Hal Foster, ed., *The Anti-Aesthetic. Essays in Postmodern Culture* (Port Townsend, WA, Bay Press, 1983), p. 128.
24. The trilogy includes *The Soft Machine* revised edn (1966), *The Ticket that Exploded* revised edn (1967) and *Nova Express* (1964). All titles published by Grove Press, New York.
25. See Samuel R. Delany, 'About 5,750 Words', in *The Jewel-Hinged Jaw. Notes on the Language of Science Fiction* (Elizabethtown, NY, Dragon Press, 1977); or Teresa de Lauretis, 'Signs of W[a/o]nder', in Teresa de Lauretis, Andreas Huyssen and Kathleen Woodward, eds, *The Technological Imagination. Theories and Fictions* (Madison, WI, Coda Press, 1980).
26. Cited in Eric Mottram, *William Burroughs. The Algebra of Need* (London, Marion Boyars, 1977), p. 40.
27. Jean Baudrillard, 'Rituals of Transparency', in Sylvere Lotringer, ed., *The Ecstasy of Communication*, trans. Bernard and Caroline Schutze (New York, Semiotext(e), 1988), p. 36.
28. Mottram, *William Burroughs*, p. 56.
29. Marshall McLuhan, 'Notes on Burroughs', *The Nation*, 28 December 1964, pp. 517–19.
30. Christopher Sharritt, 'Myth and Ritual in the Post-Industrial Landscape. The Horror Films of David Cronenberg', *Persistence of Vision*, 3/4 (1986), p. 113.
31. Jean Baudrillard, 'The Implosion of Meaning in the Media', in Baudrillard, *In the Shadow*, p. 109.
32. *The Ticket that Exploded*, p. 50.
33. William Beard, 'The Visceral Mind. The Films of David Cronenberg', in Piers Handling, ed., *The Shape of Rage. The Films of David Cronenberg* (New York, New York Zoetrope, 1983).
34. See the articles in the disturbing and entertaining Arthur and Marilouise Kroker, eds, *Body Invaders. Panic Sex in America*, (New York, St Martin's Press, 1988).
35. Carrie Rickey, 'Make Mine Cronenberg', *The Village Voice*, 1 February 1983, p.64.
36. 'The Ecstasy of Communication', p. 128.
37. One of these 'Perspectives for Conscious Alterations in Everyday Life' is reprinted in *Situationist International Anthology*, ed. and trans. Ken Knabb (Berkeley, CA, Bureau of Public Secrets, 1981), pp. 68–75.

38. William Burroughs, 'The Invisible Generation', in *The Ticket that Exploded*, p. 213.
39. Perhaps it should be noted that the RAM acronym is one familiar to computer users, and stands for Random Access Memory.
40. This exploration of sexuality is granted considerably more weight in Cronenberg's recent *Dead Ringers* (1988).
41. For an important feminist analysis of the figuration of the body, see Tania Modleski, 'The Terror of Pleasure. The Contemporary Horror Film and Postmodern Theory', in Tania Modleski, ed., *Studies in Entertainment. Critical Approaches to Mass Culture* (Bloomington, IN, Indiana University Press, 1986).
42. The phrase is borrowed from de Lauretis, 'Signs of W[a/o]nder', p. 160.
43. 'The Ecstasy of Communication', p. 132.
44. 'The Ecstasy of Communication', p. 132. Emphasis mine.
45. *The Soft Machine*, p. 155.
46. William Burroughs, *The Last Words of Dutch Schultz* (New York, Seaver Books, 1975).
47. Philip K. Dick, *Ubik. The Screenplay* (Minneapolis, MN, Corroboree Press, 1985), p. 120.
48. Karl Marx, *Capital*, vol. 1, trans. Ben Fowkes (New York, Vintage Books, 1977), pp. 163–77.
49. Marx, *Capital*, pp. 11–12.
50. See Baudrillard, 'The Precession of Simulacra', p. 12; and Frederic Jameson, 'Postmodernism, or, the Cultural Logic of Late Capitalism', *New Left Review* **146** (1984), pp. 66–8.
51. Kroker and Cook, *The Postmodern Scene*, p. 27.

# 6

# Pulpmodernism: Tarantino's affirmative action

## Peter and Will Brooker

A version of this article appeared in D. Cartmell, I. Q. Hunter, H. Kaye and I. Whelehan (eds), *Pulping fictions* (Pluto 1996)

No-one can doubt that Tarantino and his works are a cult. Over 2,000 disappointed British Film Institute members applied in advance for the 616 tickets (including overspill) available for his personal appearance and a showing of his favourite film *Rio Bravo* at the NFT at the end of January this year (1995). The box office reported up to 400 calls a day up to the Saturday of his visit; hundreds queued for stand-bys, and touts were selling tickets at four times their original price.[1]

The Tarantino phenomenon is of course inspired, somewhat uniquely, by more than his own two directed films. Other films with which he is associated include *True Romance* (screenplay), *Natural Born Killers* (screenplay) and *Killing Zoe* (associate producer). The published screenplays and sound tracks of *Reservoir Dogs* and *Pulp Fiction* have reached unprecedented sales for this kind of publication. The *Pulp Fiction* screenplay topped the 1994 pre-Christmas lists in the UK and the soundtrack reached no. 4 in the albums chart. As Mark Kermode points out, thanks to the soundtrack album, many fans 'would have known whole speeches *before* they even saw the film'.[2] This kind of exponential popularity is only further spiced by the fact that Oliver Stone has blocked the publication of the screenplay of *Natural Born Killers* and that *Reservoir Dogs* has not yet been granted a video certificate. *Pulp Fiction* renewed interest in *Reservoir Dogs* and in the other spin-offs, boosting Tarantino's reputation as writer, producer, sometime actor and populist man about cinema for our fractured, non-hierarchical times ('To be elitist about the film industry is a cancer', he has said).[3] His picture was everywhere, a portrait of the artist as young fan, the defender of popular American cinema (who cites *Rio Bravo* and Sylvester Stallone rather than *High Noon* or Anthony Hopkins), the smart kid, high school drop-out and one-time videoshop salesman who's made it, the slacker as auteur.

Much of this is reported with no more than the amused eye of the bystander used to the passing fame and spectacle expected of the postmodern. Tarantino's films themselves meanwhile have been both much praised and a cause of concern and controversy. James Wood, for example, has seen his 'brilliant' films as symptoms of our *fin de siècle* 'hectic postmodern', a period of 'trivial' and 'vacant' mass media and of a 'vaguely prurient' interest in increasing violence. Tarantino captures all this, says Wood, but is its trapped victim.[4]

Wood's comments are themselves symptomatic of a reaction to the post-modern and postmodernism whose 'final triumph', as represented by Tarantino, he says, 'is to empty the artwork of all content, thus voiding its capacity to do anything except helplessly *represent* our agonies (rather than to contain or comprehend)'.[5] In the same vein Fintan O'Toole would place Tarantino's films as 'Exhibit A in the museum of postmodern moral vacuity'. His brilliance, O'Toole thinks, shines less in his film making than in his clever exploitation of the jaded appetites of the mass culture market. What he has 'done with violence' is pornographic since it appears on screen without even the rudimentary trappings of sequential plot or any pretence 'that his characters are more than stock borrowings from old movies'. He 'has disavowed all moral or social intent and gone straight for the sadism'.[6]

Both critics speak out against postmodernism in the name of a belea-guered humanism and organicist aesthetic (Wood's notion in particular of art's function being to contain or comprehend our agonies echoes down a long tradition, most famously associated with Matthew Arnold). Not sur-prisingly this perspective requires its bad twin to sustain it. This these critics find in Tarantino and postmodernism, or what we have to say is a version of postmodernism (Wood invokes a second expression of the postmodern, though he recruits this to his own cause, in comparing Tarantino to the author Don DeLillo). This same perspective is adopted by, amongst others, Mark Kermode, though for an apparently opposite purpose. Tarantino's work is referenced to other films, Kermode has said; it is film about film, 'the entertainment value of watching it is entirely cinematic'.[7] Kermode offers this as a defence of the film's merits. We might think that this view therefore refutes Wood and O'Toole's arguments but it does not, for it is fundamentally to see the film in the same way: as empty of social and moral content. In a fuller and more explicit reading which reveals how compatible these views in fact are, Amanda Lipman detects a series of warped repeats of several actors' earlier roles in what she terms 'this rag bag of film refer-ences'.[8] Thus Bruce Willis is seen to play a version of his *Die Hard* persona, Rosanna Arquette might be her character in *After Hours*, Harvey Keitel stages a domesticated reprise of his role 'in the *Nikita* remake *The Assassin*' and John Travolta is the street boy dancer Tony Manero of *Saturday Night Fever* a few years on and a few pounds heavier. If Tarantino has anything to say in all this, Lipman concludes, it is that 'there is no morality or justice in the patterns of life or death. Instead, the nihilist argument continues, there is trivia.'[9]

If we seek neither to celebrate nor judge the film in these terms but to understand it in relation to contemporary artistic and social trends, the issue that current discussion puts before us is that of 'violence', or the rights and wrongs of a supposed new 'aesthetic of violence' (stretching from Sarah Kane's *Blasted* to Eric Cantona's temper). Manhola Dargis pigeonholed *Pulp Fiction* six months before its release as another 'bone-shattering, skin-split-ting, blood spurting' contribution to Tarantino's 'cinema of viscera ... written on the flesh of outlaw men and women'.[10] Violence is Tarantino's 'watch-word', Amanda Lipman agrees, but what he says with it is that 'Life in the

90s ... is speedy and worthless.'[11] In Kermode's view, Tarantino's work is 'so postmodern' that the portrayal of violence 'doesn't mean anything'.[12]

What, in this light, can be said if we ask less about this art's forms (which are of concern to both Wood and Kermode) than its function: who is it for and what does it do? One reply is that Tarantino's fans are young males bereft of role models needing some guidance in how to get by in a violent world. Yet some significant social facts, as well as the aesthetic experience of the film, contradict or at least qualify this, contextualising its moments of violence in a different way. *The Guardian*, for example, reported that the London NFT audience was 'a cross section of age and gender'.[13] Beyond this metropolitan audience it's a fair guess (if only a guess) that the bulk of fans – who tend to miss events in the capital – are students, both male and female. (In courses taught by the authors more women than men have volunteered class presentations on Tarantino.) Arguably, violence is an issue for these fans because it has been made one by the media. And if we say, rightly, that violence is nonetheless a real contemporary social issue we should note that, aside from the issues of class and social division it entails, this concern has brought a new critical attention to violence by women and to its cultural representation as well as to violent acts by men.[14]

If we are going to understand the relevance to this issue of Tarantino's work, it is unhelpful, not to say crass, to associate his films and postmodernism in an undifferentiated way with the amoral, superficial and self-referential portrayal of violence. We are concerned mainly here with *Pulp Fiction* but it is clear that the tone and nature of violence in this film are different from the previous *Reservoir Dogs* (both of which ought in turn to be distinguished from *Killing Zoe* and *Natural Born Killers*). The torture scene in *Reservoir Dogs* presents a different mode of violence to the careless shooting of Marvin, to cite the most obviously violent scene in the second film. It would be surprising if these scenes did not provoke a different reaction or serve a different possible 'social function', just as they function differently in the film's internal narrative worlds. More to the point, however, what viewers respond to most immediately in *Pulp Fiction* are the dialogue, and the monologues these often harbour, and above all scenes like the opening car ride, Vincent's dance at Jackrabbit Slim's 50s retro restaurant and the Wolf's clean-up campaign at Jimmie's house. These scenes are not about violence but about relationships and about style. In their dress, speech and manner, the characters display an attitude, in its fullest sense, of cool eccentricity. And again although the male characters are attractive and comic in this way to both male and female audiences, so too are Mia Wallace (Uma Thurman) and a minor character such as Jody (played by Rosanna Arquette).

We have to think beyond a traditional humanist aesthetic and more broadly than an 'aesthetic of violence' if we are to account for these features and for this kind of pleasure. We have, that is to say, to think with more discrimination and subtlety about the aesthetic forms and accents of postmodernism – so famously 'all about style' but not by that token always and only about 'merely' style. *Pulp Fiction*'s postmodernism does not produce a *hermetic* self-mirroring intertextualism nor administer *only* to male narcissism and a subordinated female gaze (less constraining perhaps than film theory sometimes likes to suppose). Nor do we have to deny the film's self-knowingness (and the audience's pleasure in this and their own) to argue that it relates to moral issues and how to live rather than kill and die. We want to suggest that *Pulp Fiction* in particular, though importantly not in isolation, is more affirmative, less vacuous and nihilistic than critics like Wood and O'Toole believe and less self-enclosed than Kermode accepts; that in keeping with its own revaluative inflection of a postmodern aesthetic it offers a 'life style' – otherwise so cheap a phrase of the end of century – which redeems and recasts the pulp of the postmodern in the very style and structure of its fictional narrative. To appreciate this we need to return firstly to the question of the film's cult status and secondly to consider its relation to the more familiar features of postmodernism.

Umberto Eco presents Michael Curtiz's *Casablanca* (1942) as an exemplary case of the cult film.[15] 'A cult movie is proof', he says, 'that, as literature comes from literature, cinema comes from the cinema' (p. 447). The cult film is characterised by an improvised, intertextual collage of stereotypical situations, or 'intertextual archetypes', already logged in the encyclopedia of cinema narrative, which when once again recycled, provoke an 'intense emotion' of recognition and the desire for repetition. But this repetition and the expression of affection for the film takes a particular form. 'A perfect movie', says Eco, 'remains in our memory as a whole' (ibid.). The cult movie, on the other hand, is imperfect, dislocated and 'unhinged . . . . It must live on, and because of, its glorious ricketiness' (ibid.). The fan will therefore recall discontinuous, selected images, or characters or snatches of dialogue, quoting 'characters and episodes as if they were aspects of the fan's private sectarian world, a world about which one can make up quizzes and play trivia games so that the adepts of the sect recognise through each other a shared expertise' (p. 446). This experience Eco suggests is culturally specific, the archetypes are 'particularly appealing to a given cultural area or a historical period' (p. 448). Rather than pursue the kind of social or cultural semiotics this would argue is appropriate to the film, however, Eco proceeds to offer a formalist and abbreviated thematic analysis, shot by shot, of the first twenty minutes of *Casablanca*. His entire discussion, moreover, is very clearly shadowed by a traditional aesthetic. Thus the cult is ramshackle and imperfect, it has no 'central idea or emotion' or 'coherent philosophy of composition' (p. 449). The cult movie indeed works 'in defiance of any aesthetic theory'; it is primitive archetype, anonymous live textuality, 'outside the conscious control of its creators' (p. 447) 'Nature', he concludes, 'has spoken in place of men' (p. 454). Though he sees a sublimity in this self-perpetuating creation it is clear that in the scale of aesthetic values Eco assumes the truly venerated terms are all on the other side of the cult film – and are much the same as those invoked by Wood and O'Toole. On this reckoning, the cult film can only be identified as the opposite of the authentic work of art understood as the conscious, coherent creation of the individual artist who 'tames' the raw matter of cultural cliché in the name of beauty and civilisation. In the postmodern film (Eco cites *Bananas, Raiders of the Lost Ark* and *ET*) the intertextuality which characterises the cult movie becomes predictably more self-conscious – for now both film maker and viewer are 'instinctive semioticians' (p. 454): a development that Eco presents with a nostalgia for what perversely appears as the innocence of the original cult film, or cult of cult films which is *Casablanca*.

Certainly *Pulp Fiction* conforms to much in Eco's description. The film's status is confirmed and re-confirmed by the mere citation of a favourite cameo role or sequence, the imitation of a look or action (the dance, the costume of black suit, white shirt, straight tie carried over from *Reservoir Dogs*), by a quoted passage of dialogue and above all by the repetition, the echoing back to the film, of individual lines and phrases ('Royale with cheese' matching Bogart's 'Here's looking at you kid' or 'Play it again Sam'). Tarantino's admirers might not all be fans, of course, and not all fans will be cult fans. It is likely, however, that all viewers will be aware to some degree of the text, or intertexts of its world of internal and on-going reference. The rituals of repetition or mirroring, a saying back to the film and other fans, can be a way of expressing common, or popular knowledge, or of displaying exceptionally detailed or new knowledge (culled, say, from a bootleg video or out of the way interview). A fan's response may be affirming and self-affirming rather than questioning or analytical, more reflexive than reflective, but if this self-generating world (producing fan upon fan, cinema from cinema) can be trivial, pedantic and exclusive it is not thereby finally confining nor isolating. Rather the reverse. Eco points to this double life of fandom in referring to the fan's 'private sectarian world' and 'shared expertise' above. There can be no solitary fan of the cult film. A cult enthusiasm is at once exclusive and shared, a socially expressed aesthetic built upon a fundamentally social emotion and experience.

The social form engendered by Tarantino's work, which helps counter the emphasis on the film's portrayal of violence as its main social content, is that of the group. According to Tarantino, before signing up for *Pulp Fiction*, Bruce Willis and his brothers would spend afternoons at home 'riffing on scenes from *Dogs*' – 'like old buddies', Mark Kermode adds, 'enjoying a communal sinagalong'.[16] Kermode talks, without further comment, of the suitability of the speeches on the *Pulp Fiction* sound-track for 'drunken rendition'.[17] If this is indeed the social form fandom takes we have some reason for thinking of its pleasures as predominantly and stereotypically 'male'. Even so, however adolescent and boorish we might find this front-room camaraderie, it is not of itself violent – any more than pub or football terrace culture are – nor necessarily amoral.

The cult world of the films also has a quite different potential, however, once again both paradoxically internalised and expanding. For the hardcore fan Tarantino as auteur has created an entire world of cross-references across not two but in the first instance at least four films. Thus Vince Vega is traceable as cousin, or brother, to Vic 'Mr Blonde' Vega in *Reservoir Dogs*, while Vic's parole officer, Scagnetti, is a central character in *Natural Born Killers*. Mr White's reference to his old flame Alabama leads us back to *True Romance*, while a scene cut from the completed *Reservoir Dogs* reveals that the nurse who Nice Guy Eddie was going to fetch for the mortally-wounded Orange is Bonnie, Jimmie's wife from *Pulp Fiction*. The path of this cross-referencing leads us to identify Mr Brown/Tarantino and Jimmie/Tarantino as one and the same man. This is the boys-own stuff of the Internet possibly, but it is only a film's width away from the erudition of literary scholarship, from learned revelations on the modernist classics or poststructuralist readings of a story by Edgar Allen Poe. That this is an active, producerly reading

of the Tarantino texts would be hard to deny. It is in the nature of intertextuality also that it extends itself, across film texts and popular media in this
case, to the music of the 1950s and 1960s on the film soundtracks, to the stories of *Black Mask* magazine, the crime writer Charles Willeford who
Tarantino alludes to, to Ralph Meeker in *Kiss Me Deadly*, to Aldo Ray in
Jacques Tourneur's *Nightfall* (a role he and Willis agreed on as a model for
Butch in *Pulp Fiction*), to the films of Roger Corman and Howard Hawkes
and to the selections from American and European cinema he introduced in
a programme of films at the London National Film Theatre.

If this appears to threaten a relation of pied-piping movie sage to cloned
disciples, winding their way down the endless by-ways of pulp (would a
true fan pause to check out all the Roger Corman films pictured on the
posters in Jackrabbit Slims?) we might remember the nature of the dispute,
as Tarantino sees it, between himself and Oliver Stone. 'He wants every single one of you to walk out thinking like he does. I don't. I made *Pulp Fiction*
to be entertaining. I always hope that if one million people see my movie,
they saw a million different movies.'[18] This unfettered libertarianism goes
hand in hand with an expanding intertextuality and contrasts not only with
the closed world the term 'cult' at first suggests but with the aesthetic ideal
of containment and the comprehension of our agonies assumed by Wood
above. Both ideas of art's form function are broadly didactic and both, contrary again to Wood's belief, have a moral aspect.

The romantic humanist aesthetic that Wood, O'Toole and Eco espouse has
long been questioned within modernism and contemporary theory alert to
the key significance of the fragment, the internally contradictory, and the
marginal. The deconstructive effect of an intertertextual postmodernism is
precisely to challenge distinctions between the original and authentic and
true, the unified, high and centred on the one hand and the copy, the false,
the low, the supplementary and marginal on the other. The problem with a
traditional aesthetic lies not so much in the position itself, however, as the
nostalgia and presumption with which it is held, leading these and other
writers to simplify and so patronise or dismiss the challenge of postmodernism. To see this tendency in contemporary culture as no more than a
nihilistic indulgence in clever-clever bricolage, a provocative but unfeeling
cultivation of excess, is to take a commentator like Jean Baudrillard and declarations on the contemporary loss of the real and any ethical perpective at
their word. There are more testing questions to ask about postmodernism's
oppositional, critical and liberating aspect and its relation to a social and cultural past and future, and there are quite obvious distinctions also between
kinds of postmodernism, or accents within the range of cultural expression
the term encompasses. If some examples of postmodern art are at once
scandalous and vacant, or 'merely' playful, others are innovative and
deeply problematising. If some are symptomatic, others are exploratory.
Like postmodern society, cultural postmodernism is various and contradictory: fatalistic, introverted, open, inventive, and enlivening. *Pulp Fiction* visits these contradictions and requires a fuller, dialectical, reading if we are to
appreciate its own double aspect.

Much that has been said above of the film's intertextuality might be glossed
by reference to what now pass as the leading features of postmodernism: its

pastiche, self-imitation, loss of affect, loss of historical sense, loss of social reference and hence critical or affirmative influence. This is the stuff of the charges brought against the film above. Unquestionably, *Pulp Fiction* echoes and alludes to other films (most conspicuously to Godard's *Bande A Part* for the dance scene in Jackrabbit Slims). It has no specific location nor setting in time. If the reference to McDonalds and Burger King in Europe, Jody's body-piercing or Jules' cellular phone indicates a present time in the late 1980s or early 90s, Vince's car is a 74 Chevy Nova, the music belongs to the 1960s and 70s, the TV references (to Kung Fu, Happy Days, and Mia's pilot Fox Force Five – both the latter already party to *la mode rétro*) suggest the late 1970s, the dialogue on occasion ('daddy-o' and 'kooties') belongs to the 50s or the 50s recycled, and the movie-star look-alike waiters and waitresses of Jackrabbit Slims itself to the no time/any time of *echt* postmodern period pastiche.

On this evidence we might indeed read the film as an amusing but pathological symptom of postmodern superficiality, unwitting proof of the randomised indifference of a thoroughly commercialised, magpie aesthetic, which blithely apes the supposed free flow of goods across the global markets of late capitalism. Yet at the same time *Pulp Fiction* displays some important contrary features. Those associated with its cult following and open, enlightening intertextuality we have already pointed to. Here we want to comment particularly on the film's episodic, circling narrative structure. This is once more a conspicuous, popularly noticed feature of the film (distinguishing it in composition and structure of feeling from *Reservoir Dogs* and other films associated with Tarantino, while suggesting a resemblance with, say, *Short Cuts* and a number of postmodern prose narratives) whose effects also have a significant bearing on the issue of violence.

The attitude towards narrative in postmodern theory is well-known, and conveniently summarised by Edward Said. Both Lyotard and Foucault, he says, have turned their attention away from the forces of radical opposition and insurgency to problem solving games, local issues, and the 'microphysics of power' surrounding the individual:

> The self was therefore to be studied, cultivated, and, if necessary, refashioned and constituted. In both Lyotard and Foucault we find precisely the same trope employed to explain the disappointment in the politics of liberation: narrative which posits an enabling beginning point and a vindicating goal, is no longer adequate for plotting the human trajectory in society. There is nothing to look forward to: we are stuck within our circle.[19]

Circling mini-narratives do not have this necessary set of implications, however. In *Pulp Fiction*, two characters, first of all, Jules and Butch undergo or contrive a transformation in which they gain new purpose and a sense of 'long-term' direction. Jules believes he has been saved from death by divine intervention and sets to reinterpret the text of Ezekiel 25:17 which he customarily recites before a killing to new ends. If he has been the 'evil man' rather than the 'righteous man' of this text, striking down those 'who attempt to poison and destroy my brothers' in a parody of the vengeful agent of the Lord, he believes he can become the blessed man who 'shepherds the weak through the valley of darkness'. He forsakes a life of violent crime for the ancient grand narrative of 'charity and good will'. ('I'm tryin', I'm tryin real hard to be a shepherd', he says, and soon after in closing his criminal life does spare Pumpkin – 'Wanna know what I'm buyin', Ringo? Your life. I'm giving you that money so I don't hafta kill your ass.') For his part Butch back-tracks on a narrative of pure self-preservation to save Marsellus from the humiliation of rape, and is able, with the 'blessing' of his enemy, to embark on the mythic narrative of a newly invented self, free of the 'violent' and crooked world of boxing.

Clearly these stories, and Butch's in particular, posit an ethical view of the world. Though it might require a transformative ephiphany to realise its 'righteous' side, this ethical view is all the same consistent, on its 'bad' side, with the emphasis on partnership and group loyalty (a textual inspiration and reinforcement to some degree surely of fan loyalty) in both *Reservoir Dogs* and *Pulp Fiction*. This ethic of comradeship is in turn grounded in the disadvantaged circumstances of the male characters as working-class professional hoodlums (a shared class identity is strongly suggested in the opening scene of *Reservoir Dogs*, where Mr White argues the importance of tipping waitresses on a minimum wage). Lives of routine danger, the films tell us, require mutual support and a code of professional conduct if they are not to flare out of routine control. Jules insists in the first scene of *Pulp Fiction* that he and Vince 'get into character' before they make the hit. The hoods in *Reservoir Dogs* are bonded at the level of their abstact common identity as colour-coded gangsters. But the coded roles that marshall their actions are evidently narrow and brittle, tested by the undertow of gossipy, bickering dialogue which squeezes past the hitman's prescribed rhetoric, and broken by the detonating crises in the films' narratives. Thus in *Reservoir Dogs* the abstract, professional code deemed necessary to survival is transgressed by the pathological Mr Blonde, and impersonated by Mr Orange. Real identities, bringing real friction and extreme violence, but also signs of a deeper comradeship, seep through their allotted anonymity and apparent sameness – as in the rapport that emerges between Mr White and Mr Orange. Both films explore the need for and fragility of fixed identities and relationships and do this analogically, through the use of stock generic characters such as 'The Undercover Cop', 'The Hitman' and 'The Boxer' and stereotypical scenarios such as 'The Heist Gone Wrong', 'The Hit', 'The Crooked Fight'. The films' characters are contained by or revert to these roles (Mr White, who has revealed himself as 'Larry', reverts to the relationship of cop and criminal once Mr Orange's duplicity is exposed). Or, on occasion, as in the examples of Jules and Butch, characters can redefine these roles and redirect their lives. Jules is finally neither 'The Hitman', nor 'The Bum' Vince says he will become: 'I'll just be Jules, Vincent,' he says, '– no more, no less.' Tarantino does not merely repeat nor pastiche the conventions of pulp cinema, therefore; he reinvents and extends these conventions, exposing their abstract 'cartoon' like rudiments, adding unexpected dialogue, fluent monologue, a concentrated intensity or relaxed attentuation of plot or hyperbole of character. He gives them new life, we might say; just as Jules and Butch and Marsellus and Mia are granted new life and, at another level, the dipping, repetitive careers of actors such as Willis and Travolta are also revived.

One remarkable instance of this inventive and affirmative mode is perhaps worth particular comment and is of interest once more in relation to the topic of violence. Escorted home from the dance at Jackrabbit Slims, Mia Wallace overdoses while Vince is in the bathroom. He races her to his dealer's and plunges a syringe into her chest, guided by a handbook for such emergencies. His efforts save her life. Like the accidental killing of the black youth in Vince's car this is a key scene in terms of the film's treatment of violence. Vince and Jules' reaction in this second case is callous in the extreme, but their combined indifference and heated bickering over the state of their clothes and of the car provoke a common audience reaction of dismay and disbelief, at their actions and the playing of the scene itself, rather than outrage. The moment edges scandalously towards slapstick and if we half suspect that their cold 'professionalism' is being parodied in this incident we know for sure that this is the intent of the following scene in which the Wolf cleans up the mess with military impersonality ('A please would be nice', Vince says huffily, as if to emphasise that common decency is not part of the Wolf's professional repertoire). Mia's 'resurrection', on the other hand, provokes a reaction of near hysterical relief. What is indeed disturbing rather than conformist about these scenes and helps re-channel stock reactions to the stock 'violence' underlying them is their mixed tone. Just as cinematic conventions are opened out, set in the fluctuating rhythms and distracting debris and dialogue of real life, so the conventions of viewing response are angled away from expectations. Scenes from the gangster genre, that is to say, are touched with unexpected comedy. Dan Glaister sees the image of 'a hypodermic needle plunged into the chest of an actress' as further evidence of Tarantino's graphic portrayal of violence[20] when in fact this is the most graphic illustration of the film's theme of re-invention and rebirth. In plain terms, Mia is brought back from the dead. What is more, Vincent's life-saving stab decisively changes the tone of the film, to the point of unsettling its assumed generic base.

Tarantino's postmodernism therefore moves off from and against a fixed base, but not so as to become aimlessly decentred. No more is the narrative of *Pulp Fiction* pointlessly circling or enclosing. One thinks of Vincent Vega's dance at Jackrabbit Slims – a controlled improvisation upon the standard form of the twist. And indeed the creative flexibility or accent which shapes the film's aesthetic and informs its ethical view is most strikingly developed in relation to this character. The 'long narratives' of hope and renewal associated with Jules and Butch strike off at a tangent from the film's main narrative movement. Vincent's fictional story, however, is entirely encompassed by it. Yet its effect, returning us to a scene before his death, is not to encircle or eliminate this character but to foreground and literally enliven him.

By implication, since he is, after all, living 'at the end', the violence of Vince's death, and other acts of violence, are perceived as matters of fiction and not 'real' at all. This is what critics of postmodernism complain of of course, seeking some effective relation of moral commentary between the two. But to be aware of fictionality does not entail a substitution of the unreal for the real so much as a recognition that the real is always constructed, its chronological plot always narrativised, our judgements upon it a matter of tone and perspective. In manipulating chronology, moreover, fiction can return us to better moments, as it does here in returning us to Vincent Vega in beach shirt and Bermudas with his buddy Jules, edgy but on top of his game, rather than the Vincent Vega who lies dead in a toilet, his white shirt blood-spattered because he was caught alone and off guard. This episode also gives us our last glimpse of Marsellus Wallace, once more the untouchable gangster king and ordering in the Wolf on his poolside phone as if his rape had never happened; which of course, at this time, it has not. Creative memory (in an era that has lost a sense of the past) defies the deadly fate of conventional linear progression or decline. Our perspective is once again angled away from the scene and sight of violence.

Vince is the only one of the four main characters to die rather than begin a new life. It is important, however, to see that this death is in a sense reasoned rather than arbitrary. In three significant moments Vincent retires to the bathroom (to talk himself into controlling the immediate future, twice to read the pulp novel *Modesty Blaise*). If these scenes function self-reflexively as an interlude to reflect upon the narrative of *this* pulp fiction and its subsequent course, they give Vince no effective guidance, since he returns to an utterly changed world – where death is threatened (Mia's, as above; Jules and the others in the cafe held up by Pumpkin and Honey Bunny) and where in the third instance he meets his own, shot by Butch with his own gun. Through Vince in particular we see the contemporary world as utterly contingent, transformed, disastrously, in the instant you are not looking. There is as they say a 'moral' here. Like Jules and Butch, Vince is given brief moments of reflection, when his story is effectively held on freeze-frame. When his narrative returns to speed, however, the world is changed around him and he adapts to it, but not in the gesture of radical self-revision that Jules and Butch bring to their equivalent moments of decision. The world of radical contingency requires a ready adjustment to the present composition and re-composition of events, a dialectical responsiveness (most decisively at a critical, life-threatening moment) that makes it possible to switch from the path of evil to the path of righteousness, to convert the fixed and routine into the original.

Perhaps after all Vince's dancing is too controlled, a set-piece without sufficient improvisation. The tension between stereotypes, from *Black Mask* and B movies, and the eccentric, transgressive variations upon them with which Tarantino invests plot and character determines the tragic outcome of *Reservoir Dogs* where Mr White must revert to type. Vince too dies as he lives, a hitman, and it is his personal tragedy that he does not exploit the moment of betweenness when in sidling out of the diner having saved the cafe, and granted Pumpkin his life, he is that hitman still but out of uniform, his gun stuck down his Bermuda shorts. Here in this moment too, he is significantly with his partner still. In a contingent world where anything might happen, including being blown away, the loner, slow to change, is surprised and lost.

But where Vince fails personally, the film's narrative does not fail him. If a fixed mode or code of conduct is ill-fitted to this world, so too is a linear narrative with beginning point, middle and end. The film's circling mini-narratives enable it to question the finality of this fated end, returning us to Vince's most potentially self-transformative moment in the diner (in which comedy serves again to unsettle the fixed type). In *this* end, the mosaic narrative movement of the film works miraculously to bring the dead

Vincent Vega back to life, revived by Tarantino; not as in a sentimental reprise, but as if to start again: to consider from a new angle what might have been. (In the scene of the Hit we see from Marvin's point of view in the bathroom; in the diner Honey Bunny's dialogue re-commences after the earlier freeze-frame, and is heard differently by Jules).

We should think then finally of an 'aesthetic of contingency' rather than of an 'aesthetic of violence'. While this describes a postmodern condition where 'anything can happen', including acts of extreme violence, it is not to endorse the undifferentiated 'anything goes' of a Baudrillardian postmodernism, or an indifference – with which the film is charged, to matters of life and death.

Tarantino's world is evidently saturated with enthusiasms, discriminations and declared preferences. It is full and affirmative rather than empty and nihilistic. His films have not sought to master, shape and control the contingent (the Wolf is the film's example of this traditional and high modernist ambition; now become, appropriately enough, mythological). Instead, both films and scripts select broadly and fluently from amongst cinematic motifs and cultural styles to assemble newly woven, open narratives which bring life to the dead, the has-been, the jaded, the banal. The past is recycled, its 'waste' products put to new creative advantage. The fixed and conventional is opened to new artistic and human connections. In this way *Pulp Fiction*, in particular, offers a *modus vivendi*; a way of telling, of living a postmodern narrative deeply embedded in a world of narratives, which in giving new life to the familiar and conventional can spin out of the hermetic enclosure both of a narrowly defined genre fiction and a traditional fiction seeking a correspondence to 'reality'. The intertextual bricolage which makes avant-garde technique a popular pleasure is joined by an underlying, if frustrated, ethic of companionship; a surviving will to do another some good. This is the best that the best of modernism ever aimed for and the best perhaps that the humanism which takes such high-minded offence at the films can aspire to.

Yet Tarantino, finally, takes on more than either of these modes. For in making it new now in the days of the postmodern, an affirmative popular art must reach lower, digging its way, eyes open, through the cultural strata to sample the mass and mess of pulp, the brutality of low and criminal life, and root it back up to the spreading generic surface of popular cinema entertainment. Vince returns to the USA at the film's beginning with a defamiliarising tale. A foreign place can sound briefly like a hood's utopia ('Oh, man, I'm goin', that's all there is to it', says Jules on hearing how polite cops must behave to drug users in Amsterdam). A traveller across cultures, as across texts, can return with a surrealising eye and a comic touch, sufficient to invert categories and raise up the lowly. 'Royale with cheese' says it all. Junk is King.

## Notes

1. *Independent on Sunday*, 27 January 1995, p. 2; *Guardian*, 30 January 1995, p. 22.
2. 'Endnotes', *Sight and Sound*, February 1995, p. 62.
3. *Guardian*, 30 January 1995.
4. *Guardian*, 19 November 1994, p. 31.

5. *Guardian*, 19 November 1994, p. 31.
6. 'Bloody Minded', *Guardian*, 3 February 1995, p. 16.
7. *The Late Show*, BBC 2, 24 January 1995.
8. *Sight and Sound*, November 1994, p. 51.
9. *Sight and Sound*, November 1994, p. 51.
10. *Sight and Sound*, May 1994, p. 6
11. *Sight and Sound*, November 1994.
12. *The Late Show*, 24 January 1995. The panellists in this discussion, including Ros Coward and Stephen Daldry, were asked by Fintan O'Toole to address the question of an 'aesthetic of violence'.
13. *Guardian*, 30 January 1995, p. 22.
14. See, for example, Helen Birch, ed., *Moving Targets. Women, Murder and Representation* (London, Virago, 1993) which includes discussion of the cases of Myra Hindley, the 'dingo baby murder' and Tracey Wigginton, and the films *Black Widow, Thelma and Louise* and *Fatal Attraction*. We might add the cases of Beverley Allitt and Rosemary West and the recent film *Heavenly Creatures*.
15. 'Casablanca. Cult Movies and Intertextual College', in *Travels in Hyperreality*, reprinted in David Lodge, ed., *Modern Criticism and Theory* (London, Longman, 1988), pp. 446–55. Following page references are given in the text.
16. *Sight and Sound*, February 1995, p. 62.
17. *Sight and Sound*, February 1995, p. 62.
18. *Guardian*, 30 January 1995, p. 22.
19. Edward Said, *Culture and Imperialism* (London, Chatto & Windus, 1993), p. 29
20. *Sight and Sound*, May 1994, p. 6.

# 7

# New Hope: the postmodern project of *Star Wars*

*Will Brooker*

Shopping in London; it's early 1996 but it feels, as the slogan had it, like a long time ago. It feels like 1977. There are life-size cardboard models of Darth Vader and C-3PO in the local Our Price, advertising the *Star Wars* trilogy on video for the last time this century. Further down the high street, W. H. Smiths has mounted a display of *Star Wars* paperbacks, the sheer range of which would surprise all but the most diehard fan: the Jedi Academy trilogy, the Corellian trilogy, the further adventures of Lando Calrissian and Han Solo. Next to the bulky volumes in their set groups of three are the flimsier illustrated teenage novels about the Junior Jedi Knights, and below those the Young Jedi Knights range, published in 1995 and clearly aimed at readers born long after the 1983 release of the most recent *Star Wars* film, *Return of the Jedi.*[1]

This is to suggest merely the films' new visibility in the populist mainstream of book and video stores; it is to neglect the role-playing department of the Virgin megastore, with its *Star Wars* New Republic Sourcebook, its Technical Companions, its Planets Collection and Twin Stars of Kira modules.[2] This is to ignore the upper floor of Forbidden Planet and its shelf of five monthly comics from *Star Wars: Tales of the Jedi* to *Star Wars: X-Wing Rogue Squadron,*[3] and the display downstairs of 1996 calendars, 'audio-book' cassettes and a recording of the 'original radio drama' retailing at over £80. Two conclusions can be drawn from this trawl; that this is a recent, on-going industry rather than a resale of old spin-offs dragged from the back of stockrooms, and that the nature of the merchandise has undergone a change since the mid-eighties, when *Star Wars* last generated any significant commercial interest.

In 1977, when *Star Wars* – 'Episode IV: A New Hope', to give it the subtitle purists prefer – was first released, its influence on the market included Walls *Star Wars* skinless pork sausages, Trebor *Star Wars* chews and Letraset notebooks with new covers hastily added proclaiming them as 'Stormtrooper's Manual' and 'Princess Leia's Rebel Jotter'. This year, apart from the videos and the apparently endless series of novels, the predominant line of merchandise lies in games for the Sega and Nintendo of which *Dark Forces*, at £49.99, is a typical example. The mini-action figures and model spacecraft so eagerly hunted out by ten-year-olds in 1980 have been hoarded for fifteen years and now fetch up to £60 on collectors' markets. Clearly, the target audience has shifted; put simply, it has grown up. Though the £80 boxed-set of the trilogy on video may have been bought by the indulgent parents of some under-tens, anecdotal evidence suggests that a great many young men in their late teens and twenties cajoled it from girlfriends as a Christmas present, and the traditional market for console games and science fiction novels suggests a similar group in terms of both age and gender.

This boom in consumer interest fits very neatly, of course, with the theatrical re-release of *A New Hope* – with revamped effects and some reinstated scenes cut from the original – scheduled for April 1997, and the first in a new trilogy promised in 1998; as such, the merchandise phenomenon can easily be traced back to efficient, long-term marketing strategies at Lucasfilm or 20th Century Fox, and would hardly bear further examination were it not for other, scattered signs of nostalgic reference to the original trilogy which suggest a wider, less quantifiable resurgence of interest and give an indication of the films' continuing cultural resonance among young men in particular.

Any list of these sources is bound to be both subjective and incomplete. It might include, however, the proliferation of *Star Wars* 'home pages' on the Internet and their print-based equivalents in amateur fanzines, of which at least seven, with titles such as *Bounty Hunter*, *Moons of Yavin* and *Holocron*, are currently available in England alone.[4] Similarly, the English cottage industry of 'small-press' comic books, with a readership predominantly of twentysomething male graduates, makes strikingly frequent reference to the *Star Wars* trilogy as a site of shared cultural knowledge: a character asks, for example, 'who did you want to get off with Princess Leia? Han or Luke? Farm-boy or pirate?' and in another title the protagonist mourns a dead friend with 'he was my Chewbacca'.[5]

This sense of the films as the formative cultural influence on a particular generation, to be celebrated a decade later in low-budget, 'independent' media forms, is echoed in a *New Musical Express* interview with the band Ash, whose second single of 1995, 'Girl from Mars', was backed with a manic reworking of John Williams' 'Cantina Band' theme from *Star Wars*; the trilogy is cited as 'an immense influence', and the band linked with Oasis and Menswear as 'part of that *Star Wars* generation' in a re-emphasis of the films' central location within the cultural capital of young British males.[6] A similar quotation and reference can be seen in American sources, both in the range of fanzines like *Star Wars Insider*, largely equivalent to their British counterparts, and in more mainstream texts which speak of the slacker or 'Generation-Y' experience, again with a striking gender-specificity. Douglas Coupland's most recent novel *Microserfs*, for instance, has its disillusioned, 26-year-old narrator Daniel filling a computer file, and pages of text, with his own random patterns of thought: buried in the outpourings are the names Han Solo and R2-D2.[7] With a comparable project and audience, the no-budget film *Clerks* – directed by 23-year old Kevin Smith in 1994 – involves its young male protagonists in a heated discussion about the contractors who built *Return of the Jedi*'s Death Star.[8]

An unsystematic and unscientific body of evidence, to be sure; but it suggests, I hope, that the resonance and meaning of the *Star Wars* films goes beyond a nostalgia imposed from 'above'. What I propose to do here is to examine the possible meanings of the films to the audience sketched in my account – that is, to the young men in their late-teens to mid-twenties who conceivably saw *A New Hope* on its first theatrical release – and, bearing in mind the right-wing connotations which the trilogy has been accused of carrying, and which have irreparably come to be borne by the term 'Star Wars' itself, the implications of this resurgence of interest and investment of nostalgia in a supposedly reactionary text.

*Star Wars* is, of course, a nostalgic text in itself and is famously cited as one of Fredric Jameson's examples of *la mode rétro*. In its pastiche of 'the Saturday afternoon serial of the Buck Rogers type' it satisfies

> a deep (might I even say repressed?) longing to experience them again: it is a complex object in which on some first level children and adolescents can take the adventures straight, while the adult public is able to gratify a deeper and more properly nostalgic desire to return to that older period and to live its strange old aesthetic artifacts through once again.[9]

The film's aesthetic of mythic recycling was noted by many reviewers at the time of its first release, who spotted allusions to 'everything from *The Searchers* to *Triumph of the Will*'[10] and either dismissed it as 'a ploddingly self-conscious pastiche' – this from a review which rather pompously traced the film's plot to *The Alamo*, its robots to *The Wizard of Oz* and its sentiment to *Lassie Come Home*[11] – or approved its project to synthesise 'a whole body of the most potent myths on which we have been raised'.[12]

As Jameson notes, though, the 'we' of this last observation was the adult public of 1977, not its children. Those seeing the film at age seven had no shared memory of Buck Rogers, *The Searchers* or *The Wizard of Oz*; *Star Wars* was no doubt, for many of its young viewers, the occasion of their first visit to the cinema, and its myths were of the first order rather than a self-conscious recycling. Here were Merlin, Ricky Nelson, the Tin Man, *The Seven Samurai* and *The Dam Busters*[13] crammed into one potent, electrifying folk story; a rush of concentrated iconography, of distilled myth. That young audience left the cinema having swallowed all the popular narratives that had thrilled their parents in one gulp; and the unprecedented, across-the-board marketing meant that for the first time children's lives were invaded by the film at every level of consumption from crisps to pyjamas to toys to lampshades. As a review in the *Evening Standard* perceptively noted, Lucas had 'manufactured a sort of "group memory" for kids who never knew the fantasies and myths that films dealt in when he was young'.[14]

Some eighteen years on, that group memory remains; and in 1995 the *Star Wars* generation began, like Lucas, to make films which recycled their own childhood myths. *Star Wars*, to 27-year-old Danny Cannon's generation, is the original; *Judge Dredd* is the nostalgia film. But something has changed; something has been lost which suggests that the continuing power of the *Star Wars* trilogy lies not simply in its Best-Of aesthetic of mythic compilation, but in its underlying ideological structure. It is in this project of the over-arching struggle, seen in terms of a 'grand narrative', that the film's reactionary political programme has been located, and which I shall consider after a brief comparison of *Star Wars* with its reworking in 1995's *Judge Dredd*.

If *Star Wars* embodies Jameson's nostalgia cinema, *Judge Dredd* works within a Baudrillardian aesthetic of pure surface, a 'dizzying collage of everybody
else's ideas',[15] a lifting of images from *Demolition Man, Terminator* 2 and
*Robocop* which themselves borrowed freely from cinema's iconographic stock-
room; in a final irony, the grimy, drizzled Mega-City One which Dredd
patrols virtually replicates the Los Angeles of *Blade Runner*, a text analysed to
within an inch of its life for its notorious plundering of *noir* and Victoriana,
Egyptian architecture and Japanese neon. That city's reappearance in *Judge
Dredd* was described by one reviewer as 'a museum-display composite seen
too many times before . . . . Now That's What I Call A Dystopia Vol 27'.[16]
Dredd himself, along with the genetically-bred soldiers he fights at the film's
climax, is a clone, one of several copies from a prototype lawman.

*Judge Dredd* opens with a text crawl giving background to the film's scenario, voiced by Darth Vader actor James Earl Jones; a device which, aimed
at precisely the audience of young men for whom the black actor's distinctive tones and the text scrolling slowly upscreen will immediately recall *A
New Hope*, is clearly intended to self-consciously reference *Star Wars* for its
nostalgic function. The pastiche goes on to incorporate from the earlier film
'the illuminating sojourn into the desert, the doomed but wise old mentor,
the overbearing martial soundtrack that John Williams himself stole from
Gustav Holst, and the ham-fisted whack of the computer equipment to get
it to operate properly'.[17] This latter telling detail occurs during an airborne
chase on jet-powered Lawmaster bikes which could, in its similarity to
*Return of the Jedi's* speeder-bike sequence, virtually have been shot from the
same storyboards. The only difference is the inevitable loss of *Jedi's* thrilling
audacity, and a surprising paucity in the later film's special effects. *Judge
Dredd's* reworking-by-numbers is simulation in Baudrillard's sense of an
endlessly self-mirroring, self-reflexive collection of images for which the
'original', if there was one, is lost in the 'uninterrupted circuit' of exchange
and duplication;[18] but it also, in the more popular sense of the word, brings
to mind the aimless pleasure of a *Star Wars* flight simulator – Disney's 'Star
Tours', or perhaps the 'Skywalker Park' of William Gibson's novel *Virtual
Light*.[19]

Aimless, for *Judge Dredd* has no aim, no point, no progression. The film's
triumphant finale centres around Dredd's refusal to be anything but a
'street judge', and his return to duty. The judicial system, shown from the
film's beginning to be brutal, militaristic and totalitarian, is reinstated, and
we as audience, like the Mega-City citizens, are encouraged to celebrate the
restoration of the old status quo. We are shown no possibility for social
change; rather, the film suggests that change is unwise, and that the devil
we know, however fascistic it may seem in its jackboots, epaulettes and
blank-eyed helmet, is preferable to the chaos presented as the only alternative.[20] Significantly, the youth of Mega-City One are seen in only two roles
and given two options; turning to crime and being policed as a juvenile
delinquent, or to the law and becoming Judge Dredd. Compare this with
the opportunity given to Luke Skywalker, and the key difference between
the two films begins to emerge. Luke is initially a disaffected teenager living
on an isolated homestead, a gentler James Dean held back by his uncle's
unambitious vision of a lifetime in farming and small business – 'you can

waste time with your friends when your chores are done'. Through his accidental discovery of a distress call from the diplomat Princess Leia, he is
offered entry into a project spanning far beyond his own limited sphere.
Luke, of course, becomes a Rebel, and he is given a cause.

> In growing up, I kept hearing from all sides that we couldn't do anything, that
> we were helpless. The only positive thing I feel I can put across in the film is to
> generate a sort of vague I-can-do-anything feeling. Once you get that feeling, it
> comes true. Be positive – you can do it.[21]

This was the project of *Star Wars* as put forward by Lucas in a *Guardian*
interview some ten months before the film opened in Britain. His hopes for
the film were echoed by a review later that year, which saw *Star Wars* as the
'triumph of faith and innocence over cynicism and despair'.[22] To claim the
same for *Judge Dredd* would be inconceivable. *Star Wars* entertains a vision
of optimistic possibility of the kind which the 'slacker' mentality – and in
Britain, the apathetic nihilism of youth portrayed in Danny Cannon's first
film, *The Young Americans*, and Paul Anderson's *Shopping*[23] – made deeply
unfashionable. However, this sense of the potential for change, the gaining
of purpose and the validity of a struggle based on principles – of new hope,
to put it at its simplest – is perhaps exactly why *Star Wars* has retained, or
regained, such poignancy among the generation now in their twenties. The
representations of youth culture over recent years, as suggested above, are
depressingly bleak narratives of joyriders, shoplifters, ravers and dealers; as
a review of *Shopping* had it, 'dull approximations of a lost generation, moving towards a self-ordained bad end like slightly disinterested lemmings.
There is practically nothing to measure their rebellion against.'[24]

*Star Wars*, by contrast, is built around a trajectory towards liberation,
emancipation and the overthrow of the tyrannical state; a narrative with
understandable resonance for a generation which has seen a single government in office for seventeen years, and for whom political change may well
seem the stuff of fairy tales. This trajectory, however, also seems to constitute one of those equally unfashionable *grands récits* of social transformation
against which Lyotard warned in 'What Is Postmodernism?';[25] and Lyotard's
suspicion of the grand narrative's 'totality' can perhaps be seen as well-
founded when we consider the wholesale appropriation of *Star Wars'* project by the Reagan administration.

Lucas went to court in 1985 in a vain attempt to sever the link between his
film title and Reagan's Strategic Defense Initiative,[26] but the words 'Star
Wars' would almost certainly have retained their secondary connotations in
the popular mind even had he won. Like Lucas, Reagan drew on the cinema of previous decades for his own myth-making, and effectively hijacked
them to his own ends. Susan Aronstein has argued that

> Apart from his freely acknowledged employment of the rhetoric and imagery
> of *Star Wars* ('the Strategic Defense Initiative has been labelled Star Wars. But it
> isn't about war. It is about peace. If you will pardon my stealing a film line . . .
> the Force is with us') most of Reagan's best lines and certainly his policies can
> be traced back to films, usually the countersubversive B movie of his own
> career, the same films that Lucas and Spielberg looked to in their revitalisation
> of early Hollywood genres.[27]

Yet it was not just Reagan who saw a right-wing project within the film's ideological premise. Years before the term 'Evil Empire' had been used to describe the Soviet Union, a newspaper editorial cartoon of 1978 showed Vader at the debating table on the side of the USSR, telling a sceptical United States team 've vant to assure you that ve have no thoughts or intentions of using space for military purposes'.[28]

Indeed, it is not hard to see some textual elements from which a reactionary reading, or reading of the film as reactionary, can be drawn. Luke Skywalker and Han Solo, for instance, embody the cowboy archetypes which Reagan so liked to evoke as the quick-shooting, frontier-taming West. J. G. Ballard's interpretation of the film as a 'parable of the US involvement in Vietnam, with the plucky hero from the backward planet . . . fighting bravely against the evil and all-destructive super-technology of the Galactic Empire'[29] falls within these parameters. Moreover, on Luke's home planet, the desert world Tatooine, the enemies are not just stormtroopers but the scavenging, scrap-dealing Jawas who attempt to cheat his uncle and the savage, alien Sandpeople; both can readily be seen as racist stereotypes of Arab culture. However, the Rebellion's struggle of opposition, couched in the vaguest terms of 'Republic' versus totalitarian Imperial state, is simply open to any and all political allegory, including Britain in India or England in Northern Ireland, and it is a tribute to Reagan's manipulation of the text that his preferred meaning has stuck so firmly to the film's key terms.

Perhaps the most extended discussion yet of the trilogy's ideological concerns can be credited to Robin Wood.[30] While Wood's inexcusably thoughtless errors – for C-3PO read 'CP-30'; for Obi-Wan 'Obi One'[31] – hardly inspire confidence in his 'close reading', he perceptively notes the dangers inherent in the Rebels' long-term project of liberation. The films' 'unease', Wood argues, lies in 'the problem of lineage: what will the rebels against the Empire create if not another empire?'.[32] This dilemma, which Wood contextualises as an American fear of Fascism from 'within' – the fear that the American democracy, founded by a nation itself revolting against British oppression, 'may carry within itself the potential to become Fascist, totalitarian, a police state'[33] – is enacted also in the ongoing question as to Luke's 'lineage'; the revelation that he is the son of 'prototypal Fascist beast' Darth Vader.

In Wood's view, symbolic resolution comes with the redemption of Vader and a celebration of 'fathericity' which restores traditional structures and excludes or suppresses women (Princess Leia), blacks (Lando Calrissian) and gays (in a bizarre reading, Wood sees C-3PO, apparently because of his 'affected British accent', as engaged in a homosexual 'pedophile relationship' with R2-D2).[34] To an extent, Wood's interpretation simply demonstrates again the readiness of the trilogy's vague terminology and stylised iconography to fit a wide variety of 'symbolic' socio-historical meanings.[35] His discussion of the oppressive and totalitarian project contained within the Rebel struggle is, though, valuable for its analysis of a dilemma clearly at the heart of the conflict between Reagan's and Lucas' 'readings'.

It is not my intention to claim that the reactionary/Republican narratives drawn from the films by Wood, Ballard and Reagan are unfounded, or based on 'misreading'. Instead, I will argue that these are not the meanings at the heart of the films' current significance in the culture of fanzines, indie bands, comics and net sites. In effect, the producers and audience behind these texts are performing a reappropriation which places different stresses and privileges different textual elements from those which were fore-grounded by the previous readings and which came to constitute the films' dominant ideological connotations. I want ultimately to suggest that this alternative reading, rather than harking back to a legitimating narrative of modernity with all its attendant dilemmas, implies instead a politically-directed postmodernism.

The project of the Rebellion in the *Star Wars* trilogy is marked from that of the Empire precisely in its aim to 'activate the differences'[36] rather than to shape the world in its own likeness. The Empire is a colonising force, impos-ing martial law on the communities within its net – we see roadblocks and armed troopers patrolling the town of Mos Eisley, for instance – and allow-ing no dissent within its own ranks. Significantly, there are suggestions in *A New Hope* of an internal conflict between the Empire's military/bureaucratic faction and its religious/feudal figurehead, Darth Vader, whose given title is Jedi Knight and Lord of the Sith. Any threat of disagreement is suppressed early in the film, however, as Vader throttles the official who scorns his 'sor-cerer's ways' declaring 'I find your lack of faith disturbing.'[37] By the start of *The Empire Strikes Back* the Imperials' military leader, Tarkin, has been killed and Vader, with the Emperor above him, takes full control. It is only when a rift occurs between Vader and his master, at the end of the third film, that the Empire begins to crumble.

The Rebellion, by contrast, thrives on difference, and builds on small pock-ets of resistance from transitory, temporary outposts such as the ice planet Hoth which the Rebels are forced to flee at the start of *The Empire Strikes Back*. These are micro-narratives of rebellion, hit-and-run raids. Leia is able to give Vader the information that her colleagues are on Dantooine, knowing that the Empire will find only deserted buildings and footprints. The Rebellion's strength is primarily in its fragmentation, the fact of its being everywhere and nowhere; its aesthetic, in effect, of the postmodern sublime.

These differences are emphasised through the costume and *mise-en-scène* attached to the two opposing sides. The Empire's ranks are clearly marked through uniform and military insignia; its stormtroopers, snowtroopers and biker-scouts are encased in black and white armour with their faces hidden, much like the Judges we applaud in Cannon's film. Vader, of course, wears a dark cloak and a casque-like helmet which both conceals his face and dis-torts his voice; again, the break-up of the Empire is signalled by the removal of this concealing apparatus at the end of *Jedi*. The Imperial warships are sleek daggers, all built around the same sharp-edged design.

The Rebellion's design aesthetic is, as Ian Saunders has suggested, one of bricolage; a mish-mash of patched-together X-Wings with Y-Wings, A-Wings and B-Wings thrown in, aided by individually-owned craft like Han Solo's smuggling vessel the Millenium Falcon. Saunders sees Solo as 'the archetyp-al bricoleur-poet', and Vader as his dialectical counterpoint:

> As Solo's career is unplanned, Vader's ambitions, like his visage, are rigidly fixed. His 'world' is the regimented artificial nation-state, the 'Death Star'; while Solo's ship is its apolitical bricolage opposite. 'What a piece of junk', says Luke

Skywalker when he first sees it. To which Solo, the ever-confident bricoleur, replies: 'She'll make .5 past light speed. She may not look like much but she's got it where it counts, kid. I've made a lot of special modifications myself.' Assembled from bits and pieces, poorly-resourced but somehow kept going by dint of ingenuity and know-how, the ship out-manoeuvres its vastly more powerful competitor through imagination and sheer cheek.[38]

Sheer cheek: this is the language not of the legitimating master narrative but of experiment and localised creativity.

Finally, the Rebellion fosters difference in its own organisation and direction. Its ranks, we see in *Return of the Jedi*, are made up of both humans and alien life forms from a bewildering variety of cultures; Chewbacca the towering, hair-covered Wookiee, of course, but also the lobster-headed Ackbar who holds the position of Admiral, and the jowled, mouse-like Nien Nunb who co-pilots the Millennium Falcon on its last raid. This is a political opposition which embraces the fantastic and the grotesque, encouraging others to its cause through an understanding of their culture and a broadening of its own; the Ewok tribe is drawn in through the droid C-3PO's relating of the Rebellion's narrative as a folk-tale complete with sound effects and actions, and in their own language. It would be possible to claim for the Ewok sequences, with their emphasis on the supernatural and the uncanny – the golden-plated C-3PO is worshipped as a god, and levitated through Luke's control of the Force – shades of the magic realism which Jameson suggests as a progressive alternative to both the ahistorical *mode rétro* and the blunted edge of avant-garde experimental cinema.[39] Significantly, the trilogy ends with songs, tribal music and joyful dance: a closure built around carnival.

The Rebellion's political meetings – before the final attacks in *A New Hope* and *Return of the Jedi* – take the form of conference-room debate rather than the formal ceremony of Vader and his master; authorities in a specific field take the floor, but those in attendance are seen to chip in with disagreement and suggestion. As such its project is similar to that described by James Donald in his discussion of the magic realist mode mentioned above; an alternative to 'one old avant-garde's death-or-glory resistance' and the other's 'utopian search for the "progressive text" that would hasten the revolution'[40]

> The emphasis . . . seems to be on experimentation, the multiplication of different narratives, and the narration of differences. The aim is no longer the silence of negation, but the noise of negotiation and dialogue. This implies neither a predisposition to compromise and quiescence, nor the pluralist assumption that 'anything goes.' Dialogue, in this view, equals conflict. Such conflict is neither an embarassment nor a sign that the process is not working. On the contrary, the discord is essential. It demonstrates the aspiration to community, a community whose form and direction cannot be determined in advance, but only in the process of the dialogue.[41]

It is this sense of a progressive community based on debate and experiment, on small-scale projects and creativity within a postmodern mode of difference and fragmentation, which I believe is currently being 'read' from the trilogy into fan culture. It can be seen in the diplomatic open spaces of the Internet with its web of *Star Wars* home pages linked across states and oceans, and their invitations to leave e-mail comments or post up subjects for discussion opening them in turn to still wider networks of debate.[42] It is at the heart of the *Star Wars* fanzine community, each promoting the others' titles and cramming pages produced on desk-top publishing packages with short stories, comic strips, board games, 'filk' songs,[43] even fairy tales,[44] and can even be located in the self-belief and playful experiment of indie bands like Ash, or the one-man, shoestring film-making of *Clerks*, a flourishing of the 'I-can-do-anything feeling' which Lucas hoped to instil.

This is the spirit behind the full-length *Star Wars* 'novels' by amateur writers,[45] advertised in fanzine columns and offered not for money but in exchange for other writing, and behind the small-press comic books written, drawn and handbound by a miniscule production team and circulated on subscription to a hundred readers; the belief that it is possible and worthwhile to work outside or in opposition to the dominant mainstream – the Boxtree and Bantam publishing houses responsible for the commercial *Star Wars* novelisations, and the 'Big Two' comic organisations, Marvel and DC – and to create a support network for small-scale creativity. This is the legacy of *Star Wars* to some of those who saw it as children, and the most optimistic reason for the trilogy's current nostalgic resonance; its suggestion that diversity, debate and the exchange of voices can be central to a community, its validation of struggle on the smallest level, and its implication that fragmentation, pastiche and bricolage, rather than leading inevitably to a superficial culture of surface, can be part of a progressive narrative of change.

## Notes

1. Most significant and critically acclaimed is Timothy Zahn's trilogy, following directly on from the events in *Return of the Jedi: Heir to the Empire, Dark Force Rising* and *The Last Command* (New York, Bantam). Others include Kevin J. Anderson's 'Jedi Academy' trilogy, Roger MacBride Allen's 'Corellian Trilogy' and the most recent bestsellers, Dave Wolverton's *The Courtship of Princess Leia* and Kevin Anderson's *Darksaber*.
2. Produced by West End Games, most of these modules and sourcebooks were published in 1994 and 1995.
3. Apart from comic adaptations of the film – invariably renamed 'Classic *Star Wars*' – Boxtree (London) publish, in 'graphic novel' format, volumes including *Dark Lords of the Sith, Dark Empire* and *Tales of the Jedi*. These were all originally published monthly by Dark Horse comics, whose range currently includes an adaptation of Zahn's novel *Heir to the Empire*.
4. Other fanzines currently available in Britain include *Luminous Beings Are We* (Essex), also linked to an Internet site, *I Have A Bad Feeling About This* (Scotland), *Telesponder* and *Force Sensitive* (London).
5. Quotations from *The Jock*, edited by Rol Hirst (Huddersfield, privately published) and *Fell, Dr L.*, edited by Andrew Pack (Lincoln: privately published).
6. Interview with Ash, *New Musical Express*, 14 October 1995, p. 34. The title of Ash's 1996 debut album, *1977*, pays further tribute to the formative influence of *A New Hope*. The album opens with the distinctive screech of a TIE Fighter, and closes with 'Darkside Lightside', a reference to the twin aspects of the Force.
7. Douglas Coupland, *Microserfs* (London, Flamingo, 1995).
8. The film also features a track by Supernova called 'Chewbacca', celebrating Han Solo's co-pilot in its chorus 'what a Wookiee'.

9. Fredric Jameson, 'Postmodernism and Consumer Society', in E. Ann Kaplan, *Postmodernism and its Discontents* (London, Verso, 1988), p. 18.
10. Derek Malcolm, *Guardian*, 13 December 1977.
11. *Glasgow Herald*, 27 January 1978.
12. David Robinson, *The Times*, 16 February 1977.
13. Although the tracing of elements in *Star Wars* to their 'source' is bound to be sub-jective, many commentators have been in agreement about these particular aspects. Ben Kenobi is clearly a Gandalf or Merlin figure, while Mark Hamill's performance as Luke Skywalker has been compared (notably by Pauline Kael) to Ricky Nelson's style of acting. C-3PO has frequently been linked to the Tin Man, and Chewbacca to the Cowardly Lion. Finally, Darth Vader's costume, and the clash of opposing Jedi schools in his duel with Obi-Wan Kenobi, seem heavily indebted to samurai iconography, and the final dogfights in the Death Star trench to films of the Second World War.
14. Alexander Walker, *Evening Standard*, 10 November 1977.
15. Joe Queenan, *The Guardian Guide*, 15–21 July 1995.
16. Jonathan Romney, *Guardian*, 20 July 1995.
17. Queenan, *The Guardian Guide*, 15–21 July 1995.
18. Jean Baudrillard, 'Simulacra and Simulations', in *Selected Writings* (Oxford, Polity Press, 1988), p. 170
19. William Gibson, *Virtual Light* (London, Viking, 1993). In the same novel, the police satellite monitoring the protagonist, Rydell, is nicknamed the Death Star.
20. This is in direct contrast with the original 'Judge Dredd' strip in *2000AD*, which was intended to satirise Dredd's unbending adherence to his absurd and brutal Law; the strip's writers have spoken in interview of their despair that a young audience began to take the character at face value.
21. George Lucas, quoted in the *Guardian*, 1 March 1977.
22. David Levin, *Daily Mail*, 1 August 1977.
23. *The Young Americans*, directed by Danny Cannon, 1993; *Shopping*, directed by Paul Anderson, 1994. The latter film also involves a nostalgic discussion of *Star Wars* toy figures; as such it parallels *Clerks* in its portrayal of a disenfranchised youth for whom the trilogy is an important cultural reference.
24. Derek Malcolm, *Guardian*, 23 June 1994.
25. Jean-Francois Lyotard, *The Postmodern Condition. A Report on Knowledge* (Manchester, Manchester University Press, 1984). Lyotard concludes 'We have paid a high enough price for the nostalgia of the whole and the one . . . let us wage a war on totality . . .' (pp. 81–2).
26. As documented in *Variety*, 3 June 1987.
27. Susan Aronstein, '"Not Exactly a Knight". Arthurian Narrative and Recuperative Politics in the *Indiana Jones* Trilogy', *Cinema Journal*, 34(4): (Summer 1995).
28. Cartoon by 'Stayskal', published by the *Chicago Tribune/New York Times* syndicate, 1978.
29. J. G. Ballard, 'Hobbits in Space?', in *A User's Guide to the Millennium* (London, HarperCollins, 1996).
30. Robin Wood, *Hollywood from Vietnam to Reagan* (New York, Columbia University Press, 1986).
31. While not wishing to labour the point, it is ironic that Wood lambasts a Roger Ebert review for the same carelessness – 'Ebert's plot synopsis sets a new record in critical inaccuracy . . .' – earlier in the same volume (p. 123). Given that the character names are listed in the on-screen credits of *Star Wars*, Wood's errors suggest a contempt for his subject; he would surely not permit an article on Hawks's films to misspell the name of a protagonist.
32. Wood, *Hollywood*, p. 170.

33. Wood, *Hollywood*, p. 169. It is perhaps the culmination of this American nightmare which *Judge Dredd* depicts with its characteristic lack of irony or critique.

34. Wood argues that Leia is reduced to a position of 'helplessness and dependency . . . there is never any suggestion that she might inherit the Force, or have the privilege of being trained by Obi One [sic] and Yoda' (p. 173). An attentive viewer would soon disprove this claim: Leia alone is able to hear Luke's mental plea for help at the end of *The Empire Strikes Back*, and knows, when Han does not, that Luke has escaped the Death Star at the close of *Return of the Jedi*. Indeed, Obi-Wan and Yoda note her potential as a replacement for Luke – 'there is another' – in *The Empire Strikes Back*, and her subsequent Jedi training is foregrounded in Timothy Zahn's novels.

35. Wood's complaints are echoed to an extent by the author Joanna Russ in her condemnation of *Star Wars* for its pleasures grounded in 'sexism, racism, heterosexism, competition and macho privilege'. Russ is quoted in John Tulloch and Henry Jenkins, *Science Fiction Audiences* (London, Routledge, 1995), p. 36. Tulloch argues, *contra* Russ, that a 'fan reading' of the film would 'stress the film's heroic treatment of resistance to totalitarian authority and the need to form alliances across multiple planetary cultures, races and genders . . . the utopianism of science fiction may emerge as much from the audience as from the producers' (p. 39). Although I think this is a simplification of the relationship between audience and text, the 'readings' which I have suggested as currently foregrounded in fan culture are indeed partly grounded in ideas of community and the embracing of difference.

36. Lyotard, *The Postmodern Condition*, p. 82.

37. The exchange is perhaps worth transcribing further as an instance of the rare conflict between Imperial characters, and of the speed with which such discourse is suppressed.

    *Vader*: The ability to destroy a planet is insignificant next to the power of the Force.
    *General Tagge*: Don't try to frighten us with your sorcerer's ways, Lord Vader. Your sad devotion to that ancient religion has not helped you conjure up the stolen data tapes. Or given you clairvoyance enough to find the Rebels' hidden- [He breaks off as Vader begins to choke him]
    *Vader*: I find your lack of faith disturbing.
    *Tarkin*: This bickering is pointless.

38. Ian Saunders, 'Richard Rorty and *Star Wars*. On the Nature of Pragmatism's Narrative', *Textual Practice*, 8(3). (Winter 1994), pp. 438–9.

39. Fredric Jameson, 'On Magic Realism in Film', *Critical Enquiry*, 12(2): (Winter 1986), p. 303.

40. James Donald, *Fantasy and the Cinema* (London, British Film Institute, 1989), p. 230.

41. Donald, *Fantasy and the Cinema*, p. 230.

42. A single net site on the trilogy will invariably promote others' sites, sometimes suggesting fifty or more. On the recommendation of one home page, I visited '*Star Wars* Central', 'Boba Fett's Home Page', 'The New Republic Central Database', 'The Ultimate Site for the Dark Side of the Force', 'Guess What . . . a *Star Wars* Page' and 'Ray-Traced Art by Anthony Yu'. Lists of 'bloopers' and memorable quotations from the trilogy on these pages are compiled by hundreds of fans e-mailing their own contributions to the collective work, and all are credited as authors, the list sometimes filling pages of text.

    Significantly, one *Star Wars* chat room is at the time of writing organising its own rebellion against the censorship inherent in Lucasfilm's official web site. Participants take an obvious pleasure in recruiting 'newbies' to their cause and signalling their loyalty through a 'Star of Alderaan' icon attached to their messages. This is a particularly ironic case of the impulse towards resistance-from-below rebounding against Lucasfilm, which now finds itself in the position of tyrannical authority.

43. Filk songs, a phenomenon apparently unique to science fiction fandom, involve new – occasionally, it has to be said, banal – lyrics put to traditional music. One example will suffice, to the tune of 'Clementine': 'Captain Solo, Captain Solo / Party to the Rebel band / Though you don't know you're a hero / Others help you understand.'

44. 'Jedi Bedtime Stories. Traditional *Star Wars* Folk and Fairy Tales', a feature in *Holocron*, December 1995.

45. For example: *The Ormand Factor* by Louise Turner, advertised in fanzines as 'a *Star Wars* novel set post-*ROTJ* and featuring Wedge Antilles and Luke Skywalker. 116 pages of text, laser printed, photocopied and comb-bound with card cover.'

I would like to thank my student at West Kent College, Phil Edmunds, for introducing me to the *Star Wars* novels and for some productive discussions about the trilogy. May the Force . . .

# 8

# Postmodern modes of ethnicity

## *Vivian Sobchack*

From Lester D. Friedman (ed.), *Unspeakable images. Ethnicity and the American cinema* (University of Illinois Press 1991)

I want to begin this exploration of the representation and cultural meanings of *ethnicity* in contemporary American cinema with a scenario set in the early 1920s. Imagine, if you will, a giant black pot has been built outside the gates of a large automobile factory in preparation for a festival sponsored by its owner, Henry Ford. The day of celebration arrives. Into the pot go 'groups of gaily dressed immigrants dancing and singing their native songs.' And out of the pot emerges 'a single stream of Americans dressed alike in the contemporary standard dress and singing the national anthem.'[1] Eventually the music of tarantellas and polkas and other ethnic dances fades away, and the rising sound of the 'Star Spangled Banner' is heard as the last of the immigrants is absorbed into an intensely patriotic, identically dressed, and utterly homogeneous American chorus.

This highly cinematic scenario seems as if it might have come from some forthcoming Monty Python or Robert Townsend film, or from a projected companion piece to Milos Forman's *Ragtime* (1981) or David Byrne's *True Stories* (1986). That is, we would be hard-pressed to take its representation as a serious or sincere and moving commentary on ethnic experience in America. Rather, its blatant lack of subtlety, its dramatic literalism in regard to the metaphor of the 'melting pot,' and its vision of a wholly assimilated, self-identical and identified American culture seems at once outrageously simple, crudely funny, and reflexively ironic. Nonetheless, it is more than likely that in the early 1920s when it was staged, this melting-pot scenario did touch the hearts of the spectators who watched it – not on a movie screen, but as the culmination of an actual public festival. At a time when a massive influx of diverse European immigrants challenged the dominant myth of American national community, main-line Henry Ford's ritual of 'forced conversion,'[2] and its celebration of total ethnic transformation and assimilation, must not only have been utterly sincere in the demands it made of its participants, but also patriotically stirring and deeply reassuring to its spectators.

Today, however, it is nearly impossible to imagine that spectators might be brought to tears by such a scene unless they were tears of laughter – for even as we live and go about our business as members of what we think of as contemporary 'American culture,' most of us are fully aware that, insofar as the term signifies a clearly bounded and unified category of social being, *there is no such thing*. The closest counterparts we can find to Ford's scenario of total conversion and assimilation occur in the fantastic and patently simulated 'small' worlds of Disneyland and other American theme parks – or in such parodic and ironic films as Woody Allen's *Zelig* (1983), Paul Mazursky's *Moscow on the Hudson* (1984), or John Sayles's *The Brother from Another Planet* (1984). All three take Ford's utopian vision of complete assimilation to a similar extreme, and yet each, in its own way, also wryly turns that vision back on itself. *Zelig*, for example, gives us a Human Chameleon as the central figure of a 'mock documentary,' someone so desirous of fitting in that he literally – and, of necessity, continually – assumes the ethnic, linguistic, and even occupational characteristics of those around him. New York, to the Russian defector in *Moscow on the Hudson*, is *all* ethnic, so assimilation ironically means *not* fitting in – just like everyone else. And in *The Brother from Another Planet*, total assimilation is viewed totally ironically as a black alien from outer space is easily absorbed into the marginalized black culture of that 'outer' (if still terrestrial) space alien-ated as Harlem. In highly conscious ways, these films foreground Werner Sollors's suggestion in *Beyond Ethnicity* that 'In America, casting oneself as an outsider may in fact be considered a dominant cultural trait . . . Every American is now considered a potential ethnic.'[3] Yet, if every American is literally and narratively 'cast' as an 'outsider' or ethnic 'other' (as they are in these films), then the meaning of 'American-ness' as it is constituted through assimilation – described as an inclusionary and culturally dominant 'sameness,' – and composed of 'insiders' loses its conceptual and experiential validity.

*Zelig*, *Moscow on the Hudson*, and *The Brother from Another Planet* are both symptomatic and explicitly aware of our contemporary confusion and ironic doubt about what, in earlier moments of our public history, seemed much more clear-cut. Today the distinctions and boundary conditions implicit in the terms *American* and *ethnic* and the concept of a unified and singular *culture* are widely and commonly experienced as problematic, if not indeed paradoxical. Likewise, the experiential ground upon which notions of 'ethnic difference' or 'assimilation' were based is no longer the same terrain traversed by the participants and spectators of Henry Ford's 'melting-pot' pageant. We now live in an age when electronic interfaces and instant communication have nearly erased the boundaries and distances of national geography. A pervasive and dispersed global network of commercial franchise has sent Kentucky Fried Chicken to Beijing and Holiday Inns everywhere – and pizza has become America's 'national' food supplanting the 'all-American' frankfurter. Multinational corporations and international co-production challenge the 'Buy American' legacy of Henry Ford to market nationally ambiguous automobiles – and movies.[4] In effect, we are hard-pressed to locate where, what, and who is either 'all-American' or 'ethnic.'

. . . In an earlier time, being ethnic meant being part of a marginalized, yet coherent and relatively stable social group – one both perceived and represented by the dominant (and unethnic or assimilated) culture and by its own members as exclusively different and other from that dominant culture by virtue of its maintenance of specific codes of language, dress, manner, kinship, social and religious structure, and of its particular history and mythology. Thus, being ethnic meant having a cultural identity structured and regulated by the constraints of *descent* – whereas being American (unethnic, assimilated) meant having a cultural identity structured and transformed by the freedoms of *consent*. As Sollors elaborates: 'Descent language emphasizes our positions as heirs, our hereditary qualities, liabilities, and entitlements; consent language stresses our abilities as mature free agents and "architects of our fates" to choose our spouses, our destinies, and our political systems.'[5] Regarded from another perspective, we can suggest that descent – with its stress on maintaining connections with cultural origins and roots – also emphasizes a 'natural' and/or 'authentic' mode of cultural identity, whereas consent – with its stress on the conscious choice and construction of social being – emphasizes the 'assumption' of cultural identity, and the latter's ultimately theatrical and 'inauthentic' nature as always a 're-presentation' of self.

We live in what seems to be the advanced stages of an age of representation, and thus we are perhaps more aware of the inauthenticity and theatricality of 'being American' than were either Ford's pageant participants or its spectators. We have been marked indelibly and made unprecedentedly self-conscious by television and its entailment of consumer culture. We exist at a moment when identity, memory, and history are re-cognized as mediated and media productions – constructed and consumable images available for countless acts of recombination, revision, and recycling. We are also part of a society which experiences the particularity of celebrity more intimately than it does the coherence of community. In this context, nearly all those visible markers that once separated the cultures of 'ethnic' descent from the 'American' culture of consent, that signaled the boundaries of otherness and gave it ethnic identity, integrity, and authenticity, are detached from their original historical roots and have become 'floating signifiers' available for purchase by anyone. Ethnicity, too, seems based on consent. We can put ourselves together in almost any fashion we like – and our self-consciousness about so inventing ourselves tends to be reflected in the fact that the fashion we like asserts this 'right of representation' through pastiche or parody, through a scavenging or playful ironizing of those costumes, speech, and manners that once were held separate and discrete and that conferred upon a portion of the culture's members their particular identity, history, and sense of community.

In such a contemporary context as ours, then, the allegorical drama of Henry Ford's melting-pot scenario is more than likely to be interpreted ironically – as a denial or interrogation of that which it also asserts. This is because the normative standard (being 'uniformly American') the scenario provided against which that value called 'ethnicity' could be clearly and simply identified is no longer perceived as having much experiential or symbolic validity. If the norm of a uniform, stable, and single notion of what it is to be American no longer holds, then a stable or sure notion of what it is to be ethnic also weakens.

. . . Rather, the constructed and provisional nature of *all* identity is what we see, and this vision of social being radically calls into question the oppositional terms and relations which, for Sollors, bound American culture as such. The notion of an 'ethnic,' 'American,' 'authentic,' or 'invented' self conflate as *all* selves are perceived as chosen and constructed by consent – even ethnic ones.

Within the context of this theatrical and 'play-full' reflexivity we have about our own personae, it is hardly surprising that a film such as Norman Jewison's *Moonstruck* (1987), for example, makes ironic its own nostalgia for the 'authenticity' of Italian-American 'experience.'[6] On the one hand, the comedy's charm emerges from its sentimental romanticism and loving celebration of a discrete ethnic community based on descent, but, on the other, its parodic bite comes from a self-mocking use of grand opera as ironic commentary on the theatrical excesses of its Italian characters and, indeed, as a gloss on the consensual construction of 'Italian-ness' itself.

It is clear, then, that since the historical occurrence of Ford's pageant in the early 1920s, various events of a social, economic, and technological kind have moved us (indeed, forced us) toward our contemporary acknowledgement of 'the mixed, plural and contradictory nature' of the age in which we live, an age 'caught between "myths of totality" and "ideologies of fracture",'[7] an age whose historically unique characteristics, cultural values, and representations have been described, theorized, and debated as *postmodern*. These descriptions, theories, and debates have implications for our understanding of the way we newly perceive and value ethnicity and for the way these new perceptions and values find representation in contemporary American cinema.

For cultural critics such as Fredric Jameson, postmodernism is virtually a global term that describes a new and unprecedented 'cultural logic'[8] – a logic that emerges from and informs all aspects of those cultures based on and homogenized by multinational capitalism and its new technologies of production, consumption, and communication. While coextensive with other and earlier logics of structuring and representing social experience (for example, realism and modernism), the new logic of postmodernism has become culturally dominant – altering the previous sense we lived and made of time, space, the world, and ourselves, and both consciously and unconsciously transforming *all* our cultural productions, whether radical and progressive or traditional and conservative. This totalized cultural transformation of sense, meaning, and value is revealed in certain novel esthetic values and features seen as characteristic of postmodern representation – among them, 'a new depthlessness, which finds its prolongation . . . in a whole new culture of the image or the simulacrum,' and 'a consequent weakening of historicity, both in our relationship to public History and in the new forms of our private temporality . . . .'[9] We are seen as living on the surface – the screen – of things, engaged with the play of display. We are seen as subjectively decentered and dislocated in space and time. Our individual identities and memories and particular histories have been objectified and circulated as images and supplanted by the simulated and extroverted memories and history given us by the visual media.

Correlatively, our social and ethnic affinities have been supplanted by affinities of consumption and cosmetic display. What once was an emotional investment in and subjective connection to a specific community and its historical past has been objectified, dispersed, and transformed into free-floating stimulation and consumer desire. This general and detached rather than specific and grounded interest in community and history leads to the practice of what Jameson describes as 'aesthetic populism' – a kind of wonderment at and valuation of everything ordinary and banal, an embrace and incorporation of the 'whole "degraded" landscape of schlock and kitsch, of TV series and *Readers' Digest* culture, of advertising and motels, of the late show and the grade-B Hollywood film, of so-called paraliterature with its airport paperback categories . . . .'[10] Lacking a sense of our roots, distanced from the gravitational pull of community and history, we have become strangers to our own lives – transients, tourists, cultural anthropologists who estheticize the everyday and wonder indiscriminately at everything.

The leveling of value described in this ultimately negative version of postmodernism is a consequence of living in a capitalist, high-tech, media culture. While in some ways liberating us from a stuffy and arbitrary allegiance to old traditions and canons, such a free-floating and indiscriminate interest in cultural flotsam and jetsam also suggests the end of old forms of human connection and cohesion, and seems to offer little hope for the kind of historical consciousness that would be responsible to either a past or a future. Bits and pieces of identities and artifacts once historically and personally located now primarily cohere in the *simulated* history and memory of the media – generally sensed as subjectively 'ours,' but given to us by others as objective images, rather like the photographs given to *Blade Runner's* replicant Rachel as testament to a memory not really her own. Increasingly estranged from a personal connection to memory and history by this pervasive awareness of mediation and its objectifications, we now nostalgically collect or schizophrenically combine the fragmented remains of history into an ahistorical pastiche put together somewhat like Madonna's costumes. Indeed, in the age of such supremely self-conscious, self-constructed, and invented presences as Madonna and Prince, it would seem that the previous historicity, specificity, and force of ethnic identification have re-solved themselves into a more general and provisional identification with individual fashion and generic subcultures.

Thus, many of the more cultish films of the 1980s seem to subsume questions of ethnicity under broader questions about the specificity, nature, and location of human identity, memory, and history in an age of media, microchips, and multinationals. We can see such inquiry going on not only in Ridley Scott's *Blade Runner* (1982) with its 'more human than human' replicants and 'less human than human' human beings, but also in Aaron Lipstadt's comic *Android* (1982). Max – the title figure and protagonist – not only contemplates the difference between humans and their simulations, but also is completely 'image conscious'; 'aware of his own existential status as an imitation,' he 'still strives to further model himself after images of images: the personae of Jimmy Stewart and Humphrey Bogart he has seen in old movies.'[11] Susan Seidelman's *Making Mr. Right* (1987) has a heroine who is an 'image consultant' and falls in love with a 'perfect man' of an android, while Paul Verhoeven's *RoboCop* (1987) gives us the cyborg Murphy, half man, half robot, who fights crime in an America ruled by corporations and pervaded by mindless television game shows and an endless stream of commercials. In an age of electronic reproduction and replication, these films and others are compelled less by the specific otherness of *ethnic* being than by the techno-logical challenge made to the generic status and sameness of *human* being.

Other contemporary films level ethnicity rather than hierarchically sub-sume it under a more general problem. That is, they dramatize its *lack* of meaningful difference from any other difference. For example, by using one performer for the two major roles in *Liquid Sky* (1983), it might be argued that Russian émigré director Slava Tsukerman was filming an allegory of that 'acute sense of doubleness' Werner Sollors identifies as marking ethnic consciousness. Yet the film's exploration of cultural identity and alienation is so diffused and dispersed that it tends to refuse such a reading. Instead, the performer's 'split subjectivity' as Margaret/Jimmy *erases* the differences between human and alien other, between gender and sexual preference, and disperses itself across the overdetermined differences within a punk-rock, new-wave, Soho, drug subculture that is fatally preyed upon by extraterrestrials who (like the subculture's own 'members') feed off its orgasmic and heroin highs. Similarly, Alex Cox's *Repo Man* (1984) may evoke traces of ethnic and racial cultures (and their stereotyping by dominant cul-ture) in the persons of two notorious Hispanic car thieves and a number of broadly drawn black characters. Nonetheless, their cultural 'otherness' or 'difference' is made narratively meaningless in a world in which everyone is equivalently other and different and wired into their own version of reality. What we get in this bizarre and episodic comedy is a leveling of difference that generates *sameness* across an endless series of small differences among small differences which ultimately do not make enough of a difference to matter. In these films and others like them cultural identity, indeed personal identity, is always provisional and always representational.

Thus ethnic consciousness is flattened into a more culturally pervasive self-consciousness. On the one hand, it is telling that it is a character named Roberta Glass who is *Desperately Seeking Susan* in Seidelman's 1985 postmod-ern comic pastiche about amnesia and switched identities. The suggestion of Jewishness about the name (and Roberta's circumstances as a bored, sub-urban New Jersey housewife) should give one pause, as should the fact that the Susan who arouses Roberta's curiosity in a personals column, the Susan she longs to be, is hardly coded as Jewish – played (and costumed) as she is by Madonna. On the other hand, the cultural and personal identities at stake in this film have little to do with Jewishness or WASPishness, so Roberta's name does not give pause. Instead, the film celebrates the picaresque possibilities of inventing and changing identities, of being differ-ent from oneself, of assuming other people's lives and living them as theatrical experience.

Most of the aforementioned films and others like them describe and dra-matize the liberating possibilities of this more generalized and provisional kind of cultural identity and identification. Only a relative few suggest that self-invention and the ability to choose and construct identity might be seri-ously problematic. Thus, it is not surprising that many of these films are *comedies* of errors, of mistaken identities. It is also not surprising that a great many also borrow upon the science fiction film – given the genre's aliens, androids, travel across time and space, and its imagination of transforma-tion.[12] As Werner Sollors points out, noting that Mario Puzo, who is Italian, wrote its screenplay, *Superman – The Movie* (1978) is 'the ultimate immigrant saga.'[13]

However, such a remark should not lead us to the immediate conclusion that these films are *repressing* their ethnic consciousness and concerns by disguising and hiding them. Rather, it might suggest that within the context of postmodern culture, those once highly charged affects generated by the representation of ethnicity in its relations to dominant culture have lost most of their emotional force. They are now weakened – more diffuse and free-floating than they are unconsciously condensed and displaced in the metaphoric representations of a 'dream work' which, of necessity, drama- tizes its repressed problematic in more psychically bearable form.[14] That is, ethnicity does not seem to be so much repressed and disguised in such films as *Blade Runner* or Jim Jarmusch's *Stranger than Paradise* (1984) as it is dis- persed and defused – explicitly part of the mise-en-scène, yet subordinate to what seem to be the more pressing problems, pleasures, dislocations, and curiosities of constructing identity in postmodern culture. It seems hardly accidental that despite the pointed punning of its title, Graham Baker's *Alien Nation* (1988), although seeming to address allegorically ethnic differ- ence and cultural discrimination in a science fiction framework, actually dif- fuses these concerns with a lack of specificity and a comic tone. The immigrant, alien 'slags' are seen as having a few ethnocentric idiosyncracies and encountering a generalized and Archie Bunkerish bigotry – but both idiosyncracy and bigotry are overcome through the generic diffusions and resolutions of the conventional 'buddy cop' narrative.

*Blade Runner* provides a related example. Its confusion and conflation of human and technological (or 'replicated') being transforms the problem of ethnic assimilation into the problem of human simulation. The narrative fact that the film's Los Angeles of 2019 is a polyglot megalopolis apparently dominated by signs of Japanese culture from SONY to sushi seems less a comment on ethnicity as a mode of being than on the objective conditions of international economics. Issues of racial discrimination, the nature of cul- tural and personal memory and history, issues of identity and its markers, or otherness and the kind of difference that makes a difference – these are dramatized through the confrontation and confusion between human and replicant, not between American and Japanese. Indeed, the Oriental domi- nation of Los Angeles in *Blade Runner* is effectively defused and diffused by the impression the mise-en-scène gives us of a cultural crazy quilt, of an eth- nic pastiche. As Jameson suggests, 'advanced capitalist countries today are now a field of stylistic and discursive heterogeneity without a norm.'[15] That is, there is a neutral mimicry of forms of ethnic specificity in *Blade Runner*, but the forms have lost their distinctive meaning, their affective content, and become blanks. Indeed, Deckard remarks upon the hybrid, pidgin lan- guage of the city – narratively commenting upon (as does the mise-en- scène's flashing signs and advertisements) what Jameson sees as 'a linguistic fragmentation of social life . . . to the point where the norm itself is eclipsed: I reduced to a neutral and reified media speech (far enough from the Utopian aspirations of the inventors of Esperanto or Basic English), which . . . becomes one more idiolect among many.'[16] Thus, 'Japanese-ness' in *Blade Runner* is not represented as a rich form of social being which generates the effects of ethnic identification. Rather, its representation constitutes part of a much cooler and more global economic code.

This dispersal, diffusion, and devaluation of ethnic specificity and identification in the cultural pastiche that marks Jameson's version of postmodernism is perhaps most blatantly articulated by the hybrid hero of W. D. Richter's *The Adventures of Buckaroo Banzai: Across the Eighth Dimension* (1984). Born of an American mother and Japanese father, Buckaroo is a race-car driver, neurosurgeon, physicist, rock star, and adventurer in time and space who lacks personhood in any psychological or historical sense. All 'image and action,' Buckaroo Banzai (much like his name) is hybrid: 'made up of pieces of the pop cultural landscape, and . . . defined moment by moment – each one erasing any smudges of history from the last – by aggressive actions.'[17] Suffering no angst about his mixed ethnic origins, no dis-ease with his lack of rootedness in time or space, Buckaroo's philosophy could stand as the celebratory slogan of those living in the ahistoricist present tense of postmodern culture: 'Remember,' he says, 'wherever you go, there you are.'

Indeed, this philosophy seems to inform the entire narrative and esthetic structure of *Stranger than Paradise* and Jarmusch's second film, *Down by Law*. Here, too, we see the vestiges of ethnic identity, traces of something which has lost nearly all its meaning – as has the specificity and distinctiveness of time and space. In *Stranger than Paradise*, sixteen-year-old Eva has come from her native Hungary to visit her cousin Willie and his friend Eddie in New York City before going to live with her aunt in Cleveland; after being bored in both New York and Cleveland, the three drive off to be bored in Florida. The cultural and geographical specificity here is hilarious by virtue of its meaningless differentiation and the characters' general indifference to it – and to everything else. Eva's 'Hungarian-ness' is barely marked and she expresses only a minimal and short-lived curiosity about things American. Wherever they go, there they are – the characters' spontaneity about going on the road and their passivity and lack of discrimination and the filmmaker's (who uses the same long takes, fades, and static set-ups to record everything and every place with an equivalent lack or plenitude of emphasis). In sum, although the cultural logic of postmodernism is liberating in its capacity for self-invention, its embrace and leveling of difference, and its effacement of discrimination, it achieves this liberation through a correlative flattening and dulling of his historical and political consciousness.

There are cultural critics, however, who offer a less global and more positive version of postmodernism. Linda Hutcheon, for example, is more sanguine than Jameson about the possibilities for responsible social and historical existence in the high-tech and consumer culture of representation, and she offers another conceptual framework within which to think about contemporary changes in the meaning and value of ethnicity. This version of postmodernism operates not within the deep structure of an informative and pervasive cultural logic, but rather as a highly explicit and reflexive 'cultural activity that can be discerned in most art forms and many currents of thought today.' For Hutcheon, 'postmodernism is a . . . phenomenon that uses and abuses, installs and then subverts, the very concepts it challenges.' It is 'fundamentally contradictory, resolutely historical and inescapably political.'[18] Rather than a weakening of historicity that leads to the nostalgic scavenging of bits and pieces of the past in which Jameson sees as 'the well-nigh universal practice today of . . . pastiche,' Hutcheon sees postmodernist representation as a culturally limited phenomenon that institutes a very specific 'critical revisiting, an ironic dialogue with the past of both art and society, a recalling of a critically shared vocabulary of . . . forms.'[19] This dialogue is not merely comic – nor is it a pastiche cannibalized, as Jameson would have it, from random bits and pieces of the past in an 'imitation of dead styles,' and in a 'speech through all the masks and voices stored up in the imaginary museum of now global culture.'[20]

Not denying many of the features Jameson describes as unique to the consumer and media culture of multinational capitalism, Hutcheon nonetheless suggests that 'contemporaneity need not signify wholesale implication without critical consciousness.' For Hutcheon, such critical consciousness is constituted in postmodern representation through parody and it is governed by irony. Neither a random cannibalization or 'ridiculing' imitation of past forms, parodic representation uses 'historical memory' and 'aesthetic introversion' systematically to initiate a 'kind of self-reflexive discourse' that 'is always inextricably bound to social discourse'[21] in its conscious recontextualization of past historical and esthetic elements in relation to a present which will change their meaning. Parody, then, is a 'repetition with critical distance that allows ironic signaling of difference at the very heart of similarity.' This repetition or formal doubling offers 'a perspective on the present and the past which allows an artist to speak TO a discourse from WITHIN it, but without being totally recuperated by it.'[22]

Here, for illustrative purposes, consider again *Moonstruck*'s reflexive use of grand opera and how, by doubling and thus drawing emphatic attention to the characters' grand – and Italian – passions, the music paradoxically both asserts and undermines their authenticity and makes us conscious of romance and specific ethnic enactments of it – as social and historical constructs. Our laughter at and affection for the characters emerge from the critical distance at which the film's parodic form positions us – and from which we can see romance and 'Italian-ness' as fictions. As Hutcheon suggests, this exposure of the fictional and ideological premises upon which specific historical and social forms of heterosexual relations and ethnicity are based, 'does not necessarily destroy their "truth" value, but it does define the conditions of that "truth". Such a process reveals rather than conceals the tracks of the signifying systems that constitute our world – that is, systems constructed by us in answer to our needs. However important these systems are, they are not natural, given or universal.'[23]

Postmodern parody with its doubling of forms, and irony with its contradictory structure of assertion and denial, constitute texts that consciously make us aware of being both cultural insiders and outsiders, of being always provisionally positioned in a plurality of histories and societies. Thus, postmodern texts create that 'acute sense of doubleness' which Sollors identifies with 'ethnic consciousness' and Hutcheon with 'critical consciousness' – both engaged in an ongoing dialogue with the premises of their culture. This is a far cry from that more systemic than systematic version of postmodernism whose pervasive cultural logic levels and flattens value, views the proliferation of distinctions and differences as finally not making much of a difference, and – by virtue of its consciousness of mediation and representation – nostalgically mourns or celebrates the end of history. This postmodernism, according to Hutcheon, is both dystopic and naive in its 'reductive belief that any recall of the past must, by definition, be sentimental nostalgia or antiquarianism.' Indeed, the formal and thematic contradictions of postmodern representation 'confront and contest any . . . discarding or recuperating of the past in the name of the future.' Parody and irony function 'to call attention both to what is being contested and what is being offered as a critical response to that, and . . . do so in a self-aware way that admits its own provisionality.'[24]

This is, in fact, precisely what certain films do in relation to the contemporary value or meaning of ethnicity: parodically and ironically contest it, and critically engage it in a dialogue with its own past meanings so as to explicitly foreground both its current value and that value's historical and cultural provisionality. These are films which do not disperse and diffuse ethnicity across other kinds of difference or subsume it under more general explorations of cultural identity. Rather, they address ethnic consciousness and its changing context directly – foregrounding it as a contradictory, paradoxical, and multivalent experience. Thus we return to those films mentioned at the beginning of this chapter which parody and ironize Henry Ford's melting-pot scenario by recontextualizing it in the present, doubling and exaggerating its formal structure, and simultaneously affirming and denying its cultural values: *Zelig, Moscow on the Hudson*, and *The Brother from Another Planet*.

*Zelig* institutes a critical dialogue with Henry Ford's celebratory notion of total ethnic conversion and assimilation (as well as the naive literalization of the melting pot) by taking it to its parodic limits. By descent, the 'originally' Jewish protagonist, Leonard Zelig, is conceived as a single 'meta-person' whose parodically continual representation both generalizes and makes literal the very structure and function of ethnic conversion and assimilation in a way that *affirms* the fact and possible value of total ethnic transformation. Assuming a multitude of body types and occupations to become 'perfectly' black, Italian, Chinese, French, Irish, Catholic, and Greek, Leonard Zelig has so deep a need to fit in with those in his immediate vicinity that he is the Human Chameleon. 'It's safe to be like the others,' he tells his psychiatrist. 'I want to be liked.' At the same time, however, his parodic and literally repetitious representation of this assimilative process denies both its successful achievement and its value. Caught up in a dynamic of continual transformation and always provisional assimilation, 'Zelig's own existence,' as the voice-over narrator tells us, 'is a non-existence'; he is 'a cipher, a non-person' rather than 'the useful *self-possessed* citizen' his psychiatrist sees as the model of civic and psychic health.

*Zelig* calls explicit attention to the fictional status of ethnic identity, interrogates the problematic nature of its specificity, and emphasizes its very existence as always provisional. On the one hand, Zelig's ability to assume the physical, linguistic, and occupational characteristics of those who surround him ironically literalizes the ethnic 'dis-ease' of the cultural Other, the desire to fit in – and, on the other hand, paradoxically points to everyone's very normal and continuous construction and revision of him or herself as always different. The newspaper headline that announces 'Human Who Transforms Self Discovered' ironically refers to us all – and denies while it affirms traditional notions of both ethnic identity and cultural assimilation.

Finally, *Zelig* is supremely reflexive and historical, its parodic documentary form both allowing Zelig's capacity for transformation and assimilation to enter into dialogue with, among other historical phenomena, Hitler's fascism and accommodating a range of voice-over commentaries and analyses from fictional documentary narrators and real cultural critics. At the film's beginning, for example, Irving Howe tells us that Zelig's 'story reflected the nature of our civilization, the character of our times, yet it was also one man's story, and all the themes of our culture were there: heroism, will, things like that.' But later he tells us that Zelig's case 'reflected the Jewish story in America – he wanted to assimilate like crazy.' The polyphony of voices and opinions and the mixture of fictional characters and real people create continual debate about the on-going and provisional nature of the construction and meaning of ethnic and American experience.

Both Moscow on the Hudson and The Brother from Another Planet also parodically repeat Ford's scenario of the assimilation of ethnic difference from a critical distance. They too insist upon and make explicit the 'ironic discontinuity . . . at the heart of continuity,' the 'difference at the heart of similarity'[25] as well as paradoxically revealing the reverse: the ironic continuity of discontinuity and the homogeneously similar experience we all have of difference. One of the characteristics of advanced capitalist society is the 'increasing tendency towards uniformity in mass culture,' a uniformity which Hutcheon sees postmodern representation as challenging, but also not denying. Postmodern representation 'does seek to assert difference, not homogeneous identity, but the very concept of difference could be said to entail a typically postmodernist contradiction: "difference unlike "otherness," has no exact opposite against which to define itself.'[26] This is precisely the theme whose contradictions are put into play in the ethnic explorations of both Moscow on the Hudson and The Brother from Another Planet.

In *Moscow on the Hudson*, an illuminating moment occurs that parallels Ford's conversion scenario in which ethnic otherness is transformed into its opposite: American sameness. The scene is at once sentimental and ironic. Lucia, the Italian heroine, joins a virtual United Nations of other former immigrants to become a citizen of the United States. The unity of the disparate congregation pledging its allegiance to America affirms and revisits Ford's melting-pot conversion. Yet it does so critically and paradoxically and the possibility of the total conversion and assimilation of ethnic Others is denied as well as affirmed. It is denied and affirmed by the black woman judge who administers the oath of citizenship, her presence a simultaneous, contradictory, and visible marker both of ultimate assimilation and social ascension, and of racial and gender otherness not all that easily assimilated or socially transcended.[27]

*Moscow on the Hudson* also tests Ford's traditional concept of otherness (which has an opposite) against the postmodern concept of 'difference' or 'differences.' The film's representation of New York suggests that *all* Americans are ethnics – whether national, racial, or religious. And it is hardly Ford's melt-ing pot. The film's primary and running joke is that no one in the melting pot has exactly 'melted' – possibly because there is virtually no one in the entire city who can serve as the 'standard American' upon whom assimilation might be modeled and against whom it might be judged. Indeed, the film begins on a bus as a Frenchman asks Vladimir, the Russian protagonist, directions while we see out the bus's window a delicatessen sign advertising 'Italian-Heroes' and a Hassidic Jew in traditional dress walks by. Thus, in context, the plot com-plication later initiated by Lucia's romantic rejection of Vladimir when she becomes a citizen because he's still an ethnic Other and not merely a 'different' American like she is functions parodically as well as sentimentally.

Indeed, throughout the film Mazursky destroys the neat binary *opposition* of Ford's vision of ethnic otherness and American sameness ironically sug-gesting that in postmodern America such a system of definition has col-lapsed because its oppositional terms have become *reversible*. Ultimately the film posits American-ness as constituted from postmodernist difference, or as Hutcheon corrects this formulation, from postmodernist 'differences, in the plural – always multiple and provisional.'[28] As well, Mazursky suggests that the vicissitudes and freedoms of capitalism are the only homogenizing characteristics of American-ness. Not only does Vladimir defect in Bloomingdales, but his assimilation into American culture is also marked primarily by his economic movement up the lowest rungs of the occupa-tional ladder – from kitchen dishwasher to selling novelties on the street to working at McDonalds to running his own hot dog stand to cab driver to limo driver to paid musician.

*The Brother from Another Planet* also simultaneously asserts and subverts the concept of ethnicity as otherness. It is a literal – and thus parodic – black comedy that plays out another highly ironic version of Ford's vision of total assimilation, but in such a manner and context that traditional ethnic other-ness and postmodernist difference are paradoxically conflated as sameness, and yet also foregrounded and maintained as two separate systems of con-ceiving ethnicity. Like *Moscow on the Hudson*, the film complicates the binary neatness of the opposition between Ford's vision of ethnic otherness and American sameness, but unlike that film, *The Brother from Another Planet* does not suggest that those oppositional terms have lost their cultural value. Instead, it parodies this opposition by narratively *repeating* it. If, as Hutcheon suggests, that parody functions as 'a critical revisiting,'[29] then the film both explicitly performs and literalizes this function with its narrative of emigration, space travel, and assimilation explicitly and critically repeat-ing and commenting upon an earlier historical narrative which did not resolve itself in happy assimilation.

Representing ethnic and immigrant otherness, a black alien from outer space lands significantly first on Ellis Island and then in Harlem – where black American Others live out their idiosyncratic differences in the homogeneous and ghettoized sameness of a terrestrial and marginalized 'outer' space. Parodying American history, the black alien is a runaway slave being tracked by two white aliens (who, along with two other white men inadvertently lost in Harlem, stand out as alien in context). Yet the otherness of the alien to his hunters is apparently not his blackness at all – but, instead, the physical characteristic of only having three toes on each foot instead of five. Foregrounded here (however cheap the joke) are both the arbitrariness and the power of the particular difference that makes a difference and thereby constitutes otherness.

In sum, Sayles wickedly presents us with a double negative of otherness and difference, effectively both erasing and foregrounding racial ethnicity as at once a double segregation of otherness and a positive assimilation to difference. In its postmodern play of paradox and contradiction, *The Brother from Another Planet* parodically revisits racial inequality and finds the mathematics yield ironic results: ethnic differences are collapsed by blackness into a homogeneous and oppositional otherness which still stands against the whiteness (and five toed-ness) of standard Americans.

These films and quite a number of others directly address the reformulation of ethnicity and ethnic consciousness in postmodern culture. This ethnic consciousness is no longer experienced as something natural based on tradition and descent or as something to be assimilated to and converted in the melting pot. Rather, it is experienced as something cultural which must be constantly invented, consented to, and negotiated with other social beings. Caught up in a dialogue with a past in which it *was* always different than it *is*, ethnicity is presently perceived as provisional, historical, and in continual transformation. It is experienced as a parodic process of self-revision through representations that are ironically aware of and explicit about the social – and symbolic – construction of reality. Contemporary ethnic differences make a different kind of difference than when Henry Ford built his melting pot. Indeed, the paradoxical and contradictory experiences of contemporary ethnic consciousness as they are parodically and ironically made explicit in postmodernist films may be seen as a positive response to the more homogenizing aspects of life in shopping-mall and television culture. 'Americans,' writes Herbert Gans, 'increasingly perceive themselves as undergoing cultural homogenization, and whether or not this perception is justified, they are constantly looking for new ways to establish their differences from each other.'[30] In the worst instance, that new way to establish our differences from each other will be the creation of another one hundred fifty-eight shades of Revlon lipstick. In the best instance, it will be the creation of a substantial, valuable, and polyvocal dialogue with our different pasts and our shared futures.

Postmodernism rejects the totalizing force of master narratives that would homogenize the diversity of cultural experiences into a single and generalized myth such as American-ness. Instead, it opts for the limited and local story that derives its primary value from a specificity that makes no general claims – or it deconstructs the master narratives and myths to expose and parody their contradictions. That is perhaps why the only films that deal explicitly with ethnic experience and that do not necessarily undermine their representations with parody or irony are biographies. Luis Valdez's *La Bamba* (1987) and *Stand and Deliver* (1988), for example, both make limited claims and do not generalize ethnic experience; both are also firmly (and by today's standards somewhat clearly) grounded in a finite historical moment. Such films as Wayne Wang's *Chan Is Missing* (1982) and *Dim Sum* (1985), Peter Wang's *A Great Wall* (1986), Spike Lee's *She's Gotta Have It* (1986) and *School Daze* (1988), and Robert Townsend's *Hollywood Shuffle* (1987) are localized films which play out the construction of American ethnic consciousness as a set of ironically small negotiations with both specific cultural traditions and dominant media representations. Extremely self-aware of their own historical vision and cultural doubleness, the larger the claims these films make about ethnic experience, the more parodic and ironic become their form and content.

In line with the contradictions of postmodernist thought, Werner Sollors writes that

> Not only the assault on ethnic boundaries but also ethnic boundary construction itself may generate innovation and modernization. As Americans of different backgrounds share larger and larger areas of an overlapping culture, they keep insisting on symbolic distinctions (often not those of 'ancient origin' but freshly invented ones), the process known as 'ethnicization.' Instead of looking at various ethnic traditions as merely growing from very parochial beginnings to modernist assimilation, we may also see ethnic identification itself as a modern phenomenon.[31]

However, also in the spirit of postmodernism, I will conclude with two contradictions which do not deny the preceding, but do make it more provisional. First, I want both to affirm and contradict Sollors by suggesting that the widespread culture awareness of the modern process of 'ethnicization' as a symbolic project makes 'ethnic identification itself' no longer a modern, but a postmodern phenomenon. And second, I want to affirm and contradict the symbolic nature of this process of 'ethnicization' by pointing to the very real effects and limitations of this symbolization and our awareness of it.

In the middle of writing this chapter, on a Sunday evening heading elsewhere, I drove through what was for me a truly foreign and clearly hostile country – a poor Mexican-American neighborhood in Watsonville, California at that moment teeming with street life, most of it male. It struck me in a way that was not at all ironic that I, a white Jewish-American woman of middle-class means, would have been afraid to get out of the car there – and rightfully so given my femaleness and their maleness, my affluence and their poverty, my whiteness and their color. It also struck me – and this *was* an ironic recognition – that I had personally and historically hierarchized the importance of the differences that made a difference in a way hardly consonant with traditions in Ford's America. Now, at least at that moment, gender and class mattered much more than racial or cultural ethnicity.

As I left those streets behind me, I realized I could not tell if their ghettoized boundaries were imposed from without or chosen from within, and it did not matter if it was a little of both. What did matter was that I had the economic and racial privilege of a 'critical distance' from which to contemplate the structure of my life-world and theirs. If parody is a critical revisiting of the 'old ethnic neighborhood' and its self-representations, before that revisiting is possible one must first have the opportunity to leave it. In sum, the one big problem with the critical distance of postmodern parody, with reflexive and self-conscious irony, with the celebration of differences and their boundaries, is that *both* parties in a cultural negotiation need to recognize and share in them if we are to talk significantly about new forms of ethnic consciousness.

# Notes

1. Robert Bellah, 'Evil and the American Ethos', in N. Sanford, C. Comstock, et al., eds, *Sanctions for Evil* (San Francisco CA, Jossey-Bass, 1971), p. 181.
2. Bellah, 'Evil and the American Ethos'.
3. Werner Sollors, *Beyond Ethnicity. Consent and Descent in American Culture* (New York, Oxford University Press, 1986), pp. 31, 33.
4. In this context it is wonderfully ironic that recently the Ford Motor Company has joined with a certain Japanese automotive corporation to produce 'all-American' vans.
5. Sollors, *Beyond Ethnicity*, p. 6.
6. The cast did, indeed, have a Brooklyn-Italian dialect coach to ensure ethnic specificity and authenticity – Julie Bovasso, who also played Aunt Rita.
7. Linda Hutcheon, 'Beginning to Theorize Postmodernism', *Textual Practice*, 1 (1987), p. 25.
8. See, for example, Fredric Jameson, 'Postmodernism, or, the Cultural Logic of Late Capitalism,' *New Left Review*, 146 (July–August 1984), pp. 53–94.
9. Jameson, 'Postmodernism', p. 58.
10. Jameson, 'Postmodernism', pp. 54–5.
11. Vivian Sobchack, *Screening Space. The American Science Fiction Film*, 2nd edn (New York, Ungar, 1987), p. 239. The last chapter, 'Postfuturism', deals at length not only with the contemporary SF film's latent and manifest representation of the cultural logic of postmodernism, but also with the new cultural functions of the 'alien other' in these films (pp. 223–305).
12. The imaginative possibilities for positive and liberating self-invention and transformation that science fiction encourages have drawn feminists to the genre. See Donna Haraway, 'A Manifesto for Cyborgs', *Socialist Review*, 80 (1985), pp. 65–107.
13. Sollors, *Beyond Ethnicity*, p. 12.
14. 'Affect,' 'condensation,' 'displacement,' 'dream work,' and 'repression' have specific meaning within the discourse of psychoanalysis and have informed much contemporary literary and film theory and analysis. For a brief elaboration of these specific meanings, see the following psychoanalytic 'dictionary': J. Laplanche and J.-B. Pontalis, *The Language of Psycho-Analysis*, trans. Donald Nicholson-Smith (New York, W. W. Norton, 1973).
15. Jameson, 'Postmodernism', p. 65.
16. Jameson; 'Postmodernism', p. 6.
17. Pat Aufderheide, 'Sci-fi Discovers New Enemies', *In These Times*, 21 November–4 December, 1984, p. 30.
18. Hutcheon, 'Beginning to Theorize Postmodernism', pp. 11, 10.
19. Jameson, 'Postmodernism', p. 64; Hutcheon, 'Beginning to Theorize Postmodernism', p. 11.
20. Jameson, 'Postmodernism', p. 65.
21. Linda Hutcheon, 'The Politics of Postmodernism. Parody and History', *Cultural Critique*, 5 (1987), p. 185, n. 18; p. 204.
22. Hutcheon, 'The Politics', pp. 185, 206.
23. Hutcheon, 'Beginning to Theorize Postmodernism', p. 19.
24. Hutcheon, 'Beginning to Theorize Postmodernism', pp. 25, 19.
25. Hutcheon, 'Beginning to Theorize Postmodernism', p. 17.
26. Hutcheon, 'Beginning to Theorize Postmodernism', p. 13.
27. In 'How American Are You if Your Grandparents Came from Serbia in 1888?', in S. TeSelle, ed., *The Rediscovery of Ethnicity* (New York, Harper & Row, 1973), Michael Novak reminds us that 'in the last decade, the word "ethnic" came to be used not so much for white ethnic groups from Europe, which were presumed

to be rapidly "melting," but as a synonym for "minorities," especially those of color: the Blacks, the Latinos, the Indians; i.e., those who visibly were *not* melting' (p. 6).

28. Hutcheon, 'Beginning to Theorize Postmodernism', p. 13.
29. Hutcheon, 'Beginning to Theorize Postmodernism', p. 11.
30. Herbert Gans, *On the Making of Americans. Essays in Honor of David Riesman* (Philadelphia, DA, University of Pennsylvania Press, 1979), p. 215.
31. Sollars, *Beyond Ethnicity*, pp. 244–5.

# 9

# Recoding narratives of race and nation

*Kobena Mercer*

From *Black film, British cinema* (The Institute of Contemporary Arts 1988)

The prolific activity of the black independent film movement stands out as an area of development in contemporary film culture that is unique to Britain in the 1980s. The conference on which this publication is based[1] focussed on three recent products of this activity – *The Passion of Remembrance, Playing Away* and *Handsworth Songs* – to take stock of developments in the black independent film and video sector and unravel the controversies generated by the new wave in black film-making. The conference identified important shifts and changes in conditions of production and reception which have enabled the emergence of a younger generation of black British film-makers and widened the circulation of black films in the public domain. In the process it brought together a range of critical reflections which begin to clarify why 'race' has become the subject and the site of so many controversies in British film-making today.

As an active intervention in the cultural politics of cinema, the starting point was to unpack the contradictory responses to the new black British films. The sheer range of conflicting views and opinions surely indicate that something important is going on. Take the case of *Handsworth Songs* (director John Akomfrah, 1987), Black Audio Film Collective's documentary-essay on the civil disobedience that erupted in reaction to the repressive policing of black communities in London and Birmingham in 1985. On the one hand, the film received critical acclaim, and won many prizes including the prestigious Grierson Award from the British Film Institute. On the other, one reviewer in a black community newspaper, *The Voice*, received the film with the dismissive remark, 'Oh no, not another riot documentary' and in *The Guardian* the film was subject to a serious and fierce intellectual polemic from novelist Salman Rushdie. Whereas the film-makers conceived their experimental approach to the documentary genre as a strategy, 'to find a structure and a form which would allow us the space to deconstruct the hegemonic voices of British television newsreels',[2] Rushdie argued that, on the contrary, 'the trouble is, we aren't told the other stories. What we get is what we know from TV. Blacks as trouble; blacks as victims.'

What is at issue goes beyond a dispute over the merits of one particular film. The contradictory reception of *Handsworth Songs* is but one aspect of the growing debates that have focussed attention on issues of race and ethnicity in film and television during the 80s. Other film-making groups such as Ceddo, Sankofa and Retake have also been at the centre of recent controversies arising out of the cultural politics of black representation. Sankofa's innovative dramatic feature. *The Passion of Remembrance* (director Maureen Blackwood and Isaac Julien, 1986) interlaces a rendition of black family life around its central character, Maggie Baptiste, with a series of fragmented reflections on race, class, gender and sexuality as issues demanding new forms of representation. Yet in pursuit of such forms, the mixture of conventional and avant-garde styles in the film has bewildered audiences and critics, black and white alike. Retake's first feature, *Majdhar* (director Ahmed Jamal, 1984) revolves around a young Asian woman whose 'independence' brings conflicting choices and options and for this reason the film provoked intense criticism not only within Asian communities here in Britain, but across the front pages of the national press in Pakistan. Ceddo, an Afro-Caribbean workshop based in London, have produced a documentary on the 1985 'riots' – *The People's Account* (director Milton Bryan, 1986) – yet although the film was financed by Channel 4, and scheduled for a slot in the 'People to People' series, it has still not been screened on television, as the Independent Broadcasting Authority has demanded editorial changes which the film-makers regard as tantamount to state censorship – a demand which they have resisted.

These developments have taken place in the independent sector, on the fringes of mainstream film culture; but the controversies are of a piece with the contradictory reception of *My Beautiful Laundrette* (director Stephen Frears, written by Hanif Kureishi, 1985). As a relatively low-budget independent production, partly funded by Channel 4, this film took many by surprise with the unexpected scale of its popularity. Few would have anticipated that a gay romance between a British-born Asian and an ex-National Front supporter, set against the backdrop of Thatcherite enterprise culture, would be the stuff of which box office successes are made! Yet it is precisely this 'crossover' phenomenon – whereby material with apparently marginal subject matter becomes a commercial success in the marketplace – that pinpoints shifts on the part of contemporary audiences.

This trend, underpinning the success of recent black American independent films like Spike Lee's *She's Gotta Have It* and Robert Townsend's *Hollywood Shuffle*, indicates that the market is not defined by a monolithic 'mass' audience, but by a diversity of audiences whose choices and tastes occasionally converge. Horace Ove's *Playing Away* (1987, written by Caryl Phillips) pursued such a 'crossover' strategy, staging a tense but often comic encounter between a black inner-city cricket team and their white counterparts in the English countryside. But the film was summarily dismissed by Barry Norman – presenter of BBC's popular film review programme – who felt that as a black director Ove should confine himself to stories about black experiences. This reveals a rather narrow view of black film-making, and one unfortunately held by many critics: it therefore underscores the need for a more adequate critical framework for the evaluation of black film – the issue motivating Rushdie's polemic and elaborated upon by Julian Henriques' article included in this ICA Document.

Criticism entails more than the ability to define or discriminate between bad and good movies. It plays a crucial mediating role between film-makers and audiences that often determines the distribution and circulation of the films as much as their artistic and cultural validation. In respect of this latter role, it is now necessary to re-evaluate traditional criteria for film criticism as, in many instances, these criteria have been based on a narrowly Eurocentric canon. Moreover, in so far as criticism reflects upon the social significance of cinema – as that cultural arena in which, as Ray Durgant once put it, society reflects upon and adjusts its image of itself – the recent controversies and debates around race and ethnicity demand a reconsideration of what we mean when we talk about a specifically 'British' film culture.

In the case of *My Beautiful Laundrette* for example, a critical discourse needs to account for the fact that, despite its success, many people actively disliked the film – and did so for very different reasons. Among the Asian communities, angry reactions focussed on the less than favourable depiction of some of the Asian characters which, when read as emblematic of the community, were seen as reinforcing certain ethnic stereotypes. Norman Stone on the other hand singled out *Laundrette* and *Sammie* and *Rosie Get Laid* in his appraisal of British cinema, for portraying a 'negative image' of contemporary England. Stone regarded the films as inherently 'disgusting' and symptomatic of the artistic and economic 'sickness' of the British film industry, which he traced to the malignant influence of 'left' intellectuals from the 1930s and 60s. In counterpoint, one example of 'good' British film-making that Stone selected for praise was *A Passage to India* (director David Lean, 1987), an epic adaptation of the literary classic reframed for cinema in what has become known, after the success of television drama such as *Jewel in the Crown* (Granada TV, 1983), as the 'Raj nostalgia mode'.[3]

What is at issue here is not simply that different readers produce contradictory readings of the same cultural texts or that an ethnically diverse society throws up conflicting ideological viewpoints. More fundamentally, this critical exchange highlights the way image-making has become an important arena of cultural contestation – contestation over what it means to be British today; contestation over what Britishness itself means as a national or cultural identity; and contestation over the values that underpin the Britishness of British cinema as a *national* film-culture.

Such issues provide the scope and context of the introductory dossier and conference papers documented here. As a way into the debates it would be worthwhile to draw out the paradox upon which black independent film-making is poised – as this encapsulates some of the reasons for its current resurgence which has been described as, 'the most intellectually and cinematically innovative edge of British cultural politics'.[4] The fact of the matter is that black film-making in Britain is a marginal cultural practice, but as it expands and becomes progressively de-marginalised, its oppositional perspectives reveal that traditional structures of cultural value and national identity are themselves becoming increasingly fractured, fragmented and de-centred.

A consistent thematic concern with contradictory experiences in the formation of black British identity runs throughout black film-making in Britain as a generic characteristic. Far from being a parochial concern, this theme raises questions of representation that speak directly to the experience of cultural fragmentation and displaced selfhood that has become such a general preoccupation in postmodern trends in the arts. Reflecting on 'identity' in a previous ICA Document and on the feeling of displacement entailed by the experience of migration from colonial periphery to post-colonial metropolis, Stuart Hall has commented on the nature of this paradox:

> Now that, in the postmodern age, you all feel so dispersed, I become centred. What I've thought of as dispersed and fragmented comes, paradoxically, to be *the* representative modern experience![5]

To the extent that the convergence of concern with identity in postmodernism has been diagnosed as a response to, 'a crisis of cultural authority, specifically of the authority vested in Western European culture and its institutions',[6] black film-making offers a unique set of perspectives on the fluctuation and potential break-up of hierarchical distinctions between 'high' arts and 'popular' culture, between what is valorised as 'universal' and what is dismissed as 'particular', between identities that have been centralised and those which have been marginalised.

Like other expressive and artistic practices that have developed in the midst of that peculiar collision of cultures and histories that constitutes 'black Britain', black independent film is part of a shift registering a new phase in what Hall describes as the 'politics of representation'. As an element in this general process of cultural relativisation, black film-making not only critiques traditional conceptions of Britishness, which have depended on the subordination of 'other' ethnic identities, but calls the very concept of a coherent national identity into question by asserting instead what Colin MacCabe describes as a 'culture of differences'. This introduction outlines the institutional shifts that have contributed to the de-marginalisation of black film; the widening range of aesthetic strategies which this has made possible; and the reconstitution of audiences in relation to the increasingly local and global (rather than 'national') diversification of audiovisual culture.

## Historical formation

The public profile of black independent film-making today might give the impression that this is a 'new' area of activity which only began in the 80s. But it did not; film-makers of Asian, African and Caribbean descent, living or born in Britain, have been a part of the black arts movement since the 1960s. The previous 'invisibility' of black film-making reflects instead the structural conditions of marginality which have shaped its development. An indication of just how recently conditions have changed can be gleaned from the fact that *The Passion of Remembrance* and *Handsworth Songs* were the *first* black-directed feature films to begin theatrical exhibition at a West End London venue, a standard *rite-de-passage* in film culture. This shows how far things have come since the mid-70s when Horace Ove's *Pressure* was the first black feature film to be made in Britain, or the early 60s when the very first films by black directors were made by Lionel Ngakane and Lloyd

Reckord. But, it also indicates how far conditions have yet to change before black film is regarded as an integral aspect of British cinema. The story of its development so far must be told, as Jim Pines has argued, as a struggle against conditions of 'recurrent institutional and cultural marginalisation'.[7]

As an industrialised art-form, film-making involves a complex division of labour and intensive capital investment and funding: the crucial issue for black film-makers therefore has been access to resources for production. 'Independent' film-making is usually taken to refer to production outside the commercial mainstream, which is dominated by multinational capital and the profit motive. Although the term is something of a misnomer, for as James Snead remarks, 'independent' film is often highly *dependent* on funding from public institutions, it could be said that black film-making has been 'independent' by default as the struggle for access has been engaged on both fronts. The commercial marketplace has provided employment for a few individual film-makers, but not a secure environment for black film-making as a cultural movement. Rather, the grant-aided or subsidised sector has provided the context in which black film-making has grown. Yet even here black film-makers have had to struggle to secure their rights to public funding. As a result of this, alongside the general struggle to establish and secure black rights, what has changed in the past decade is the institutional recognition of black people's rights to representation within film-culture.

The 80s have inaugurated shifts in the policy and priorities of cultural institutions in the public sphere and this has helped to widen opportunities for access to production. These changes in the institutional framework of funding have expanded the parameters of the black independent sector and opened up a new phase which contrasts starkly with the conditions under which the pioneering generation of black film-makers worked. The earliest films – *Jemima and Johnny* by Lionel Ngakane and *Ten Bob in Winter* by Lloyd Reckord (both made in 1963) – were produced without the support of public funds. Like Ove's first films, *Baldwin's Nigger* (1969) and *Reggae* (1970), they were largely financed by the film-makers themselves, who often demonstrated entrepreneurial flair by raising money from unlikely sources.

Ove's first feature length film, *Pressure*, marked a turning point in 1974, as it was the first film by a black director to be financed by the British Film Institute. The BFI's production of *A Private Enterprise*, a dramatic feature set in the Asian community co-written by Dillip Hiro in 1975, and *Burning an Illusion* by Menelik Shabazz in 1981, signalled growing institutional recognition of black film-making within the terms of 'multicultural' funding policy. Yet although this recognition drew black film-makers into the remit of the subsidised independent sector, marking an advance from the previous period, the time interval between productions and the comparatively modest budgets of the productions themselves suggest that, even within the terms of 'official' multicultural policies, black film-making remained marginal in relation to the general growth of the independent sector during the 1970s.

Various factors contributed to the shifts of the 80s which, if they can be traced to a single source, occurred outside the institutions of British society in the political events of 1981; 'riots' or 'uprisings', the term varies with your viewpoint. Over and above their immediate causes as a response to new, quasi-military forms of policing in the Thatcherite era, the events had the

symbolic effect of marking a break with the consensus politics of multiculturalism and as such announced a new phase of 'crisis-management' in
British race-relations. In the wake of 'The Scarman Report', political expediency – the need to be seen to be doing something – was a major aspect of
the 'benevolent' gestures of many public institutions, hurriedly redistribut-
ing funding to black projects. Politically, the eruption of civil disorder
expressed protest at the structural marginalisation of black voices and opinions within the polity and encoded militant demands for *black representation*
within public institutions as a basic right. Culturally, this demand generated
a veritable renaissance of black creativity – from literature, music and theatre to photography, film and video[8] and in relation to audiovisual media in
particular, this surge of activity coincided with the advent of Channel 4,
which proved to be crucially important for black film-makers and audiences
alike.

It has been said, apropos the economic decline of the British film industry
in the post-war period, that 'British cinema is alive and well and living on
television' as TV has provided a unique point of entry into the profession
for many writers and directors. With its official mandate to encourage innovative forms of programme making, Channel 4 contributed significantly to
the expansion of the independent film production sector. The Channel was
also mandated to provide for the unmet needs of various 'minority' audiences, and as a new model of public service broadcasting which explicitly
recognised the diversity of audiences in a plural society, its brief on 'multicultural' programming aroused high expectations about black representation. Early programmes like *Eastern Eye* and *Black on Black* received
enthusiastic welcome from Asian and Caribbean audiences, primarily
because they filled some of the gaps – the absence of black images – in the
more entrenched tradition of public service which assumed a single, mono-
cultural 'national' audience.

However, while Channel 4 brought TV into line with the ethos of multiculturalism, the multicultural consensus was itself being thrown into question
by more radical aspects of black politics and its cultural expression in the arts.
Criticisms were made of the 'ghettoisation' that circumscribed such 'ethnic
minority' slots on Channel 4. Indirectly, this led to the formation of numerous black independent production companies with the aim of delivering
alternative films and programmes to television.[9] Similar critiques were
voiced by the independent film-makers' lobby and the women's lobby and
alongside these the Black Media Workers Association formed in 1982 to campaign for an equal distribution of employment and commissions. The
BMWA's objectives shifted from the monitoring role of earlier initiatives such
as the Campaign Against Racism in the Media[10] and were oriented towards
pragmatic concerns such as ensuring access to independent production.

Channel 4 has since revised its ethnic programming – *Bandung File, Club
Mix* and *The Cosby Show* replaced the earlier output after Farrukh Dhondy
assumed the position of Commissioning Editor for Multicultural Programmes.
For all the criticisms of 'minority broadcasting' (which have come from the
right as much as the left), it should be noted that Channel 4 has taken the
lead in encouraging television to rethink its attitude to the cultural diversity
of its nation-wide audience. The BBC's self-critique – *The Black and White*

*Media Show*[11] – suggests an indication of the extent to which issues of race and black representation have been acknowledged or at least 'accommodated' as part of contemporary television: the title of the programme puns on 'The Black and White Minstrel Show', one of the BBC's most popular light entertainment shows which only ended, after much complaint, in 1978.

At another level, the limits of tokenism were inscribed as a political shift from multicultural to anti-racist policy. In relation to the local state this process was led by the radical Labour administration of the Greater London Council between 1982 and its abolition, as a result of central government legislation, in 1986. Beyond mere expediency, the GLC took up demands for black representation in political decision-making and opened up a new phase of local democracy involving constituencies marginalised from parliamentary politics. At a cultural level, the GLC also inaugurated a new attitude to funding arts activities by regarding them as 'cultural industries' in their own right. Both of these developments proved important for the burgeoning black independent film sector, particularly for the younger generation of film-makers who formed workshops.

By prioritising black cultural initiatives either by direct subsidy or through training and development policies (as well as numerous public festivals and events), the GLC marked a break with the piecemeal and often patronising funding of so-called 'ethnic arts'.[12] Emphasising broadly educational objectives, the GLC's extensive black and Third World film exhibition programmes such as 'Third Eye' in 1983, were also important as they brought a range of new or rarely seen films into public circulation. The 'Third Eye' symposia in 1985 gathered together film-makers from Britain, the US, Africa and the Indian sub-continent to map out an agenda for alternative interventions in production and distribution and highlighted, on the one hand, common experiences of marginalisation, and on the other, the impact of black and Third World feminism on issues of representation.[13] Like the conference on 'Third Cinema: Theories and Practices', held at the Edinburgh Film Festival in 1986, such events have placed black British film-making within an international context and helped to clarify the innovative qualities that differentiate black independent film from the 'first cinema' of the commercial mainstream and the 'second cinema' of individual auteurism.[14]

At the same time however, such events have also brought to light important differences within the black British film-making community. In one sense these differences concern the diverse ideological emphases and aesthetic strategies pursued by black film-makers in the 80s; but they are also structural in nature and stem from the different modes of production of workshops and production companies. Independent production companies – which include Anancy Films, Azad Productions, Kuumba Productions, Penumbra Productions and Social Film and Video, for example – operate within the orbit of the television industry and as such compete in the marketplace for commissions and finance for individual productions. Workshops on the other hand – such as Black Audio, Cardiff Film and Video Workshop, Ceddo, Macro, Retake, Star and Sankofa – are grant-aided and operate in the public sector context of subsidised independence. Whereas the former tend to adhere to the professionalised codes of mainstream working practices, often revolving around the individual director or producer, the workshops are committed to 'integrated practice' which entails activity around areas of training, education, developing audience-outreach and networks of alternative distribution and exhibition as much as producing films themselves, often through collectivist working methods. In this respect the workshops have been enabled by a unique trade agreement between ACTT, the film-makers' union, and a range of public institutions including Channel Four – the Workshop Declaration (established in 1982) – whereby groups involved in such cultural activities and with a minimum of four staff can be accredited or franchised and thus receive financial support.

Arguments have raged over which mode of production offers a greater degree of autonomy and independent decision-making. Production companies may claim that by working within conventional patterns, black film-makers can negotiate a wider potential audience and thus overcome the risk of 'ghettoisation'. Workshops on the other hand have argued that 'integrated practice' makes the development of a distinct black film culture possible, and thus allows black film-makers the space in which to address issues of concern to black audiences as a specific 'community of interest' and the space in which to explore black aesthetics. The debate is by no means resolved. In any case, it should be noted that the arguments are of a piece with the different tendencies within the independent sector generally: the work of an independent director such as Ken Loach contrasts with the more 'oppositional' orientation of the workshop movement which began with groups such as the London Film-Maker's Co-op set up by Malcolm LeGrice and others in the mid-1960s. With regard to the specificity of black film-making however, it is important to recognise that the emergence of workshops has widened the range of issues that black practitioners have been able to take on, bringing questions of audience and distribution into the arena of funding and development. In contrast to previous periods, the structural shifts of the 80s have diversified the range of ideological and aesthetic options for black independent film practices. It is this qualitative expansion of approaches to representation that informs the intensity of the debates on aesthetics in the contemporary situation.

## Displacing the burden of representation

Culturally, definitions of 'independent cinema' embrace such a variety of specific traditions – from combative documentary in the Third World or counter-informational video newsreels addressing local/regional community audiences, to EuroAmerican 'art' cinema or formalist experimentation, accommodated in rarefied art galleries and museums – that its coherence as a classificatory term seems questionable. This is especially so when it comes to black independent film in Britain as each of these traditions are relevant to the 'hybridised' cultural terrain in which it has evolved. In addition there is another problematic area of definition concerning the use of the term 'black' as a political, rather than racial category. Throughout the 70s and 80s, the re-articulation of this term as an inclusive political identity based on alliances between Asian, African and Caribbean peoples in a shared struggle against racism, has helped to challenge and displace commonsense assumptions about 'blackness' as a fixed or essential identity.

A grasp of both these areas of contested definition is necessary for an understanding of the cultural struggle around the social production of imagery that black film-making has engaged. In this sense it would be more helpful to emphasise the 'oppositional' aspects of both terms so that rigidly essentialist or normative definitions may be avoided in favour of a relational and contextual conception of black independent film as a kind of counter-practice that contests and critiques the predominant forms in which black subjects become socially visible in different cultural forms of representation. A consistent motivation for black film-makers has been to challenge the pre-dominantly stereotypical forms in which blacks become visible either as 'problems' or 'victims', always as some intractable and unassimilable Other on the margins of British society and its collective consciousness. It is in rela-tion to such dominant imagery that black film-making has brought a politi-cal dimension to this arena of cultural practice. And it is from this position that adequate consideration can be given to questions such as whether a distinctly *black* visual aesthetic exists or not; whether realism or modernism offers the more appropriate aesthetic strategy; or whether black film can be exhaustively defined as that produced 'by, for, and about' black people. These issues are taken up in detail by the contributions of Judith Williamson and Paul Gilroy, and, from the comparative angle of black American inde-pendent film, by James Snead. To begin to clarify what is at stake, it would be relevant to start with the question of stereotyping as this has formed the background against which recent debates have highlighted the complexity of race and ethnicity vis-à-vis the politics of representation.

Through a variety of genres, from dramatic fiction to reportage and docu-mentary, black film-makers have had to contend with the ideological and cultural power of the codes which have determined dominant representa-tions of race. Stereotypes are one product of such audiovisual codes, which shape agreed interpretations of reality in a logic that reproduces and legiti-mates commonsense assumptions about 'race'. More broadly, in the struggle against the hegemonic forms of racial discourse supported by racial and eth-nic stereotypes, black film-practices come up against the master-codes of what Jim Pines describes as the 'official' race-relations narrative. Within the logic of its narrative patterns, blacks tend to be depicted either as the source and cause of social problems – threatening to disrupt moral equilibrium – or as the passive bearers of social problems – victimised into angst-ridden sub-mission or dependency. In either case, such stories encode versions of reality that confirm the ideological precept that 'race' constitutes a 'problem' per se.

From films of the colonial period, such as *Sanders of the River* with its dichotomy of 'good native'/'bad native', to films of the post-war period of mass immigration and settlement such as *Sapphire* or *Flame in the Streets* which narrate racial antagonism in a social realist style, the predominant forms of racial representation in British cinema and television have pro-duced a 'problem-oriented' discourse.[15] In seeking to find a voice and a means of cinematic expression able to challenge and displace the authority of this dominant discourse, black film-making has negotiated a specific, if not unique, set of representational problems that constitute a particularly difficult 'burden of representation'. To evaluate how different filmic strategies have sought to unpack this burden we need to examine the contradictory effects of realism and how this impinges on the cinematic investigation of the contradictory experiences of black British identity.

A cursory overview of black films made in Britain would show the preponderance of a 'documentary realist' aesthetic in both dramatic fiction and documentary films. This emphatic insistence on the 'real' – often expressed as a desire to 'correct' media distortions and 'tell it like it is' – should be understood as the prevailing mode in which a counter-discourse has been constructed against the dominant versions of reality produced by the race-relations master narrative. From a context-oriented point of view the 'reality-effect' so powerfully conveyed by documentaries such as *Step Forward Youth* (director Menelik Shabazz, 1977) and *The People's Account* (Ceddo, 1987) is an important rhetorical element by which the 'authority' of dominant media discourses is disrupted by black counter-discourse. Furthermore, within campaigning or counter-informational documentary such as *Blood Ah Go Run* (Kuumba Productions, 1982) for instance, issues of form are necessarily and justifiably subordinate to the conjunctural imperative to interrupt the dominant racial discourse. Thus it could be argued that the operation of four filmic values within this mode of practice, transparency, immediacy, authority and authenticity – (which are aesthetic principles central to the realist paradigm) – constitute the means of encoding alternative forms of knowledge to 'make sense' of processes and events from a black perspective. In this sense the focal concern with the politicising experiences of black youth in 70s films demonstrates a counter-reply to the criminalising stereotypes of dominant media discourses which amplified 'moral panics' around race and crime.

Similarly, a film such as *Blacks Britannica* (made in 1979, by an American TV company, WGBH-Boston, but cited here as it is widely read and circulated as a film encoding a black British perspective) interrupts commonsense understandings of race by 'giving voice' to those silenced and marginalised by dominant versions of reality. Like *Riots and Rumours of Riots* (director Imruh Bakari Caesar, 1981), the combination of oral testimony, didactic voice-over and political analysis advanced in the films by black activists and intellectuals, presents an 'alternative definition of the situation' and one that emphasises the historical legacy of imperialism and colonialism as a factor in Britain's recurrent crises of race-relations. The oral histories of black community life in four British cities offered by *Struggles for the Black Community* (director Colin Prescod, 1983 and produced by the Institute of Race Relations) cut across the de-historicising logic of the race-relations narrative which seems to be premissed on a 'profound historical forgetfulness . . . a kind of historical amnesia . . . which has overtaken the British people about race and Empire since the 1950s'.[16]

In such instances then, documentary realism has had an overdetermined presence in framing black versions of reality: the 'window on the world' aesthetic does not perform the naturalising function which it does in broadcast news; rather, by encoding versions of reality from black viewpoints, it renders present that which is made absent in the dominant discourses. As a conjunctural intervention, the use of documentary realist conventions empowers the articulation of counter-discourse. Yet as Pines notes, although perspectives coded as 'black' at the level of reference and theme differentiate such work from dominant discourse, at the level of film-form and cinematic expression these films often adhere to the same aesthetic principles as the media discourses whose power and ideological effects they seek to resist. Pointing to the relational nature of this constitutive paradox, Pines argues that

> This is also one of the ways in which black films are marked off from other kinds of independent work, because institutionalised 'race-relations' has a marginalising effect structurally and tends to reinforce rather than ameliorate the 'otherness' of the subject – which documentary realism historically and representationally embodies. Within this set of relations, therefore, it has been difficult for black practitioners to evolve a cinematic approach which is unaffected by the determinants of 'race-relations' discourse or which works outside documentary realism.[17]

The contradictory effects this gives rise to can be appreciated mostly in relation to narrative fiction as the aspiration to authenticity or 'objectivity' entailed by realism becomes more problematic when brought to bear on the contradictory *subjective* experiences of black British identity. Narrative closure, the tying up of the threads that make up a fictional text, is regarded as characteristic of cinematic realism; but the symptomatic irresolution of the story told in *Pressure* suggests some of the limitations of documentary realism in the attempt to re-code the race-relations narrative.

The film's central protagonist, a British-born black school leaver, becomes increasingly disillusioned as he realises that racial discrimination prevents him from attaining conventional goals and expectations, such as a career. The youth becomes estranged from his parents, who believed that because he was born in Britain he would have the advantage of being able to 'assimilate' into British society. He drifts into street-corner society and after an encounter with the police, he joins his Caribbean-born brother in a separatist 'Black Power' organisation. The plot describes the politicisation of his identity or rather, a growing awareness of the contradictions inherent in the very idea of a black British identity where, ideologically, society regards the two terms as mutually exclusive.

In presenting this dilemma in dramatic form *Pressure* constructs an important statement, but in the telling, in its mode of enunciation through documentary realism, the linear development of the story recapitulates the themes of 'inter-generational conflict' and 'identity-crisis' established by the epistemology of the classic race-relations narrative. We are left with an angst-ridden black subject, pathologised into a determinate non-identity by his very marginality.

As Pines has argued, the narrative logic in *Pressure* remains within the problem-oriented discourse of both social realist drama and race-relations sociology. Consequently, the dream sequence at the end of the film, when the youth enters a country-mansion and sadistically stabs at the carcass of a pig, and the final scene of a protest march outside a court-house in the rain, evoke not only the impotence or hopelessness of a politicised black identity, but a certain powerlessness on the part of the film itself, as if it cannot find a successful means of escaping from the master codes that circumscribe it. Ove's rendition of a hostage scenario that occurred in the mid-70s, *A Hole in Babylon* (BBC, 1979) also conveys a pessimistic view of black protest politics. But the crisis of narrative resolution in *Pressure* should not be attributed to its author; on the contrary it must be read as symptomatic of a heroic, but compromised struggle with the master narrative of race relations discourse.

In subsequent black narrative fiction films we see the development of different modes of story-telling within this problematic of 'identity'. *Burning an Illusion*, by Menelik Shabazz narrates a black woman's awakening sense of black consciousness as she discards the signs of her colonised self – 'Mills and Boon' novels and a straightened hairstyle – to rediscover her 'roots' and a politicised self-image. While the linear plot and mode of characterisation are similar to *Pressure* (as the central protagonist is taken to embody a general or 'typical' experience), the shift of emphasis from black/white confrontation to gender politics *within* a black community setting displaces the binary polarisation in which black identity is reactively politicised by its 'opposition' to white authority alone. Yet, by the same token, because the woman's transformation is narratively motivated by her boyfriend's encounter with police and then prison, *Illusion* has been criticised for presenting what is really a male-oriented idea of black women's experiences as the female protagonist is at all times *dependent* upon the 'politicising' role of the male character.[18]

The elision of specificity in the pursuit of 'authenticity' within documentary realism also affects Retake's first feature film, *Majdhar* ('mid-stream'). The story concerns a young woman brought to England from Pakistan by her husband, who then abandons her and thus throws her into a complex set of choices. The protagonists speak with neutral accents, an important aspect of the characterisation and chosen by the film-makers to pre-empt the 'goodness, gracious, me' Asian stereotype. Yet, paradoxically, this seems inadvertently to confirm the 'torn between two cultures' thesis which implies that, for Asian women, independence is synonymous with Western, or in this case English middle-class, culture. What is at stake in each of these films is a struggle to re-tell stories of black British identity, whether set in Asian or Afro-Caribbean contexts, within a code or a language which positions that identity as a 'problem'.

Sankofa's feature film, *The Passion of Remembrance*, marks a turning point not because it transcends this problematic, but because it self-consciously enunciates an explicit attempt to break out of the constraints of the master code. The 'slice of life' drama that unfolds around the 'Baptiste' family is coded in realist fashion, but by foregrounding conflicts around gender and sexuality from black feminist and gay perspectives at the level of character, the story dismantles the myth of a homogenous 'black community' and emphasises the plurality of identities within black society. The family drama is cut across by a dialogue between the emblematic black female and male figures which takes place in an abstract space: along with the 'scratch video' footage that features in the realist sequences, the effect is to disrupt conventions such as narrative continuity. In the process, the layering of diverse rhetorical and textual strategies thematises the question of memory in shaping political identities, calling up images of previous symbols in

black politics to challenge the latent heterosexism of certain cultural nation-
alist discourses in the present.

The plurality of filmic styles and ways of seeing not only deconstructs the
aesthetic principles of documentary realism, but reflexively demonstrates
that the film, as much as its subject matter, is a product of complex cultural
construction. The break with naturalistic conventions in *Passion* should not
be read, within this synoptic and summary overview, as a sign of teleologi-
cal 'progress'; rather, its significance is that, along with documentary-texts
such as *Territories* and *Handsworth Songs*, its cinematic self-consciousness
demonstrates a conception of representation not as mimetic correspondence
with the 'real', but as a process of selection, combination and articulation of
signifying elements in sound and image. This is certainly informed by the
aesthetic principles of modernism (and as such, inscribes the influences of
an engagement in theories and methods available from an education and
training in British art schools, polytechnics and universities), but it would be
reductive to compare the newer film-language experiments to earlier black
films in a rigid 'realist/modernist' dichotomy.

Rather, as the choral refrain in *Territories* implies – 'we are struggling to
tell a story' – what is at issue is a widening range of strategic interventions
against the master codes of the race relations narrative. These are brought to
bear on the same sets of problems, such as 'identity', but articulated in such
a way as to reveal the nature of the problems of representation created by
the hegemony of documentary realism in racial discourse. Indicatively, collage and intertextual appropriation feature significantly in the more recent
films whose formal strategy critiques rather than confirms the modernist
tenet of pure formalism. Because the self-reflexive qualities of films like
*Passion* or *Territories* are specifically oriented and directed to problems of
racial representation, they implicitly critique the celebration of cinematic
abstraction that characterises aspects of the Euro-American avant-garde. In
this sense, as critiques of modernism, the films are of a piece with the
deconstructive impulse that figures in various aspects of post-modernism.
As Dick Hebdige suggests,

> In films like *Handsworth Songs* and *Territories* the film-makers use everything at
> their disposal: the words of Fanon, Foucault, CLR James, TV news footage,
> didactic voiceover, interviews and found sound, the dislocated ghostly echoes
> of dub reggae, the scattergun of rap – in order to assert the fact of difference ...
> Deconstruction here takes a different turn as it moves outside the gallery, the
> academy, the library to mobilise the crucial forms of lived experience and resis-
> tance embedded in the streets, the shops and clubs of modern life.
> Deconstruction here is *used* publicly to cut across the categories of 'body' and
> 'critique', the 'intellectual' and 'the masses', 'Them' and 'Us', to bring into being
> a new eroticised body of critique, a sensuous and pointed logic – and to make it
> bear on the situation, to make the crisis *speak*.[19]

Thus *Territories*, for example, which begins as a documentary 'about'
Notting Hill Carnival as a phenomenon of diaspora culture, appropriates
the subversive logic of Carnival itself to creolise and effectively 'carnivalise'
the filmic text. The fragmentary collage gives rise to a surplus of connotations not as textual 'free play' but as a hybridised mode of enunciation that
returns again to the topic of identity and self-image. In this way, the film

foregrounds the complex intersections of 'difference' – racial, sexual, gen-dered, class-based, ethnic – as the unstable terrain on which identity is con-structed: the image of the two youths embracing while the Union Jack burns in the background replays the antimonies of black Britishness as merely one ambivalent identity amongst others. Similarly, the carnivalesque transcoding of found footage in *Handsworth Songs* subverts the linear logic of narrative closure by invoking multiple chains of semantic association in a dream-like manner that engages the spectator, affectively and cognitively, in a 'critical reverie'.

The dialogic tendencies that inflect aspects of these films implies an aware-ness that the struggle to find a voice does not take place on a neutral or 'innocent' cultural terrain, but involves numerous modes of *appropriation* that dis-articulate and re-articulate the given signifying elements of hegemonic racial discourse.[20] In this sense, this kind of cultural practice celebrates the 'in-between-ness' of the black British condition, not as pathology but as a position from which critical insight is made possible. Theoretically, this implies an epistemological break with sociological orthodoxies, a cut in the race-relations master narrative, that reveals the productivity of the historical collision of cultures that Homi Bhabha describes as 'hybridity' and which Paul Gilroy discusses in terms of syncretic forms of cultural production spe-cific to diasporean conditions of fragmentation and displacement.[21] And, without constructing a monologic opposition between the old and the new in black film-making, it is precisely the variety of representational strategies in contemporary practices that begins to dismantle the burden of representa-tion. As John Akomfrah of Black Audio Film Collective describes it:

> Almost everybody who works here has in many ways been influenced by or has engaged with or has been genuinely interpellated by a whole series of film making discourses, some European, some Third World, others British. I think what one attempts to do is to reformulate the filmic agenda, in which the strat-egy simultaneously undermines and inaugurates a new black cinema; where it is apparent that questions of anger or of reflexivity are not enough; that the moral imperative which usually characterises black films, which empowers them to speak with a sense of urgency, that one needs a combination of all those things to speak of black film-making.[22]

The variety of film-making strategies today – made possible by shifts at the point of production and funding – is important because the rationing of resources plays a decisive role in determining the cinematic qualities of a film. The aesthetic traits that figure prominently in black film-making are not determined by the artistic consciousness of the author(s) alone, but by extra-textual factors such as budgets and funding. The contemporary diver-sification of aesthetic forms entails the awareness that the rationing of funds imposes a double bind on black creativity: because access and opportunities are regulated, such that films tend to get made only one at a time, there is an inordinate pressure on each individual film to be 'representative' or to say as much as possible in one single filmic statement. This precisely is the 'burden of representation' succinctly pinpointed by one of the characters in *Passion* who comments, 'Every time a black face appears on the screen we think it has to represent the whole race', to which comes the reply, 'But there is so little space – we have to get it right.' Martina Attille explains the nature of this dilemma as it arose in the making of *Passion*:

> There was a sense of urgency to say it all, or at least to signal as much as we could in one film. Sometimes we can't afford to hold anything back for another time, another conversation or another film. That is the reality of our experience – sometimes we only get the *one* chance to make ourselves heard.[23]

What is at issue is a question of power, a question of *who* has power over the apparatus of image-making.

As Judith Williamson noted in her review of *Passion*, 'The more power any group has to create and wield representations, the less it is required to *be* representative.' This concerns the politics of marginalisation in the struggle for access to production, for as Williamson adds, 'the invisible demand to "speak for the black community" is always there behind the multicultural-ism of public funding'.[24] There is, in effect, a subtle 'numbers game' in play: if there is only *one* black voice in the public discourse, it is assumed that that voice 'speaks for' and thereby 'represents' the *many* voices and viewpoints of the group that is marginalised from the means of representation in society. Tokenism is one particular effect of this state of affairs: when films are funded with the expectation that they 'speak for' a disenfranchised community, this legitimates institutional expediency (it 'demonstrates' multicultur-alism) *and* the rationing of meagre resources (it polices a group's social rights to representation). The very notion that a single film or cultural arte-fact can 'speak for' an entire socio-ethnic community reinforces the per-ceived marginality and 'secondariness' of that community.

What is at stake is the way in which the discursive parameters and enun-ciative modalities of black cinematic expression have been regulated and 'policed' by hierarchical relations between 'minority' and 'majority' dis-course. In legal terms, a 'minor' is a subject whose speech is denied access to 'truth' (children cannot 'give evidence'), like an infant (literally, without speech), a social minor has not aquired the right-to-speak. The sometimes paternalistic attitudes which have underpinned the parsimony of multicul-tural funding police black film-making in much the same way: as 'ethnic minority arts', black films have been funded and thus black film-makers have been given the right-to-speak, on the implicit expectation that they 'speak for' the community from which they come. The critical difference in the contemporary situation thus turns on the decision to speak *from* the specificity of one's circumstances and experiences, rather than the attempt, impossible in any case, to speak *for* the entire social category in which one's experience is constituted.

Certain dialogic tendencies which foreground the mode of filmic enuncia-tion – specifying 'where' the films are speaking from – threaten to overturn or at least destabilise the way in which black film discourses have been policed by the burden of representation. And, as Stuart Hall points out, this involves the reconsideration of 'ethnicity' as the acknowledgement of the contextual and historically-specific place from which one speaks. It under-mines the transcendental and universalist claims of Western discourses which arrogate for themselves the right-to-speak on behalf of all of us while marginalising and repressing those voices that speak from its margins, into ethnic particularism. Within the British context, the hybridised accents of black British voices begin to unravel the heteroglossia, the many-voicedness and variousness of British cultural identity *as it is lived*, against the centrifugal and centralising monologism of traditional versions of national identity.

## Notes

1. 'Black Film/British Cinema', was held on 6 February 1988 at the ICA and sponsored by the Production Division and former Ethnic Advisor of the British Film Institute. The title, incidentally, was derived from a day event organised by Peter Hames at Stoke Regional Film Theatre in November 1987.
2. Reece Auguiste, 'Handsworth Songs. Some background notes', *Framework*, **35** (1988), p. 6.
3. See, Salman Rushdie, 'The Raj Revival', *Observer*, April 1984, reprinted in John Twitchin, ed., *The Black and White Media Book* (Stoke-on Trent, Trentham Books, 1988), p. 130; and Farrukh Dhondy, 'Ghandi. Myth and Reality', *Emergency*, **1** (1984).
4. Paul Willemen, 'The Third Cinema Question. Notes and Reflections', *Framework*, **34** (1987), p. 36.
5. Stuart Hall, 'Minimal Selves', in Lisa Appignanesi, ed., *Identity*, ICA Documents, **6** (1988), p. 44.
6. Craig Owens, 'The Discourse of Others. Feminists and Postmodernism', in Hal Foster, ed., *Postmodern Culture* (London, Pluto, 1985), p. 57.
7. Jim Pines, 'The Cultural Context of Black British Cinema', in Mbye Cham and Claire Andrade-Watkins, eds, *BlackFrames. Critical Perspectives on Black Independent Cinema* (Cambridge, MA, MIT Press, 1988), p. 26. This publication was produced as part of 'Celebration of Black Cinema', a programme featuring a range of black British film, held in Boston, April 1988.
8. An overview of black arts in the 80s is provided by, Kwesi Owusu, ed., *Storms of the Heart. An Anthology of Black Arts and Culture* (London, Camden Press, 1988).
9. For a critique for Channel 4's initial entertainment and current affairs programmes addressed to the Afro-Carribbean communities, see Paul Gilroy, 'Bridgehead or Bantustan?', *Screen*, **24** (4–5) (1983).
10. See, Phil Cohen and Carl Gardner, eds, *It Ain't Half Racist Mum* (Comedia/Campaign Against Racism in the Media, 1982): for reflections on a BBC 'Open Door' programme produced by CARM, see Stuart Hall, 'The Whites of their Eyes. Racist Ideologies and the Media', in G. Bridges and R. Brunt, eds, *Silver Linings* (London, Lawrence & Wishart, 1981).
11. See Twitchin, *The Black and White Media Book*, and on Channel 4's minority programmes in relation to the audience, see David Docherty, David Morrison and Michael Tracey, *Keeping Faith? Channel 4 and its Audience* (London, Broadcasting Research Unit/John Libbey, 1988).
12. Funding policies in relation to the black arts movement are critically examined in Kwesi Owusu. *The Struggle for Black Arts in Britain* (London, Comedia, 1986).
13. The event, organised by Parminder Vir and co-ordinated by June Givanni, is documented in *Third Eye. Struggle for Black and Third World Cinema* (London, GLC Race Equality Unit, 1986).
14. For two conflicting accounts of the event, see my report in *Screen* **27**:6 (1986) and David Will's report in *Framework* 32/33 (1986). The rather ethnocentric views expressed in the latter are the subject of a counter-reply in Clyde Taylor, 'Eurocentrics vs. New Thought at Edinburgh', *Framework*, **34** (1987). Proceedings from the conference are published as *Questions of Third Cinema*, Jim Pines and Paul Willemen, eds, (London, British Film Institute, 1988).

15. See, Jim Pines, 'Black in Films. The British Angle', *Multiracial Education*, 9:2 (Special Issue on Race and the Media) (1981). The analysis of ethnic stereotyping is also discussed by Homi Bhabha in his influential essay, 'The Other Question. The Stereotype and Colonial Discourse', *Screen*, **24** (4) (1983).
16. Stuart Hall, 'Racism and Reaction', in *Five Views on Multiracial Britain*, (London, Commission for Racial Equality, 1979), p. 25; see also. Hall, 'The Whites of their Eyes'.
17. 'The Cultural Context of Black British Cinema, p. 29.
18. See Sally Sayers and Layleen Jayamanne, 'Burning an Illusion', in Charlotte Brundson, ed., *Films for Women* (London, British Film Institute, 1986); see also, Martine Attille and Maureen Blackwood, 'Black Women and Representation' in the same volume.
19. Dick Hebdige, 'Digging for Britain. An Excavation in Seven Parts', in *The British Edge* (Boston, Institute of Contemporary Arts, MA, 1987).
20. I have drawn on Bahktin's concept of dialogism, developed in *The Dialogic Imagination* (University of Texas, 1981), in my essay, 'Diaspora Culture and the Dialogic Imagination. The Aesthetics of Black Independent Film in Britain', in *BlackFrames*. See also, on the range of arguments around aesthetics, contributions to *Undercut* 17 (London Film-Makers Co-op, 1988) from the 'Cultural Identities' conference held at the Commonwealth Institute in March 1986.
21. Bhabha's concept of 'hybridity' is developed in 'Signs Taken for Wonders. Questions of Ambivalence and Authority Under a Tree Outside Delhi, May 1817', in Henry Louis Gates, Jr. ed., *Race, Writing and Difference* (University of Chicago, 1988). Gilroy's discussion of syncretism and diasporean culture is developed in *There Ain't No Black in the Union Jack* (London, Hutchinson, 1988) (esp. Ch. 5, 'Diaspora, Utopia and the Critique of Capitalism').
22. In Paul Gilroy and Jim Pines, 'Handsworth Songs. Audiences/Aesthetics/Independence', interview with Black Audio Film Collective, *Framework*, 35 (1988), p. 11.
23. In 'The Passion of Remembrance. Background', *Framework*, **32/33**, p. 101, and reprinted in *Black Film. British Cinema* (London, ICA, 1986), pp. 53–4.
24. *New Statesman*, 5 December 1986.

# Television

## Hyperreality and hybrid selves

In all Jean Baudrillard's dystopian rhetoric, his pronouncement that the Gulf War would not and did not happen is perhaps the most notorious. Baudrillard's 'The reality gulf' reprinted here, would be called apocalyptic were it not for his insistence that apocalypse itself has become redundant and transferred, with the concepts of religion and armed struggle, into a zone of virtuality and simulation. Television is central to Baudrillard's account – a metaphor for and major accomplice in creating the undifferentiated flatness of postmodern experience. Its role as a 'record' of reality, as in the case of the US *vérité* documentary on the Loud family which he comments on in 'The end of the panopticon' below, comes, in its very immediacy, to usurp its real life referent, just as its absorbing emotional content contributes to a pervasive loss of affect. By extension, a war in which the saturation coverage of 24-hour television broadcasts could bring 'surgical strikes' into the home the moment they occurred constructed an unprecedented immediacy and interaction between the viewer and the distant real-life conflict. CNN viewers were engaged in the spectacle of warfare as never before. Yet, according to Baudrillard, this experience constituted a gross deluding of the television spectator, a mass succumbing to the simulation of war behind which no 'real' war was taking place.

Christopher Norris counters Baudrillard on the Gulf War with a list of 'real' mass destruction, civilian deaths and human tragedies. Suspecting a basic obscenity behind Baudrillard's assertions, Norris seeks to recover the concepts – 'truth', 'ideology', 'critique' – which Baudrillard would claim are long discredited. Norris insists that, on the contrary, the mass viewing public must be helped to realise that 'there *is* (must be) some ultimate reality behind appearances, and that truth will surely come to light in the long run' (p. 170).

Norris's committed humanism and Baudrillard's deliberately provocative soothsaying clearly operate at such different levels of discourse that the two commentaries can barely engage with each other, let alone find any common ground. They do share an assumption, however, of mass-media dis-information and some concern with the gullibility or otherwise of a collective audience whose knowledge of the war came largely through television – an audience from which both writers significantly retain a critical distance.

Marie Gillespie's investigation of West London Punjabi teenagers' response to the televised conflict adds a valuable dimension to this debate. Baudrillard's notion of the viewer as 'hostage' becomes strikingly appropriate in terms of the multiple, often contradictory positions these young viewers occupy, shifting their own identificatory roles between allies and Muslim, 'here' and 'there', according to the demands of home and school, India and Britain.

Gillespie's empirical study brings a lived complexity to notions of postmodern schizophrenia. In some contexts these teenage viewers question the propaganda, misinformation and loaded statistics of the news reports, yet in others boast of enjoying the spectacle of 'precision bombing' as a sophisticated video game. Not surprisingly, this turns out also to be a gendered response. At the heart of their viewing experience, though, is the very real shared knowledge that as British Asians, they occupy a position between cultures and experiences that feels more uneasy than liberating.

'The television generation is a grim bunch', Marshall McLuhan had observed in *The Medium is the Massage*. 'It is much more serious than children from any other period' (p. 152). Punjabi teenagers in Southall are in one way the heirs to this seriousness. Yet in another direction 'the television generation' means the cartoon teenagers, Beavis and Butt-Head, whose sordid lives are dominated by the screen and the 24-hour saturation not of CNN but MTV. If this appears to offer a pathetic extreme of self-reflexivity, in which teenage viewers gaze at two on-screen teenagers, themselves engaged in the very act of endless TV-viewing, it should be noted that Beavis and Butt-Head, rather than mindlessly consuming, converse with, mock, imitate and critique the music videos they watch, in a dialogue which displays considerable subtlety and cultural capital, their expertise as television 'readers' echoing the fluidity and sophistication displayed by Gillespie's teenage subjects. Douglas Kellner's study suggests how, in the face of a moral panic against the programme's alleged influence on American teenagers, the alienated and disenfranchised lifestyles of Beavis and Butt-Head, rather than shaping anti-social behaviour, accurately reflect and articulate the experiences of the 'slacker' generation.

As Kellner observes, the motifs and references of *Beavis and Butt-Head*, to say nothing of the characters' own understanding of the world, are entirely derived from previous television culture. History, so often prophesied as the first casualty of postmodernism, has indeed been reduced in Butt-Head's living room to a bizarre montage of half-remembered clips. McLuhan's references to George Washington, Franklin and even Kennedy would be lost on the duo who struggle to identify 'that dude on the dollar'. This, like its tamer predecessors, *The Simpsons*, *Moonlighting* and *Max Headroom*, is what Umberto Eco terms 'neo-television', talking less about the 'outside' world and increasingly about television itself, rebounding off its own in-jokes and cross-references until conventions of realism threaten to implode.

In a mode which current vernacular might term 'Brecht-lite', signifiers of artifice are now used to serve, albeit playfully, as guarantors of 'authenticity'. Just as, in Eco's account, a visible boom-mike would be included to suggest live transmission even for recorded programmes, so *Wayne's World* foregrounds its amateurish cue-cards, count-downs and 'extreme close-ups' and

*The Larry Sanders Show* devotes more screen-time to the writing and rehearsal of its sketches than to the polished final product. Even Max Headroom's stutters and jump-cuts were artificial devices to simulate an authentic – that is, imperfect – computer-generated host from an actor in a latex mask.

Jim Collins continues this navigation of neo-TV's often bewildering intertextuality with his observation of *LA Law* characters watching *thirtysomething* and Bart Simpson recognising himself as a cartoon character on his own (cartoon) television set. Collins' account of the marketing strategies behind *Twin Peaks*, itself now effectively canonised as postmodern TV, suggests a multiple address not merely in the programme's 'eclectic' drawing on soap, Gothic horror, police drama and Tibetan spiritualism, but in its being targeted at various audiences as, on the one hand, a cinematic, 'avant-garde' addition to the Lynch *oeuvre* and, on the other, a low-level soap serial. Collins suggests, though, that a 'postmodern cultural literacy' enables the individual viewer to enjoy the text in both ways, and that the TV 'spectator-as-*bricoleur*' has the power actively to create and adapt meanings according to his or her own needs.

Collins' viewers are 'hyperconscious' and a match it would seem for the hyperreality of postmodern image culture. Lynne Joyrich's findings on the fundamental gendering of television and postmodernism suggest there is quite another aspect to this detached intertextuality, however. Two generations of TV commentators, as she argues, from McLuhan, Eco and Baudrillard, to Fiske and others, have implicitly conceptualised TV and postmodernism as feminine. The result, in her view, has been not simply hyperreality and its accompanying ironies and knowingness, but 'hypermasculinity', a compensatory physical exaggeration or numerical dominance and ideological foregrounding of the male on screen, as witnessed, respectively, in her examples, in *Max Headroom* and *Miami Vice*.

This might bring us to reconsider the utopian-sounding prospect sketched by Collins and others. But so, too, might the other two examples of types of viewers presented here: the media-literate but immature social outcasts, Beavis and Butt-Head, and the teenagers of Gillespie's study, caught in a running, skilful dialogue with media texts. The latter's attitude and identities, in particular, bear all the ambiguities of postmodern instability: complex and mobile, certainly, but as fraught as they are fluid. Both medium and viewers, we are led to conclude, are contradictorily placed: at once socially and ideologically constructed and open to re-invention.

## Further reading

Allen R. C. (ed.) 1992. *Channels of discourse. Reassembled.* London: Routledge.

Baehr H. and Dyer G. (eds) 1987. *Boxed in. Women and television.* London: Pandora Press.

Baudrillard J. 1994. *The Gulf War did not take place*, trans. Paul Patton. Sydney: The Power Institute.

Brunsdon C. 1993. Identity in feminist television criticism. *Media, Culture and Society* 15(2), 309–20.

Denton R. E. (ed.) 1993. *The media and the Persian Gulf War.* Westport, CT: Praeger.

Ferguson M. 1991. Marshall McLuhan revisited. 1960s Zeitgeist victim or pioneer postmodernist? *Media, Culture and Society* 13(1), 71–90.

Fiske J. 1991: Postmodernism and television. In Curran J. and Gurevitch M. (eds), *Mass media and society*. London: Arnold.

Grossberg, 1987: The in-difference of television. *Journal of Communication Inquiry* **10**(2) 28–46.

Hartley J. 1992. *Tele-ology. Studies in television*. London: Routledge.

Joyrich L. 1988. All that television allows. TV melodrama, postmodernism, and consumer culture. *Camera Obscura* **16**, 128–53.

Kellner D. 1990. *Television and the crisis of democracy*. Boulder, CO: Westview.

Kellner D. 1992: *The Persian Gulf TV War*. Boulder, CO: Westview.

MacCabe C. (ed.) 1986: *High theory/low culture. Analysing popular television and film*. Manchester: Manchester University Press.

Mellencamp P. (ed.) 1990. *Logics of television*. Bloomington, IN: Indiana University Press.

Morley D. 1986. *Family television. Cultural power and domestic leisure*. London: Comedia.

Williams R. 1974. *Television. Technology and cultural form*. London: Fontana.

Williams R. 1989. *Raymond Williams on television*, ed. A. O'Connor. London: Routledge.

**See also the journals:**

*Camera Obscura*: Special Issue 'Television and the Female Consumer', **16** (Jan. 1988).

*Media Culture and Society*: 'Postmodernism', **13**(1) (Jan. 1991).

# 10

## The medium is the massage

*Marshall McLuhan*

From Marshall McLuhan and Quentin Fiore, *The medium is the massage*
(Penguin/Bantam 1967)

All media work us over completely. They are so persuasive in their personal, political, economic, aesthetic, psychological, moral, ethical, and social
consequences that they leave no part of us untouched, unaffected, un-
altered. The medium is the massage. Any understanding of social and
cultural change is impossible without a knowledge of the way media work
as environments.

All
media
are
extensions
of
some
human
faculty –
psychic
or
physical

. . . Ours is a brand-new world of allatonceness. 'Time' has ceased, 'space'
has vanished. We now live in a *global* village . . . a simultaneous happening.
We are back in acoustic space. We have begun again to structure the primordial feeling, the tribal emotions from which a few centuries of literacy
divorced us.

We have had to shift our stress of attention from action to reaction. We
must now know in advance the consequences of any policy or action,
since the results are experienced without delay. Because of electric speed,
we can no longer wait and see. George Washington once remarked, 'We
haven't heard from Benj. Franklin in Paris this year. We should write him a
letter.'

At the high speeds of electric communication, purely visual means of
apprehending the world are no longer possible; they are just too slow to be
relevant or effective.

Unhappily, we confront this new situation with an enormous backlog of outdated mental and psychological responses. We have been left d-a-n-g-l-i-n-g. Our most impressive words and thoughts betray us – they refer us only to the past, not to the present.

Electric circuitry profoundly involves men with one another. Information pours upon us, instantaneously and continuously. As soon as information is acquired, it is very rapidly replaced by still newer information. Our electrically-configured world has forced us to move from the habit of data classification to the mode of pattern recognition. We can no longer build serially, block-by-block, step-by-step, because instant communication insures that all factors of the environment and of experience coexist in a state of active interplay.

. . . Television completes the cycle of the human sensorium. With the omnipresent ear and the moving eye, we have abolished writing, the specialized acoustic-visual metaphor that established the dynamics of Western civilization.

In television there occurs an extension of the sense of active, exploratory touch which involves all the senses simultaneously, rather than that of sight alone. You have to be 'with' it. But in all electric phenomena, the visual is only one component in a complex interplay. Since, in the age of information, most transactions are managed electrically, the electric technology has meant for Western man a considerable drop in the visual component, in his experience, and a corresponding increase in the activity of his other senses.

Television demands participation and involvement in depth of the whole being. It will not work as a background. It engages you. Perhaps this is why so many people feel that their identity has been threatened. This charge of the light brigade has heightened our general awareness of the shape and meaning of lives and events to a level of extreme sensitivity.

It was the funeral of President Kennedy that most strongly proved the power of television to invest an occasion with the character of corporate participation. It involves an entire population in a ritual process. (By comparison, press, movies, and radio are mere packaging devices for consumers.) In television, images are projected at you. You are the screen. The images wrap around you. You are the vanishing point. This creates a sort of inwardness, a sort of reverse perspective which has much in common with Oriental art.

The television generation is a grim bunch. It is much more serious than children of any other period – when they were frivolous, more whimsical. The television child is more earnest, more dedicated.

Most often the few seconds sandwiched between the hours of viewing – the 'commercials' – reflect a truer understanding of the medium. There simply is no time for the narrative form, borrowed from earlier print technology. The story line must be abandoned. Up until very recently, television commercials were regarded as simply a bastard form, or vulgar folk art. They are influencing contemporary literature. *Vide* 'In Cold Blood,' for instance. The main cause for disappointment in and for criticism of television is the failure on the part of its critics to view it as a totally new technology which demands different sensory responses. These critics insist on regarding television as merely a degraded form of print technology. Critics of television have failed to realize that the motion pictures they are lionizing

– such as 'The Knack,' 'Hard Day's Night,' 'What's New Pussycat?' would prove unacceptable as mass audience films if the audience had not been preconditioned by television commercials to abrupt zooms, elliptical editing, no story lines, flash cuts.

# 11

## A guide to the Neo-Television of the 1980s

*Umberto Eco*

From *Framework* 25, 19–27 (1984)

*The following notes explain the differences between Neo-Television and Paleo-Television. They deal with the most sadistic American show, technical innovations, the behaviour of the Neo-TV viewer, and furthermore, they offer a word of prophecy.*

Once upon a time there was Paleo-Television. It was produced in Rome or Milan for everyone. It spoke of the appointment of ministers and it saw to it that the public only learnt about harmless things, even if it meant telling it lies. With the multiplication of channels, privatisation and the arrival of new electronic devilries, we are now living in the era of Neo-Television. It was once possible to compile a small dictionary of Paleo-TV with the names of its protagonists and the titles of its programmes. With Neo-TV this wouldn't be possible. This is not just because the number of protagonists and programmes is infinite (and no one can remember or recognise them), but also because the same characters play different roles, depending on whether they are speaking on state or private screens. A small dictionary of Neo-TV cannot, therefore, be anything other than a review of new forms of behaviour, and a sketch of general outlines, tendencies and coming developments. Studies have already been carried out on the character of Neo-TV (for example, the recent research done at Bologna University on television entertainment programmes on behalf of the Parliamentary Commission).[1] The small dictionary which follows does not attempt a résumé of research in the field, but casts an eye over the panorama that it has brought to light. It is a small dictionary of mutating television for a public of mutants.

The principal characteristic of Neo-TV is that it talks less and less about the external world. Whereas Paleo-TV talked about the external world, or pretended to, Neo-TV talks about itself and about the contact that it establishes with its own public. It does not matter what it might say, nor what it might be talking about (now more than ever, since the public, armed with remote control, decides when to let it speak and when to switch channels). Neo-TV, in order to survive this control, seeks to hold the viewer by saying to him: 'I am here, it's me, I am you.' The maximum amount of news that Neo-TV provides, whether it is dealing with missiles or with Stanley who has pushed over a wardrobe, is this: 'I am telling you (and that's the miracle of it) that you are watching me; if you don't believe me, try me by ringing this number and I'll answer.'

After a lot of doubts, finally one thing is certain: Neo-Television exists. It is true because it is, without a shred of doubt, a television invention.

## TV and truth

Experiments in the 1960s taught us that for many underdeveloped viewers the evening's viewing was understood to be a continuum without distinctions between truth and fiction. The underdeveloped viewer believed that the facts of the news programme were as fictional as drama, or that drama was truth like the weather forecast. Then viewers learnt to distinguish between genres according to how characters looked at the camera.

## Looking and not looking at the camera

The viewer had learnt that whoever spoke looking directly at the camera (like the newsreader) was bound to be telling the truth; he spoke about something that had really happened. Instead, whoever did not look at the camera and spoke as if the camera watched him through a key-hole (as happens with actors), was a fictional character. Then there was the quiz- or variety show-compère; he spoke the truth when he looked at the camera and announced the name of a guest, but also when he didn't do so – when he was putting a question to a competitor to which he knew the right answer. But in the same programme, the comic, and sometimes the presenter himself, used to look at the camera and say something made-up, such as a joke or a story. Now it's all changed. On Altra Domenica on Neo-TV, Arbore used to look at the camera, and it was obvious that he made up stories. Certain interviewees on chat shows do not look at the camera, yet they are presumed to be sincere. When can you assume that whoever is speaking wants to tell the truth?

## The 'hold-all' programme

To confuse our ideas the 'hold-all' programme has arrived in which a conductor talks, plays music, introduces a drama programme and perhaps a documentary or a debate, and even reads the news. At this point the overdeveloped viewer mixes up the genres. He suspects that the bombardment of Beirut is a show and that the audience of youngsters who are clapping on the Beppe Grillo show is made up of human beings.[2]

## The boom-mike

On Paleo-TV there was a cry of alarm which was a prelude to warning letters, sackings and the collapse of promising careers; it was: 'Boom-mike in shot.' The boom-mike was not allowed to be seen, and the same applied to its shadow (indeed, its shadow was greatly feared). Television pathetically insisted on presenting itself as reality, and hence it had to hide artifice. Then the boom-mike made its appearance on the quiz show, on the news and on various experimental shows. Television no longer hides artifice, rather, the presence of the boom-mike assures (even when it's not the case) that the transmission is live. It is the presence therefore of the boom-mike which now serves to hide artifice.

### The TV camera

The TV cameras were also not meant to be seen. Now, they too are seen. By showing them the television is saying: 'I am here, and if I'm here, this means that in front of me, and in front of you, there's reality; that's TV which is filming. The proof is that if you say "hi" in front of the TV camera, they see you at home.' The disquieting fact is that if you see a TV camera on television it is certain not to be the one that is filming (unless there is a complex mis-en-scène using mirrors). Hence, every time the TV camera appears, it is telling a lie.

### The telephone on the news

Paleo-TV showed comedy characters who used to talk to the telephone, and it used to give information about real or supposed events that were taking place outside television. Neo-TV uses the 'phone to say: 'I am here, linked to my inside with my own brain, and to my outside with you who are watching me at this moment.' The newsreader uses the telephone to talk to the producer; an intercom would do just as well, but the voice of the producer would be audible, whereas it must remain mysterious – the television speaking with its own secret, intimate recesses. But what the newscaster hears is true and crucial. He says: 'Wait, the newsfilm is coming', and justifies long seconds of waiting because the film must come from the right place at the right moment.

### The 'Portobello' telephone

The telephone on 'Portobello' and similar programmes put television's big heart in touch with the public's big heart.[3] It is the triumphant sign of direct access, it is umbilical and magic. You are us, you can come and become part of the show. The world which TV talks about to you is the relationship between us and you. The rest is silence.

### That TV announcer is a wreck

The woman TV announcer is one of the most touching developments of Paleo-TV. It made sense when there was only óne TV and a single channel: it reinforced television's role as domestic hearth. Like the hostess, the announcer took us by the hand during a voyage in a closed box to tell us what we would see and how we should see it. On account of this she was chosen from the petit bourgeoisie, was attractive but hardly sensual, and was advised by a dress-maker capable of titillating the worst instincts of the majority of the day; that is to say, of the viewers living in remote areas never previously exposed to the models of the dominant class. The announcer was, in her style and speech-rhythms, in harmony with the programmes she presented, which were full of circus jugglers and comics adept at long pauses full of double entendres.

Now that there are many TV channels, and you come across this one or that one by chance, the presenter is no longer needed. Now that television space costs money because it is sold to advertisers, the announcer constitutes a huge waste. Now that the TV stations use many American and Japanese programmes which move at high speeds, the appearance of the announcer lacerates, so to speak, the television time which is monstrously stretched like a plastic-bag pulled beyond the limits of its elasticity. Now that the programmes inform the viewers about how the fashionable dress, the announcer with her pompom, her chemises à la Eva Braun and her necklines à la Red Cross, seems to come from another planet.

Certain private television stations try to get around the difficulty by having a slightly whorish announcer who seems to invite the viewer to follow her into the screen while the midnight logo descends. But the compulsive viewer is not fooled and is already moving the thumb greedily in search of the latest soft-porn.

## The auction phone

Private Neo-TV invented the auction. With the auction-phone-in, the public seems to be setting the pace of the show itself. In fact, the calls are all vetted, and it is reasonable to suspect that they use the gaps to make false calls to raise the bids. If only one viewer phoned, then the item would be sold at a very low price. It is not the auctioneer who induces the viewers to spend more, it's one viewer that induces another, or rather, the telephone. The auctioneer is innocent.

## Applause

On Paleo-TV applause had to seem to be real and spontaneous. The public in the studio applauded when a sign lit up, but the public in front of the screen had not to know. Evidently the public has learnt this and Neo-TV makes no such pretences; the presenter says: 'Now let's give him a good hand', the public in the studio claps, and those at home are happy because they know that the clapping is no longer artificial. It doesn't matter to the viewer whether it is spontaneous, but rather whether it's really television.

## The provinces

Paleo-TV wanted to be a window that looked out from the most far-flung provinces onto the wide world. Independent Neo-TV (starting from the state model of 'It's a Knock-Out') points the TV cameras on the provinces, and shows the public of Piacenza the people of Piacenza – which has gathered together to listen to a Piacenza watchmaker's advertisement, while a Piacenza presenter makes coarse jokes about the 'tits' of a Piacenza woman, who takes it all uncomplainingly so that she can be seen by the public of Piacenza while she wins a pressure-cooker. It's like looking through the telescope from the wrong end. Nothing like that boring 'Hamlet' stuff.

## The auctioneer

The auctioneer is simultaneously salesman and actor. But an actor who tries to play the part of a salesman would not be convincing. The public knows salesmen as people who persuade them to buy a second-hand car, a roll of material or marmot's fat at the village fair. The auctioneer must be handsome (or fat, or a flashy dresser) and should speak like his viewers, i.e., with an accent and with the odd ungrammatical expression, and say 'that's it' and 'interesting offer', just as the people who really sell do. He must say: 'Eighteen carats, Signora Ida, I don't know if I make myself understood.' In fact, he doesn't have to; he needs only express the same amazement as the buyer in the presence of the goods. In his private life he is probably very upright and honest, but on the screen he must have a roguish air, otherwise the public will not trust him. Salesmen are like that.

## The promotion of bad habits

Once upon a time there were swear words that were said at school, at work and in bed. Then you had to control your habits a bit in public, and Paleo-TV (subject to censorship and designed for an ideal public, both meek and Catholic) spoke in a cleaned-up way. Independent television, instead, wants the public to recognise itself and to say: 'That's really us.' Thus, the comedian or presenter who asks a riddle when looking at a woman spectator's bottom, uses bad language and makes double entenders. Adults find themselves again – finally TV is like life. Children think that that must be the right way to behave in public – just as they have always suspected. It's one of the few occasions on which Neo-TV tells the absolute truth.

## The masochistic viewer

Neo-TV, especially the independent channels, exploits to the limit the viewers' masochism. The presenter puts questions to meek housewives which should make them die of shame, and they play ball, between feigned (or genuine) blushes, and behave like little whores. This form of TV sadism has reached its height in America with a new game in Johnny Carson's extremely popular 'Tonight Show'. Carson recounts the plot of some hypothetical drama, à la Dallas, in which idiotic, wretched, disfigured and perverted characters appear. While he speaks, the TV camera frames the face of a spectator, who, in the meanwhile, sees himself on a TV screen above his head. The spectator laughs with delight as he is depicted as a sodomite and child-exploiter, while a woman spectator enjoys being put in the shoes of a drug-addict or of a congenital mental defective. Men and women (that the camera has, in fact, already maliciously picked out on account of some physical defect or over-pronounced feature) laugh happily at feeling themselves derided in front of millions of viewers. Anyway, they think, it's only a joke. But they really are objects of derision ('sputtanati').

## Babel's film-library

The forty- and fifty-year-olds know what hard work and research went into recovering an old film by Duvivier in an out-of-the-way cinémathèque. Now the magic of the cinéthèque is over, Neo-TV gives us Totò, an early Ford and perhaps some Meliès all in one evening. We acquire a film-culture. But for one old Ford, there are ten indigestible crusts and fourth-rate films. The old hands of the cinéthèques still know how to tell the difference but as a result they search the channels only for the films they have already seen. Thus their film-culture does not develop. The young identify every old film with the cinéthèque film so their culture regresses. Fortunately there are some papers which give some guidance. But how can one read the papers if one has to watch television?

## The rhythm

American TV, for which time is money, imposes a rhythm on all its programmes, a jazz-type rhythm. Italian Neo-TV mixes American material and home-made (or Third World, e.g., Brazilian) material which have an archaic rhythm. Hence, the time of Neo-TV is an elastic time composed of snatches, accelerations and decelerations.

## Remote control

Fortunately the viewer can impose his own rhythms by selecting hysterically with his remote control. Have you ever tried watching TV news on two state channels, switching in hiccup fashion from one to the other so that you always see the same item of news twice, and never the one you are waiting for? Or brought in a 'pie-in-the-face' at the moment when the old mother is dying?

Or intercut the Starsky and Hutch gymkhana with a slow dialogue between Marco Polo and a *bonze*? In this way we all create our own rhythms and watch TV in the same manner as when we listen to music pressing our hands over the ears; it's us who decides what will become of Beethoven's 'Fifth' or of 'Bella Gigugin'.[4] Our TV evenings no longer tell us whole stories; it's all a 'trailer'. The dream of the historical avant gardes come true.

## The video tape recorder

With Paleo-TV there was little to see and it was all to bed before midnight. Neo-TV has tens of channels and they are on late into the night. Appetite comes from eating. The VTR lets us see so many more additional programmes – hired and bought films and programmes that were broadcast when we were not at home. How wonderful, one can now spend 48 hours a day in front of the TV, so there's no more need to come into contact with that remote fiction – the real world. Moreover, events can be made to go backwards and forwards, in slow-motion and speeded up. Just think, watching Antonioni at Mazinga's rhythm.[5] Now unreality is within everyone's grasp.

## Teletext

It is now one of the new possibilities, but there are already others, and there will be others in infinite number. One will read train timetables, stock exchange prices, and encyclopedia entries on the TV. But when everything, absolutely everything, even the interventions of members of the board of directors, will be able to be read on the screen, who will need to know the times of trains or shows, or the weather forecast? The screen will give information on an outside world where no one will go any more. The project for the new MiTo, that is the Milan-Turin megapolis, is based in large part on contacts via the TV screen. At this point, one can no longer see why it's necessary to improve the motorway or the railways since no one will need to go from Milan to Turin, or vice versa. The body becomes useless, and the eyes are all you need.

## Battlestar Galactica

One can buy electronic games, make them appear on the TV and the whole family can play at destroying Darth Vader's space fleet. But when – given that one has so many things to see already, including taped material?

In any case the galactic battle is no longer played in the bar between a coffee and a telephone call, but all day until you get spasms (because you know you only stop because someone is breathing down your neck, but at home you can carry on forever), and this will have the following effects: it will teach children to have optimal reflexes so that they will then be able to fly a supersonic fighter. It will get both adults and infants used to the idea that to make ten space-ships disintegrate is in fact nothing special – a missile-war will be reduced to a human scale. When we then really make war, we will be destroyed in a split-second by the Russians, who are free from Battlestar Galactica. Because, I don't know whether you've tried it, but after playing for a couple of hours at night in a restless half-waking and half-sleeping state, you see flashing lights and the trails of tracer projectiles. The retina and the brain are pulped. It's like when a camera flash has flashed in your eyes. For a long time you see a dark spot in front of you. It's the beginning of the end.

## Notes

1. Since 1975 a Parliamentary Commission has replaced Government in exercising ultimate control over state broadcasting.
2. Beppe Grillo is a madcap Genoese comic who has a show on a private TV station and specialises in political satire.
3. 'Portobello' was an extremely popular show in which members of the audience put things up for sale. In 1983 it was hit by scandal when its presenter was arrested under suspicion of involvement in the Neapolitan camorra.
4. 'Bella Gigugin' is a popular song going back to the Risorgimento.
5. 'Mazinga' is a Japanese sci-fi cartoon typical of a genre which has invaded Italian TV.

With thanks to Zyg Baranski for help with notes and translation.

Translated from an article in the weekly magazine *L'Espresso* (30 January 1983) by Bob Lumley.

# 12

## The end of the panopticon

## *Jean Baudrillard*

From *Simulacra and simulation*, trans. Sheila Faria Glaser (University of Michigan 1994)

It is still to this ideology of lived experience – exhumation of the real in its fundamental banality, in its radical authenticity – that the American TV vérité experiment attempted on the Loud family in 1971 refers: seven months of uninterrupted shooting, three hundred hours of nonstop broadcasting, without a script or a screenplay, the odyssey of a family, its dramas, its joys, its unexpected events, nonstop – in short, a 'raw' historical document, and the 'greatest television performance, comparable, on the scale of our day-to-day life, to the footage of our landing on the moon.' It becomes more complicated because this family fell apart during the filming: a crisis erupted, the Louds separated, etc. Whence that insoluble controversy: was TV itself responsible? What would have happened *if TV hadn't been there*?

More interesting is the illusion of filming the Louds *as if TV weren't there*. The producer's triumph was to say: 'They lived as if we were not there.' An absurd, paradoxical formula – neither true nor false: utopian. The 'as if *we* were not there' being equal to 'as if *you* were there.' It is this utopia, this paradox that fascinated the twenty million viewers, much more than did the 'perverse' pleasure of violating someone's privacy. In the 'vérité' experience it is not a question of secrecy or perversion, but of a sort of frisson of the real, or of an aesthetics of the hyperreal, a frisson of vertiginous and phony exactitude, a frisson of simultaneous distancing and magnification, of distortion of scale, of an excessive transparency. The pleasure of an excess of meaning, when the bar of the sign falls below the usual waterline of meaning: the nonsignifier is exalted by the camera angle. There one sees what the real never was (but 'as if you were there'), without the distance that gives us perspectival space and depth vision (but 'more real than nature'). Pleasure in the microscopic simulation that allows the real to pass into the hyperreal. (This is also somewhat the case in porno, which is fascinating more on a metaphysical than on a sexual level.)

Besides, this family was already hyperreal by the very nature of its selection: a typical ideal American family, California home, three garages, five children, assured social and professional status, decorative housewife, upper-middle-class standing. In a way it is this statistical perfection that dooms it to death. Ideal heroine of the American way of life, it is, as in ancient sacrifies, chosen in order to be glorified and to die beneath the flames of the medium, a modern *fatum*. Because heavenly fire no longer falls on corrupted cities, it is the camera lens that, like a laser, comes to pierce lived reality in order to put it to death. 'The Louds: simply a family who agreed to deliver themselves into the hands of television, and to die by it,' the director will say. Thus it is a question of a sacrificial process, of a sacrificial spectacle offered to twenty million Americans. The liturgical drama of a mass society.

TV vérité. A term admirable in its ambiguity, does it refer to the truth of this family or to the truth of TV? In fact, it is TV that is the truth of the Louds, it is TV that is true, it is TV that renders true. Truth that is no longer the reflexive truth of the mirror, nor the perspectival truth of the panoptic system and of the gaze, but the manipulative truth of the test that sounds out and interrogates, of the laser that touches and pierces, of computer cards that retain your preferred sequences, of the genetic code that controls your combinations, of cells that inform your sensory universe. It is to this truth that the Loud family was subjected by the medium of TV, and in this sense it amounts to a death sentence (but is it still a question of truth?).

*End of the panoptic system.* The eye of TV is no longer the source of an absolute gaze, and the ideal of control is no longer that of transparency. This still presupposes an objective space (that of the Renaissance) and the omnipotence of the despotic gaze. It is still, if not a system of confinement, at least a system of mapping. More subtly, but always externally, playing on the opposition of seeing and being seen, even if the panoptic focal point may be blind.

. . .We are witnessing the end of perspectival and panoptic space (which remains a moral hypothesis bound up with all the classical analyses on the 'objective' essence of power), and thus to the *very abolition of the spectacular*. Television, for example in the case of the Louds, is no longer a spectacular medium. We are no longer in the society of the spectacle, of which the situationists spoke, nor in the specific kinds of alienation and repression that it implied. The medium itself is no longer identifiable as such, and the confusion of the medium and the message (McLuhan) is the first great formula of this new era. There is no longer a medium in the literal sense: it is now intangible, diffused, and diffracted in the real, and one can no longer even say that the medium is altered by it.

Such a blending, such a viral, endemic, chronic, alarming presence of the medium, without the possibility of isolating the effects – spectralized, like these advertising laser sculptures in the empty space of the event filtered by the medium – dissolution of TV in life, dissolution of life in TV – indiscernible chemical solution: we are all Louds doomed not to invasion, to pressure, to violence and blackmail by the media and the models, but to their induction, to their infiltration, to their illegible violence.

But one must watch out for the negative turn that discourse imposes: it is a question neither of disease nor of a viral infection. One must think instead of the media as if they were, in outer orbit, a kind of genetic code that directs the mutation of the real into the hyperreal, just as the other micromolecular code controls the passage from a representative sphere of meaning to the genetic one of the programmed signal.

It is the whole traditional world of causality that is in question: the perspectival, determinist mode, the 'active,' critical mode, the analytic mode – the distinction between cause and effect, between active and passive, between subject and object, between the end and the means. It is in this sense that one can say: TV is watching us, TV alienates us, TV manipulates us, TV informs us . . . In all this, one remains dependent on the analytical conception of the media, on an external active and effective agent, on 'perspectival' information with the horizon of the real and of meaning as the vanishing point.

Now, one must conceive of TV along the lines of DNA as an effect in which the opposing poles of determination vanish, according to a nuclear contraction, retraction, of the old polar schema that always maintained a minimal distance between cause and effect, between subject and object: precisely the distance of meaning, the gap, the difference, the smallest possible gap, irreducible under pain of reabsorption into an aleatory and indeterminate process whose discourse can no longer account for it, because it is itself a determined order.

It is this gap that vanishes in the process of genetic coding, in which indeterminacy is not so much a question of molecular randomness as of the abolition, pure and simple, of the *relation*. In the process of molecular control, which 'goes' from the DNA nucleus to the 'substance' that it 'informs,' there is no longer the traversal of an effect, of an energy, of a determination, of a message. 'Order, signal, impulse, message': all of these attempt to render the thing intelligible to us, but by analogy, retranscribing in terms of inscription, of a vector, of decoding, a dimension of which we know nothing – it is no longer even a 'dimension,' or perhaps it is the fourth (which is defined, however, in Einsteinian relativity by the absorption of the distinct poles of space and time). In fact, this whole process can only be understood in its negative form: nothing separates one pole from another anymore, the beginning from the end; there is a kind of contraction of one over the other, a fantastic telescoping, a collapse of the two traditional poles into each other: *implosion* – an absorption of the radiating mode of causality, of the differential mode of determination, with its positive and negative charge – an implosion of meaning. *That is where simulation begins.*

Everywhere, in no matter what domain – political, biological, psychological, mediatized – in which the distinction between these two poles can no longer be maintained, one enters into simulation, and thus into absolute manipulation – not into passivity, but into *the indifferentiation of the active and the passive*. DNA realizes this aleatory reduction at the level of living matter. Television, in the case of the Louds, also reaches this *indefinite* limit in which, vis-à-vis TV, they are neither more nor less active or passive than a living substance is vis-à-vis its molecular code. Here and there, a single nebula whose simple elements are indecipherable, whose truth is indecipherable.

# 13

## The reality gulf

*Jean Baudrillard*

from the *Guardian*, 11 January 1991

From the start it was clear that this war would not exist. After the 'hot' war, and then after the cold war, we now have the dead war. The thawing of the cold war has left us in the embrace of a corpse of war, needing to handle this decomposing cadaver which no one within the confines of the Gulf has managed to revive. What the United States, President Saddam Hussein and the local powers are fighting over in the Gulf is in fact the corpse of war.

War itself has entered a definitive crisis. It is too late for a hot third world war. The moment has passed. It has been distilled in the course of time into the cold war and there will be no other. Some may have thought that the end of the eastern block, by taking the wraps off deterrence, might open up new 'areas of freedom' for war.

That hasn't happened. The deterrent has not been taken to its intended conclusion. In fact, quite the reverse. The reciprocal deterrent between the two blocks worked because of what might be termed the excess of the means of destruction. Today, though, it works even better as a total self-deterrent, which has gone so far as to create the self-dissolution of the eastern block.

Yet it is also a profound self-deterrent for US might and for western power in general. This power has also been cowed and paralysed by its own strength. It is incapable of using its position within the balance of power. That is why the Gulf War will not happen.

This phenomenon – the marginalisation of war into interminable suspense (rather like a form of psychoanalysis) – is neither reassuring nor comforting. Looked at like this, the non-event of the Gulf is at least as serious as the possibility of war. It is the equivalent of that destructive period in which a corpse rots, a period which causes nausea and impotent lethargy. In both cases, our rituals and symbolic defences are very weak. We are incapable of even putting an end to war, and so we live through the experience with the self-same shameful indifference as with the hostages.

The manipulation and negotiation over hostages is a degenerate form of war which perfectly embodies this 'non-war'. Hostage-taking and blackmail are the purest products of the era of deterrence. The hostage has replaced the warrior. Even by pure inactivity he takes the limelight as the main protagonist in this simulated non-war. The warriors can be buried in the desert, while the hostages occupy centre-stage. Today's hostage is a phantom player, a walk-on who fills the impotent vacuum of modern war. So we have the hostage at a strategic site, the hostage as a Christmas present, the hostage as a bargaining counter and as a liquid asset.

President Saddam has turned himself into the capitalist of the value of hostages, the commercial vulgariser of a hostage market, replacing the market in slaves and workers. He has cheapened the powerful value of hostages, in the same way as the value of war has been cheapened. The low-value hostage has become the symbol of weak war. In its debility, replacing the warlike challenge, it has become synonymous with the debility of war.

It affects us all. We are all hostages to media intoxication. We are all manipulated in the general indifference, induced to believe in the coming war as we were once induced to believe in revolution in Romania, under house arrest to the pretend war. We are all in place as strategic hostages.

Our strategic site is the television screen, from which we are daily bombarded, and in front of which we also serve as a bargaining counter. In this sense, President Saddam's grotesque charade is performed as a diversion – both from war and from active international terrorism. At least such 'soft' terrorism enables President Saddam to put an end to 'hard' terrorism (whether Palestinian or some other). In this guise he reveals himself, as in many other ways, as the perfect accomplice of the West.

The difficulties of the path to war have led to the triumph of blackmail as a strategy. It is the triumph of blackmail and the end of true threats. In the case of Iran, there was an element of true threat; with President Saddam there is nothing but blackmail. What makes President Saddam so despicable is his vulgarisation of everything. He has debased the challenge of religion into a false holy war. He has made the sacrificial hostage into the commercial hostage. He has made war itself into an impossible farce.

Of course the West did a lot to help, by encouraging him to believe he had won the war against Iran, and so fostering the illusion of further victory, this time against the West. The only enjoyable aspect of this whole story is the sight of this chicken coming home to roost.

We are experiencing neither the logic of war nor the logic of peace. We are experiencing the logic of deterrence, inexorably pursuing its course for the last 40 years. It is working itself out as a logic of weakness, through events that are becoming ever weaker, whether in eastern Europe or the Gulf or as exemplified by the vagaries of our French politicians.

The United Nations has given the green light to a diluted kind of war – the right to war. It is a green light for all kinds of precautions and concessions, making it a kind of extended contraceptive against the act of war. First safe sex, now safe war. A Gulf War would not even register two or three on the Richter scale this way. It is unreal, war without the symptoms of war, a form of war which means never needing to face up to war, which enables war to be 'perceived' from deep within a darkroom.

We ought to have been on our guard because of the disappearance of the declaration of war. There can be no real war without a declaration – it is the moment of passing from word to deed. Once that disappears, then the operations of war disappear, too (French soldiers were even armed at one time with fake bullets!). Then the ending of the war disappears, too. The distinction between victors and vanquished ceases. War becomes interminable because it never began.

We dreamed of a pure war – a strategic orbital war purged of all local and political details. Now we have fallen into its feeble alternative – a derisory fantasy in which the adversaries outdo each other in de-escalation, as if the outbreak of war, the true event of war, had become intolerable. Thus everything transfers itself into a 'virtual' form and so we are confronted with a virtual apocalypse. That is much more dangerous in the long term than a genuine apocalypse.

In Aristotle, the chain of logic passes in the other direction, from the virtual to the actual. This is the basis for the widespread belief according to which a new army must eventually be forced into action, and an accumulation of troops in the desert of Saudi Arabia can only lead to a violent solution. But this is a realist Aristotelian logic to which we no longer subscribe. We must now be satisfied with virtual reality which, contrary to the Aristotelian perception, deters from passage to the deed.

In our fear of the real, of anything that is too real, we have created a gigantic simulator. We prefer the virtual to the catastrophe of the real, of which television is the universal mirror. Indeed it is more than a mirror: today television and news have become the ground itself, television plays the same role as the card which is substituted for territory in the Borges fable.

War has not escaped this process. Even soldiers have not been able to retain for themselves the privilege of real war. Arms have not kept the privilege of the value of their use. Deterrence has passed this way and it spares nothing. Arms have mislaid their real function, their function of death and destruction. They are hooked by the lure of war just as others are hooked by power's lure.

PS: It is perhaps rash to demonstrate the reasons for the impossibility of a war just at the very moment when it is supposed to happen and when the signs of its outbreak are accumulating. But wouldn't it have been even more stupid not to seize the opportunity?

# 14

## 'Postscript' (Baudrillard's second Gulf War article)

## Christopher Norris

From *Uncritical theory. Postmodernism, intellectuals and the Gulf War* (Lawrence & Wishart 1992)

On 29 March 1991, shortly after the official cessation of hostilities, Baudrillard produced another essay, 'The Gulf War Has Not Taken Place', published in *Libération*. Considering what had happened in the interim it is remarkable indeed that Baudrillard found no reason to retract or significantly revise his original theses. Of course he acknowledges – albeit in passing – that this 'simulated' war has not been *entirely* a product of mass-media illusionist techniques; that large numbers of Iraqi conscripts and civilians had been killed by the Allied aerial bombardment; that massive damage had been inflicted on the country's urban infrastructure; that the so-called 'smart' or precision laser-guided bombs which figured so prominently in news coverage in fact made up a small fraction of the total Allied armoury, far outnumbered by the weapons of indiscriminate mass-destruction used against 'front-line' and other targets; that the US call for an internal insurrection that would 'finish the job' (i.e. put an end to Saddam's rule) and the subsequent failure to back that call with any measure of logistical or diplomatic support had created a catastrophe of appalling scale among the Kurdish and Shi'ite populations; that large areas of Kuwait had been laid waste by an Iraqi scorched-earth policy which the Western 'experts' had mostly discounted as an idle (because physically impossible) threat; and that US-Allied claims on a range of issues – from casualty figures to strategic interests, regional policy, aims for post-war 'reconstruction' etc – had been shown up as a propaganda package designed to head off domestic opposition.

All these points Baudrillard effectively concedes, along with several others (e.g. the extent and influence of media disinformation) which might seem to mark a decisive shift on the question of whether the war had indeed 'taken place'. But no: he sticks to his original position, declaring it a species of mass-hallucination, a 'virtual' engagement played out in the absence of anything that corresponded to a genuine 'war' as hitherto known or experienced. For this was a conflict where the massive imbalance of forces meant that the outcome was never in doubt; where the Allied and Iraqi strategies were so utterly disparate as to make comparisons (or talk of 'victory') beside the point; where the combatants occupied different worlds of time and space, different orders of 'reality' created – at least on the US side – by a hyperreal technology preventing any sense of direct, 'face-to-face' contact; where 'advance' and 'retreat' were meaningless terms, given the absence of any real terrain (as apart from the simulated war-game scenarios) by which to measure such claims; and where Saddam's 'defeat' turned out to be a mode of shrewdly timed strategic withdrawal, a move whose consequence (the deployment of his best-equipped troops against the Kurdish and Shi'ite internal opposition) amounted to a moral and political defeat for the Allies and their management of post-war public opinion. All of which Baudrillard takes as confirming his initial hypothesis: that this would be a fictive or fabulous war, a conflict of rival imaginary realms in which the stakes were unamenable to any analysis in real-world, rational, truth-seeking terms.

His essay concludes with the following remarks, aimed squarely at those readers who might be so naive as to think that his predictions had been somehow falsified by the event. 'In the case of this war', he writes,

> it is a matter of the vivid illustration of an implacable logic, one that renders us incapable of envisaging any other hypothesis save that of its real occurrence. The realist logic that lives off the illusion of a final outcome ... [For] the final solution of an equation as complex as a war is never to be found in the evidence of the war itself. It is a matter of grasping, without prophetic illusions, the logic of subsequently unfolding events. To be 'for' or 'against' the war is idiotic if one doesn't give a moment's thought to the probability of this war, its credibility, its realist credentials. All ideological or political speculations amount to a form of mental deterrence (stupidity). Through their immediate consensus on the evidence they heighten the unreality of this war, they reinforce the bluff by their unwitting readiness to be duped.
>
> The true belligerents are those who thrive on the ideology of the truth of this war, despite the fact that the war itself exerts its ravages on another level, through faking, through hyperreality, the simulacrum, through all those strategies of psychological deterrence that make play with facts and images, with the precession of the virtual over the real, of virtual time over real time, and the inexorable confusion between the two. If we have no practical knowledge of this war – and such knowledge is out of the question – then let us at least have the sceptical intelligence to reject the probability of all information, of all images whatever their source. To be more 'virtual' than the events themselves, not to reestablish some criterion of truth – for this we lack the means. But at least we can avoid being dupes and, to this end, reimmerse (*replonger*) all that information and the war itself into the element of virtuality from which they took rise. To turn deterrence back against itself. To be metereologically sensitive to stupidity in all its forms. (1991: my translation)

One could scarcely wish for a clearer statement of the moral and political nihilism that follows from Baudrillard's far-out sceptical stance on matters of truth and falsehood. Of course there is a need to question immediate appearances, to doubt what is proferred in the way of 'on-the-spot' evidence, and always to allow that the unfolding of subsequent events – like those in Kurdistan – may necessitate a large-scale adjustment in our view of what actually occurred (or was envisaged all along) behind the smokescreen of propaganda coverage. But we can only be in a position to make such judgments if we continue to seek out the best available sources of information, and moreover to interpret that evidence according to the standards of veridical utterance, of enlightened participant debate, and of ethico-political accountability. On Baudrillard's view these ideas are just a species of intellectual and moral 'stupidity', a failure to grasp that the Gulf War was unreal (or 'virtual') through and through, and that anyone thinking to discuss it in terms of truth *versus* falsehood – or reality *versus* 'ideological' illusion – is committing the greatest stupidity of all, one that plays straight into the hands of those with an interest in maintaining such delusive ontological distinctions. If there is any effective power of resistance then it will only come about – as he argues in *Fatal Strategies* – when 'the masses' evince such a total indifference to issues of media truth and falsehood that the whole apparatus of public-opinion management collapses into manifest nonsense (Baudrillard, 1989).

At this point notions like 'truth', 'ideology' and 'critique' will have lost their old power to hold the intellectuals in thrall, as well as their other, socially legitimizing function: that of convincing the populace at large that there *is* (must be) some ultimate reality behind appearances, and that truth will surely come to light in the long run, whatever the extent of current mass-media disinformation. For it is this belief – as Baudrillard sees it – that prevents 'the masses' (i.e. the captive TV viewers, tabloid readers, opinion-poll respondents etc) from perceiving the enormous confidence-trick that has been practised in the name of a liberal democracy where 'truth' is defined purely and simply according to current consensual norms. To this extent the Gulf War was merely an extravagant example of what has long been the case with regard to our reliance on information-sources with not the least semblance of 'authentic' truth-telling warrant. So the best – indeed the only – lesson to be learned from it is the need to exercise a 'sceptical intelligence' that refuses to be taken in *not* by 'appearances' (since appearances are all we have), but by the thought that there exists a truth 'behind' appearances, a level of rock-bottom factual appeal and ethical responsibility which may yet be invoked by investigative journalists, critical intellectuals, and others with a principled interest in exposing the extent of mass-media complicity. Such ideas made sense – as Baudrillard implicitly concedes – during that period when wars were conducted in the 'real' time and space of a battlefield encounter where talk of 'victory', of advance and retreat, of tactical superiority and so forth could at least be gauged against the evidence supplied by first-hand (or front-line) sources. But in the Gulf War no such standards could possibly apply since combatants, strategists, politicians, commentators, readers and viewers alike were all locked into a gigantic simulation-machine which programmed their every last thought and perception.

The result, in Baudrillard's sublimely offensive simile, is much like that of the air-burst bombs which the Americans deployed to such appalling effect against large concentrations of Iraqi soldiers and other (unspecified) targets. For the saturation coverage through channels like CNN had this much in common with the saturation bombing: that it produced, in his words,

> an unbearable atmosphere of deception and stupidity ... And if people were vaguely aware of having been caught up in this surfeit (*assouvissement*) and this illusory yet undeluding play of images, still they revelled in this deception and remained fascinated by the evident staging of this war, an effect with which [or

to which] we were innoculated by every means, through our eyes, through our senses, through discourse ... In the Gulf, no matter what (*rien de tel*), it was as if the outcome had been devoured in advance by a parasitic virus, the retro-virus of history. This is why one could offer the hypothesis that this war would not have taken place. And now that it is over, one can finally take account of its non-occurrence (*on peut enfin se rendre compte qu'elle n'a pas eu lieu*). (Baudrillard, 1991)

One is tempted to treat all this – in Dr. Johnson's phrase – as a piece of 'unresisting imbecility' to which it would be wasted effort to return any kind of rational rejoinder. But whatever their provocative or mischievous intent, Baudrillard's 'arguments' have generated widespread discussion and have been taken seriously by a sufficient number of commentators to require something more than a knock-down commonsensical riposte, like Johnson's celebrated kicking of the stone to 'refute' the claims of Berkeleian transcendental idealism. In fact this analogy is very much to the point since Berkeley's position has a good deal in common with Baudrillard's stance of thoroughgoing cognitive and epistemological scepticism. In both cases the most effective response is one that goes by way of that critical tradition whose first major spokesman was Kant, and whose later representatives (from Marx to Habermas) have sustained the project of enlightened *Ideologiekritik*, whatever their undoubted differences of view as regards the best means of so doing. One measure of postmodernism's retrograde stance – its intellectual and political bankruptcy – is the way that its proponents have either (like Lyotard) misread certain crucial passages in Kant, especially those concerning the sublime, or otherwise (like Baudrillard) consigned the whole legacy of critical-emancipatory thought to the dustbin of outworn 'Enlightenment' ideas. His Gulf War articles should be enough to settle any remaining doubts on that score.

## References

Baudrillard J. 1989: *Fatal strategies*. London: Pluto Press.
Baudrillard J. 1991: La guerre du Golfe n'a pas eu lieu. *Libération* (29 March).

# 15

## Ambivalent positionings: the Gulf War

*Marie Gillespie*

from *Television, ethnicity and cultural change* (Routledge 1995)

For Southall youth and their families, TV coverage of the Gulf War highlighted the contradiction of being addressed by the news media as part of the British nation, while at the same time the national status and loyalty to Britain of 'Asian immigrants' was being more insistently questioned than is usually the case in public discourse (for a fuller discussion than is possible here, see Gillespie, 1994). The outbreak of war precipitated an intensification of debate among young people in Southall about national, political, religious and ethnic allegiances. One of the most persistently surprising aspects of the discussions held by young people in the first weeks of the Gulf War was the constant shifting of categories used to describe the adversaries. The opponents on either side of the equation vary, as at various moments the war is seen to be a confrontation between the Middle East and America; Christians and Muslims; east and west; Arabs and Allies; blacks and whites. In their discussions young people experimented with a variety of positions, moving across and between these categories. Initially, however, attention focussed on the dramatic coverage of the 'precision bombing' and ambivalences were played down in favour of a more generally humanist approach. I shall begin by describing some of the more general responses to the war, and those which are age and gender related, before proceeding to an analysis of young people's experimentation with identities.

One of the most immediate and obvious effects of the outbreak of the Gulf War was the sudden change in personal and domestic routines. Many young people in Southall claimed that their families, like those elsewhere, were glued to their TV set during the first week of the war. Those who had cable TV (20 per cent of the survey sample) felt themselves to be especially privileged, since CNN's coverage of the war was considered far superior to that of the national news networks. But the sense of exhilaration that some derived from CNN's dramatic, live footage was countered by a pervasive feeling of nervousness. War provokes fear, especially fear of death. The initial Allied attacks led to anxieties that the war might spread to Britain, even to Southall. Some, usually younger teenagers such as this 15-year-old Muslim boy, seemed confused as to whether it was a nuclear war:

*Adnam*: They're not only destroying a country but also the world, all of them, all these nuclear war planes that they're hitting is, in the end, going to destroy

the world. It's frightening, I don't want to die young! In the end they're probably going to destroy everyone ... sometimes I have a feeling that I'm going to
die cos it's just possible that they shoot something over here or in the middle
of the core of the earth and they might just destroy us all.

Adnam's apocalyptic vision rather dramatically expresses the more general
sense of fear and uncertainty about the possible consequences of the war
that were prevalent among many of the younger teenagers in its first week.
Anxieties about growing up in a world already 'spoilt' by adults were frequently expressed: 'We're young and we have open minds, older people
tend to have tunnel vision and have fixed ideas and this leads to conflict ...'
(Kirit). Empathy was most clearly aroused when the victims of war were
perceived as family members. Indeed, it is as if the poignancy of the human
casualties of war is only fully appreciated with reference to family tragedies.
The irreparable and enduring consequences of the war, especially in breeding hatred in the world, were often discussed in an emotionally charged
atmosphere during school breaks, especially by girls. Sameera, a 16-year-old
Muslim, said:

Those people out there who are dying, they are ordinary people, like us, they
are mothers and fathers, sons and daughters, you feel for them whether they're
Muslims or Christians, black or white, I mean, they're all human beings.

However, several weeks later, a widespread shift in attitude was apparent.
The war had become 'boring'. Some complained that some of their favourite
programmes, like *Home and Away* and *'Allo 'Allo*, had been cut in favour of
war coverage. Others felt that the TV coverage was excessive and that the
war was dominating their lives at home and at school. However, the language of war remained as a new set of military terms and idioms was
acquired, undoubtedly encouraged by the tabloid press, and put to use in
everyday talk. For example, one girl, suffering from an outbreak of acne,
was approached by a boy who jibed, 'That's a pretty bad Scud attack on
your face.' She slapped his. Young people also became familiar with a new
cast of political, military and journalistic characters who they could exploit
for the purposes of insult. Gulf jokes, from the sick to the silly, began to circulate and humour became a common way of dealing with war, especially
among boys. Some enjoyed pointing out ironies in the situation, in this case
incidentally implying a disidentification with the British nation: 'Britain
built all these bunkers for Iraq and now [laughs] the silly bastards can't even
blow up their own bunkers.' Such casual and lighthearted talk was typical
of the very competitive style of interaction among some boys for whom
scoring a point or 'having a laugh' in an all-male peer context takes precedence or who would be seriously challenged by any deeper or more serious
discussion of the issues.

Clear gender differences emerged in perceptions of news coverage and in
patterns of identification with the military and journalists. The parallels
which have been pointed out by many cultural critics, between the TV representation of the Gulf War (and other recent wars) and the imagery of video
games appear to have played a role in these gendered responses. TV viewers
consume close-up images of distant wars in the security of their homes.
Responses to the outbreak of the war and its imagery reveal a shifting sense

of involvement and detachment, proximity and distance, threat and security. In an essay on the Falklands War, Williams (1989) refers to the 'culture of distance' which TV has helped to create. He argues that very precise images of 'wars of distance' are already built into contemporary audio-visual culture and that these serve to blunt our perceptions and sensibilities:

> In every games arcade we can press buttons and see conventionally destructive flashes on targets . . . What difference is represented when the flash of a hit can be remembered to contain and to be destroying a man? [The pervasiveness of such imagery] may already, in many minds, have blurred the difference between the exercise and the actuality, between the rehearsal and the act . . . for it is one of the corroding indulgences of the culture of distance that to the spectator the effect, at least, offers to be the same. (1989: 16)

That the media contribute to a desensitising of our responses to human tragedy, or compassion fatigue, has long been argued by media effects researchers. Such arguments need to be treated with some caution, as does any implication that viewers somehow confuse or cannot distinguish between a real, televised war and a video-game war. However, it seems that at times a blurring of the difference certainly occurred, especially among boys, for whom playing video games is a daily activity. Thus Williams's argument needs gendering. The seductiveness of the imagery of this techno-war was clearly apparent among boys, many of whom expressed a fascination with war technology – a fascination which boys' comics and action-packed war videos, as well as games, have partly created and heavily exploit.

During the first week of the war, it was quite common to hear some boys engaged in an enthusiastic debate about the relative merits of Scuds and Patriots and the thrilling nature of 'precision' bombing. In reply to a comment that the war was getting boring one boy retorted: 'No way man, the war's all right, all right as long as the blowing up and killing goes on!' This kind of 'gung-ho' remark was more common among the disaffected 'dossers', or 'low achievers' of the school who would not, or could not, debate the war at a more sophisticated level. It was also an attempt to shock and attract attention in the presence of peers and of myself – perhaps more a product of rivalry among boys wishing to present a 'hard' image than genuine insensitivity to the casualties of war. Yet many boys did become intrigued by the images of 'spectacular destruction'. For example, Perminder complained that she had not seen her boyfriend since the outbreak of the war:

> He doesn't come to school any more, he just stays at home, glued to the set, and his mates go round and they sit there all day waiting for another Scud missile attack. I think there's something gross about that myself . . . and now all he talks about when he phones is Scud missiles, interceptors and all that. I don't know what he's going on about half the time.

Certainly teenage boys in Southall, socialised into a video culture of macho heroics (Sylvester Stallone, Arnold Schwarzenegger and Co.) consume many more war-based videos and video games than girls. Boys display their fascination with images of war, violence and aggression and appear to find warfare far more compelling and fascinating than girls. Several girls criticised boys for treating the war like a video game: 'It's just like a film but we know this is real. In films war is glorified but here it's not . . . some of the boys treat it as if it's just a video game, they don't seem to care.' As many young people pointed out, it was easy in the early days of the war to ignore its human casualties since the visual emphasis in news reports was on the military technology. Gita exclaimed:

> All you see are Scud missiles flying around in the sky and interceptors colliding in space – it's like *Star Wars*. You never see anyone being killed, just buildings being destroyed, it's as if this was a war without human beings.

Further gender differences emerged in the patterns of identification. Nobody identified with 'war leaders'. Boys tended to identify most with the pilots who acquired heroic status, expressing sympathy with them because of the dangers they faced. The most compelling TV interviews were considered to be those with pilots returning from sorties, still flushed with excitement and fear, who talked openly about the air attacks. Their accounts of the war were seen to be more authentic than any others. For girls, the point of identification was the TV journalist Kate Adie. She was admired as a heroine, a 'woman at war', willing to brave danger so that the viewers 'back home' could be informed.

> *Gurinder*: I think Kate Adie's great, she's stuck there in that army hut. It must be rough for her but I think she's a really good reporter . . . she seems to get to the bottom of what's going on . . . . I bet a lot of the soldiers fancy her in her camouflage uniform [giggles].

The nurses were a further point of identification for many girls:

> *Kerenpaul*: Humara keeps saying that she wants to go there as a nurse and we tease her that she only wants to go for all the dishy soldiers . . . . I would go, not for the soldiers [laughs] but to help people. I would, I really would like to go . . . if anything watching the Gulf War has shown me that being a soldier is not glamorous or fun, it's a job in which people get paid to kill others.

These gendered points of identification with protagonists in the war as televisual spectacle, linking to other points of identification in audiovisual culture (video war games and war videos for boys, women TV reporters and hospital dramas for girls), suggest efforts to deal with the disruptive and anxiety-provoking nature of the war or its coverage, by resorting to already familiar genres. But, at least for more reflective individuals, these strategies could only momentarily suppress awareness of the political complexities of the war, and of the ways in which they were personally implicated in these complexities, as citizens of Britain whose 'Britishness' is only one facet of their cultural identity. It is time to turn to young people's criticisms of the war coverage, their concerns about the local effects of the war, and the contradictory and ambivalent positions which they experimented with in relation to national and cultural identity, in the course of discussions about the war.

Clearly, to follow the war news in any detail required a degree of competence and motivation, which some young people simply did not possess. It was noticeable that in the sixth-form common room, where much of this data was gathered, the most serious and extended discussions of the war and its coverage took place among A-level students who very consciously brought their subject knowledge, notably of history, economics and English literature, to bear on discussions. Far from taking an uncritical view of TV's coverage of the war, most young people seem to adhere to a conspiracy theory of the media. The most common refrain was that the news is biased: 'It only shows you one side of the story, it makes out that everything that the Allies do is right!' The news coverage of the Gulf was seen as little more than propaganda:

> *Pritpal*: A lot of my friends they just believe what they see in the news but if you didn't question the news it could brainwash you, I mean how do we really know what's going on? How do we know that the government isn't misleading us? . . . They said that the Allied attacks had 80 per cent 'success rate', now they're saying that 80 per cent 'found their target' but didn't necessarily bomb them, so that's the news misleading people innit?

Others commented upon the prevalence of images of bloodsoaked Israeli casualties and the absence of images of Iraqi casualties; the abundance of images of 'successful' Allied attacks and absence of 'successful' Iraqi attacks; the time and space given to justifying the Allied intervention as legitimate and lack of attention given to Saddam Hussein's point of view; the portrayal of American war leaders as heroes and of Saddam Hussein as a villain, 'a Hitler', 'The Butcher of Baghdad' – labels circulated by the tabloid press.

> *Hersh*: I limit myself to news about the war because I know there's a lot of propaganda and that it's not really truthful . . . for example, I heard that the Ministry of Defence has issued a 32-point plan for censoring news.

Most young people realised that the war was censored on both sides and that TV's coverage of the war was selective, biased and partial. But this was necessary, they variously argued, for the sake of national security; to keep up public morale; to sell newspapers and fill air time; to avoid a public backlash by those who have relatives risking their lives and fighting out there; and to reinforce public opinion that the Allies are right. The old cliché – truth is the first casualty of war – was reiterated by many. Most realised that truth is filtered and as Kashif stated: 'News, like a poem, has to be interpreted.'

Critical distance is also apparent in comments about the portrayal of the Iraqi people:

> *Jagdeep*: It's as if the ordinary Iraqi people have no dignity, they are not given the dignity of human beings and that's not right, that makes me feel sad because it's as if their lives are worth nothing but the life of one British soldier is precious.

Those – a minority – who gave their full support to the Allies were seen to have derived all their views, exclusively, from the media. Having no alternative source of information, they were regarded as victims of propaganda:

> *Abjinder*: [Among my friends] the ones who think America are right are the ones who've been watching the news and taken it for granted, they've taken all their views from there and been influenced by it quite a lot so they're not really thinking for themselves and they haven't got any other news or views to compare it with, they just soak up the propaganda.

The economic as well as the human consequences of war were discussed, not simply in terms of the rise in the price of petrol, but also in terms of local employment. As Heathrow Airport is one of the main local employers, within a month of the outbreak of war, hundreds of parents were made redundant or had their hours reduced due to restrictions on air travel. Security at the airport tightened dramatically and parents brought home news about armed police on patrol; fears of terrorist attacks at the airport, and elsewhere, were rife, and many young people expressed fears about their parents' safety. Clearly, the local repercussions of such a devasting global event also serve to mediate responses to the war and its representations, bringing it closer to home and reminding young people of the interdependence of the local and global spheres.

The war provoked a heightened sense of vulnerability to racist attack and awareness of the threats posed to young people's religious identity, as well as their ambivalent nationality and citizenship status. Many young Muslims were deeply worried about the effects of the war on their religion and its possible consequences for themselves. News of the summary deportation of a number of Muslims from Britain led to fears that they, too, might be deported. The imminence of Ramadan, a forty-day period of fasting from sunrise to sunset, was another focus of concern:

> *Adil*: This war is going to badly affect my religion, soon it will be Ramadan and there should be peace – Muslims are taught that we shouldn't fight one another – it says so in the Koran – they shouldn't be fighting.

Some were distressed that the war would violate the sanctity of Mecca, the most sacred place of worship for Muslims worldwide. It would, some argued, prevent Muslims from performing the *haj*, the pilgrimage to Mecca which all Muslims are expected to make in the course of their lifetime. Others worried about the presence of 'Christian' soldiers in Mecca and the likelihood of their eating pork and drinking alcohol, which are strictly forbidden by the Koran.

Differences between parental and peer viewpoints were also most intense for young Muslims, who often expressed the need to find a delicate balance between the two, though rarely so poignantly as did Kashif:

> For me the war is a conflicting factor. I come to school and the Gulf War is somewhere and then I go home and its different. My mother she sees the war on TV and she tells me I should even go and fight if need be . . . . She is on Saddam Hussein's side, like she preaches that Islam is behind Saddam Hussein and she is behind Islam. It's like here [school] I almost live in both worlds, here, it's like 'our side' and then I go home and and it's like 'Saddam Hussein is Nawab' [prince] and stuff. At home I have to keep the family order so I can't exactly have opposing views to my parents, like showing them opposing views and when I go to a highly English area, I have to keep social order, you know, whatever the public view is, you might have your own views but you can't express them as well. I might say I'm for Saddam Hussein and then 4,000 English people will come down on me . . .

Kashif is clear on the nature of the contradictions experienced by many of his Muslim peers:

> The news talks about the anger of British Muslims and their loyalty to Islam but what is a British Muslim? Is he more British or more Muslim? You can't exactly

have an equal choice of both, it's difficult to say but I think I'm more western-ised, I wouldn't say I'm British because we're in two societies at the same time, one is Islamic society, but not to the true extent, and the other is westernised society, but bearing away from it. If you look at the small things in these soci-eties they are totally different, like your behaviour, your duties and your role in the family.

Kashif is both 'westernised' and Muslim in varying degrees in different situations. He shifts his position according to context in order, as he says, to keep both the family order, based upon Islam, and the social order, based upon western views. Trying to cope with the variety of roles he has to play and the expectations demanded of him is assisted by the distinction he makes between his public and private selves. In front of his father he will confirm his role as a 'pure Muslim' in order to avoid conflict and resent-ment. Similarly, at school he finds that he takes the Allies' side: 'Like here when I say "we" I mean the Allies but at home I say "them".' This shifting of positions according to different contexts is commonplace; indeed, the ability to deal with contradiction, ambivalence and ambiguity pragmatically, while as far as possible remaining true to oneself inwardly, is seen to be a sign of maturity. In Southall, this type of skill is another facet of the adulthood asso-ciated with understanding news. Kashif accepted that his strategy was nec-essary to 'keep the peace' and 'social order'.

Many young Muslims questioned the legitimacy of the war and the justi-fications for the Allied interventions given in the British news media: 'Kuwait stole Iraqi oil during the Iran/Iraq war and so they owed Saddam Hussein money which he was entitled to.' Similarly, although few young Muslims actively support Saddam Hussein, they try to understand his point of view. Some held him in some esteem for standing up to the powerful forces of the west which are seen to dominate the world. Farida: 'In a way Saddam Hussein has already won the war – he has done the impossible, he has stood up to the west and in most Arabs' eyes that means he has won!'

A further set of opposed standpoints is derived from parents' views of the war, which are premised on sharp distinctions drawn between the East and the West, and often reflect their allegiances within Indian subcontinental politics. Navdeep, a 17-year-old Sikh boy:

I get quite a lot from my parents . . . they have lived through past experiences and they know for a fact that there is a divide between East and West, so when we listen to them we get their image as well, so we think within that frame as well and I believe that they've gone there just to show western superiority . . . .

It is partly through news viewing in the family that young people gain insight into their parents' political views, since this is a context in which political opinions are often expressed. Nirmal, an 18-year-old Hindu boy:

My dad overreacts to everything on the news, especially Indian politics . . . he keeps going on that the British are making all this propaganda about Russia cos, you know, India is an ally of Russia.

Indian subcontinental politics is relevant to many parents', and therefore also young people's, views. During the Cold War India was seen to be an ally of Russia, in contrast to Pakistan which received American support. Thus young Hindus and Sikhs claimed that parents of Indian background tended to have an anti-American stance already, which made it easy for them to be critical of the Allies. Anti-American views of course do not coincide at all with the dominant accounts of the conflict circulated by the British media which supported and justified the Allied attacks. As Shelley, an 18-year-old Hindu boy, explained:

> Our dads are anti-American because of the way they dominate the world and think they own the world. They think they are the world's policeman . . . they have their own theories about why America is involved in the Middle East and like in the Pakistan–Indian border dispute, America is supplying Pakistan with weapons, they seem to have a lot of proof so they believe it . . . they say the Americans are evil . . . watching the news with my dad, it's a one-way slag off of America.

It is not surprising, then, that many young people in Southall take a critical approach to the western media's portrayal of the war. Their parents' past experiences of colonialism and the struggle for independence, followed by migration and settlement in Britain, have sensitised them politically in ways which differ markedly from the average member of the British public. The argument, prevalent in the media at the time of the Gulf War, that the American presence in the Middle East is justified as an act of retaliation against Iraq's violation of the UN agreement and in order to protect the human rights of Kuwaitis, was given short shrift by many, such as this 16-year-old Hindu boy:

> *Hersh*: They [the Americans] don't really care about the people or the human rights, there were no human rights in Kuwait or Saudi Arabia, Saudi Arabia has been condemned by Amnesty International for torture and in Kuwait only 7 per cent of the population have been allowed to vote . . . . I think they should have human rights and that those people should not be killed because they happen to live in a certain country.

The notion of human rights returns repeatedly in discussions: this is doubtless connected with the fact that at age fifteen all these students study the topic of human rights in their Humanities lessons. Thus a conception of human rights combined with a widespread condemnation of war, *per se*, was the basic stance adopted by most young people. This also fed into their views on the 'racial' and racist dimensions of the conflict.

Many young people in Southall felt threatened by the rise in racist attacks in Britain and in America which accompanied the war. As Anopama, a 16-year-old Sikh girl exclaimed:

> It's not just Muslims that are being attacked! Did you hear that Sikhs were attacked in Chicago, Sikhs were attacked! Sikhs were threatened because people thought they were Iraqis, we're all Pakis as far as some people are concerned.

It was felt that the war itself could be seen as a 'race war', and the consequent sense of vulnerability – though more pronounced among parents than young people – emerges clearly in the following exchange among a group of Sikh and Hindu girls:

> *Anopama*: Doesn't this Iraqi war seem like a 'race' war? [chorus of 'Yeah!'] It's like two different races fighting against each other but America just doesn't want to admit it, they cover it up.

*Reena*: What if there's a huge backlash here?

*Anopama*: If the war started here where would we fit in? We call ourselves British . . .

*Reena*: No one cares if we're British or about where we come from, we're just all coloured.

*Herjinder*: We're not British and we're not Indian, if you went to live in India you wouldn't fit in there.

*Anopama*: We can't fit in, we can't, if I'm here I'm a Paki and there I'm a *gora* [white person] in my jeans, innit?

*Herjinder*: We can't think their way, there are a lot of differences between east and west.

*Anopama*: We can take the best of both worlds but if there was a rift between India and England where would we fit in?

*Reena*: We think west laws here in school and we go home and they inflict east laws on us there.

*Anopama*: When Saddam Hussein calls for a holy war where does that leave us Sikhs and Hindus?

The heightened sense of vulnerability and insecurity that the Gulf War provoked is revealing of deeper ambiguities concerning definitions of self in relation to significant 'others'. The fact of being addressed by the news media as a member of the British public was severely undermined by the rise in racist attacks around Britain and the widespread questioning of Muslims' loyalty to Britain and to the Allies during the war. The war coverage heightened young people's awareness of how they are perceived by 'others', members of the British public in particular; and this in turn generated debate about the vulnerability of their position in Britain, and about the difficulties of 'fitting in' both 'here' and 'there' – in India and in Britain, at school and at home.

The Gulf War and other international, national and local news events, mediated by multiple, culturally diverse information channels, impinge in various ways on life in Southall. The debates precipitated by such news events – or rather, by such plural news coverages and the diverse interpretations of them – prompt teenagers to become acutely conscious of the diversity of positions they are obliged, invited or able to choose to take up, in varying contexts, as members of internally diverse diaspora 'communities' and as British citizens. They find themselves constantly needing to ask 'Who am I?', 'Where do I speak from?' and 'Who is speaking on my behalf?' as well as 'Who is speaking to me?', and they answer these questions differently, and often ambivalently, in different circumstances. The skills involved in negotiating these questions of identity from context to context are learned in the process of graduation from child to adult status in the eyes of families and peers; and this process is accelerated when, in response to dramatic public events, young people are (or feel) called upon to take up explicit positions as if to resolve ambiguities and ambivalences, which, however, remain. Of all events, war most powerfully insists on a thinking in terms of stark binary oppositions – us and them, friend and foe. Such terms reveal themselves as woefully inadequate to the complexities of these young people's sense of hybrid national and cultural identity.

# References

Gillespie M. 1994: The gulf between US: Punjabi Londoners, television and Gulf War. *Indo-British Review.*
Williams R. 1989: *Raymond Williams on television. Selected writings*, ed. A. O'Connor. London and New York: Routledge.

# 16

## *Beavis and Butt-Head*: no future for post-modern youth

*Douglas Kellner*

From *Media culture* (Routledge 1995)

Animated cartoon characters Beavis and Butt-Head sit in a shabby house much of the day, watching television, especially music videos, which they criticize in terms of whether the videos are 'cool' or 'suck.' When they leave the house to go to school, to work in a fast food joint, or to seek adventure, they often engage in destructive and even criminal behavior. Developed for MTV by animated cartoonist Mike Judge, the series spoofs precisely the sort of music videos played by the music television channel.[1] *Beavis and Butt-Head* quickly became a cult favorite, loved by youth, yet elicited spirited controversy when some young fans of the show imitated typical Beavis and Butt-Head activity, burning down houses, and torturing and killing animals.[2]

The series provides a critical vision of the current generation of youth raised primarily on media culture. This generation was possibly conceived in the sights and sounds of media culture, weaned on it, and socialized by the glass teat of television used as pacifier, baby sitter, and educator by a generation of parents for whom media culture, especially television, was a natural background and constitutive part of everyday life. The show depicts the dissolution of a rational subject and perhaps the end of the Enlightenment in today's media culture. Beavis and Butt-Head react viscerally to the videos, snickering at the images, finding representations of violence and sex 'cool,' while anything complex which requires interpretation 'sucks.' Bereft of any cultivated taste, judgment, or rationality, and without ethical or political values, the characters react in a literally mindless fashion and appear to lack almost all cognitive and communicative skills.

The intense alienation of Beavis and Butt-Head, their love for heavy metal culture and media images of sex and violence, and their violent cartoon activity soon elicited heated controversy, producing a 'Beavis and Butt-Head' effect that has elicited literally thousands of articles and heated debates, even leading to U.S. Senate condemnations of the show for promoting mindless violence and stupid behavior.[3] From the beginning, there was intense media focus on the show and strongly opposed opinions of it. In a cover story on the show, *Rolling Stone* declared them 'The Voice of a New Generation' (August 19, 1993) and *Newsweek* also put them on its cover, both praising them and damning them by concluding: 'The downward spiral of the living white male surely ends here: in a little pimple named Butthead whose idea of an idea is, "Hey, Beavis, let's go over to Stuart's house and light one in his cat's butt"' (October 11, 1993). 'Stupid, lazy, cruel; without ambitions, without values, without futures' are other terms used in the media to describe the characters and the series (*The Dallas Morning News*, August 29, 1993) and there have been countless calls to ban the show.

Indeed, a lottery prize winner in California began a crusade against the series, after hearing about a cat that was killed when kids put a firecracker in its mouth, imitating Beavis and Butt-Head's violence against animals and a suggestion in one episode that they stick a firecracker in a neighbor boy's cat (*The Hollywood Reporter*, July 16, 1993). Librarians in Westchester, New York ranked *Beavis and Butt-Head* high 'on a list of movies and television shows that they think negatively influence youngsters' reading habits,' because of their attacks on books and frequent remarks that books, or even words, 'suck' (*The New York Times*, July 11, 1993). Prison officials in Oklahoma banned the show, schools in South Dakota banned clothing and other items bearing their likeness (*Times Newspapers Limited*, October 11, 1993), and a group of Missouri fourth graders started a petition drive to get the program off the air (*Radio TV Reports*, October 25, 1993).

Yet the series continued to be highly popular into 1994, and it has spawned a best-selling album of heavy metal rock, a popular book, countless consumer items, and movie contracts in the works. *Time* magazine critic, Kurt Anderson, praised the series as 'the bravest show ever run on national television' (*The New York Times*, July 11, 1993) and there is no question but that it has pushed the boundaries of the permissible on mainstream television to new extremes (some critics would say to new lows).

In a certain sense, *Beavis and Butt-Head* is 'postmodern' in that it is purely a product of media culture, with its characters, style, and content almost solely derivative from previous TV shows. The two characters Beavis and Butt-Head are a spin-off of Wayne and Garth in *Wayne's World*, a popular *Saturday Nite Live* feature, spun off into popular movies. They also resemble the SCTV characters Bob and Doug McKenzie, who sit around on a couch and make lewd and crude remarks while they watch TV and drink beer. Beavis and Butt-Head also take the asocial behavior of cartoon character Bart Simpson to a more intense extreme. Their comments on the music videos replicate the popular Comedy Central Channel's series *Mystery Science Theater 3000*, which features two cartoon stick figures making irreverent comments on god-awful old Hollywood movies and network television shows. And, of course, the music videos are a direct replication of MTV's basic fare.

*Beavis and Butt-Head* is interesting for a diagnostic critique because the main characters get all of their ideas and images concerning life from the media and their entire view of history and the world is entirely derived from media culture. When they see a costumed rapper wearing an eighteenth-century-style white wig on a music video, Butt-Head remarks: 'He's dressed up like that dude on the dollar.' The 1960s is the time of hippies, Woodstock and rock 'n' roll for them; Vietnam is ancient history, collapsed into other American wars. Even the 1950s is nothing but a series of mangled media cliches: on Nelson, the twins of 1950s teen idol Ricky Nelson, Butt-Head remarks that: 'These chicks look like guys.' Beavis responds: 'I heard that these chicks' grandpa was Ozzy Osbourne.' And Butt-Head rejoins: 'No way. They're Elvis's kids.'

The figures of history are collapsed for Beavis and Butt-Head into media culture and provide material for salacious jokes, which require detailed knowledge of media culture:

> *Butt-Head*: What happened when Napoleon went to Mount Olive?
>
> *Beavis*: I don't know. What?
>
> *Butt-Head*: Pop-Eye got pissed.

Moreover, Beavis and Butt-Head seem to have no family, living alone in a shabby house, getting enculturated solely by television and media culture. There are some references to their mothers and in one episode there is a suggestion that Butt-Head is not even certain who his father is, thus the series presents a world without fathers.[4] School is totally alienating for the two, as is work in a fast-food restaurant. Adult figures who they encounter are largely white conservative males, or liberal yuppies, with whom they come into often violent conflict and whose property or goods they inevitably destroy.

There is a fantasy wish-fulfillment aspect to *Beavis and Butt-Head* that perhaps helps account for its popularity: kids often wish that they had no parents and that they could just sit and watch music videos and go out and do whatever they wanted to (sometimes we *all* feel this way). Kids are also naturally disrespectful of authority and love to see defiance of social forces that they find oppressive. Indeed, Beavis and Butt-Head's much maligned, discussed, and imitated laughter ('Heh, heh, heh' and 'Huh, huh') may signify that in their space *they rule*, that Beavis and Butt-Head are sovereign, that they control the television and can do any damn thing that they want. Notably, they get in trouble in school and other sites of authority with their laugh, but at home they can laugh and snicker to the max.

And so the series has a utopian dimension: the utopia of no parental authority and unlimited freedom to do whatever they want when they want to. 'Dude, we're there' is a favorite phrase they use when they decide to see or do something – and they never have to ask their (absent) parents' permission. On the other hand, they represent the consequences of totally unsocialized adolescent behavior driven by aggressive instincts.[5] Indeed, their 'utopia' is highly solipsistic and narcissistic with no community, no consensual norms or morality to bind them, and no concern for other people. The vision of the teenagers alone in their house watching TV and then wreaking havoc on their neighborhood presents a vision of a society of broken families, disintegrating communities, and anomic individuals, without values or goals.

Beavis and Butt-Head are thus left alone with TV and become couch-potato critics, especially of their beloved music videos. In a sense, they are the first media critics to become cult heros of media culture, though there are contradictions in their media criticism. Many of the videos that they attack are stupid and pretentious, and in general it is good to cultivate a critical attitude toward culture forms and to promote cultural criticism – an attitude that can indeed be applied to much of what appears on *Beavis and*

*Butt-Head.* Such critique distances its audience from music video culture and calls for making critical judgments on its products. Yet Beavis and Butt-Head's own judgments are highly questionable, praising images of violence, fire, naked women, and heavy metal noise, while declaring that 'college music,' words, and any complexity in the videos 'suck.'

Thus, on one level, the series provides sharp social satire and critique of the culture and society. The episodes constantly make fun of television, especially music videos, and other forms of media culture. They criticize conservative authority figures and wishy-washy liberals. They satirize authoritarian institutions like the workplace, schools, and military recruitment centers and provide critical commentary on many features of contemporary life. Yet, the series undercuts some of its social critique by reproducing the worst sexist, violent, and narcissistic elements of contemporary life, which are made amusing and even likeable in the figures of Beavis and Butt-Head.

Consequently, *Beavis and Butt-Head* is surprisingly complex and requires a diagnostic critique to analyze its contradictory text and effects. There is no denying, however, that the *Beavis and Butt-Head* effect is one of the most significant media phenomena of recent years.[6] Like Linklater, Judge has obviously tapped into a highly responsive chord and created a media sensation with the characters of Beavis and Butt-Head serving as powerfully resonant images. In 1993, while lecturing on cultural studies, wherever I would go audiences would ask me what I thought of *Beavis and Butt-Head* and so I eventually began to watch it and to incorporate remarks on the series into my lectures.[7] If I was critical or disparaging, young members of the audience would attack me and after a lecture at the University of Kansas, a young man came up, incredulous that I would dare to criticize the series, certain that Mike Judge was a great genius who understood exactly how it was for contemporary youth, with no prospects for a job or career, and little prospect for even marriage and family and a meaningful life. In this situation, I was told, what else can young people do except watch MTV and occasionally go out and destroy something?

In a sense, the series thus enacts youth and class revenge against older, middle-class and conservative adults, who appear as oppressive authority figures. Their neighbor Tom Anderson – depicted as a conservative World War II and Korean war veteran – is a special butt of their escapades and they cut down trees in his yard with a chain saw, which, of course, causes the tree to demolish his house, assorted fences, power lines, and cars. They put his dog in a laundro-mat washing machine to clean it; they steal his credit card to buy animals at the mall; they lob mud baseballs into his yard, one of which hits his barbecue; and otherwise torment him. Beavis and Butt-Head also blow up an Army recruiting station with a grenade, as the officer attempts to recruit them; they steal the cart of a wealthy man, Billy Bob, who has a heart attack when he sees them riding off in his vehicle; and they love to put worms, rats, and other animals in the fast food that they are shown giving to obnoxious white male customers in the burger joint where they work.

Beavis and Butt-Head also love to trash the house of their 'friend' Stewart whose yuppie parents indulgently pamper their son and his playmates.

Stewart's permissive liberal parents are shown to be silly and ineffectual, as when his father complains that Stewart violated his parents' trust when he let Beavis and Butt-Head in the house after they caused an explosion which blew the wall out. The mother gushes about how cute they are and offers them lemonade – in fact, few women authority figures are depicted.

The dynamic duo also torment and make fun of their liberal hippie teacher, Mr Van Driessen, who tries to teach them to be politically correct. They destroy his irreplaceable eight-track music collection when he offers to let them clean his house to learn the value of work and money. When he takes them camping to get in touch with their feelings and nature, they fight and torment animals. In fact, they rebel against all their teachers and authority figures and are thus presented in opposition to everyone, ranging from conservative males, to liberal yuppies, to hippie radicals.

Moreover, the series presents the revenge of youth and those who are terminally downwardly mobile against more privileged classes and individuals. Like the punk generation before them, Beavis and Butt-Head have no future. Thus, while their behavior is undeniably juvenile, offensive, sexist, and politically incorrect, it allows diagnosis of underclass and downwardly mobile youth who have nothing to do, but to destroy things and engage in asocial behavior.

From this perspective, *Beavis and Butt-Head* is an example of media culture as popular revenge:[8] Beavis and Butt-Head avenge youth and the downwardly mobile against those oppressive authority figures who they confront daily. Most of the conservative men have vaguely Texan, or Southwestern, accents, so perhaps the male authority figures represent oppressive males experienced by Judge in his own youth in San Diego, New Mexico and Texas. Moreover, Beavis and Butt-Head's violence is that of a violent society in which the media present endless images of the sort of violent activities that the two characters regularly engage in. The series thus points to the existence of a large teenage underclass with no future which is undereducated and potentially violent. The young underclass Beavis and Butt-Heads of the society have nothing to look forward to in life save a job at the local 7-Eleven, waiting to get held up at gunpoint. Consequently, the series is a social hieroglyphic which allows us to decode the attitudes, behavior, and situation of large segments of youth in contemporary U.S. society.

For a diagnostic critique, then, it is wrong to simply excuse the antics of Beavis and Butt-Head as typical behavior of the young. Likewise, it is not enough simply to condemn them as pathological.[9] Rather the series reveals how violent society is becoming and the dead-end futures of downwardly mobile youth from broken homes who are undereducated and have no real job possibilities or future. Indeed, the heavy metal culture in which Beavis and Butt-Head immerse themselves is a way for those caught up in dead-end lives to blot everything out, to escape in a world of pure noise and aggression, and in turn to express their own aggression and frustrations through heavy metal 'head-banging.' Thus, when Beavis and Butt-Head play the 'air guitar,' imitating heavy metal playing during the music videos, they are signalling both their aggression and the hopelessness of their situation.

Beavis and Butt-Head's narcissism and sociopathic behavior is a symptom of a society that is not providing adequate nurture or support to its citizens.

It is indeed curious that many of the most popular media culture figures could easily be clinically diagnosed and analyzed as narcissistic: Rush Limbaugh, Andrew Dice Clay, Howard Stern, and other popular media figures are examples of empty, insecure, and hostile individuals who resort to extreme behavior and assertions to call attention to themselves. In turn, they tap into audience aggression and frustrations and become popular precisely because of their ability to articulate inchoate social anger. Indeed, compared to a Rush Limbaugh, Beavis and Butt-Head are relatively modest and restrained in their narcissism.

Beavis and Butt-Head, Rush Limbaugh, and other figures of contemporary U.S. media culture also think they know things, but are know-nothings in the good old tradition of American anti-intellectualism. These figures are basically buffoons, sometimes entertaining and often offensive, who in the classical syndrome of narcissism are empty, insecure, and aggressive. They masquerade their emptiness and insecurity in verbal bravado and aggressiveness and attention-seeking action. They also display classic symptoms of fear of women, who they continually objectify, and engage in puerile and infantile sexual jokes and gesture. Beavis and Butt-Head are classic teenagers whose hormones are out of control and who cannot control them, and their elders like Howard Stern and Andrew Dice Clay exhibit similar symptoms. These figures of popular entertainment are all white boys, incapable of taking the position of the other, of empathizing with the other, or of respecting differences. They are all extremely homophobic, though Beavis and Butt-Head are obviously repressing homosexual proclivities signalled in all the 'butt' jokes, 'suck' references, and Butt-Head's injunction: 'Hey, Beavis pull my finger.'

In a sense, *Beavis and Butt-Head* is an example of what has been called 'loser television,' surely a new phenomenon in television history. Previous television series tended to depict wealthy, or secure middle-class, individuals and families, often with highly glamorous lives. It was believed that advertisers preferred affluent environments to sell their products and so the working class and underclass were excluded from network television for decades. Indeed, during the Reaganite 1980s, programs like *Dallas*, *Dynasty*, and *Life Styles of the Rich and Famous* celebrated wealth and affluence. This dream has been punctured by the reality of everyday life in a downsliding economy, and so a large television audience is attracted to programs that articulate their own frustration and anger in experiencing downward mobility and a sense of no future. Hence, the popularity of new 'loser television,' including *The Simpsons, Roseanne,* and *Beavis and Butt-Head*.

Thus, the MTV show *Beavis and Butt-Head* allows a diagnostic critique of the plight of contemporary youth in disintegrating families, with little education, and with no job possibilities. Beavis and Butt-Head's destructiveness can be seen in part as an expression of their hopelessness and alienation and shows the dead-end prospects for many working-class and middle-class youths. Moreover, the series also replicates the sort of violence that is so widespread in the media from heavy metal rock videos to TV entertainment and news. Thus, the characters' violence simply mirrors growing youth violence in a disintegrating society and allows the possibility of a diagnostic critique of the social situation of contemporary youth.

Yet the show *is* highly violent and has already had spectacular violence effects. In the *Liquid Television* animated short that preceded the series, Judge shows Beavis and Butt-Head playing 'frog baseball,' splattering frogs and bashing each other with baseball bats (an image immortalized on one of many Beavis and Butt-Head t-shirts). In other shows, they use lighters to start fires, blow up a neighbor's house by sniffing gas from the stove and then lighting it, and engage in multifarious other acts of mayhem and violence. A Los Angeles area school teacher discovered that about 90 percent of her class watched the show and invited a local fire department official to speak to her class:

> after several students wrote about playing with fire and explosives in their autobiographical sketches. Some examples: 'A major "Beavis and Butt-Head" fan, Jarrod Metchikoff, 12, used to "line them (firecrackers) up in a tube and shoot them in the sewer pipe" until his mother found out. Brett Heimstra, 12, said he set off firecrackers in manholes and sewers until his mother discovered them and he "heard some stuff about how it's dangerous." Elizabeth Hastings, 12, said she knows a boy who lights firecrackers in portable toilets.' (*Los Angeles Times*, October 16, 1993)

The fire official told the students 'about a 10-year-old Orange County boy who lost use of his hand after an explosion caused by WD-40 and a cigarette lighter' (ibid.). After the initial reports of cruelty to animals and fans of the show starting fires, many more such reports came in. The fire chief in Sidney, Ohio, 'blamed MTV's cartoon for a house fire started by three girls' (*The Plain Dealer*, October 14, 1993). Further: 'Austin, Texas, investigators say three fires started by kids may have some connection to the show' (*USA Today*, October 15, 1993). And Houston teenage fans of the show were blamed for setting fires near the Galleria mall (*Radio TV Reports*, October 25, 1993).

Intense criticism of the show's violence – and Congressional threats to regulate TV violence – led MTV to move back its playtime to later in the evening and there was a promise not to replay the more violent episodes, or to show Beavis and Butt-Head starting fires, or Beavis shouting 'Fire! Fire!' but the series had already become part of a national mythology and its popularity continued apace.[10] Indeed, media culture is drawn to violence and taboo-breaking action to draw audiences in an ever-more competitive field. Thus, the program's excesses are directly related to a competitive situation in which commercial media are driven to show ever more violent and extreme behavior in the intense pressures for high profits – a trend that many believe will accelerate as the number of TV channels grows and competition becomes fiercer.

And so we see how media culture taps into its audience's concerns and in turn becomes part of a circuit of culture, with distinctive effects. Media cultural texts articulate social experiences, transcoding them into the medium of forms like television, film, or popular music. The texts are then appropriated by audiences, which use certain resonant texts and images to articulate their own sense of style, look, and identity. Media culture provides resources to make meanings, pleasure, and identity, but also shape and form specific identities and circulate material whose appropriateness may insert audiences into specific positions (i.e. macho Rambo, sexy Madonna, disaffected Slackers, violent Beavis and Butt-Head, and so on).

The *Beavis and Butt-Head* effects were particularly striking. Not only did the show promote acts of violence and copious discussion of media effects, but the characters became models for youth behavior, with young people imitating various of their tics and behavior patterns. Of course, the series generated a large consumer market of 'Beavis and Butt-Head' products, which in turn proliferated its images and effects. For example: 'Mask-maker Ed Edmunds of Distortions Unlimited says he's sold 40,000 Beavis and Butt-Head masks, his top sellers for this Halloween season' (*U.S.A. Today*, October 26, 1993). In 1994, Beavis and Butt-Head combs, calendars, and even day-planners were on the market.

The show also strongly influenced musical tastes and sales, providing a boon for heavy metal rock. Studies showed that sales jumped of every video played on the show, including ones Beavis and Butt-Head panned.[11] The *Beavis and Butt-Head* effect even became part of political contestation:

> It was only a matter of time before 'Beavis Clinton' and 'Butt-Head Gore' T-shirts began appearing on the streets of Washington. The hapless, ugly, dumb cartoon characters have been altered to look like the leaders of the free world, thanks to local political entrepreneurs and T-shirt creators Kathleen Patten, Beth Loudy and Chris Tremblay. On the shirts, Beavis is sporting a Fleetwood Mac T-shirt and is seen asking Butt-Head, 'Eh, do you think we'll get re-elected?' To which the veep, wearing the Greenpeace whale logo, says: 'Huh ... nope'. (*Washington Times*, October 26, 1993)[12]

Previous studies of media effects seem blind to the sort of complex effects of media culture texts of the sort I have discussed in analyses of the *Rambo* effect, the *Slacker* effect, and the *Beavis and Butt-Head* effect. In each case, figures and material were taken from these texts and were used to produce meaning, identities, discourse, and behavior. The media provide symbolic environments in which people live and strongly influence their thought, behavior, and style. When a media sensation like *Beavis and Butt-Head* appears, it becomes part of that environment, and in turn becomes a new resource for pleasures, identities, and contestation.

Thus, it is totally idiotic to claim that media culture has no discernible effects, as in the dominant paradigm from the 1940s, which lasted several decades.[13] Yet it is equally blind to blithely claim that audiences simply produce their own meanings from texts and that the texts do not have their own effectivity. As my discussions have shown, media culture has very powerful effects, though its meanings are mediated by audiences and even a figure like Rambo can be a contested terrain in which different groups inflect its meanings in different ways.

The *Slacker* and *Beavis and Butt-Head* effects that I have just discussed crystallize the experiences and feelings of alienation and hopelessness produced by a disintegrating society and shape these experiences into identification with slackers, rockers, heavy metal and nihilistic violence of the sort engaged in by Beavis and Butt-Head. Popular media texts tap into and articulate feelings and experiences of their audiences and in turn circulate material effects that shape thought and behavior. The texts of media culture thus have very powerful and distinctive effects and should thus be carefully scrutinized and subject to diagnostic critique.

## Notes

1. *Beavis and Butt-Head* was based on an animated short by Mike Judge, in which the two characters play 'frog baseball,' shown at the Sick and Twisted Animation festival and taken up by MTV's animated series *Liquid Television*. The series itself premiered in March 1993, but because there were only four episodes, the show went on hiatus, returning May 17 after Judge and his team of creative assistants put together thirty-two new episodes (*The San Francisco Chronicle*, June 29, 1993). The series tripled MTV's ratings and MTV ordered 130 more episodes for 1994 (*The New York Times*, October 17, 1993).
2. An October 9, 1993, story in the *Dayton Daily News* reported that a 5-year-old boy in Dayton, Ohio, ignited his bedclothes with a cigarette lighter after watching the pyromaniac antics of Beavis and Butt-Head, according to his mother. The boy's younger sister, aged 2, died in the ensuing blaze. The mother said her 5-year-old son had become 'obsessed' with *Beavis and Butt-Head* and imitated the characters' destructive behavior. I provide more examples of the *Beavis and Butt-Head* effect throughout this section.
3. An October 23, 1993, Senate Hearing on TV violence focused media attention on the show, though U.S. Sen. Ernest Hollings (D-SC) botched references to it, saying: 'We've got this – what is it – Buffcoat and Beaver or Beaver and something else ... I haven't seen it; I don't watch it; it was at 7 o'clock – Buffcoat – and they put it on now at 10:30, I think' (*The Hartford Courant*, October 26, 1993). Such ignorance of media culture is often found in some of its harshest critics.
4. Their family genealogy in a book on the series puts a question mark in the place of both of their fathers (Johnson S. and Marcil E. *Beavis and Butt-head. This book sucks* (New York: Pocket Books) 1993). So far, their mothers have not been shown, though there are some references to them. It is also unclear exactly whose house they live in, or are shown watching TV in, and whether they do or do not live together. One episode suggests that they are in Butt-Head's house and that his mother is (is always) out with her boyfriend, but other episodes show two beds together in what appears to be their highly messy bedroom and as of early 1994, their parents have never been shown.
5. Psychoanalysts like to identify Beavis and Butt-Head with the Freudian Id, with uncontrolled aggression and sexual impulses that they cannot understand or control (they were often shown masturbating, or talking about it, and Beavis uncontrollably 'moons' attractive female singers while watching music videos). There is also a barely repressed homo-erotic element to their relationship, expressed in the endless 'butt' jokes and references, their constant use of 'sucks,' and other verbal and visual behavior ('Hey Beavis, pull my finger!').
6. Margot Emery was taking a midterm examination in a mass communications theory course for master's degree candidates at the University of Tennessee at Knoxville when she found, on the last page, a question about ... Beavis and Butt-Head. Novelist Gloria Naylor, Hartford Stage Company artistic director Mark Lamos and other distinguished panelists were discussing stereotypes in art, especially the depiction of Jews in 'The Merchant of Venice,' when unexpectedly the talk swung around to ... Beavis and Butt-Head. Fred Rogers of 'Mister Rogers' Neighborhood' was being honored for his work by the Pittsburgh Presbytery and wound up discoursing upon ... Beavis and Butt-Head. Thomas Grasso, a prisoner whose main problem these days is deciding whether he'd rather have the state of Oklahoma execute him or the state of New York imprison him for a very long time, recently wrote a poem comparing Gov. Mario Cuomo and a New York corrections official to ... Beavis and Butt-Head. In fact, it has become so rare to read 10 pages of a magazine, to

browse one section of a newspaper or to endure 30 minutes of television or radio talk without bumping into some knowing reference to the animated MTV dullards. (*The Hartford Courant*, October 26, 1993)

7. Via MTV marathons of the series in summer 1993, January 1994, and Steve Best's collection, I was able to see almost every episode of the series. I also did extensive Nexis data-base searches for mainstream media references to and debates over the series and through the Fall of 1993 and into 1994, there were literally hundreds of references to the series. There also appeared a best-selling album of the heavy metal that Beavis and Butt-Head celebrate, a best-selling book, and movie deals in the works. Consequently, one can also easily speak of the *Beavis and Butt-Head* effect.

8. On this concept and a wealth of examples, see Kellner 'Ideology, Marxism and Advanced Capitalism'. *Socialist Review*, **42**: 37–65, 1978.

9. After a Washington, D.C. psychologist said that Beavis and Butt-Head's humor sounded like the antics of normal youth, she frantically called back the reporter after seeing that night's episode, leading her to comment on voice mail: 'I totally condemn this program. I do not see any shred of normal adolescent behavior here. It's one of the most sadistic, pathological programs I've ever seen. I would not recommend it to anyone of any age' (*The Washington Times*, October 17, 1993). The same story noted that an advocate of People for the Ethical Treatment of Animals stated: 'Psychiatrists will tell you that almost every major serial killer has animal abuse in their background. Beavis and Butt-Head not only torture animals, but they are preoccupied with fire, and those are two of the three predictors of adult criminal behavior.'

10. MTV's parent company Viacom was engaged at the time in a much-publicized battle to merge with Paramount and the conglomerate obviously did not want too much bad publicity. Thus, MTV had to walk the line between preserving its most profitable and popular product and avoiding excessive media criticism. The result was compromises that softened the edge of *Beavis and Butt-Head*, while attempting to preserve the show's popularity. As of spring 1994, the MTV strategy has worked with the show continuing to be highly popular with controversy diminishing.

11. The group White Zombie's album *La Sexorcisto: Devil Music Vol. 1*, for example,

> wasn't selling enough to make the nation's Top 100 charts, averaging only about 2,000 copies a week. But the group's video has been a fixture on 'Beavis and Butt-Head' since the summer, and the exposure – along with the bratty teens' words of praise – have propelled the album into the national Top 30. Estimated sales now: more than 500,000 copies . . . . Rick Krim, MTV's vice president of talent and artists relations, explains the response to the 'Beavis and Butt-Head' exposure. 'We had liked the Thunder video and supported it with play on the various specialty shows,' he says. 'That never really sparked significant album sales, the Beavis and Butt-Head exposure sure did. The sales response was pretty immediate . . . . Almost everything that gets played on the show gets some sort of sales bump from it (*Billboard*, September 4, 1993).'

12. Such an anti-Clinton move could backfire as younger voters might interpret the association to suggest that Clinton and Gore are 'cool' and thus come to support them.

13. I am speaking of Lazarsfeld's 'two step flow' model which claimed that media culture had no direct effects, that its effects were modest and minimal, and mediated by 'opinion leaders' who had the more important effects on consumer and political behavior, social attitudes, and the like (see Katz E. and Lazarsfeld P. F. *Personal influence* (New York: The Free Press) 1955 and the critical discussion of its effects in Gitlin T. Media sociology: the dominant paradigm. *Theory and Society* **6**: 205–53, 1978).

# 17

# Television and postmodernism

*Jim Collins*

From R. C. Allen (ed.), Channels of discourse, reassembled. *Television and contemporary criticism* (Second edition) (Routledge 1992).

The development of some kind of working relationship between television and postmodernism within the realm of critical studies is inevitable, almost impossible, and absolutely necessary. Inevitable, because television is frequently referred to as the quintessence of postmodern culture, and postmodernism is just as frequently written off as mere 'television culture.' Close to impossible, because of the variability of both television and postmodernism as critical objects; both are currently undergoing widespread theorization in which there are few, if any, commonly agreed-upon first principles. Necessary, because that very lack, the absence of inherited critical baggage, places television studies in a unique position vis-à-vis postmodernism. Unlike the critical work devoted to other media, television studies does not have to 'retrofit' critical paradigms developed in modernist or premodernist periods and therefore should ideally be able to provide unprecedented insights into the complex interrelationships between textuality, subjectivity, and technology in contemporary cultures.

There is no short definition of *postmodernism* that can encompass the divergent, often contradictory ways the term has been employed. One reason for this divergence is that the term is used to describe: (1) a distinctive style; (2) a movement that emerged in the sixties, seventies, or eighties, depending on the medium in question; (3) a condition or milieu that typifies an entire set of socioeconomic factors; (4) a specific mode of philosophical inquiry that throws into question the givens of philosophical discourse; (5) a very particular type of 'politics'; and (6) an emergent form of cultural analysis shaped by all of the above.

This terminological confusion is exacerbated by the contentiousness of the various definitions. As Jonathan Arac has written, 'It remains even now typically the case that to "have a position" on postmodernism means not just to offer an analysis of its genesis and contours, but to let the world know whether you are for it or against it, and in fairly bold terms.'[1] One could argue that the chief drawback of most of this work is that the latter inevitably takes precedence over the former, producing little in the way of actual description but a great deal in the way of critical ax grinding. But although easy moralizing about postmodernism may often reveal little besides the presuppositions of the critical languages used to demonize or valorize it, the contested nature of the term – the fact that no definition of contours can ever be ideologically neutral, that description is inseparable from evaluation – reveals one of the most significant lessons of postmodern theory: all of our assumptions concerning what constitutes 'culture' and 'critical analysis' are now subject to intense debate.

If there is a common denominator in all of these contentious definitions of postmodernism, it is the determination to define it as something other than *modernism*, a term that is likewise given variable status. Modernism is generally characterized in one of two ways, depending on the individual critic's perspective on postmodernism: as a heroic period of revolutionary experimentation that sought to transform whole cultures, in which case postmodernism is seen as a neoconservative blacklash; or as a period of profound elitism, in which case postmodernism signals a move away from the self-enclosed world of the avant-garde back into the realm of day-to-day life.

. . . Although it is possible to list the tell-tale stylistic features of postmodern design – the move away from abstraction and geometrics to the overly familiar and mass-produced; the replacement of purity with eclecticism, internationalism with cultural specificity, and invention with rearticulation – the cultural significance of these changes and their ideological ramifications remains a matter of intense debate. It is also especially difficult to relate television to these debates in any kind of one-to-one correspondence. Television, unlike architecture, literature, or painting, never had a modernist phase that could serve as a point of departure for postmodern television. The emergence of postmodernism is decidedly an 'uneven' development; its appearance and eventual impact vary from one medium to another.

Because neither an etymology, nor an evolutionary schema, nor an all-encompassing theoretical paradigm can provide an adequate working definition of postmodernism that allows for diverse applications to television, I will set forth a series of recurring themes developed by theoreticians working in different media that, in aggregate, provide a sense of the conflictedness but also the potential cohesiveness of postmodern theory. These themes, considered together, allow for a reconsideration of the semiotic, technological, and ideological dimensions of television.

## A semiotics of excess: 'The bombardment of signs'

One of the key preconditions of the postmodern condition is the proliferation of signs and their endless circulation, generated by the technological developments associated with the information explosion (cable television, VCRs, digital recording, computers, etcetera). These technologies have produced an ever increasing surplus of texts, all of which demand our attention in varying levels of intensity. The resulting array of competing signs shapes the very process of signification, a context in which messages must constantly be defined over and against rival forms of expression as different types of texts frame our allegedly common reality according to significantly different ideological agendas.

Television is obviously a central factor in this information explosion.

Many critics on both the left and the right insist that television is likewise instrumental in the devaluation of meaning – the reduction of all meaningful activity to mere 'non-sense', to a limitless televisual universe that has taken the place of the real. Such critics as Allan Bloom and Jean Baudrillard have made grandiose claims about the destructive power of mass culture (most especially television).[2] The former has claimed that television has brought about the ruination of true learning and morality. The latter has claimed that contemporary culture *is* television culture – endless simulations in which reality simply disappears. In Bloom's view, the culprit is not television alone, but the more general democratization of culture, which threatens the elite values that once formed the basis of real learning: the acquisition of Truth. But to Baudrillard (who is no more a postmodernist than Bloom), television is cause as well as symptom, allegedly constructing a seamless realm of simulations that hinder our acquisition of the *really real*.

The problem with these critiques is their contention that all signs are encoded and decoded according to exactly the same logic, or encoded so differently that, as a whole, they produce one and only one effect. They insist that the technological developments of the recent past have made 'meaning' an antiquated concept, because all signs are supposedly exhausted, mere electronic pulses disconnected from any referent. The chief limitation of these critics who are so anxious to demonize television is that they insist on making dire predictions about the devastating effects of this technological explosion (which alters everything, everywhere, in the same way), but they fail to recognize that the rate of absorption of those technological changes has increased commensurately. The medium may indeed be the message, but twenty minutes into the future the technological novelty is already in the process of being absorbed. In the same way that a figure of speech enjoys a certain novelty at its initial appearance but then begins to become absorbed into the category of the already familiar, the 'figures of technology' that produce an initial disorientation are quickly made manageable (*secondarized*) through different strategies of absorption as they are worked over by popular texts and popular audiences. This absorption/secondarization process involves the manipulation of the array by texts operating within it – television programs (as well as rock songs, films, bestsellers, and so forth) that demonstrate an increasingly sophisticated knowledge of the conditions of their production, circulation, and eventual reception.

A recent episode of *Northern Exposure* illustrates this absorption process quite clearly. When Holling, the local tavern owner, acquires a satellite dish that receives two hundred worldwide channels, his girlfriend Shelley quickly becomes a television addict, her entire life suddenly controlled by the new technology. She becomes maniacal in the process, and we see her calling the shopping channel to order thousands of dollars worth of kitsch items. The determination of her character by television programs is stressed repeatedly, as she dances to music videos or dresses up as a Vanna White wannabe to watch *Wheel of Fortune*. But by the end of the program she has confessed her televisual sins, in a mock confessional to the local disk jockey-priest, and resolves to watch selectively. Meanwhile the central character, Dr. Joel Fleischmann, envisions his failed love affair in terms of old black-and-white Hollywood films, including a silent-movie version of the final scene from

*The Graduate*, with himself as the star. Other characters recognize his need for what they call 'closure' in his relationship, and they decide to provide this by enacting a movie fantasy of how his relationship should have ended. The closure of both plot lines epitomizes the absorption of media culture, not just through parody but through its secondarization by texts and audiences that rearticulate it according to their own needs, a process thematized by the program itself.

## Irony, intertextuality, and hyperconsciousness

The all-pervasiveness of different strategies of rearticulation and appropriation is one of the most widely discussed features of postmodern cultural production. Umberto Eco has argued that this ironic articulation of the 'already said' is the distinguishing feature of postmodern communication. In his often-quoted example, he insists that we can no longer make innocent statements. A lover cannot tell his beloved, 'I love you madly,' because it would very probably produce only a laugh. But if he wants to make such a declaration of love, he could say, 'As Barbara Cartland would put it, "I love you madly."' The latter indicates a mutual awareness of the 'already said,' a mutual delight in ironically manipulating it for one's own purposes.[3] This emphasis on irony is often written off as mere 'camp' recycling, but such a view fails to account for the diversity of possible strategies of rearticulation, which range from the simple revivalism found in the buildings of Robert Stern, the interior design collections of Ralph Lauren, or the clothing of Laura Ashley to the more explicitly critical reworking of the 'already said' in films like *Thelma and Louise*, the photographs of Barbara Kruger, or the radicalized cover versions of pop standards by the Sex Pistols or The Clash, in which the past is not just accessed but 'hijacked,' given an entirely different cultural significance than the antecedent text had when it first appeared. What is postmodern in all of this is the simultaneity of these competing forms of rearticulation – the 'already said' is being constantly recirculated, but from very different perspectives ranging from nostalgic reverence to vehement attack or a mixture of these strategies. Linda Hutcheon argues very convincingly that what distinguishes postmodern rearticulations of the past is their ambivalent relationship to the antecedent text, a recognition of the power of certain texts to capture the imagination, but at the same time a recognition of their ideological or stylistic limitations (this ambivalent parody will be discussed in more detail below).[4]

There is no other medium in which the force of the 'already said' is quite so visible as in television, primarily because the already said is the 'still being said.' Television programming since the fifties has depended on the recycling of Hollywood films and the syndication of past prime-time programs. The proliferation of cable channels that re-present programs from the past four decades of television history marks the logical extension of this process, in which the various pasts and presents of television now air simultaneously. Television programming as accessing of the accumulated past of popular culture ranges from K-Tel offers for old *Honeymooners* and *I Love Lucy* episodes to the explicitly parodic demolitions of television programs to be found on *In Living Color, David Letterman*, and *Saturday Night Live*. This diversity in the forms and motivations of televisual rearticulation is even more apparent in the simultaneous but conflictive 're-presentations' of early sitcoms on rival cable networks. The Christian Broadcasting Network and Nickelodeon both broadcast series from the late fifties and early sixties, but whereas the former presents these series as a model for family entertainment the way it used to be, the latter offers them as fun for the contemporary family, 'camped up' with parodic voice-overs, super-graphics, and reediting designed to deride their quaint vision of American family life, which we all know never really existed even 'back then.'

The foregrounding of intertextual references has become a marker of 'quality television' (for example, prime-time network programs like *Hill Street Blues* and *St. Elsewhere*, which reflect a more sophisticated 'cinematic style,' feature ensemble casts, etc.) as well. Jane Feuer has traced this self-conscious intertextuality as it developed in the MTM style, but more recently, as 'quality television' has developed across production companies and networks, the explicit referencing has played a vital role in situating a given program in relation to other forms of quality and nonquality programs.[5] During the 1990 fall season, for example, Michael and Hope of ABC's *thirtysomething* referred to watching *L.A. Law*, while on NBC's *L.A. Law*, attorney Anne Kelsey spoke of wanting to get home and watch *thirtysomething* because it was 'responsible television.'

This sort of referencing-as-positioning is not restricted to quality TV. On a recent episode of *Knots Landing* (a nighttime soap that airs opposite *L.A. Law* and makes no claims whatsoever to be quality television), two minor characters argue about their favorite TV programs. One states that he has to turn down a dinner invitation because 'I forgot to set my VCR. I gotta see what Corbin Bernsen is wearing tonight.' When his friend states that he 'never watches that show' because he's a 'newshound,' the *L.A. Law* fan says derisively, 'News my foot. You're crazy about Diane Sawyer.' When his colleague protests that 'she's very intelligent,' his friend responds, 'Right, you're in love with her mind.' The referencing here, within the context of an evening soap, presupposes three important factors: (1) that viewers will possess a televisual literacy developed enough to recognize programs from the actors' names and that they will know the television schedule well enough to appreciate the reference to the programs that air opposite *Knots Landing* on the two other major networks (*L.A. Law* and *Prime Time Live*); (2) that VCR time-shifting is now commonplace, especially for dedicated viewers of *L.A. Law* but also for those fans who exist within the fictional world of programs that air on competing channels; and (3) that the 'irresponsible,' nonquality program informs us why viewers *really* like quality television – for the wardrobes and the sexiness of the stars involved, which, as the characters of *Knots Landing* know, constitute the *real* pleasure of the televisual text.

These intertextual references are emblematic of the *hyperconsciousness* of postmodern popular culture: a hyperawareness on the part of the text itself of its cultural status, function, and history, as well as of the conditions of its circulation and reception. Hyperconsciousness involves a different sort of self-reflexivity than that commonly associated with modernist texts. Highly self-conscious forms of appropriation and rearticulation have been used by postmodern painters, photographers, and performance artists (David Salle, Cindy Sherman, Laurie Anderson, and others), and their work has enjoyed a great deal of critical attention. In the 'meta-pop' texts that we now find on television, on newsstands, on the radio, or on grocery store book racks, we encounter, not avant-gardists who give 'genuine' significance to the merely mass cultural, but a hyperconscious rearticulation of media culture by media culture.[6]

The self-reflexivity of these popular texts of the later eighties and early nineties does not revolve around the problems of self-expression experienced by the anguished creative artist so ubiquitous in modernism but instead focuses on antecedent and competing programs, on the ways television programs circulate and are given meaning by viewers, and on the nature of televisual popularity. A paradigmatic example of this is the opening scene of *The Simpsons' Thanksgiving Special* (1990), in which Bart and his father, Homer, are watching television in their living room on Thanksgiving morning. *The Simpsons*, as a concept, is already a mean-spirited parody of the traditional family sitcom, and this particular scene adds an attack on the imbecilic chatter of 'color commentators.' But the scene goes beyond simple parody. As they watch the Thanksgiving Day parade, Bart keeps asking Homer to identify the balloon float characters, complaining that they could use some characters that 'were made in the last fifty years.' His father tells him that the parade is a tradition, that if 'you start building a balloon for every flash-in-the-pan cartoon character, you'll turn the parade into a farce.' At this point the television-within-the-television depicts a Bart Simpson balloon floating by while the 'real' Bart Simpson looks on. Thus Bart watches himself as a popular phenomenon on television. *The Simpsons* television program thereby acknowledges its own characters' status as popular icons whose circulation and reception are worked back into the 'text' itself.

## Subjectivity, bricolage, and eclecticism

The 'Bart watches Bart' example may be emblematic of a postmodern textuality, but what are the effects of this hyperconscious irony on television viewers? Is its ultimate effect emancipatory, leading to a recognition that television's representations are social constructions rather than value-neutral reflections of the 'real' world? Or does this irony produce a disempowering apathy, in which no image is taken at all seriously? John Caughie has described this problem very effectively:

> The argument, then, is that television produces the conditions of an ironic knowingness, at least as a possibility . . . [which] may offer a way of thinking subjectivity free of subjection . . . Most of all, it opens identity to diversity, and escapes the notion of cultural identity as a fixed volume . . . But if it does all this, it does not do it in that utopia of guaranteed resistance which assumes the progressiveness of naturally oppositional readers who will get it right in the end. It does it, rather, with terms hung in suspension . . . tactics of empowerment, games of subordination with neither term fixed in advance.[7]

The crux of the matter here is the notion of the subject that is presupposed. Caughie's insightful point about irony vis-à-vis subjectivity suggests that television viewers are individual subjects neither completely programmed by what they are watching nor completely free to choose as self-determining individuals, captains of their fates, masters of their souls.[8] One of the significant developments in postmodern theory (put forward in an increasing number of disciplines) is the recognition that a new theory of the subject must be developed, one that can avoid the deterministic conception of the individual as programmable android without resurrecting a romantic 'Self' that operates as a free agent, unfettered and uninfluenced by ideology.

[...] The concept of the postmodern subject as multiple and contradictory, acted upon but also acting upon, has also led to reconsideration of the 'effects' that popular culture, most especially television, has on its viewers. The *hypodermic* model of media effects (in which mass media allegedly 'injects' values directly into passive viewers) has been challenged by John Fiske, Ien Ang, and others who share a cultural studies perspective.[9] Many of them use de Certeau's concept of 'poaching' to characterize audiences' skillful abduction of televisual texts, focusing on the ways in which audiences make the meanings they want or need out of television programs.[10] It is at this point that British cultural studies begins to share a number of concerns with postmodern theory per se, positing a subject who operates as a technologically sophisticated *bricoleur*, appropriating and recombining according to personal need. The term *bricolage*, developed by anthropologists to describe the ways primitive tribespeople piece together a meaningful cosmogony (or simply a way of operating) out of random elements they encounter in their day-to-day lives, has recently been applied to the behavior of individuals in contemporary media cultures. The culturalist and postmodernist positions differ, however, in regard to 'mass culture.' The former presupposes that mass culture may still be pernicious and homogeneous, but that it may be transformed into something resembling a genuine folk culture at the moment of reception because viewers tend to disregard the intended effects of television and take from it what best fits into their lives. This is a very attractive political position in that it allows for the continued demonization of capitalism and mass culture while it celebrates the resourcefulness of ordinary people. However, it fails to recognize the eclecticism of postmodern cultural *production*.

Many television programs, films, popular songs, and other manifestations of popular culture are already the result of sophisticated forms of *bricolage*, already conscious of the multiple ways they might be understood. As I have mentioned above, Charles Jencks insists that one of the distinguishing features of postmodern architecture is 'radical eclecticism'.[11] The work of Charles Moore, James Stirling, and Hans Hollein juxtaposes styles, materials, and conventions hitherto thought to be thoroughly incompatible. Michael M. J. Fisher and George Lipsitz contend very convincingly that this eclecticism, this creation as *bricolage*, is also a feature of the ethnic and racial subcultures that are so prominent in American popular culture. 'It is on the level of commodified mass culture that the most popular, and often the most profound, acts of cultural *bricolage* take place. The destruction of established canons and the juxtaposition of seemingly inappropriate forms that characterize the self-conscious postmodernism of "high culture" have long been staples of commodified popular culture.'[12]

The eclecticism associated with postmodernism takes on a more complicated dimension in regard to television. Individual programs like *Pee-Wee's Play House*, *Max Headroom*, and *Twin Peaks* are as radically eclectic in their use of diverse stylistic conventions as any postmodern building. Furthermore, the eclecticism of television textuality operates on a technological/institutional level as well because it has been institutionalized by cable television and the VCR, which together produce infinite programming variations. Postmodernist eclecticism might only occasionally be a preconceived design choice in individual programs, but it is built into the technologies of media-sophisticated societies. Thus television, like the postmodern subject, must be conceived as a *site* – an intersection of multiple, conflicting cultural messages. Only by recognizing this interdependency of *bricolage* and eclecticism can we come to appreciate the profound changes in the relationship of reception and production in postmodern cultures. Not only has reception become another form of meaning production, but production has increasingly become a form of reception as it rearticulates antecedent and competing forms of representation.

## Commodification, politics, value

Another major concern of postmodern cultural analysis has been the impact of consumerism on social life. Fredric Jameson argues that postmodernism is best understood as the end result of capitalism's relentless commodification of all phases of everyday existence. He sees pop culture's radical eclecticism as mere 'cannibalization' of the past and as 'sheer heterogeneity' without 'decidable' effects.[13] For Jameson, all such cultural activity is driven by the logic of 'late' capitalism, which endlessly develops new markets that it must neutralize politically by constructing a vision of success and personal happiness, expressible solely through the acquisition of commodities.

The relevance of Jameson's work for television studies has already been explored by a number of critics, not surprising given the advertiser-driven nature of the medium in the United States, where commercials not only interrupt programs but have actually emerged as a form of programming. The blurring of the distinction between programs and commercials has become even greater with the development of 'infomercials,' shopping channels, product lines generated by Saturday morning cartoons (as well as by evening soaps like *Dynasty*), and so on. If television is defined by its semiotic complexity, its intertextuality, and its eclecticism, it is also just as surely defined by its all-pervasive appeals to consumerism.

The problem for television studies, as it tries to come to terms with postmodernism, is how to reconcile the semiotic and economic dimensions of television. Stressing the semiotic to the exclusion of the economic produces only a formalist game of 'let's count the intertexts,' but privileging the economic to the point that semiotic complexity is reduced to a limited set of moves allowed by a master system is just as simplistic. The attempt to turn television into a master system operating according to a single logic is a fundamentally nostalgic perspective; the culture of the 1990s, though judged to be the sheer noise of late capitalism, is nevertheless expected to operate according to nineteenth-century models of culture as homogeneous totality.

Making postmodernism coterminous with late capitalism offers a theoretical neatness by providing an all-purpose, master explanation: postmodern culture is a symptom of more fundamental economic and political trends. But this position is fraught with a number of problems. The limitations of this view of postmodernism become especially apparent in Jameson's notion of 'cognitive mapping'.[14] He argues that a new aesthetics that will make sense of multinational capitalism has yet to emerge and that there exists as yet no way of mapping the chaotic spaces of postmodern cultures. But the 'map' he hopes will be drawn will not be acceptable to him unless it envisions this space according to the contours of traditional Marxist theory. Jameson doesn't entertain the notion that mere mass culture may itself provide a mapping function or that television is not just a chaotic terrain in need of mapping but is itself a proliferation of maps. Lifetime, MTV, Black Entertainment Television, and the Family Channel all envision contemporary cultural life from specific generational, racial, and gendered perspectives. Taken together, they don't coalesce into one big picture but rather a composite of overlapping views that visualize the terrain of contemporary life in reference to its specific uses. The desire to formulate one master map, despite the multiple ways that the terrain can be envisioned and put to use by individual subjects as *bricoleurs*, exposes not just the limitations of traditional Marxist paradigms, but also the need to develop far more sophisticated forms of materialist analysis that recognize the multiple uses and effects of consumerism.[15]

. . . Within this politics of diversity and difference, 'value' is not abandoned – only absolute 'truth values,' or what Herrnstein Smith has called the automatic 'axiomatics' of traditional critical theory that relied on transcendent, universal qualities as proof or verification for all evaluation. She insists that both value and evaluation are radically contingent. 'That which we call "value" may be seen neither as an inherent property of objects, nor an arbitrary projection of subjects but, rather, as the product of the dynamics of some economy or, indeed, of any number of economies (that is, systems of apportionment and circulation of "goods") in relation to a shifting state, of which an object or entity will have a different (shifting) value.'[16]

The ramifications of this point for television study – specifically for developing a theory of postmodern television – are far reaching, because Smith argues that we need to continue to debate the value of any given text but also insists on the contingent nature of those judgments. Evaluation always depends on criteria that are culturally determined and therefore culturally specific rather than transcendent. This is a vitally important point, because it allows for an analysis of television that recognizes the variable nature of televisual signs. Their value cannot be explained in reference to one logic but will be channel-, program-, and audience-sensitive. Even more important, by focusing on the dynamics of the economies that determine these shifting values, we can begin to understand the interconnectedness of the semiotic and the economic dimensions of postmodern television.

## *Twin Peaks*

In order to demonstrate how the various themes of postmodern theory might be considered together in reference to a single television series, I will focus on *Twin Peaks*, because it became a cultural phenomenon that epitomizes the multiple dimensions of televisual postmodernism. *Twin Peaks* was not 'postmodernist' just because it involved David Lynch, a bona fide postmodernist filmmaker, or because it depended on a number of postmodern stylistic conventions, or because it generated so many commodity intertexts (*The Secret Diary of Laura Palmer, Dale Cooper: My Life, My Tapes*, and a soundtrack album, among other things). Rather, the circumstances that allowed for its development and the ways in which it circulated are emblematic of postmodern culture and represent the confluence of a number of factors that give postmodern television its historical specificity.

The appearance of *Twin Peaks* on prime-time network television was due in large part to the impact of cable and VCR technology. The advent of cable systems that offer dozens of alternatives to the 'big three' networks and the ubiquity of the VCR, which offers an even broader range of entertainment, led to a significant decline in the networks' share of the total viewing audience. In 1979, 91 percent of viewers were watching network programs during prime time, but by 1989 the number had dropped to 67 percent.[17] This viewer migration to cable and videocassettes has been portrayed in near-catastrophic terms by the networks, because those households that are able to afford cable and VCRs are precisely the households network advertisers most want to reach. Particularly prized within this audience segment are 'yuppie' viewers, who not only purchase expensive consumer goods but also tend to consume other forms of entertainment – on broadcast television, videotape, cable, and pay-per-view and at movie theaters.

The development of *Twin Peaks* reflects a fundamental change in the way the entertainment industries now envision their publics. The audience is no longer regarded as a homogeneous mass but rather as an amalgamation of microcultural groups stratified by age, gender, race, and geographic location. Therefore, appealing to a 'mass' audience now involves putting together a series of interlocking appeals to a number of discrete but potentially interconnected audiences. The promotion of *Batman: The Movie* by the various components of Warner Communications serves as the paradigmatic example here. D.C. Comics were used to secure the preteen and early teen audience, while MTV and Prince helped to lure the female teen audience. The original development of *Twin Peaks* involved exactly this sort of appeal to a number of distinct audiences. As producer Mark Frost himself acknowledged, he hoped the series would appeal to 'a coalition of people who may have been fans of *Hill Street, St. Elsewhere*, and *Moonlighting*, along with people who enjoyed the nighttime soaps' – along with, of course, the people who watch neither anymore, now that cable and VCR have become household fixtures.[18] The emergence of 'coalition audiences' as a marketing strategy parallels the development of 'coalition politics' in contemporary political theory. Culture industries and political activists both recognize the fragmentary nature of 'the public' and realize that effective mobilization of 'public opinion' is possible only through strategies of amalgamation.

The media blitz that surrounded the premiere of *Twin Peaks* is quite literally a textbook example of the skillful manipulation of the discourses of cultural legitimation that have hitherto been used to attribute value to media other than television. The full-page ad that appeared in the *New York Times* the day the pilot premiered (6 April 1990) is a case in point. In bold, oversized letters we are told: 'Twin Peaks – the series that will change TV,' according to *Connoisseur* magazine. Two evaluative criteria are reiterated throughout the glowing reviews quoted in the ad – a romantic-modernist glorification of originality and the shock of the new it produces, and an all-purpose notion of connoisseurship (see Fig. 17.1). Throughout this initial wave of reviews in the popular press, *Twin Peaks* is valorized in cinematic terms, a medium that, judging by these reviews, enjoys a far higher degree of cultural status than television, especially when it involves David Lynch, already promoted as a genius director.

Many reviews bestowed automatic status on the program because it was the product of an *auteur* – a filmmaker with a recognizable signature. Richard Zoglin's review in *Time* (9 April 1990), entitled 'Like Nothing Else on Earth: David Lynch's *Twin Peaks* may be the most original show on TV,' describes the 'Lynchian touches' and the director's art school training. The notion that great television might be made only by a great filmmaker also pervades Terence Rafferty's review in *The New Yorker* (9 April 1990). After referring to Lynch as an 'all-American surrealist,' Rafferty states that 'within five minutes of the opening of *Twin Peaks* we know we're in David Lynch's world – unmistakable even on a small screen.' The reliance on this evaluative criteria appears in its most bald-faced form in *Newsweek*'s cover story (1 October 1990) on Lynch, in which an 'avant-garde' portrait of the director is accompanied by the graphic, 'David Lynch – The Wild at Art Genius Behind *Twin Peaks*'.

The discrete filmlike nature of the pilot was emphasized explicitly in an ad quoted in the television spot that ran during the week of the premiere: 'It's must-see, must-tape television,' a statement that stresses the singularity of the program. After the first few episodes had appeared, however, the avant-garde *auteur* mode of evaluation began to dissipate as *Twin Peaks* came to be conceived no longer as a discrete cinematic pilot, but rather as a television serial. The next major article in *Time* (7 May 1990) concerns the *Twin Peaks* 'mania,' how it has become a topic of 'coffee wagon' conversation around offices. The article refers to the show's 'trendiness' and includes a chart detailing the character configuration, complete with cutesy hearts and coffee cups, all of which emphasize its soap opera dimensions. The article features, interestingly, this quote from a regular viewer: 'It's only a TV show, but you feel like a cultural idiot if you can't quote it on Fridays.' At this point, when *Twin Peaks* is no longer being described as 'hauntingly original,' it returns to being just TV.

The issue of 'cultural literacy,' raised indirectly by the viewer's statement, involves this very shift in evaluative criteria. What does it mean to be 'culturally literate' about *Twin Peaks*? Should one regard it as an unprecedented *auteurist*/avant-gardist incursion into the vast wasteland of mere TV? Or should one adopt a sense of knowing detachment that asserts, 'I know it's just all TV trash, but I enjoy it ironically'?[19] The answer is not a

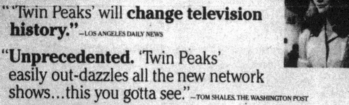

# "'Twin Peaks'– the series that will change TV."

—CONNOISSEUR MAGAZINE

"Something of **a miracle.** The most **hauntingly original** work ever done for American TV." —TIME MAGAZINE

"The year's best show! **Grade: A +**" —ENTERTAINMENT WEEKLY

"'Twin Peaks' **extends the boundaries** of network television." —GQ MAGAZINE

"'Twin Peaks' will **change television history.**" —LOS ANGELES DAILY NEWS

"**Unprecedented.** 'Twin Peaks' easily out-dazzles all the new network shows...this you gotta see." —TOM SHALES, THE WASHINGTON POST

"**Intelligent, gorgeously filmed** and highly stylized. TV has never seen a small town like 'Twin Peaks'. " —NEWSDAY

"'Twin Peaks'...**like nothing else** on television." —LOS ANGELES TIMES

New Series

▲ **TWIN PEAKS** ▲

Special Preview Tonight
9/8:00 Central ⓐ

**Fig. 17.1**

matter of either/or but *both*, because a postmodern cultural literacy recognizes exactly this kind of variability. *Twin Peaks* is a polysemic phenomenon alternately valorized as would-be cinema and would-be soap opera. The cover stories on *Twin Peaks* that appeared in *Newsweek*, *Rolling Stone*, and *Soap Opera Weekly* (16 October 1990) reflect the polysemic nature of signs that constitute this program. The *Newsweek* 'Wild at Art' cover features only Lynch as mad genius, whereas the *Rolling Stone* cover shows three of the program's stars vamping it up. *Soap Opera Weekly* features a large photo of lynch with smaller inset photos of the stars, but surrounds both with other soap stories and photos – 'Behind the scenes at *The Bold and the Beautiful*,' 'It's not all Romance at *Lovings* Dual Wedding' – in addition to the 'curious Revelations' from *Peaks* cast members. In each case, the significance or cultural resonance of the series changes fundamentally in accordance with the evaluative criteria employed by each magazine as it frames the phenomenon according to its own discursive agenda.

Although the press coverage of the *Twin Peaks* phenomenon accentuates its polysemic, multiaccentual nature, the semiotic variability of the program is not restricted to the diverse ways it is given significance at the point of reception. The style of *Twin Peaks* is aggressively eclectic, utilizing a number of visual, narrative, and thematic conventions from Gothic horror, science fiction, and the police procedural as well as the soap opera. This eclecticism is further intensified by the variable treatment each genre receives in particular scenes. At one moment, the conventions of a genre are taken 'seriously'; in another scene, they might be subjected to the sort of ambivalent parody that Linda Hutcheon associates with postmodern textuality. These generic and tonal variations occur within scenes as well as across scenes, sometimes oscillating on a line-by-line basis, or across episodes when scenes set in paradigmatic relationship to one another (through the use of the same character, setting, or soundtrack music) are given virtually antithetical treatments. The movement in and out of parodic discourse is common in all of the episodes. For example, in the pilot, when Dale Cooper and Harry Truman are going through Laura Palmer's diary and personal effects, the dialogue, delivery, and soundtrack music all operate according to the conventions of the Jack Webb police procedural. But the 'just the facts, ma'am' tone of Cooper's discourse about cocaine, safety deposit boxes, and court orders is shattered by the concluding line of the scene, which is delivered in exactly the same manner: 'Diane, I'm holding in my hand a box of chocolate bunnies.'

This sort of tonal variation has led a number of critics to conclude that *Twin Peaks* is mere camp, an ironic frolic among the rustic bumpkins and the TV trash they devour along with their doughnuts. But the series is never just camp; the parodic perspective alternates with more straightforward presentation, encouraging an empathetic response rather than the ironic distance of the explicitly parodic. In the third episode, for example, when Dale Cooper explains his 'deductive technique involving mind-body coordination' – complete with a blackboard, a map of Tibet, and rock throwing the scene becomes a thoroughgoing burlesque of the traditional final scene of detective novels, films, or television programs when the detective explains how he/she solved the crime, usually through a hyperrational deduction process. The introduction of the Dalai Lama, dream states, and rocks transports ratiocination (crime solving by rational deduction) into the realm of irrational spirituality, thereby parodying one of the fundamental 'givens' of detective fiction. The absurd misuse of conventions defies the viewer to take the scene seriously. However, the scene at the end of episode fifteen in which Leland, possessed by Bob, brutally murders Maddie is one of the most horrifying murder scenes ever to appear on prime-time television; it defies the viewer *not* to empathize with the innocent victim, not to be deeply disturbed by the insanity and violence, which are intensified by the editing and sound distortions.

The death of Leland at the end of episode seventeen exemplifies not just this scene-to-scene variation but also the paradigmatic variation mentioned above, in which the same textual elements from earlier episodes are repeated but given completely different inflections. As Leland dies in Cooper's arms, he realizes that he has killed three young women, including his daughter Laura, and in the moments when he is dying, the framing, dialogue, acting style, reaction shots, and nondiegetic music all contribute to the pathetic nature of the scene, encouraging the viewer to empathize wholeheartedly with the horrified father. Particularly interesting here is that two key elements contributing to this pathos were used parodically in earlier episodes: Cooper's Tibetan spiritualism, previously used as a signifier of his goofiness, is here given integrity as something that comforts the dying man, describing what he apparently sees at the point of death; and 'Laura Palmer's Theme,' previously used parodically to accompany any number of 'soap opera' love scenes, here accompanies a scene of tragic paternal love.

It could be argued that this tonal oscillation and generic amalgamation, in which viewers are encouraged to activate ever-shifting sets of expectations and decoding strategies, is simply one of those 'Lynchian tricks' – that in *Twin Peaks*, as in *Blue Velvet*, Lynch labors to catch his viewers *between* sets of expectations, producing the shock of the newly juxtaposed. Although this oscillation in tonality is undeniably a characteristic of Lynch's more recent projects, it is also reflective of changes in television entertainment and of viewer involvement in that entertainment. That viewers would take a great deal of pleasure in this oscillation and juxtaposition is symptomatic of the 'suspended' nature of viewer involvement in television that developed well before the arrival of *Twin Peaks*. The ongoing oscillation in discursive register and generic conventions describes not just *Twin Peaks* but the very act of moving up and down the televisual scale of the cable box. While watching *Twin Peaks*, viewers may be overtly encouraged to move in and out of an ironic position, but watching other television soap operas (nighttime or daytime) involves for many viewers a similar process of oscillation in which emotional involvement alternates with ironic detachment. Viewing perspectives are no longer mutually exclusive, but set in perpetual alternation.[20]

What distinguishes *Twin Peaks* from, say, *Dallas* or *Knots Landing* is not that it encourages this alternation in viewing positions but that it explicitly acknowledges this oscillation and the suspended nature of television viewing. In other words, *Twin Peaks* doesn't just acknowledge the multiple subject positions that television generates; it recognizes that one of the great pleasures of the televisual text is that very suspension and exploits it for its own ends.

If the postmodern condition is one in which we as individual subjects are constantly engaged in the process of negotiating the array of signs and subject positions that surround us, *Twin Peaks* and other forms of hyperconscious popular culture address themselves directly to this condition, situating themselves exactly in the arcs and gaps that result when these positions don't coalesce. By taking the array as their 'setting' and redefining 'narrative action' in terms of the exploitation of the array, these texts redefine the nature of entertainment in contemporary cultures. The concerns of postmodern television and postmodern theory, then, are thoroughly intertwined, because both are responses to the contingent, conflicted set of circumstances that constitute cultural life at the end of the twentieth century.

## Notes

1. Jonathan Arac, *Critical Genealogies* (New York, Columbia University Press, 1987), p. 284.
2. Allan Bloom, *The Closing of the American Mind* (New York, Simon & Schuster, 1987); Jean-Louis Baudrillard, 'The Implosion of Meaning in the Media and the Information of the Social in the Masses', in Kathleen Woodward, ed., *Myths of Information. Technology and Post-Industrial Culture* (Madison, WI, Coda Press, 1980), pp. 137–48.
3. Umberto Eco, postscript to *The Name of the Rose* (New York, Harcourt Brace Jovanovich, 1984).
4. Linda Hutcheon, 'The Politics of Postmodernism, Parody, and History'. *Cultural Critique*, 5 (Winter 1986–87), pp. 179–207.
5. Jane Feuer, 'The MTM Style', in Jane Feuer, Paul Kerr, and Tise Vahimagi, eds, *MTM. 'Quality Television'* (London, British Film Institute, 1984), pp. 32–60.
6. Jim Collins, 'Appropriating Like *Krazy*. From Pop Art to Meta-Pop', in James Naremore and Patrick Brantlinger, eds, *Modernity and Mass Culture* (Bloomington, IN, Indiana University Press, 1991), pp. 203–23.
7. John Caughie, 'Playing at Being American. Game and Tactics', in Patricia Mellencamp, ed., *Logics of Televisions. Essays in Cultural Criticism* (Bloomington, IN, Indiana University Press, 1990), pp. 54–5.
8. For a detailed analysis of the changes in theories of the subject, see Paul Smith, *Discerning the Subject* (Minneapolis, MN, University of Minnesota Press, 1988).
9. John Fiske, 'Popular Discrimination', in James Naremore and Patrick Brantlinger, eds, *Modernity and Mass Culture* (Bloomington, IN, Indiana University Press, 1991), pp. 103–16; Ien Ang, *Watching 'Dallas'. Soap Opera and the Melodramatic Imagination*, trans. Della Couling (London, Methuen, 1985).
10. Michel de Certeau, *The Practice of Everyday Life* (Berkeley, CA, University of California Press, 1984).
11. Charles Jencks, *The Language of Post-Modern Architecture*, 5th edn (New York, Rizzoli, 1987).
12. George Lipsitz, 'Cruising around the Historical Bloc. Postmodernism and Popular Music in East Los Angeles', *Cultural Critique*, 5 (Winter 1986–87), p. 161.
13. See Fredric Jameson, 'Postmodernism, or, the Cultural Logic of Late Capitalism', *New Left Review*, 146 (July/August 1984), and 'Postmodernism and Consumer Society', in Hal Foster, ed., *The Anti-Aesthetic. Essays on Postmodern Culture* (Port Townsend, WA, Bay Press, 1983), pp. 111–25.

14. Fredric Jameson, 'Cognitive Mapping', in Cary Nelson and Lawrence Grossberg, eds, *Marxism and the Interpretation of Culture* (Urbana, IL, University of Illinois Press, 1988), pp. 347–57.
15. See especially Hilary Radner, *Shopping Around. Feminine Culture and the Will to Pleasure* (New York, Routledge, 1992).
16. Barbara Herrnstein Smith, 'Value without Truth Value', in John Fekete, ed., *Life after Postmodernism* (New York, St. Martin's Press, 1987), p. 1.
17. *Entertainment Weekly*, 4 March 1990.
18. *Time*, 9 April 1990, p. 97.
19. Ang, *Watching 'Dallas'*.
20. Jane Feuer, 'Reading *Dynasty*. Television and Reception Theory', *South Atlantic Quarterly*, **88**: 2 (Spring 1989), pp. 443–60.

I would like to thank Ava Preacher Collins and Hilary Radner for their contributions to the completion of this manuscript.

# 18

# Critical and textual hypermasculinity

## Lynne Joyrich

From P. Mellencamp (ed.), *Logics of television* (Indiana University Press and BFI 1990)

I'd like to begin my discussion of TV, postmodernism, and the cultural connotations of femininity by referring to an image from David Cronenberg's
film *Videodrome*. In this film, video signals are used to literally open their
viewers to total control: exposure to these signals transforms the human
body into a living VCR which can then be penetrated by videotapes, preventing the subject from differentiating reality from video simulation. Not
only does this illustrate the worst fears of mass culture critics (fears concerning the power of the media to seduce and rape the viewer), but it clearly and
violently marks the receptive TV body as feminine – the tapes are thrust into
a gaping wound that pierces the hero's stomach. *Videodrome* thus brings
together the image of the cyborg body – a postmodern hybrid of human, animal, and machine – and the image of the 'feminine body' – a body yielding
to manipulation, too close to the image to properly evaluate it.[1]
   Such conceptual ties between TV, postmodernism, and femininity (or,
more accurately, the meanings our culture assigns to 'femininity') are symptomatic of shifting gender relations in our technologically mediated culture.
Television, today's cyborgian 'machine-subject,'[2] can be seen as playing out
these relations in all their contradictions, revealing a terrain in which gender figures prominently in a network of differences we have only begun to
explore. By 'reading' several television texts against texts marking TV's critical reception, I will attempt to map out the connections forged between TV
and postmodern culture, focusing on the veiled references to sexual difference and the figuration of gender constituted within this field.
   Noting the ways in which TV has been portrayed as feminine in both film
and mass culture criticism – a situation exacerbated by the fluctuating
ground of postmodernism – I argue that while such tropes of analysis are
seductive, they are also potentially dangerous, encouraging critics to ignore
the complexities and contradictions of gender inscription as well as the other
fields of difference (race, class, age, and so on) which traverse the TV text
and audience alike.[3] In fact, attending to the complex dynamics of gender
within both television and TV criticism might lead us to a very different conclusion from that implied by *Videodrome*'s sexual imagery. Despite the prevalence of such figures and images in accounts of TV, we cannot simply claim

that television is itself either feminine or feminizing. Rather, this ontological premise recuperates the feminine and the critical insights of feminism within a new version of masculinity which inhabits television studies as well as television texts. In other words, the focus on TV as 'feminine' masks a deeper cultural concern with masculinity – a concern which may express itself through the construction of a 'hypermasculinity' that renders the presence of women within TV representation and TV criticism unnecessary.

Several theorists have noted that consumer culture and the culpable masses blamed for its existence have often been figured as feminine. Tania Modleski examines this aspect of historical accounts and emphasizes the problems involved in either simply condemning or celebrating these feminine inscriptions.[4] Andreas Huyssen has also explored attacks on sentimental culture – slurs based on fears of the engulfing ooze of the masses which provoked the 'reaction formation' of a virile and authorial modernism. Yet he concludes his analysis by claiming that such gendered rhetoric has diminished with the decline of modernism: 'mass culture and the masses as feminine threat – such notions belong to another age, Jean Baudrillard's recent ascription of femininity to the masses notwithstanding . . . .'[5] Nonetheless, despite Huyssen's optimistic conclusion, such gendered imagery can still be seen in many analyses of television. While, as Huyssen argues, the 'great divide' between art and mass culture may have narrowed (or even imploded) in the postmodern age, this rupture does not necessarily extend to a generalized dissolution of binary categories of analysis. Rather than an age in which bipolar thinking is no longer operative, we exist in a transitional space in which new dichotomies are erected as fast as the old ones break down. In fact, the very rupture of traditional modes of thought provokes a panicked attempt to create new divisions rather than working to dispel our society's felt need for oppositions. Thus, the kind of binary divisions used to discount mass art by the modernist critics Huyssen discusses continue to exert an influence over critics associated with the rise of postmodern theory in spite of their apparent reluctance to condemn all forms of mass and subcultural production. In other words, distinctions of value seem to hold sway within the realm of mass texts themselves even if the grand opposition between high and low art can no longer describe today's aesthetic theory or practice. Television theorists regularly define their object through such polarities; by constructing a duality in which television is placed in opposition to some other, more 'respected' medium, these theorists articulate cultural and textual difference in terms that are reminiscent of what is still posed as the dominant binarism of our culture – sexual difference.

In *Understanding Media*, for example, Marshall McLuhan compares today's media to the previously dominant print, arguing that the new holistic and participatory modes promote a 'global embrace' and the implosion of margin to center. Associating these media with the nonconformity of criminals, children, blacks, cripples, and women, McLuhan distinguishes the heterogeneity of television from the regularity of book culture.[6] The 'rational' form of print, allied with 'literate man,' is uniform, linear, and isolated – it is, like film, a 'hot' medium based on exclusion. It thus creates the centralized, autonomous subject motivated toward impersonal domination, expansionism, and departmental organization. On the other hand, the 'irrational' media of the electric age, particularly television, return us to the mythical form of the icon in which distance – the distance between subjects as well as the distance between sign and referent – is abolished. The mosaic of TV requires the involvement of all senses in a tactile, primitive intimacy that produces, according to McLuhan, retribalization, organic interlacing, proximity, and empathy.

These qualities are clearly drawn from sterotypes of femininity, and while McLuhan values them, he nonetheless believes that what he terms the 'threat from within the gates' (the new media) must be kept under control by the masculine logic of print.[7] This phrase comes from Hegel who, in theorizing the disruption provoked by Woman, writes that the community 'creates its enemy for itself within its own gates, creates it in what it suppresses, and what is at the same time essential to it – womankind in general. Womankind – the everlasting irony in the life of the community – changes by intrigue the universal purpose of government into a private end . . . .'[8] McLuhan's metaphor for the disruptive media then clearly genders television as feminine – intrinsically feminine if 'the medium is the message.' Any enthusiasm he expresses for the organic qualities of television thus evades important historical questions. For example, McLuhan's claim that TV is inherently decentralized allows him to ignore the fact that it is very much economically centralized and that its femininity consists more in the gender of its primary consumers than in its moral or aesthetic nature. Ignoring the particular social construction of both TV and femininity, McLuhan produces a celebratory reading of television in which sexual difference, once again polarized and essentialized, is made to uphold a historically specific mode of consumption.

Several other critics comparing television to earlier media similarly figure opposition in gendered terms. John Fiske and John Hartley, for example, use McLuhan to support their theory of television as our culture's bard, also describing it as immediate and illogical, failing to support the individualism upheld by linear, abstract print. Arguing that TV is criticized merely because it fails to conform to the standards of 'Rational Man,' they too employ unacknowledged gender codes in their evaluation of television as a 'separate but equal' medium. While Fiske and Hartley do not recognize their oppositions as gendered ones, their description of television as an intimate, personal, familiar medium, working to bond all viewers in an inclusive world, repeats common sexual stereotypes.[9] The cultural denigration of television is thus related to the marginality of an unnamed femininity – as Fiske and Hartley claim, TV is scorned merely for being TV: nonlinear, illogical, and unmasculine.[10]

Similarly, John Ellis compares television to the cinema, arguing that today, the culturally respectable is equated with the cinematic. According to Ellis, cinema's mode of narration constructs a scenario of voyeurism, granting the spectator power over the image and centering the look on the female body. TV, on the other hand, has little narration in the cinematic sense: it offers itself as an immediate presence, failing to produce a sufficiently voyeuristic position for its viewers. TV involves what Ellis calls 'the glance' – a look without power – rather than cinema's gaze. The viewer then delegates his/her look to television itself, forging a sense of intimacy as events are shared rather than witnessed.[11] In other words, the glance of the TV viewer is a domestic, distracted, and powerless look that implies continuous co-presence – a 'feminine' look that is too close to the object to maintain the gap essential to desire and full subjectivity.

As this brief survey shows, the use of feminine imagery to describe our 'lowest' cultural form (in opposition to whatever is held up as more respectable and 'masculine' – print or film) has not faded away with the passing of modernism.[12] In fact, such gender implications take on new meaning in the postmodern age as the threat of fluctuating signs, unstable distinctions, and fractured identities provokes a retreat toward nostalgia for firm stakes of meaning.[13] As the '"natural" grounding principle' once seemingly offered by sexual difference erodes, new anxieties are created which are often projected onto television (a medium which stands as the ultimate in fluctuating signs even as it tries to remain a bastion of family values). Describing television in a world in which distance and contemplation are impossible, for example, Baudrillard writes, 'the opposing poles of determination vanish according to a nuclear contraction . . . of the old polar schema which has always maintained a minimal distance between a cause and an effect, between the subject and an object . . . .'[14] In the circular logic of simulation, classical reason threatens to vanish, and separate positions merge. In Baudrillard's words, 'positivity and negativity engender and overlap . . . there is no longer any active or passive . . . linear continuity and dialectical polarity no longer exist.'[15] As dialectics collapse, the oppositions which maintain sexual difference and the stability of the sexed gaze seem to shift, if not fully disappear.

This collapse of the oppositions which have always upheld the primacy of the masculine subject is further suggested in Baudrillard's description of television as he discards what film theory has taken to be the terms of sexual difference: 'TV is no longer the source of an absolute gaze . . . no longer . . . a system of scrutiny . . . playing on the opposition between seeing and being seen . . . .'[16] In rejecting the applicability of the categories subject/object, active/passive, and seeing/being seen, Baudrillard rejects the divisions that have been seen by many feminist film critics as constitutive of the male spectator.[17] In other words, for Baudrillard, postmodernism – and television in particular – seems to disallow the security and mastery of the masculine position, and as this stable site disappears, we are all left floating in a diffuse, irrational space – a space traditionally coded as feminine.

In the essay 'In the Shadow of the Silent Majorities,' Baudrillard describes the masses as soft and sticky, lacking attribute and reference. They are like a black hole that engulfs all meaning in an implosion of the social, an overpresence that collapses inward, producing a lack of distance or defining feature, and through this account, the masses are figured in clichés of femininity. But like women, the masses have access to a certain excess – they over-conform and over-consume, reduplicating the logic of the media. Referring, like McLuhan, to Hegel's analysis of 'womankind,' Baudrillard writes that this 'destructive hyper-simulation' is 'akin to the eternal irony of femininity of which Hegel speaks – the irony of false fidelity, of an excessive fidelity to the law, an ultimately impenetrable simulation of passivity and obedience . . . which annuls . . . the law governing them . . . .'[18] This theorization of subversive hyperconformity is very familiar. It mimics both Luce Irigaray's analysis of feminine mimicry – a playful repetition in which women resubmit themselves to a masculine discourse so as to show they remain 'elsewhere' – and the notion of feminine masquerade elaborated, for example, by Mary Ann Doane in which women flaunt their femininity in order to hold it at a distance.[19]

Yet as many critics have noted, Baudrillard (unlike Irigaray and Doane) is not advocating acts of political resistance – he assumes the position of the feminine in order to stress the vacuum of the enveloping mass rather than the possible differences that may be constituted within it. He thus argues against those theorists who 'would like to make a new source of revolutionary energy (in particular in its sexual and desire version). They would like to . . . reinstate it in its very banality, as historical negativity. Exaltations of micro-desires, small differences, unconscious practices, anonymous marginalities . . . and to transfer it back to political reason.'[20] For Baudrillard, the goal of politicizing such fields is an impossible one. Substituting the fear of an all-consuming mass for the older notion of an all-controlling industry, he insists upon the anonymity of the feminized masses who are neither subject nor object.[21] In rejecting any theory of subjectivity which might valorize the deconstruction of identity (in a play of differences) as politically progressive, Baudrillard sentences the political (and political resistance) to annihilation. Nonetheless, as 'a direct defiance of the political,' the masses' feminine hyperconformity, their ironic excess, is still a show of strength, a mode of resistance escaping control.[22] In this way, Baudrillard employs the concept of the feminine, but deprives it of the progressive force suggested by some feminist critics – he simply recasts the division between mass culture and high culture in terms of a routine gender dichotomy.

Baudrillard is not the first male theorist to claim the position of the feminine as a way to signify ironic strength (whether deemed political or not). His analysis of hyperaffirmation recalls Jacques Derrida's discussion of the feminine in *Spurs* (part of which occurs, interestingly, in a section entitled 'Simulations'). Considering Nietzsche's 'affirmative woman,' Derrida writes, 'she plays at dissimulation, at ornamentation, deceit, artifice, at an artist's philosophy. Here is an affirmative power . . . .' Woman is thus an indeterminable identity, 'a non-figure, a simulacrum.'[23] It is the very breakdown in logic that dismays readers of Baudrillard's *Simulations* that delights Derrida here, and the creation of a space between the self and the image through an exaggeration of this breakdown, the hypersimulation associated with feminine irony, is the only 'hopeful' possibility that even Baudrillard seems to offer.

Yet feminists must approach a hope figured as feminine salvation with suspicion. As Modleski points out, figuring both the masses and their subversive mode as feminine does not necessarily give feminists concerned with the historical and cultural position of women any cause for celebration. Noting the (masculine) sexual indifference that arises when the position of feminine difference is claimed by everyone, Modleski insists that the ascription of femininity to the anonymous mass glosses over crucial distinctions.[24] Attending similarly to Nancy Miller's warning, we must not lose sight of the ways in which a theoretical position that deems the question 'who speaks?' irrelevant can also maintain the institutional silencing of women. As Miller states, 'Only those who have it can play with not having it.'[25]

Not only must we be leery of male theorists playing with the demise of a social and political representation that we have never had, but we must not obscure the differences that do exist for men and women within the realm of mass culture. Returning to Huyssen's claim that images of a feminized mass culture no longer apply to the postmodern world, let me continue his point: 'If anything, a kind of reverse statement would make more sense: certain forms of mass culture, with their obsession with gendered violence, are more of a threat to women than to men. After all, it has always been men rather than women who have had real control over the productions of mass culture.'[26] In other words, while television spectatorship may be figured as generically feminine, two crucial differences are overlooked: the historical split between consumption and production (in which women are the primary consumers while men largely control television production) and TV's reaction against the feminine through the construction of a violent hypermasculinity.

Turning first to the issue of a gendered consumption, many television critics and historians have explored the material conditions of female consumption, women's viewing patterns, and advertisers' address to this audience.[27] Furthermore, several theorists suggest a relationship between constructions of femininity and the consumer subject. Elsewhere, I have argued that such theoretical accounts of femininity accord in many ways with popular images of women in relation to looking and buying.[28] In the popular imagination, the woman is too close to what she sees – she is so attached that she is driven to possess whatever meets her eye (or, as the pun suggests, her 'I'). The labels commonly applied to film and television genres addressing a female audience – 'weepies' and 'tearjerkers' – convey the same assessment: there is an almost physical closeness assumed to exist between the overinvolved female spectator and the image which forces her tearful response. Such everyday appraisals of women as subjects who lack the distance required for 'proper' reasoning and viewing are mirrored by theoretical and psychoanalytic accounts of femininity which similarly stress women's lack of subject/object separation.[29]

While feminist theorists may offer these tropes of female proximity, fluidity, and 'nearness' as a subversive or hopeful alternative to the masculine model of identity, such overpresence cannot be divorced from consumer desires. As several critics have remarked, it is the emphasis on self-image that invites the consumer to attend to the images of advertised products, and the woman who must purchase in order to enhance her own status as valued commodity becomes the prototypical consumer – the same overpresence that ties her to the image allows her to be situated as both the subject and the object of consumerism at once.[30] It is thus no coincidence that (what has been seen as) the particular 'feminine' textuality of television supports the psychology of the perfect consumer. One of TV's most devalued genres, the soap opera, clearly exposes this intersection of cultural notions of femininity and consumerism: within the form seen by many critics as emblematic of female subjectivity, there are almost twice as many commercials as occur on prime-time TV. Furthermore, television theorists have suggested a relationship between soap opera form – a continuously interrupted present which refuses closure – and the effectivity of its commercials which, rather than truly interrupting the soap opera, continue its narrative patterns while offering 'oases of narrative closure.'[31]

Yet the conditions that link consumerism and femininity (both related to an overidentification with the image and commodity object) affect all of postmodern culture – today men also attend to self-image and their value of exchange, similarly losing the distinction between subject and object that has characterized the female consumer. Not only, then, are women presumed to be the best of consumers, but all consumers are figured as feminized – a situation yielding tension in a culture desperately trying to shore up traditional distinctions even as its simulations destabilize such attempts. As the distance between subject and object diminishes in the weightless space of postmodern culture, the threat of feminization as well as an all-encompassing consumerism hangs over all subjects, and television (discussed, like femininity, through tropes of proximity, overpresence, and immediacy) is central to this process.

While TV's appeal then does not stop with women, its consumers have been belittled in such terms in the critical and popular imagination alike, provoking contemptuous assessments of genres in addition to those traditionally associated with female audiences. Music Television, for example – a form which also addresses a culturally devalued (but economically desirable) audience, youths in this case – further reveals the relations between a fractured Oedipal logic, postmodern form, and consumerism: these videos completely dissolve the distinction between program, product, and ad in texts which can only be described as commercials for themselves.[32] TV soap operas and music videos, the programs most disparaged, are thus in many ways the most telling, displaying the conventions of continuity and difference, presence and interruption, viewing and consuming invoked by the television apparatus. In other words, the forms that seem to best illustrate TV's specificity also reveal a consumerism associated with the address to an audience deemed infantile or feminine, a spectator 'not fully a man.'

Yet as the 'feminine' connotations attached to television and consumer closeness are diffused onto a general audience, contradictions of gender and spectatorship emerge, and television is placed in a precarious position as it attempts to induce consumer overpresence even as it tries to achieve cultural status by mimicking the more respectable cinema. It is interesting in this context to look at texts which exaggerate or foreground the specific representational strategies and discursive configurations of contemporary television. For example, a program such as ABC's on-again, off-again series *Max Headroom* rejects the cinematic model as it self-consciously announces television's difference, and as it calls attention to the characteristics of television (which are, as we have seen, shot through with connotations of gender), it would also seem to be among the shows most vulnerable to charges of feminization.

*Max Headroom* does, in many ways, raise this fear as it both extends and defends itself against the vacuum of simulation and the threat of a feminized world. In the premiere episode, for example, we are introduced to Max, a computer-generated 'video subject' who is born in an attempt to answer an enigma. The enigma at the root of this 'birth' centers on a mysterious death and cover-up – an event investigated by ace news reporter Edison Carter, the man who furnished the mind given to Max. In the scene

in which this enigma is made visible, we see a large and lazy man at home in his armchair, watching television as an ad comes on the air. The ad he sees makes use of a diegetically new representational form – instead of presenting a logical and linear argument, a miniature narrative, or a coherent series of associational images, it involves a rapid flow of sound and images, chaotically thrown together so that nothing can be clearly identified or isolated. In other words, this ad is simply an intensified microcosm of TV as we, the home viewers, know it. The effect of this commercial on the diegetic viewer, however, is that of a literal inflation – the man swells up as consumer s(t)imulation builds inside of him until he actually explodes (or, for Baudrillard, implodes). What we witness, then, can almost be described as a form of hysterical pregnancy – TV provokes a generation of sensations, meaning, and animated force until this energy short-circuits and bursts to the surface, destroying the human body but providing the narrative origin of the cyborg, Max. Because Edison Carter has seen this event (although on videotape), he is captured, and his brain is scanned by a computer in order to disclose the full extent of his knowledge. In the process, Max Headroom is created. Eventually, of course, Edison recovers, solves the case, and reports the crime through another simulation – he broadcasts the contents of Max's memory which contains the videotape of the viewer explosion.

Exploring the sexual and textual issues raised in this episode, it is first of all apparent that TV is caught up in a web of simulations – any access to 'the real' is mediated through a series of video images (the original video ad, the videotape of the ad and explosion, the computer scan of Edison's memory of the tape, and finally, Edison's retaping of Max's computerized memory of the tape – a broadcast which is at that point at least four times removed). In the show's brief second run, such simulations are even further exaggerated. While Max gained Edison's mind in the opening season, in the 'second premiere' Max returns the favor, allowing Edison to be programmed with the contents of his computerized memory in order to save Edison from 'going out of his head' after being brainwashed by some junk food and its accompanying prize.[33] The question, then, of whose mind either Edison or Max can go out of (or into) raises the ultimate problem of simulation and its twisted yet seemingly all-encompassing order. *Max Headroom*, in other words, presents a completely technologically mediated world, the ultimate in postmodern hyperreality that, as the program's logo tells us, is only twenty minutes into our own future. Furthermore, in its form as well as content, this show draws on postmodern textual devices – the program is known for the ways in which it refuses to subordinate its visual effects to a clear narrative progression and multiplies the look through a dense layering of simulated images and a fractured diegesis. As this program plays with TV's multiplicity of signs, time flow and shifting space, editing techniques derived from advertising, and fluctuating levels of reality/reproduction/fabrication, it carries TV form to its limits, shifting the critique of television into a celebration of its specificity.

But like critical accounts of television, *Max Headroom*'s depiction of TV simulation is not divorced from questions of gender: this scene figures both the receptive TV body and the threat of a simulated world in terms of denigrating images of femininity. The viewer-victim, while a man, is an emasculated one –

flabby and passive, he sits in front of his TV set until his body blows up in the pregnancy that ultimately results in Max. As (literally) a 'talking head,' Max himself is likewise feminized – he lacks the body of a man and constantly tries to sort out a man's sexual memories that he can't really understand. While Max masquerades as male, his constantly shifting contours provide him with a fluctuation of being that refuses even the illusion of unity and stability. Unable to differentiate himself from the matrices that bear him, he does not master the order of hyperreality but can only flow within it, losing the distinction between self and other that is (however fictionally) required to attain the status of a man. This condition, however, is not confined to Max – even the experts of this simulation, the computer operators who help Edison solve his cases, lack powerful masculinity: Max is created by a pre-adolescent (and pre-sexual) whiz kid, while Edison's computer guide is female. Here, as in Baudrillard's vision, the dangers of hyperreality, as well as its perpetrators, are feminized.

Yet while it plays with textual figures and devices that have been theoretically linked not only to postmodernism but also to feminine subjectivity, various strategies with which to contain TV's 'feminine' connotations are also employed. *Max Headroom* literally splits its hero in two, displacing postmodern consumer consciousness onto Max and leaving Edison Carter free to play the role of traditional hero. While Max is there for comic effect (much of the show's humor is based on his lack of a stable identity and his literal existence in the perpetual present of the TV mosaic – in the show's jargon, Max is 'in the system,' essentially bound to the flow of TV), it does, nonetheless, take a 'real man' to free us from the adverse effects of this simulated world. Edison Carter, a typical melodramatic hero, battles crime and exposes wrongdoing in order to keep his world in line. This program thus exists in the tension between modern and postmodern forms, projecting the 'feminine' cyborgian elements onto a dominated other (Max) while still allowing its male protagonist to control the diegetic space and the flow of the narrative.

In a similar way, television as a whole exists in an odd tension, balanced between the modern and the postmodern (its reliance on melodrama, for example, in the midst of its own self-referential texts) and between culturally constituted notions of the feminine and the masculine (both sustaining and rejecting the positions offered by critical, as well as commercial, discourses). This places television in a curious bind – a situation perhaps most evident in many prime-time programs which, in order to be 'culturally respectable' and appeal to male viewers, attempt to elevate the infantile and deny the feminine conventionally associated with television (particularly with the texts I have noted). A common strategy of television is thus to construct a violent hypermasculinity – an excess of 'maleness' that acts as a shield. In this way, TV's defense against the feminine may be seen to correspond with television theory's attempts to dispense with the same – by their either resisting the feminine position (as many television texts do) or else incorporating and so speaking for it (as occurs in many recuperative critical texts, as discussed above), the real presence of women within these particular TV representations and critical texts is deemed unnecessary.

Within the realm of TV itself, there are a number of possible methods of defense. By aiming for the status of 'quality' television (producing texts that

can function under the name of an author), creating 'proper' spectator distance by mimicking cinematic conventions, or obsessively remarking the masculinity of their thematics, some programs attempt to evade TV's feminization. Yet attempts at denial and male masquerade can produce problems which emerge on the surface of 'masculine' texts.[34] Faced with the contradictions created by the imperative to inscribe order in a medium that disallows resolution and the demand to be 'manly' in the 'feminized' world of TV, these texts yield a realm of masculine excess that demonstrates their fragile position within both TV's hyperreality and a 'hypermasculinity' that is its defense.

In her article on televised sports, Margaret Morse notes that despite cultural inhibition, 'the gaze at "maleness" would seem necessary to the construction and . . . replenishment of a shared . . . ideal of masculinity'[35] – an ideal that, in the light of my earlier remarks on consumer culture, particularly needs replenishing. Morse examines the discourse on sport as 'a place of "autonomous masculinity," freed even from dependence on woman-as-other to anchor identity.'[36] Sport, however, is not the only area in which the male body is displayed. In her analysis of *Magnum, p.i.*, for example, Sandy Flitterman traces the mobilization of the male spectacle, revealing the ways in which an eroticized masculinity is foregrounded.[37] Furthermore, such displays do not necessarily establish a masculinity free from relation to the feminine, despite their location within the (generally) all-male preserves of sports and the cop/detective show. They can instead be seen as an attempt to save masculinity even in the 'feminized' world of TV, even in the vacuum of a crisis-ridden postmodernism (which, not incidentally, also includes the crisis of Vietnam – a crisis in masculinity which has been dealt with explicitly in several cop/detective shows, including *Magnum, p.i.*, and which may also be partially responsible for the popularity of the genre in general).[38]

Even more than *Magnum, p.i.*, *Miami Vice* is a show of male excess and display which can be analyzed as a response to a feminine 'contagion.' In his insightful analysis, Jeremy Butler reveals the ways in which *Miami Vice* aspires to the cultural position of the cinema through its use of *film noir* conventions.[39] Yet *Vice* differs from *film noir* in some important ways. In place of the duplicitous woman – the trouble that sets the cinematic plot in motion – the motivating forces in *Miami Vice* are all men. Women may be visible as background detail or decor, but in a world in which male criminals are the primary enigmas and objects of voyeurism, the woman is divested of all potency, including, and most importantly, her power of masquerade, her ability to manipulate her feminity. Here, the power of masquerade belongs to men, most frequently Crockett and Tubbs who display themselves as criminals in order to lure their prey into captivity. (This display can also be seen in the ways in which the images of Crockett and Tubbs have been taken up by advertising and fashion – again, it is the male image which is now the focus, the men who masquerade.) While *film noir* investigates female identity and masquerade, *Miami Vice*'s central dilemma revolves around the identity of 'V/vice' and the possibility of differentiating between the cops and the crooks, the men and their roles.[40] Clearly at stake here is a question of masculinity in a world in which all stable distinctions have dissolved, in which the feminized object of the look and trouble of the text constitute a position shared by everyone. This is a crucial question for postmodern, post-Vietnam America as well as an issue for television – the 'feminine' cultural form of our time.

An episode entitled 'Duty and Honor' (one of the episodes confronting Vietnam) exemplifies the textual disturbances provoked by such displays of manliness. The narrative traces the paths of both an assassin – a black Vietnam veteran, called only 'the Savage,' who is responsible for a series of prostitute murders (all of the victims are marked by the words 'VC Whore' despite the fact that most of them are not Vietnamese) – and a Vietnamese police officer, a former friend of Lieutenant Castillo who comes to Miami to solve the murders that have haunted the two since their meeting in Vietnam. From our first sight of the Savage, he is marked as an object of the gaze as he appears before a mirror, eyeing himself and rehearsing a pose. He is thus constituted as spectacle – the spectacle of a perfect machine, a cyborg weapon of war, and a feminized icon demanding to be looked at.

Discussing the spectacle of the cyborg body as well as the aesthetic of slow motion, Morse analyzes the athlete in terms of the cultural fantasy of the perfect machine body, a body moved by an 'inner logic' beyond space and time, at one with nature and 'unimpeded by acts of the ego.' In the ritualized experience of this unified 'flow,' she writes, 'man can overcome his separateness from nature, God, other men and his own body, and achieve grace, signified by slow motion.'[41] In other words, as a cyborg body, an object displayed for the fascinated gaze, the male athlete can ritually experience a subjectivity usually coded as feminine. This analysis of slow motion applies to the visual style of *Miami Vice*, and specifically here to the cyborg, the Savage, who is positioned as both a (feminized) visual object and a perfect machine of death. His status as image is constantly emphasized as we see him primp in a black leather coat, repeating a gesture of smoothing his hair. In one scene, he even competes with a televised display of male body-building as he yells at his landlady for watching too much TV and failing to look at him when she speaks.

As both spectacle and object of the investigatory gaze, the Savage is assigned the role traditionally aligned with femininity. In fact, as the narrative progresses, we learn that he is literally feminized; he has been castrated in Vietnam, the reason for his hatred of Vietnamese women and their simulated stand-ins. Hypermasculinity as a response to such feminization, the underlying structure of texts of male spectacle, is then made manifest in the episode's central murder scene.[42] The scene is marked by a flattened pictorial space fully dominated by the Savage. Staring into the camera, he is posed against a stark wall, apparently naked, with an enormous knife emerging from the bottom of the frame. Sharing the prostitute's point of view, we see the Savage approach and almost leap into the camera, returning the look of the spectator with a violent retribution that obscures our vision and concretizes the excess of his status as spectacle as well as the discord of such hypermasculinity, a reaction to castration.

In the logic of the episode, this castration is infectious – after the introductory flashback to the initial crime in Vietnam, the episode begins as Sonny Crockett is interrupted at the height of a sexual encounter by the news of the latest homicide. Sonny is also a Vietnam vet, and there is an odd mirroring thus established between two 'couples': Sonny and the Savage, and Castillo and Nguyen Van-Trang, Castillo's former partner. In both couples, each 'partner' has immediate knowledge of the other which goes beyond language but is distorted by a masquerade. Furthermore, in these 'pairs,' the conventional terms of sexual difference have been displaced onto racial difference, a situation also key to *Miami Vice*'s primary partnership – that of Crockett and Tubbs. In this episode, however, the focus shifts to the couples Sonny and Savage, Castillo and Trang – two familiar heroes and their 'others.' Sonny mirrors the Savage in two scenes as shots of his search for the killer are intercut with shots of the Savage looking for prostitutes. Finally, Sonny exhibits the contagion of feminization by smoothing his hair in the characteristic gesture of his prey moments before the Savage arrives and is instantly recognized through the crowd (although Sonny has never seen him before) while making the same gesture.

While the chase scene locates Sonny and the Savage as (literally) moving down 'parallel roads,' the successful joining of Castillo and Trang is located in the hope for an impossible future world. It is only after Trang has saved Castillo from attack, tenderly examined his wound, and quickly disappeared that Castillo reads of his friend's masquerade – Trang is an alias, assumed for undercover work in South Vietnam and Miami. While he remains unnamed, his voice-over explains his real status as colonel in the Army of the Republic of Vietnam, his new understanding of the Savage as victim (of the true savages in both of their countries who nurture war), and his appreciation of Castillo's care despite the masquerade. He ends his letter asking for friendship: 'I dream of a more perfect world in which we could also be comrades.' The dream of male bonding, occurring against a backdrop in which it is impossible to distinguish opposing sides, assert right or wrong, or secure masculinity apart from a violent defense, is here played out in all its excess and contradiction.

While the politically progressive 'message' of this episode is striking in relation to the usual fare of TV cop shows, it exposes the problematic of which I am speaking in chillingly clear terms, embodying the hypermasculine defense against a feminization associated with TV, postmodernism, and post-Vietnam America in the cyborg character of the Savage. As such, it reveals TV's masquerade of masculinity – a masquerade which may be seen as a violent response to the feminine connotations attached to television and its receptive viewers. In other words, while theoretical and popular discourses alike may figure television in terms of femininity, we should not accept such views uncritically, failing then to notice other crucial differences which run through television – differences related to class and racial positioning, for example – as well as the contradictions of gender that do exist within television's multiple address. While the gender inscriptions of US broadcast television are complex, intertwined, and unstable, it is important to note that even the temporary securities offered in shows of male spectacle require the neutralization or absence of women (while still disavowing any overt homosexual eroticism). The family offered is a family of man, and the gender positions cast are significant for both the men and women watching. In a medium in which the familial is the dominant theme as well as mode of address, this is the final irony that cannot yet be explained by current theories of sexual and textual difference – the masculine threat that lurks 'within the gates' of a medium deemed feminine.

## Notes

1. The concept of the cyborg body comes from Donna Haraway, 'A Manifesto for Cyborgs. Science, Technology, and Socialist Feminism in the 1980s', *Socialist Review*, 80 (Mar.–Apr. 1985), pp. 65–107. See also Tania Modleski's discussion of *Videodrome* in 'The Terror of Pleasure. The Contemporary Horror Film and Postmodern Theory' in Tania Modleski, ed., *Studies in Entertainment. Critical Approaches to Mass Culture* (Bloomington, IN, Indiana University Press, 1986), p. 159.
2. The term 'machine-subject' comes from Margaret Morse who analyzes the ways in which TV seems to address its viewers from a position of subjectivity in 'Talk, Talk, Talk – The Space of Discourse in Television', *Screen*, 26:2 (Mar.–Apr. 1985), p. 6.
3. For a related analysis, see Patrice Petro, 'Mass Culture and the Feminine. The "Place" of Television in Film Studies', *Cinema Journal*, 25:3 (Spring 1986), pp. 5–21.
4. Tania Modleski, 'Femininity as Mas(s)querade. A Feminist Approach to Mass Culture', in Colin MacCabe, ed., *High Theory/Low Culture* (New York, St. Martin's Press, 1986), pp. 37–52.
5. Andreas Huyssen, 'Mass Culture as Woman. Modernism's Other', in *After the Great Divide. Modernism, Mass Culture, Postmodernism* (Bloomington, IN, Indiana University Press, 1986), pp. 62 and 53–5.
6. Marshall McLuhan, *Understanding Media. The Extensions of Man* (New York, McGraw, 1964), pp. 16–17.
7. McLuhan, *Understanding Media*, p. 17.
8. Georg W. F. Hegel, *Phenomenology of Mind*, trans. J. B. Baillie (New York, Harper, 1967), p. 496.
9. John Fiske and John Hartley, *Reading Television* (New York, Methuen, 1978). See, for example, pp. 15, 85–7, 112, and 116–26. The chart of oppositions between television and literate media that Fiske and Hartley offer in this book (pp. 124–5) mirrors the one that Fiske employs to differentiate feminine and masculine forms in *Television Culture* (New York, Methuen, 1987), p. 203.
10. According to Fiske and Hartley, it is in the space between TV's irrational mode and the masculine logic of print that the viewer can position him/herself so as to decode TV differently. Through the (unspoken) metaphors of sexual difference, then, these theorists construct a theory of television's difference – a view that echoes a common position in literary theory which has also aligned textual difference with figures of femininity.
11. John Ellis, *Visible Fictions* (London, Routledge, 1982). See, for example, pp. 57, 116, 137–9, 141–3, 146.
12. Perhaps the most obvious case of this tendency to associate television with the feminine is the Lacanian reading offered by Beverle Houston in the article 'Viewing Television. The Metapsychology of Endless Consumption', *Quarterly Review of Film Studies*, 9:3 (Summer 1984), pp. 183–95. I don't discuss this analysis in the text precisely because the thesis that TV is feminine is so clear in her work. The more interesting cases, in my opinion, are those in which gendered metaphors creep into discussions of television by critics not expressly making this claim.
13. See, for example, Huyssen's discussion of nostalgia as a response to postmodernism's 'various forms of "otherness"' (including feminism) on pp. 199 and

219–20. Janice Doane and Devon Hodges discuss the anxiety provoked by the erosion of traditional categories of gender in *Nostalgia and Sexual Difference. The Resistance to Contemporary Feminism* (New York, Methuen, 1987).

14. Jean Baudrillard, *Simulations* (New York, Semiotext[e], 1983), p. 56.

15. Baudrillard, *Simulations*, pp. 30–1. See also pp. 52, 54.

16. Baudrillard, *Simulations*, pp. 52, 54.

17. See, in particular, Laura Mulvey, 'Visual Pleasure and Narrative Cinema', *Screen*, 16(3): (Autumn 1975), pp. 6–18. Recently, many feminist film theorists have retheorized spectatorship so as to account for shifting and contradictory identifications and more powerful and pleasurable positions for the female viewer. See, for example, Elizabeth Cowie, 'Fantasia', *m/f*, 9 (1984), pp. 71–105; Teresa de Lauretis, *Alice Doesn't. Feminism, Semiotics, Cinema* (Bloomington, IN, Indiana University Press, 1984); Tania Modleski, *The Women Who Knew Too Much. Hitchcock and Feminist Theory* (New York, Methuen, 1988); Kaja Silverman, *The Acoustic Mirror. The Female Voice in Psychoanalysis and Cinema* (Bloomington, IN, Indiana University Press, 1988); and Linda Williams, 'Something Else Besides a Mother. *Stella Dallas* and the Maternal Melodrama', *Cinema Journal*, 24(1): (Fall 1984), pp. 2–27.

   In discussing the female spectator in the latter part of this paper in terms of narcissism and tropes of proximity, I am not claiming that these are the only or essential positions available for an actual female viewer. Rather, I am focusing on the *representation* of women in both popular and critical accounts of cinematic spectatorship. In other words, the historically and culturally sanctioned positions for female viewers are quite limited even though other constructions of viewing pleasure are certainly possible, particularly for viewers who have been positioned 'differently' by the discourses of feminism.

18. Jean Baudrillard, *In the Shadow of the Silent Majorities . . . or The End of the Social and Other Essays* (New York; Semiotext[e], 1983), p. 33.

19. Luce Irigaray, *This Sex Which Is Not One*, trans. Catherine Porter (Ithaca, NY, Cornell University Press, 1985), pp. 76, 150–1; and Mary Ann Doane, 'Film and the Masquerade. Theorizing the Female Spectator', *Screen*, 23: 3–4 (Sept.–Oct. 1982), pp. 74–88. Doane employs and expands the concept of masquerade developed by Joan Riviere in 'Womanliness as Masquerade', in Henrik Ruitenbeek, ed., *Psychoanalysis and Female Sexuality* (New Haven, CT, College and University Press, 1966), pp. 209–20. Also see Mary Ann Doane, 'Masquerade Reconsidered. Further Thoughts on the Female Spectator', *Discourse*, 11(1): (Fall-Winter 1988–89), pp. 42–54.

20. Baudrillard, *In the Shadow*, pp. 40–1. See also p. 39.

21. Rey Chow, 'Tofu. The Protein and Protean Dietetics', Cornell Graduate Student Conference on the Culture Industry, Cornell University, New York, April 1987.

22. See Baudrillard, *In the Shadow*, p. 39.

23. Jacques Derrida, *Spurs. Nietzsche's Styles*, trans. Barbara Harlow (Chicago, IL, University of Chicago Press, 1978), pp. 67, 57, 49.

24. Modleski, *The Women Who Knew Too Much*, pp. 50–51.

25. Nancy Miller, 'The Text's Heroine. A Feminist Critic and Her Fictions', *Diacritics*, 12: 2 (Summer 1982), p. 53. Also addressing this issue is Naomi Schor, 'Dreaming Dissymmetry. Barthes, Foucault, and Sexual Difference', in Alice Jardine and Paul Smith, eds, *Men in Feminism* (New York, Methuen, 1987), pp. 98–110; and Patricia Mellencamp who examines sit-com simulations that are inflected differently by the female voice in 'Situation Comedy, Feminism, and Freud. Discourses of Gracie and Lucy', in Modleski, *Studies in Entertainment*, especially p. 87.

26. Huyssen, 'Mass Culture as Woman', p. 205. The 'threat to women' revealed by mass culture's gendered violence can also be seen in my example of *Videodrome* – a

film that thus demonstrates how TV has been figured as feminine as well as how this figuration masks a violent hypermasculinity.

27. See, for example, the essays in *Camera Obscura*'s special issue on 'Television and the Female Consumer', *Camera Obscura*, 16 (Jan. 1988), and in the anthology *Boxed In. Women and Television*, ed. Helen Baehr and Gillian Dyer (New York, Pandora Press, 1987).

28. Lynne Joyrich, 'All That Television Allows. TV Melodrama, Postmodernism, and Consumer Culture', *Camera Obscura*, 16 (Jan. 1988), pp. 141–7.

29. See, for example, Nancy Chodorow, *The Reproduction of Mothering. Psychoanalysis and the Sociology of Gender* (Berkeley, CA, University of California Press, 1978); Carol Gilligan, *In a Different Voice. Psychological Theory and Women's Development* (Cambridge, MA, Harvard University Press, 1982); Irigaray, *This Sex Which Is Not One*; and Michèle Montrelay, 'Inquiry into Femininity', *m/f*, 1 (1978), pp. 83–102. For an illuminating discussion of such tropes of feminine proximity, see Mary Ann Doane, *The Desire to Desire. The Woman's Film of the 1940s* (Bloomington, IN, Indiana University Press, 1987).

30. On advertising and self-image, see T. J. Jackson Lears, 'From Salvation to Self-realization. Advertising and the Therapeutic Roots of Consumer Culture, 1880–1930', in Richard Wightman Fox and T. J. Jackson Lears, eds, *The Culture of Consumption. Critical Essays in American History, 1880–1980* (New York, Pantheon, 1983), pp. 3–38. Relating this to the specific position of women is Rosalind Coward, *Female Desires. How They Are Sold, Bought, and Packaged* (New York, Grove Press, 1985), and Doane, *The Desire to Desire*, especially pp. 13 and 22–33.

31. See Sandy Flitterman, 'The *Real* Soap Operas. TV Commercials', in E. Ann Kaplan, ed., *Regarding Television. Critical Approaches – An Anthology* (Frederick, MD, University Publications of America, 1983), pp. 84, 94. See also the essays on soap by Tania Modleski, Charlotte Brunsdon, and Robert Allen in the same volume.

32. On MTV and postmodernism, see, for example, E. Ann Kaplan, *Rocking Around the Clock. Music Television, Postmodernism, and Consumer Culture* (New York, Methuen, 1987); Peter Wollen, 'Ways of Thinking about Music Video (and Postmodernism)', *Critical Quarterly*, **28**: 1–2 (Spring–Summer 1986), pp. 167–70; and the essays on music video in *Journal of Communication Inquiry*, **10**(1)(1986).

33. After *Max Headroom*'s initial introduction in the US on March 31, 1987 (a remake of the original British text), its 'second premiere' aired on ABC on April 28, 1988. Throughout this episode, we witness an argument between the two heroes which erupts when Max (who gets better ratings) steals Edison's airtime. When Max is later projected into Edison's brain in order to provide what is referred to as 'a jumpstart' (a phrase which implies that Edison too is a technological being, another cyborg), they continue the argument. Edison exclaims, 'You're always in my way – you're too close to me,' and Max responds, 'I can't help being that close and being a threat to you.' Edison then asks, 'Have you any idea what it's like having a part of me competing against me?' to which Max replies, 'And have you any idea what it's like just being a part?' This exchange, coupled with the plot concerning the power of consumerism, is interesting for the ways in which it explicitly employs the tropes of 'nearness' and overpresence that have been raised in both popular and critical portrayals of the cyborg, the female, and the 'consuming' body. Furthermore, it reveals the threat to a (presumed) separate and unified male subject that is posed by such 'feminized' objects as well as by the operations of postmodern culture which confuse the distinction between part and whole, self and 'other.'

34. The analysis of such shows as 'hysterical' texts that yield contradictions emerging as textual fissures suggests a reading of these programs as 'male melodramas.' Noting that melodrama's search for clearly marked oppositions historically

arises in periods of crisis, one can analyze television – the medium of hyperreality which is defined as *the* age of crisis – as the melodramatic forum of postmodernism. Because of both the specific suitability of melodrama for television and the demands of postmodernism, even genres not typically associated with the melodrama – such as the cop show – have turned toward the more personal issues associated with melodramatic form, thereby inheriting some of this genre's tensions as well as the tensions provoked by such generic hybrids. See Joyrich, 'All That Television Allows', pp. 129–53.

35. Margaret Morse, 'Sport on Television. Replay and Display', in Kaplan, *Regarding Television*, p. 45.
36. Morse, 'Sport on Television', p. 44.
37. Sandy Flitterman, 'Thighs and Whiskers – the Fascination of *Magnum, p.i.*', *Screen*, **26**(2) (Mar.–Apr. 1985), pp. 42–58.
38. The crisis in masculinity provoked by Vietnam has also been discussed by Andrew Ross, 'Masculinity and *Miami Vice*. Selling In'. *Oxford Literary Review*, 8:1–2 (1986), p. 150. Comparing *Miami Vice* to *film noir*, Jeremy Butler reminds us of the historical connection between *noir* style and postwar disillusionment – a connection which suggests that the popularity of *Miami Vice* may be related to post-Vietnam despair. See '*Miami Vice*. The Legacy of Film Noir', *Journal of Popular Film and Television*, **13**(3) (Fall 1985), p. 129.
39. For Butler's analysis of these issues of sexual difference, see pp. 129–30, 132–3.
40. On this core dilemma, see Butler, '*Miami Vice*', pp. 131–2. On the double meaning of 'Vice' as it relates to masquerade and the 'right stuff' of masculinity, see Ross, 'Masculinity and *Miami Vice*', p. 152.
41. Morse, 'Sport on Television', pp. 44, 56.
42. In other words, in 'Duty and Honor' (which NBC first aired on February 6, 1987) hypermasculinity can be seen as a response to (or defense against) the literal embodiment of the Oedipal structure and the castrating woman.

# Video

## Commerce and collage

Unlike cinema, postmodern video tends to resist the standard separation of 'commercial' and 'avant-garde' forms. In both the experimental mode dissected here by Fredric Jameson and the endless spool of music advertisements which E. Ann Kaplan freeze-frames for analysis, the same key terms recur: eclecticism, diversity, flow and, most regularly, 'bricolage'. At moments this method serves conventional ideologies, at others their opposite, but often, too, at its most interesting, video works to re-articulate this distinction.

It is this sense of variety and potential that Peter Wollen cautiously greets at the opening of this section. Music video signals a breakdown of categories and a challenge to genre distinctions, combining record sleeve, fashion catwalk, film pastiche and live performance. Wollen identifies its aesthetic of appropriation and replication, its use of found material and fragmentation of existing texts, its plundering of 'the image-bank and the word-hoard' as essentially postmodern, yet warns against an over-optimistic celebration of the form.

Wollen's description of music video as 'the adolescence of postmodernism' finds telling echoes in the specific MTV texts singled out by E. Ann Kaplan. While she notes the claims made for music video as a means of transcending genres and resisting binary categorisation, her examples are shown to construct an uneasy scenario where the objectification and exploitation of women is offset by a 'playful' mode of intertextual quotation. In Madonna's *Material Girl* promo, for example, the male teenage spectator of MTV is offered the conventional pleasures of voyeurism and spectacle with the postmodern twist of 'irony' as a get-out clause. Likewise, in Kaplan's analysis, the twelve-year-old girls drawn into Madonna's image are seduced into the patriarchal constraints of the 'look' and denied an effective critical voice.

Kaplan's discomfort with these two videos leads her to draw a distinction between 'co-opted' postmodern video and a more progressive group of texts which she links to a modernist and avant-garde tradition. While allowing that the diversity and flow of MTV's commercial postmodernism incorporates 'transgressive' moments in such varied forms as Tina Turner and Laurie Anderson, Kaplan favours the deconstructive strategies of independent film-makers such as Laura Mulvey and Sally Potter. Kaplan's 'utopian' postmodernism would, therefore, be reached less through music video, as Wollen anticipates, than through more overtly transgressive texts which, as she admits, inevitably imply a minority audience and exhibition in 'alternative spaces'.

Fredric Jameson highlights the difficulties of interpretation and the search for a core meaning, or referent, behind the blitz of freewheeling signifiers that characterise postmodern video. His autopsy of the experimental work *AlienNATION* involves a freezing of the 'total flow' comparable to that performed by Kaplan on MTV, and suggests that the deconstructive text by its very nature problematises any notion of communicating a single 'progressive' meaning to its audience. Indeed, the revelation of what the text is 'about' comes as a banal reduction of the work, a simplification of a text whose nature actively resists meanings to corny 'thematisation'. Jameson implies that while the spectator is unable to resist constructing 'meaningful' interpretation from the most obscure stream of images, each individual spectator may draw several conclusions from the same work.

This perception of the ambiguity of experimental video may to some degree unsettle the optimism of the final two accounts, which look to video's potential for the critical articulation of gender, ethnic and sexual difference. Patricia Mellencamp's admiring assessment of Cecilia Condit's work presents a concrete example of the deconstructive mode advocated by Kaplan: a remaking of Oedipal and Lacanian 'grand narratives', a transgression of the binary codes which position women as enunciated other, and a foregrounding of multiple differences 'among women' and 'within women'. Condit's videos achieve this hetereogeneity through a montage of documentary footage, Hitchcockian pastiche and a multiplicity of female voices, evoking the Bakhtinian grotesque and the oral tradition of the folk and fairy tale.

In similar vein, Pratibha Parmar presents her juxtaposition of government Aids warnings with spoken testimonies from lesbians and gay men, disrupting Indian cinema's 'male gaze' through strategic re-editing, and British imperial history with diverse images of resistance through Asian music. Thus, the postmodern aesthetic of quotation and re-working is employed as a weapon against structures of racism, sexism and homophobia. In common with Mellencamp, Parmar embraces postmodern video as a vehicle for the expression of diversity and difference, extending this to her own coding as black and lesbian 'other'. Within this reading, the schizophrenia and decentring often theorised as symptomatic of the postmodern condition acquire a specific relevance to the cultural experience of the 'marginalised' subject in British society. In Parmar's work, the postmodern concepts of dislocation and dispersal are wedded to the 'diasporian sensibilities' of black experience and to the negotiations required against 'the racism of the white gay community, and . . . the homophobia of communities of color' (p. 281).

If these essays appear to situate video uncomfortably between two modes, one compromising 'progressive' content for popularity and the other sacrificing accessibility for a transgressive, deconstructive project, Parmar's account of her own *Bhangra Jig* suggests a further option. Challenging orthodoxies, incorporating popular voices and broadcast several times in one week on

British television, *Bhangra Jig* points to a third way, beyond the ambivalence of commercial MTV and the obscurity of 'alternative' works. Here, perhaps, a 'hybrid aesthetic' emerges to see postmodern video through its difficult adolescence

## Further reading

Cubitt S. 1991: *Timeshift. On video culture.* London: Routledge.

Cubitt S. 1993: *Videography. Video media as art and culture.* London: Macmillan.

Ellis J. 1982, rev. 1992: *Visible fictions. Cinema, television, video.* London: Routledge.

Fiske J. 1986: MTV. Post structural post modern. *Journal of Communication Enquiry* 10:1, 74–9.

Frith S., Goodwin A. and Grossberg L. (eds) 1993: *Sound and vision. The music video reader.* London and New York: Routledge.

Goodwin A. 1987: Music video in the (post) modern world. *Screen* **28**(3): 36–55.

Gray A. 1992: *Video playtime. The gendering of a leisure technology.* London: Routledge.

Hebdige D. 1988: *Hiding in the light. On images and things.* London: Routledge.

Levy M. 1989: *The VCR age. Home video and mass communications.* London: Sage.

Schwichtenberg C. (ed.) 1992: *The Madonna connection.* Boulder, CO: Westview.

Watts M. 1996: Electrifying fragments. Madonna and postmodern performance. *New Theatre Quarterly* 12: **46**: 99–107.

See also the journal: *Screen*: 'Video Issue', **36** (2): (Summer 1995).

# 19

## Ways of thinking about music video (and postmodernism)

*Peter Wollen*

From C. MacCabe (ed.), *Futures for English* (Macmillan 1988)

Music video is generally reckoned to have begun in Britain as a promotional tool ('pop promos') and then to have taken off as an international and television phenomenon with the launch of MTV (Music TeleVision) in the United States on 1 August 1981: the first mass-audience, twenty-four hour, cable music station.

Not only does music video raise a number of semiotic and aesthetic questions, about the relationship between musical, graphic and performance forms, for instance, but it also exemplifies in capsule many of the cultural traits which have given currency to the idea of 'postmodernism'. We can group these under three heads. First, crossover between: (1) the fine arts/avant-garde tradition, (2) the mass-media, (3) vernacular culture (or sub-cultures), (4) the new technologies (mainly electronic) associated with the 'communications explosion' and the 'information revolution'. It is important to stress that both the fine arts and the mass media have themselves evolved and changed in relation to vernacular culture and new technologies and that this, in turn, has transformed the terms of the old avant-garde/kitsch debate.

This has been particularly clear in the world of music. Both the music industry and the avant-garde were forced to respond to the new popular music 'from below' which followed the advent of rock'n'roll and which coincided with new electronic technology that transformed both performance and post-production. In a way, music video simply represents the extension of this into the television industry, at the same time as video art locked in with new trends in music (often, as with Philip Glass or Laurie Anderson, difficult to characterise as 'pop' or 'avant-garde' any longer).

Thus, music video itself challenges the distinction between television and video art, which had already grown up by analogy with the avant-garde/kitsch, fine art/graphics and literature/pulp polarities. Both have converged in the experimental use of new post-production technologies. The input from vernacular culture is much more mediated than it was in the music world, though if home video technology were to become more widely available, this too would change.

Second, the breakdown of genre distinctions and the development of new mixed-media forms. Music video, of course, is just such a form, combining elements of live musical performance, film and TV to produce a kind of electronic mini-operetta, or, to put it another way, an animated record sleeve, extended in time, and with its own sound-track. This strange grafting of packaging on to capsule opera and dance both combines and transforms its varied ingredients in a novel blend to make a miniature 'total work-of-art', to use Wagner's phrase.

But the most significant hybridisation brought about by music video is the breakdown of the distinction between programme and ad. In origin and, from the point of view of the music industry, in function, music videos are an advertising vehicle, promoting the sale of records. In fact, MTV is often credited with the resurgence of the fortunes of the music industry in the United States. In form, too, music videos have much in common with the more sophisticated ads, and there has also been a rapid crossover between the two (e.g. Michael Jackson's Pepsi ads).

But music videos are treated by the television industry as programmes (e.g. the Max Headroom Show in Britain, produced by Chrysalis Records). Of course, this was already the case on radio, where records are programme material for the broadcaster and promotion for the record company. Music videos, however, are both ads for (image) and samples of (sound) the product they are promoting. At the same time, they are increasingly becoming commodities in their own right, which can be bought as video cassettes. Here we have a quite new and complex form of interaction between programming and marketing.

Besides music performance, TV show and ad/packaging, there is a fourth element being hybridised by music video: the fashion event. Fashion already had a close relationship with music performance and with the packaging of musicians as 'images' witness the straddling of the music world, the performance world and the fashion world by David Bowie and Malcolm McLaren. Fashion, in its turn, has been moving into performance as the traditional catwalk has been supplemented by music, lighting, dance and even embryonic narrative. Music video is the culmination of this trend.

Thirdly, the art of postmodernism is one whose typical forms are eclecticism and historicism. Its characteristic modes are those of appropriation, simulation and replication. It plunders the image-bank and the word-hoard for the material of parody, pastiche and, in extreme cases, plagiarism. As Jean-Luc Godard once said, 'Everything can be put in a film. Everything should be put in a film. It's all there and it's all mixed up. That's why I'm so attracted by TV.' Postmodernism takes the modernist forms of the ready-made and collage and lets them loose in Malraux's Imaginary Museum, recycling, not found objects, but found images and fragments of found text.

It is as if the relation between nature and culture has shifted radically. In an age marked by an ever-increasing and ever-accelerating proliferation of signs, of all types, the immediate environment becomes itself increasingly dominated by signs, rather than natural objects or events. The realm of signs becomes not simply a 'second nature' but a primary 'reality'. (The quotes around 'reality' mark the effacement of the traditional distinction between reality and representation in a world dominated by representation, as described, for example, by Baudrillard, in vatic terms.)

As Benjamin's 'age of mechanical reproduction' is replaced by our 'age of

electronic reproduction', the trends which he discerned are further extended. Reproduction, pastiche and quotation, instead of being forms of textual
parasitism, become constitutive of textuality. Repetition and citation become
the typical forms of postmodern cultural production. Clearly, these developments reflect the massive capacity for information storage made possible by
the invention first of photography, then of audio and videotape, then of the
computer. We can expect the production of both image and sound to
become more and more a matter of combining and altering already existing
images and sounds extracted from one or other information store.

Music video, with its emphasis on post-production technology and
departure from the reproduction of live performance, is already replete
with quotation and allusion, ranging from pastiche of Hollywood film styles
(*film noir*, science fantasy) through Fritz Lang's *Metropolis* to images taken
from Magritte or Warhol (purloinment upon purloinment). At the same
time, the music is also ceaselessly recycling itself. Malcolm McLaren's *Fans*,
for instance, is a 'bricolaged' mix of opera (*Carmen, Madame Butterfly*), rap,
and self-referential material from McLaren himself. Songs are made out of
found music, images out of found footage.

Clearly, postmodernist forms, like those to be found in music video,
demand a postmodernist aesthetic. The polarised distinction between
avant-garde and kitsch, high and low art; the doctrine of the purity of genres; the cluster of aesthetic concepts around the idea of artistic originality –
all these are useless for any serious engagement with a hybrid and technologically sophisticated form such as music video. The whole apparatus of
levels, standards, hierarchies, boundaries, limits, centres and sources needs
to be re-thought.

This is not to say that music video should be welcomed uncritically or
unquestioningly. It is rather that the necessary criticism and questioning
demands new concepts and new attitudes. The old critical apparatus has
tended, in practice, to lead either to an exaggerated cultural pessimism or to
a polemical over-enthusiasm. It would be too easy to inflect a traditional
aesthetic with a critique of the spectacle and the commodity-form and
denounce music video out of hand. Or, conversely, to extol it as a form
which infects mainstream television with a subversive new mode of *significance*, associated with the youth audience and youth sub-cultures. Neither
of these approaches will do.

Artistic innovation is always ambiguous. On the one hand, it represents a
phase of transition from one aesthetic orthodoxy to another. In this sense,
the modernist chapter of art history, once consecrated in museum, university
and concert hall, is inevitably ordained to be challenged and eventually
superseded by the next chapter – postmodernism becoming, in its turn, a
new orthodoxy. Postmodernism is then simply the mode of art appropriate
to the next epoch, marked by new technologies and audiences. On the other
hand, artistic innovation is also the bearer of a subversive and corrosive
potential, one which challenges and contradicts established aesthetic norms
and, thus, if pushed far enough, the role of art itself.

In Ernst Bloch's terms, even music video, trashy, glitzy and prematurely
hackneyed as it often is, still can contain a *novum*, an instance of the radically
new which has never yet been. We need an open aesthetics, future-oriented,

to deal with an art which is still in process, not yet sedimented or stereotyped. Music video is still an arena of possibilities: its identity is still unsettled. Bloch argued that the human condition, like adolescence, was defined by its possible futures, its unidentified desire and unarticulated want. Music video is a form of the adolescence of postmodernism. It still holds the utopian possibility of being on its way to somewhere else, somewhere which is not necessarily television, but could be displaced into another kind of form and institution, by a knight's move. That is why music video is worth listening to, watching, theorising, learning from.

# 20

## Feminism/Oedipus/postmodernism: the case of MTV

### E. Ann Kaplan

From E. Ann Kaplan (ed.), *Postmodernism and its discontents* (Verso 1988), including an extract from E. Ann Kaplan, *Rocking around the clock. Music television, postmodernism and consumer culture* (Routledge 1987)

Feminist theorists have been preoccupied with the problem of Oedipus at least since Roland Barthes's convincing elaboration of Freud's 'discovery' of links between narrative and the oedipal complex. If classical narrative 'has the movement of a passage, an actively experienced transformation of the human being ... into man',[1] then it seemed essential, in a first move, for female artists to avoid the processes involved in classical narrative.[2] Correlatively the same theories provoked feminist critics into analyzing the passive position, subject to the Law of the Father, that women have occupied in traditional narratives.

Feminists films (produced as texts counter to dominant ones in the mid-1970s) of necessity used alternative aesthetic strategies in their attempt to avoid the oedipal paradigm centered around the phallus as signifier. Some of the feminists developments took as their starting point Kristeva's postulation of a pre-oedipal, pre-linguistic terrain which Kristeva found in the largely male artistic avant-garde (Joyce, John Cage). Others were attracted by her use of Bakhtin's carnivalesque and polyphony as ways to avoid the phallic, monologic text inevitably representing woman in oppressive ways. Still others, influenced by Brecht, Russian Formalism and Louis Althusser, constructed the well-known polarity whereby the classical realist text, seen as embodying dominant ideology, was pitted against the subversive, non-realist, non-narrative and avant-garde text. The binarisms in classical realist texts were said to function as what Althusser has called Ideological State Apparatuses – that is, as creating and positioning us as subjects who are then made to stand in a specific relation to each other and the State – which Althusser sees as primarily serving the ruling classes. The oedipal scenario (as revised by Lacan) is central for Althusser; it remains among the primary psychic mechanisms by which means we are 'hailed' as subjects.

Some feminists, following Kristeva, began to argue that modernism itself could be equated positively with a subversive 'feminine', since modernist literary techniques deliberately violated traditional forms that embodied (whether explicitly or implicitly) the oedipal scenario. Others saw modernism as misogynist and as problematic for feminist theory and practice because of its high culture, elitist discourse (epitomized by Ortega y Gasset).[3] From this point of view, the 'separateness of the aesthetic from the rest of human life'[4] is antithetical to feminism. Yet even the critics and artists making this objection wanted to retain modernism's transgressive stance.

In different ways, then, popular culture theorists in the 1970s and early 1980s took for granted that the concept of transgression as it had been developed by the great modernists was most useful in criticizing dominant narrative paradigms and in conceptualizing (and creating) counter-texts. Feminists, that is, adapted modernist strategies to their own distinctive ends: since women were writing and creating in an historical moment far different from that of the early decades of the century, modernist strategies functioned differently, taking on different meanings. But broadly speaking these strategies are still best categorized as modernist.

Two reactions to 1970s theories must be briefly mentioned here. First, the anti-narrative text was itself criticized in the mid-1980s as in its turn doing violence to women by denying the audience pleasure. In 'Oedipus Interruptus', Teresa de Lauretis began to question the 'active-passive and gaze-image dichotomies in the theorization of spectatorship'[5] that had led to concepts of the anti-narrative text; she began to rethink 'the possibilities of narrative identification as a subject-effect in female spectators'. She proposes a feminist cinema that would be 'narrative and oedipal with a vengeance', since it would aim to enact the contradiction of female desire in the terms of narrative (p. 40). In this way, feminist cinema could avoid 'the stoic, brutal prescription of self-discipline that seemed inevitable at the time [the early 1970s]' (p. 39).

In a second reaction against seventies theories, feminists analyzing popular culture began to move beyond showing merely that the oedipal scenario positions/limits/represses woman. Exploring the woman's melodrama in film and soap operas on television, they showed the ways in which some dominant texts are able to expose the constraints the oedipal scenario imposes and to reveal gaps where the female spectator is able to retrieve something for herself (for example, through the mothering relation or through female–female bonding). Some argued, in a manner similar to nineteenth-century feminists, that the patriarchally defined feminine, which includes emotionalism, relatedness, connectedness, can be used to further women's own, human ends. The ensuing debate, often articulated as being between so-called 'essentialist' and 'anti-essentialist' feminists (a debate I have analyzed elsewhere)[6] reached its logical extreme in Toril Moi's recent *Sexual/Textual Politics.*[7]

In both the first and second theoretical moves by feminist film and television theorists, women were seen to 'need' narrative. In the first case, feminist film-makers needed narrative as the system against which to create counter-narratives questioning how women had been represented and throwing representation itself into crisis; in the second move, feminists needed narrative as a form within which to position women differently. In this latter, narrative's link to desire is seen as something women have a stake in preserving: to refuse narrative is to refuse pleasure.

But does the postmodern discourse that swept across the American intellectual horizon in the mid-1980s on its way from France require narrative equally? Is narrative a viable concept in the wake of Baudrillard and Lyotard (who represent opposing if complementary positions)?

I want to explore the implications of postmodernism as a putative new cultural moment, as a theoretical and critical concept, and as a variously valued (anti-)aesthetic for feminist theories of narrative as sketched briefly above, particularly in the light of Craig Owens's observation that discussions of sexual difference have been signally absent from writings about postmodernism.[8] How does postmodernism as a theory and as deployed in popular culture affect feminist theory and aesthetic practice?[9] Does postmodernism change female representation, female spectatorship? Does it hinder or advance feminist cultural aims? I will consider these questions through the optic of Music Television as a postmodern cultural institution: specific rock videos exhibited on the channel will help to clarify theoretical points.

Some broad distinctions will be useful in answering the questions just posed. Music Television belongs in the 'co-opted' category by virtue of its being a commercial station, produced and exhibited within a profit-making institution. Its postmodern (anti-)aesthetic strategies need to be considered within that larger context rather than in and for themselves. If some of the devices approximate those used in the 'utopian' postmodern texts, we must nevertheless ask if such a text can be produced within the commercial framework.

Several critics who include popular texts in their discussion of the 'utopian' postmodern appear to accept that possibility. Some apply to the latter area theories not originally developed with popular culture in mind; or they use a theorist like Bakhtin, who wrote about a very different kind of popular culture preceding mechanization. Indeed, many such scholars look to Bakhtin as the one thinker who can provide a theoretical opening to a utopian text or to cultural alternatives.[10] Bakhtin's concept of dialogism, as rewritten by Kristeva, has seemed particularly useful in avoiding the traps and dead-ends of binarism. As is well known, the early Kristeva searches for a text where sex and other differences are transcended, where the metaphysical category of difference no longer exists: we see this in her concept of the 'semiotic' and in her reworking of Bakhtin's notion of the carnivalesque, 'where discourse attains its "potential infinity" . . . where prohibitions (representation, "monologism") and their transgression (dream, body, "dialogism") coexist'.[11] It is what she finds in Sollers's *H* which 'is music that is inscribed in language, becoming the object of its own reasoning, ceaselessly, and until saturated, overflowing, and dazzling sense has been exhausted . . . It whisks you from your comfortable position; it breaches a gust of dizziness into you, but lucidity returns at once, along with music . . .' (p. 7).

Similarly, the following theorists seem to be agreed in imagining a kind of art that does not take its shape from running counter to the dominant system, but is anti-essentialist, plural, where discourses are not hierarchically ordered, where sex and other differences are transcended, where the metaphysical category of difference no longer exists. This is what White and Stallybrass demand when they note the need for a concept of carnival to be linked to notions of transgression and symbolic inversion if it is to designate 'not just an infraction of binary structures, but movement into an absolutely negative space beyond the structure of significance itself'.[12]

This is what Lyotard is reaching for in his rejection of the master narratives of the past, and in his nostalgic attempt to return to something preceding modernism but nevertheless beyond it;[13] Robert Stam similarly envisions 'a fundamentally non-unitary, constantly shifting cultural field in which the most varied discourses exist in shifting multivalenced oppositional relationships'.[14] And it seems to be what Fred Pfeil has in mind in his discussion of possibilities within what he calls 'the culture of the PMC' (i.e. the Professional–Managerial Class), when he hopes that 'much of what we now call postmodernism might be turned and engaged in more progressive political directions . . .'. Pfeil is fully aware that the figurations he has in mind 'are at present no more than trace elements of a dream whose concrete realization would require on all sides enormous amounts of hard work and painful struggle'.[15]

Recently certain feminist film and literary theorists have begun to consider this same option. Teresa de Lauretis, for example speaks about the need for texts that construct a new aesthetic in a specific female and heterogeneous address – an address which insists on a series of different spectator positions through which one becomes involved in a process toward subjectivity, rather than being fixed.[16] And Alice Jardine has raised the possibilities for new ways of thinking woman in her exploration of 'gynesis' as this has been recently deployed in texts by French male theorists.[17]

This sort of utopian postmodernism builds on, and carries to its own subversive ends, certain strands of high modernism. Not all modernism was co-opted into mainstream culture; resistant trends (Eisenstein, Buñuel, Brecht – what Paul Willemen calls the 'true' avant-garde because it subverted art's autonomy in favor of a reintegration of art and life)[18] may be seen as precursors of the utopian postmodern briefly outlined above.

Let me now return to the question of whether this sort of art can ever be produced within dominant *commercial* culture: if not, how does the commercial institutional context constrain meanings and influence reception? The question is complicated because what is new about much recent popular culture – especially MTV – and what marks it as different from high modernism is the very intermingling of modernist/avant-garde and popular aesthetic modes that may also be characteristic of the 'utopian' postmodern. Some theorists (e.g. Stam and Pfeil) obviously believe that commercial culture provides at least limited space for a subversive postmodern, although they are scarcely clear about precisely what aesthetic terrain they have in mind when they speak about the utopian possibilities. We can imagine texts which transcend binary categories within an avant-garde context of production and exhibition (largely the terrain on which people like Kristeva, Cixous, de Lauretis think); but I am wary of such claims being made for the sphere of popular culture as it exists at present. Or at least, we need to address the contradictions and constraints of any 'spaces' we may find in mass texts. Do mixings of the popular and the avant-garde transcend binary oppositions or decenter the subject in a way that leads to something new? Or are they rather an example of Baudrillard's implosion or collapsing of meanings into something undesirable?

The answer to this question is intricately tied to one's theory about the TV apparatus. This phrase refers to the complex of elements including the machine itself and its various sites of reception from the living-room to the bathroom; its technological features (the way it produces and presents images); its mixture of texts, inclusion of ads, commentaries, displays; the central relationship of programming to the sponsors, whose own texts, the ads, are arguably the *real* TV texts;[19] the unbounded nature of the texts and reception; the range of potentialities one can produce through operating the machine.

Baudrillard's image is compelling: 'With the television image – television being the ultimate and perfect object for this era – our own body and the whole surrounding universe become a control screen.'[20] Situated in the illusory position of mastery and control, the spectator can play with various possibilities, none of which, however, makes the slightest difference to anything. Have we (as Baudrillard would argue) replaced Marx's 'drama of alienation' with the 'ecstasy of communication', and Freud's old 'hot sexual obscenity' with 'the contactual and motivational obscenity of today'?[21] Is TV, as Kroker and Cook argue, 'the real world of postmodern culture which has *entertainment* as its ideology, the *spectacle* as the emblematic sign of the commodity form, *lifestyle advertising* as its popular psychology, pure, empty *seriality* as the bond which unites the simulacrum of the audience, *electronic images* as its most dynamic, and only form of social cohesion . . . the diffusion of a *network of relational power* as its real product'?[22]

I am persuaded by much of Baudrillard's and Kroker's and Cook's scenario for where high culture is headed, and the role the TV and the computer screens play in it. The somewhat complicit vision in texts like *Blade Runner*, *Videodrome* and *Max Headroom* on the one hand, or the more subversive one in those like *The Man Who Fell to Earth* or *Brazil*, no longer seem impossible. I agree with Kroker that the enemy is partly liberal humanist philosophy with its easy compromises and denials; but I have trouble with Baudrillard's notion that the resistance of the object (i.e. 'infantilism, hyperconformism, total dependence, passivity, idiocy') is the proper response to the dangerous 'hegemony of meaning'.[23] In either case, however, once the signifiers have been freed from their signifieds, once the fixed frameworks and constraints of traditional gender-based genres have been relinquished, we have no way of controlling what comes into the space. Both positive and negative things may happen, particularly for women.

MTV is a useful area within which to debate competing claims about postmodernism, and by which to distinguish the postmodern from the transgressive text. It also provides an occasion to ask how we can create a popular culture that will move beyond dominant binary oppositions (and the classical realism within which such binarisms are encased), without the collapse of oppositions being recuperated through their reduction to empty surfaces.

Many rock videos have been seen as postmodern insofar as they abandon the usual binary oppositions on which dominant culture depends.[24] That is, videos are said to forsake the usual oppositions between high and low culture; between masculine and feminine; between established literary and filmic genres; between past, present and future; between the private and the public sphere; between verbal and visual hierarchies; between realism and anti-realism, etc. This has important implications for the question of

narrative as feminists have been theorizing it, in that these strategies violate
the paradigm pitting a classical narrative against an avant-garde anti-narrative, the one supposedly embodying complicit, the other subversive, ideologies. The rock video reveals the error in trying to align an aesthetic strategy
with any particular ideology, since all kinds of positions emerge from an
astounding mixture of narrative/anti-narrative/non-narrative devices. The
five video types I have outlined elsewhere in an effort to organize the multitude of rock videos on the channel are only broad categories that by no
means cover all the various possible combinations of narrational strategies.[25]

Narrative/non-narrative is no longer a useful category within which to
discuss videos. What is important is, first, whether or not any position mani-
fests itself across the hectic, often incoherent flow of signifiers which are not
necessarily organized into a chain that produces a signified, and, second,
what are the implications of the twenty-four-hour flow of short (four-
minute or less) texts that all more or less function as ads.

In line with Baudrillard's theory, MTV partly exploits the imaginary
desires allowed free pay though the various sixties liberation movements,
divesting them, for commercial reasons, of their originally revolutionary
implications.[26] The apparatus itself, in its construction of a decentered, fragmented spectator through the rapid flow of short segments, easily reduces
politics to the 'radical chic' ('USA for Africa') or the pornographic (Rolling
Stones' 'She Was Hot').

Yet, paradoxically, MTV's chosen format of short texts enables exhibition of
thematic and aesthetic positions that criticize the status quo. That is, MTV's
twenty-four-hour rapid flow of short segments on the one hand renders all of
its texts 'postmodern' because of the manner of their exhibition (i.e., a stream
of jumbled, hectic signifiers for which no signified was intended or has time
to be communicated; the reduction of all to surfaces/textures/sounds/the visceral and kinaesthetic: the hypnotizing of the spectator into an exitless, schizophrenic stance by the unceasing image series); yet, on the other hand, if we
rather artificially 'stop the flow', we can find individual texts that in their
four-minute airplay do offer subversive subject positions.

Since the subject positions the channel offers are important for the female
spectator, let me 'stop the flow' for the purposes of analysis, fully aware that
what one finds in this process differs from what one experiences as a 'normal' spectator. The existence of alternative subject positions is theoretically
important, even if such positions are normally swept up in the plethora of
more oppressive ones. Hence, I will look briefly at strategies in a typical
'postmodern' video having negative results for women, and then at videos
leaning in the avant-garde, transgressive direction descending from high
modernism and opening up useful space for the female spectator.

Take for instance Tom Petty and the Heartbreakers' 'Don't Come Around
Here No More'. This video, like many others, stands in a strange intertextual
relationship to a well-known original – here Lewis Carroll's *Alice in
Wonderland*. The text cannot be labelled 'parody' in the modernist sense that
Jameson has outlined; and yet it is clearly playing off the original. It thus
falls between parody and actually moving beyond the binarisms of conventional narrative. The issue of the gaze becomes confused: we have a sense of
the text playing with oedipal positionings in the apparent sadism enacted

on Alice's body, in the monstrous father torturing the child; but it deflects this reading by the semi-comic, self-conscious stance it takes toward what it is doing, and by the brilliance of its visual strategies. One becomes entranced by the visual and aural dimensions, which overwhelm all others. One holds in abeyance the reaching for a signified and is absorbed in the surfaces/textures/shapes/sounds which dominate reception channels.

The pastiche mode makes it difficult to say that the text is taking a sado-masochistic pleasure in violence against women, so that while the imagery offends the female spectator she fears she is being trapped into taking it too seriously. The video just might be intending reference to the sadism in the original *Alice*; it might even be 'exposing' male abuse of the female body through the grotesque image of Alice's body being eaten as cake. But one cannot be sure. The spectator is made to doubt through this sort of play, which characterizes the co-opted postmodern.

Madonna's successful 'Material Girl' positions the spectator equally uncomfortably, while not addressing or moving beyond established polari-ties in the manner of the utopian text. 'Material Girl' stands in a strange intertextual relationship to Howard Hawks's film, *Gentlemen Prefer Blondes*. It offers a pastiche of Monroe's 'Diamonds Are a Girl's Best Friend' number, while declining any critical comment upon that text. In this video, Madonna may be said to represent a postmodern feminist stance by combining seduc-tiveness with a gutsy kind of independence. She incorporates the qualities of both Jane Russell and Monroe in Hawks's film, creating a self-confident, unabashedly sexual image that is far more aggressive than those of the Hollywood stars. An analysis of the main shots and use of diegetic spaces demonstrates the ways in which conventions of the classic Hollywood film, which paradoxically provided the inspiration for the video, are routinely violated. Even in a video that at first appears precisely to remain within those conventions – unlike many other videos whose extraordinary and avant-garde techniques are immediately obvious – regular narrative devices are not adhered to. But the video violates classic traditions even more with its sound–image relations.

This aspect of the video brings up the question of the rock video's uniqueness as an artistic form, namely as a form in which the sound of the song, and the 'content' of its lyrics, is prior to the creation of images to accompany the music and the words. While there are analogies to both the opera and to the Hollywood musical, neither form prepares for the rock video in which the song–image relationship is quite unique. The unique-ness has to do with a certain arbitrariness of the images used along with any particular song, with the lack of limitations spatially, with the fre-quently extremely rapid montage-style editing not found generally (if at all) in the Hollywood musical song/dance sequences, and finally with the precise relationship of sound – both musical and vocal – to image. This relationship involves (a) the links between musical rhythms and significa-tions of instrumental sounds, and images provided for them; (b) links between the significations of the song's actual *words* and images conjured up to convey that 'content'; (c) links between any one musical phrase and the accompanying words, and the relay of images as that phrase is being played and sung.

This is obviously a very complex topic – far beyond my scope here – but let me demonstrate some of the issues in relation to 'Material Girl', where again things are far simpler than in many videos. On the visual track there are two distinct but linked discourses, that involving the D's desire for Madonna I (his determined pursuit and eventual 'winning' of her), and that of Madonna I's performance, where she plays Madonna II, the 'material girl'. These discourses are not hierarchically arranged as in the usual Hollywood film, but rather exist on a horizontal axis, neither subordinated to the other. In terms of screen time, however, the performance is given more time.

When we turn to the soundtrack, we find that, after the brief introductory scene in the screening room (a scene, by the way, often cut from the video), the soundtrack consists entirely of the lyrics for the song 'Material Girl'. This song deals with the girl who will only date boys who 'give her proper credit', and for whom love is reduced to money. Thus, all the visuals pertaining to the D–Madonna I love story do not have any correlate on the soundtrack. We merely have two short verbal sequences (in the screening room and dressing room) to carry the entire other story: in other words, soundtrack and image track are not linked for that story. An obvious example of this discrepancy is the shot of Madonna I (arriving at the studio in the flashy car) rejecting her rich lover: Madonna lip-synches 'That's right' from the 'Material Girl' song – a phrase that refers there to her only loving boys who give her money – in a situation where the opposite is happening: she *refuses* to love the man who is wealthy!

In other words, the entire video is subordinated to the words with their signifieds that refer in fact only to the stage performance. The common device in the Hollywood musical of having the dance interlude simply an episode in the main story seems here to be reversed: the performance is central while the love story is reduced to the status merely of a framing narrative. Significant here also is the disjunction between the two stories, the framing story being about a 'nice girl', and the performance being about the 'bad' girl: but even these terms are blurred by the obvious seductiveness of the 'nice' girl, particularly as she walks at the end toward the car in a very knowing manner.

We see thus that the usual hierarchical arrangement of discourses in the classical realist text is totally violated in 'Material Girl'. While Madonna I is certainly set up as object of the D's desire, in quite classical manner, the text refuses to let her be controlled by that desire. This is achieved by unbalancing the relations between framing story and performance story so that Madonna I is overridden by her stage figure, Madonna II, the brash, gutsy 'material girl'. The line between 'fiction' and 'reality' within the narrative is thus blurred: this has severe consequences just because the two women are polar opposites.

In *Gentlemen Prefer Blondes*, on the other hand, no such confusion or discrepancy exists. From the start, Monroe's single-minded aim is to catch a rich man, and she remains fixed on that throughout. The function of her performance of 'Diamonds Are a Girl's Best Friend' is partly simply to express what has been obvious to the spectator, if not to Esmond, all along; but also to let Esmond get the idea, were he smart enough. Lorelei sings a song that expresses her philosophy of life, but we are clear about the lines between the stage-fiction and the context of its presentation, and Monroe as a character in the narrative. Part of the confusion in the Madonna video comes about precisely because the scene of the performance is not made very clear and because the lines between the different spaces of the text are blurred.

The situation in 'Material Girl' is even more problematic because of the way that Madonna, as historical star subject, breaks through her narrative positions via her strong personality, her love of performing for the camera, her inherent energy and vitality. Madonna searches for the camera's gaze and for the TV spectator's gaze that follows it because she relishes being desired. The 'roles' melt away through her unique presence and the narrative incoherence discussed above seems resolved in our understanding that Madonna herself, as historical subject, is the really 'material girl'.

It is perhaps Madonna's success in articulating and parading a desire to be desired – the opposite of the self-abnegating urge to lose oneself in the male evident in many classical Hollywood films – that attracts the hordes of twelve-year-old fans to her performances and videos. A cross between a bag-lady and a bordello queen, Madonna's image is a far cry from the 'patriarchal feminine' of women's magazines; yet it remains within those constraints in still focusing on the 'look' as crucial to identity. Madonna's narcissism and self-indulgences co-opt her texts back into a consumerist postmodernism, as do also the seductive participatory rhythms of this and other pop rock melodies. Such melodies bind the female spectator to the images so that the repressive aspects slip by unnoticed because of the comforting, appealing beat.

Some videos on the channel do use the new form in ways reminiscent of a transgressive/modernist mode. They use narrative in differing degrees and in various ways, much as did the great modernists, and they employ realist or non-realist strategies as befits a particular moment in a text. There is no set form for videos offering a critique of dominant female representations or of woman's position in male culture as signs for something in the male unconscious. The videos range from the black-comedy parody in Julie Brown's 'The Home Coming Queen's Got a Gun', to a sophisticated feminist critique of female representations and of woman's construction as passive sexual object in Annie Lennox's and Aretha Franklin's 'Sisters Are Doin' It for Themselves' and Tina Turner's 'Private Dancer'; to Laurie Anderson's anti-narrative, deconstructive video 'Language is a Virus', which attacks dominant bourgeois culture generally and commercial TV in particular.

We can thus see how difficult it is to make a case for MTV as progressive or retrogressive in its narrative modes. In a sense, those categories do not apply. MTV is something else – or it is elsewhere. It defies our usual critical categories while not setting up something we can recognize as liberating in new ways such as those Derrida and Kristeva search for.

Let me conclude by summarizing the contradictory aspects of postmodernism for feminist cultural concerns. Contemporary feminism, as a political and cultural discourse, has assumed a set of strategic subjectivities in order to attack the old patriarchal theorists. Feminists have both made use of and criticized the powerful, often subversive discourses of both Marx and Freud in creating the feminist stance against dominant gender constructs. If those discourses are seen as no longer relevant, on what ground can any strategic feminism stand? We might hope that we no longer needed such feminism, that we could work toward transcending 'death-dealing binary oppositions of masculinity and femininity', but events like the recent 'Baby M' case show how distant is American culture from any such stage. Does postmodernism make feminism archaic as a theory, while refusing to address the remaining oppressive discourses that perpetuate woman's subordination? For Kroker and Cook, technology is the only remaining ideology; feminists, however, can see in the Baby M case how various gender ideologies interact with new technologies in a complex, often contradictory manner.

The postmodernism that is produced by the collapse of the enlightenment project and of the belief in the transcendental (male) subject benefits women when it leads to the utopian postmodern text discussed earlier. And even in the commercial postmodernism exemplified in MTV, we saw that there are benefits for the female spectator: the breaking up of traditional realist forms sometimes entails a deconstruction of conventional sex-role representations that opens up new possibilities for female imagining. The four-minute span does not permit regression to the oedipal conflicts of the classical Hollywood film that oppresses women. Meanwhile, the fragmentation of the viewing subject perhaps deconstructs woman's conventional other-centered reception functions – woman positioned as nurturer, caregiver – releasing new ways for the female spectator to relate to texts. Postmodernism offers the female spectator pleasure in sensations – color, sound, visual patterns – and in energy, body movement. Madonna represents new possibilities for female desire and for the empowered woman, even if we would want these forms of desire and empowerment to be only a transitional phase.

On the other hand, we could argue that commercial postmodern culture builds on and satisfies already dominant masculine qualities such as violence, destruction, consumption, phallic sexuality, and appropriation of the female in the non-male image. In much postmodernism, the domestic and the familial – modes that in the past offered some satisfaction to women – no longer function. It is possible that the new 'universe of communication' is attractive to some male theorists seeking relief from Baudrillard's old 'Faustian, Promethean (perhaps Oedipal) period of production and consumption', just because women have begun, through feminist discourse, to make and win demands within that system and to challenge male dominance there.

But the postmodern discourse theorized by Kroker and Cook is not antifeminist; rather, it envisions a world beyond feminism as we have known it in the past twenty-five years. In the postmodern world, both men and women are victims; all bodies are 'invaded' and exploited because they are no longer adequate to the advanced technologies. Marilouise and Arthur Kroker are concerned about the (ab)use of women's bodies in fashion and about the reduction of woman to a baby-making 'machine' through new reproductive technologies. These devices alienate woman from her body and disconnect her from the baby she produces. But the Krokers also point out the new 'fallen' image of the penis in the age of AIDS and other sexual viruses, and many other ways in which humans, as we have conceived of them for centuries, are being drastically altered by electronic implants and additions.

Indeed, a movie like *Videodrome* is surprising more for its representation of the male than of the female body. Female figures in the film interestingly fall back into traditional stereotypes (the masculinized 'bitch' woman, the over-sexed, masochistic woman), but we see the male body invaded and made monstrous in the hero's machine-produced hallucinations. It is true that the horrific deformation of the body involves its turning into a kind of vagina-like, bloody opening,[27] but this is a reference to the horror of technology that deforms all bodies and blurs their gender distinction. There are as many images of castration (the deformed arm, the powerless gun) as of female orifices. The point is that the hero's body turns into a playback machine; the body is controlled by electronic frequencies that prevent the owner from controlling himself. We have entered a Baudrillardean world (Brian Oblivion being a thinly disguised Baudrillard) in which there is no 'reality' other than video; the human body is reduced to the video machine – it and the TV set are one and the same.

As feminists we need to listen to the discourse for what it can tell us about the possible future: as an ethics of description, the postmodern discourse of this kind may warn against the devastating results of the abuse of science and technology by capital. Popular culture theory needs to attend to the Baudrillard/Kroker accounts, while avoiding their more seductive but improbable extremism. In what is hopefully only a transitional phase, we need more than ever to construct critical analyses of the new cultural scene, and the shift in consciousness wrought by science and technology; we need to engage in work that will redress dangerous directions, or prevent what is envisaged from coming to be. As humans implicated against our wills in the effects of new technologies, we also still exist as historical subjects in specific political contexts: we must continue feminist struggles wherever we live and work, at the same time being aware of the larger cultural constructions that implicate us and for which feminist ideologies may no longer be adequate.

In terms of cultural studies, the first two of my triology of male theorists (i.e. Barthes and Bakhtin) are useful particularly as they have been theo-rized by French feminists (Kristeva, Cixous, Montrelay); Lacan, Althusser and Foucault are equally important, again in connection with French femi-nists (Cixous, Irigaray). Let me conclude by listing the different kinds of cul-tural work that feminists need to be doing: I will discuss this work in terms of the three main categories discussed above, namely: (a) the modernist/transgressive text; (b) the 'utopian' postmodern text; and (c) the 'popular/commercial' postmodern text.

First, feminists must continue to make use of transgressive strategies, as some feminist film-makers have been doing (e.g., Mulvey and Wollen's *Riddles of the Sphinx*, Sally Potter's *Thriller* or her *Gold-diggers*, *Sigmund Freud's 'Dora'*; Trinh T. Minh-ha's *Naked Spaces – Living Is Round*, among oth-ers). In this way, feminists can continue to question and undo the patriar-chal construction of femininity, to pose the problem of representation, to demonstrate the social constructions of gender. Unlike the high modernists (most of whom were male, many misogynist), such feminists have the bene-fit of recent work on deconstruction, and can employ sophisticated theories of representation and gender that have also recently been developed through semiotics and psychoanalysis. Inevitably, such texts will be produced and exhibited mainly in alternate spaces, given the demands they make on the viewer through their counter-text strategies. However, we should not underestimate the impact of such texts, now that they are making their way into the academy.

Such texts vary in their strategies, particularly in relation to the use or non-use of narrative. Some feminists, like Teresa de Lauretis, keenly aware that narrative movement is that of masculine desire, 'the movement of a passage, an actively experienced transformation of the human being into . . . man', nevertheless are wary of the automatic adoption of anti-narrative devices. De Lauretis argues that we must create a new kind of narrative, based not on male desire but rather on a different kind of desiring. Other feminists believe that all narrative involves essentializing (i.e., positing some 'female' desire in place of the prior 'male' desire) and that, therefore, we can offer a truly transgressive position only through anti-narrative techniques.

This work needs to be differentiated from a second feminist concern, which we could position within the 'utopian' postmodernism discussed above. Here, feminists theorize and try to construct texts that radically decenter, disrupt and refuse all categories hitherto central in Western thought, much in the manner of Derrida. The efforts in the transgressive sort of text should provide the groundwork for the utopian postmodernist text in leading us through the problems and tangles of binary oppositions toward a glimpse of how the beyond might appear.

An important third area of work needs to address the possibilities within what I have called the dominant 'co-opted' postmodernism of our time. Here it seems to me that we can bring to bear tools developed just prior to the postmodern moment in analyzing women in popular culture (the classical Hollywood melodrama, 1950s television, the soaps). An important issue here is the degree to which the new co-opted postmodernism is an aggressive attempt to recover popular culture, traditionally linked to a scorned 'feminine', for males. We can begin to analyze the implications of the changes in films and in television shows that earlier addressed a specifically female audience – and that therefore spoke to women's special needs, fantasies and desires within partriarchy. If postmodernism takes away such gaps, perhaps it offers other possibilities. We need to explore fully the contradictions involved in 'co-opted' postmodernism, for once the fixed frameworks and traditional gender-oriented genres are relinquished, once signifiers are freed from the constraints such frameworks and genres impose, then both negative and positive outcomes for women may occur. Since co-opted postmodernism addresses a mass female audience, it is perhaps the most important terrain for feminist cultural studies. We need actively to resist and challenge the male qualities of violence, aggression ann misogyny that mark much co-opted postmodernism and toward which women are being drawn in the mistaken belief, perhaps, that this offers liberation from earlier 'feminine' constraints. We also need to recognize the genuine places where new possibilities are offered to the female spectator by virtue of prior genre constraints being lifted.

We cannot expect a commercial medium like MTV to resist the pressures of what may indeed be a deep cultural change. And we need to see post-modernism of both kinds in the context of the great modernist movement, of the search for an alternative consciousness, cultural practice and representation to the dominant. Unfortunately, we cannot actually produce the positive or utopian postmodernism until we have managed to challenge the symbolic order sufficiently to permit its articulation. That is, we have to work through the binary oppositions by constantly challenging them before we can be beyond them. Much utopian postmodernism does just that: it stands on the shoulders of modernism and the great modernist thinkers, while struggling to move beyond their critical categories and aesthetic strategies. It moves through them by meditating upon the possibility of transcending them.

But much of what people celebrate as liberating in what I call 'co-opted' postmodernism is an avoidance of the struggle, an attempt to sidestep the task of working through the constraining binary oppositions, including sexual difference. The liberating elements in some popular culture like rock videos are important, but often superficial. Women are invested in culture's move beyond dysfunctional gender polarities, but a superficial collapsing of previously distinct female representations, for instance, gets us nowhere. This sort of strategy, as many others evident in rock videos, is preferable to the old 'realist-talking-heads', essentializing and monolithic (male) discourse of the past. But we must still be wary of making too extreme claims for what is going on. We must also be wary of assuming the acceptance by historical female subjects of the co-opted postmodernist world. Work needs to be done on the various kinds of resistances these subjects devise in the face of the commercial and technological onslaughts.

As cultural workers, we do not want to return to the error of insisting upon fixed points of enunciation, labelled 'truth'; rather, as Tony Bennett and Ernesto Laclau have both pointed out,[28] we must continue to articulate oppositional discourses – recognizing them as discourses rather than an ontological truth that theory has cast doubt on – if we are to construct new subjects capable of working toward the utopian postmodernism we all hope will be possible. This means not validating or celebrating the erosion of all categories and differences and boundaries – as Baudrillard and his followers sometimes appear to do. Feminists in particular need to continue to construct strategic subjectivities, and to use the category 'woman' as a tool to prevent the too easy and too early collapsing of a difference that continues to organize culture. As long as that difference operates, we need to counter it with the only tools we have, while simultaneously working toward a much more difficult transcendence – or, in Craig Owens's words,[29] toward a concept of difference without opposition.

## Notes

1. Stephen Heath, quoted by Teresa de Lauretis, 'Oedipus Interruptus', *Wide Angle*, 7: 1 & 2 (1985), pp. 34–40.
2. Marthe Robert, *The Origin of the Novel*, trans. Sacha Rabinovitch (Bloomington, IN, Indiana University Press, 1980), which discusses and further develops Freud's early essays on 'Creative Writing and Day Dreaming', and on 'The

Family Romance'. See also Roland Barthes, *The Pleasure of the Text* (New York, Hill & Wang, 1975). For excerpts from theoretical texts by French feminists dealing with alternative textual strategies, see Elaine Marks and Isabelle de Courtivron, *New French Feminisms* (Amherst, MA, University of Massachusetts Press, 1980).

3. See Jose Ortega y Gasset, *The Dehumanization of Art* (1925) (Princeton, NJ, Princeton University Press, 1948).

4. Martha Rosler, 'Notes on Quotes', *Wedge*, 2 (Fall 1982), p. 69.

5. De Lauretis, 'Oedipus Interruptus', p. 38. Page numbers refer to this version.

6. E. Ann Kaplan, 'Feminist Film Criticism. Current Issues and Problems', *Studies in the Literary Imagination*, 19: 1 (Spring 1986), pp. 7–20.

7. Toril Moi, *Sexual/Textual Politics. Feminist Literary Theory* (London, Methuen, 1985).

8. See Craig Owens, 'The Discourse of Others. Feminists and Postmodernism', in Hal Foster, ed., *The Anti-Aesthetic. Essays on Postmodern Culture* (Port Townsend, WA, Bay Press, 1983), p. 61.

9. Given the focus of this article, it will not be possible to deal with how postmodernism affects all the different kinds of feminisms; hence, I shall beg the reader's indulgence for an analysis positing a generalized 'feminism' that necessarily embodies my own biases.

10. The reasons for this are fascinating, and perhaps have to do with Bakhtin's links to both Freud and semiotics, while not adhering to either theory fully. See Robert Stam's essay in this volume.

11. See Julia Kristeva, 'Word, Dialogue, and Novel', in Leon S. Roudiez, ed., *Desire in Language. A Semiotic Approach to Literature and Art*, trans. Thomas Gora, Alice Jardine and Leon S. Roudiez (New York, Columbia University Press, 1980), p. 79. Subsequent page references appear parenthetically.

12. See Allon White and Peter Stallybrass, *The Politics and Poetics of Trangression* (London, Methuen, 1986), p. 18.

13. Jean-François Lyotard, *The Postmodern Condition. A Report on Knowledge*, trans. Geoff Bennington and Brian Massumi (Minneapolis, MN, University of Minnesota Press, 1984).

14. Robert Stam, 'Mikhail Bakhtin and Left Cultural Critique', in Colin MacCabe, ed., *Futures for English*.

15. Fred Pfeil, 'Makin' Flippy-Floppy. Postmodernism and the Baby-Boom PMC', in Mike Davis, Fred Pfeil and Michael Sprinker, eds, *The Year Left. An American Socialist Yearbook* vol. I, (London, Verso, 1985), pp. 272, 292.

16. See Teresa de Lauretis, 'Aesthetic and Feminist Theory. Rethinking Women's Cinema', *New German Critique*, 34 (Winter 1985), pp. 154–75.

17. Alice A. Jardine, *Gynesis. Configurations of Woman and Modernity* (Ithaca and London, Cornell University Press, 1985).

18. See Paul Willemen, 'An Avant Garde for the Eighties', *Framework*, 24 (Spring 1984), pp. 53–73. One of the issues complicating the debates about postmodernism has of course been the different theories of modernism from which critics start. Willemen's article is a useful clarification of some of the confusions around modernism.

19. See Sandy Flitterman, 'The *Real* Soap Operas. TV Commercials', in E. Ann Kaplan, ed., *Regarding Televisions Critical Approaches – An Anthology* (Los Angeles, CA, The American Film Institute, 1983), pp. 84–97.

20. Jean Baudrillard, 'The Ecstasy of Communication', in Foster, *The Anti-Aesthetic*, p. 127.

21. Baudrillard, 'The Ecstasy of Communication', pp. 130–1.

22. Arthur Kroker and David Cook, *The Postmodern Scene. Excremental Culture and Hyper-Aesthetics* (New York, St Martin's Press, 1986), p. 279.

23. Jean Baudrillard, 'The Implosion of Meaning in the Media and the Implosion of the Social in the Masses', in K. Woodward, ed., *The Myths of Information Technology and Postindustrial Culture* (Madison, WI, Coda Press, 1980), pp. 138–48.

24. For example, see the issue of the *Journal of Communication Inquiry*, 10: 1 (Winter 1986), devoted to Music Television.
25. See my *Rocking Around the Clock. Music Television, Postmodernism and Consumer Culture* (London and New York, Methuen, 1987), Chapter 3.
26. Let me note here to avoid confusion that in the following comments I am talking about the 'model' spectator the apparatus constructs, rather than about the possible modes of specific reception – including resistance – individual historical spectators may engage in. In interviews with teenagers, it became clear that historical subjects are not necessarily *tabulae rasae*, soaking up spectator positions, but employ a number of strategies to subvert or alter what they are given. Some teenagers turn off the sound and put on their own, preferred music to accompany images; others talk and comment about the images, ridiculing and spoofing the stars. Female spectators apparently manifest less of this behaviour, but a complexly organized reception study would be necessary to establish the validity of generalization.
27. See Tania Modleski, 'The Terror of Pleasure. The Contemporary Horror Film and Postmodern Theory', in Tania Modleski, ed., *Studies in Mass Entertainment Critical Approaches to Mass Culture* (Madison, WI, University of Wisconsin Press, 1986), p. 163.
28. See Tony Bennett, 'Texts in History. The Determinations of Readings and Their Texts', in D. Attridge, G. Bennington and R Young, eds, *Post-Structuralism and the Question of History* (Cambridge, Cambridge University Press, 1987); and Ernesto Laclau, 'Populist Rupture and Discourse', *Screen Education*, 34: (Spring 1980).
29. See Craig Owens, 'The Discourse of Others'.

# 21

## Surrealism without the unconscious

*Fredric Jameson*

From *Postmodernism, or, the cultural logic of late capitalism* (Duke University Press and Verso 1991)

It has often been said that every age is dominated by a priviledged form, or genre, which seems by its structure the fittest to express its secret truths; or perhaps, if you prefer a more contemporary way of thinking about it, which seems to offer the richest symptom of what Sartre would have called the 'objective neurosis' of that particular time and place. Today, however, I think we would no longer look for such characteristic or symptomatic objects in the world and the language of forms or genres. Capitalism, and the modern age, is a period in which, with the extinction of the sacred and the 'spiritual,' the deep underlying materiality of all things has finally risen dripping and convulsive into the light of day; and it is clear that culture itself is one of those things whose fundamental materiality is now for us not merely evident but quite inescapable. This has, however, also been a historical lesson: it is because culture has *become* material that we are now in a position to understand that it always *was* material, or materialistic, in its structures and functions. We postcontemporary people have a word for that discovery – a word that has tended to displace the older language of genres and forms – and this is, of course, the word *medium*, and in particular its plural, *media*, a word which now conjoins three relatively distinct signals: that of an artistic mode or specific form of aesthetic production, that of a specific technology, generally organized around a central apparatus or machine: and that, finally, of a social institution. These three areas of meaning do not define a medium, or the media, but designate the distinct dimensions that must be addressed in order for such a definition to be completed or constructed. It should be evident that most traditional and modern aesthetic concepts – largely, but not exclusively, designed for literary texts – do not require this simultaneous attention to the multiple dimensions of the material, the social, and the aesthetic.

It is because we have had to learn that culture today is a matter of media that we have finally begun to get it through our heads that culture was always that, and that the older forms or genres, or indeed the older spiritual exercises and meditations, thoughts and expressions, were also in their very different ways media products. The intervention of the machine, the mechanization of culture, and the mediation of culture by the Consciousness

Industry are now everywhere the case, and perhaps it might be interesting to explore the possibility that they were always the case throughout human history, and within even the radical difference of older, precapitalist modes of production.

Nonetheless, what is paradoxical about this displacement of literary terminology by an emergent mediatic conceptuality is that it takes place at the very moment in which the philosophical priority of language itself and of the various linguistic philosophies has become dominant and well-nigh universal. Thus, the written text loses its privileged and exemplary status at the very moment when the available conceptualities for analyzing the enormous variety of objects of study with which 'reality' presents us (now all in their various ways designated as so many 'texts') have become almost exclusively linguistic in orientation. Media analysis in linguistic or semiotic terms therefore may well appear to involve an imperializing enlargement of the domain of language to include nonverbal – visual or musical, bodily, spatial – phenomena; but it may equally well spell a critical and disruptive challenge to the very conceptual instruments which have been mobilized to complete this operation of assimilation.

As for the emergent priority of the media today, this is scarcely a new discovery. For some seventy years the cleverest prophets have warned us regularly that the dominant art form of the twentieth century was not literature at all – nor even painting or theater or the symphony – but rather the one new and historically unique art invented in the contemporary period, namely film; that is to say, the first distinctively mediatic art form. What is strange about this prognosis – whose unassailable validity has with time become a commonplace – is that it should have had so little practical effect. Indeed, literature, sometimes intelligently and opportunistically absorbing the techniques of film back into its own substance, remained throughout the modern period the ideologically dominant paradigm of the aesthetic and continued to hold open a space in which the richest varieties of innovation were pursued. Film, however, whatever its deeper consonance with twentieth-century realities, entertained a merely fitful relationship to the modern in that sense, owing, no doubt, to the two distinct lives or identities through which, successively (like Virginia Woolf's *Orlando*), it was destined to pass: the first, the silent period, in which some lateral fusion of the mass audience and the formal or modernist proved viable (in ways and resolutions we can no longer grasp, owing to our peculiar historical amnesia); the second, the sound period, then coming as the dominance of mass-cultural (and commercial) forms through which the medium must toil until again reinventing the forms of the modern in a new way in the great auteurs of the 1950s (Hitchcock, Bergman, Kurosawa, Fellini).

What this account suggests is that however helpful the declaration of the priority of film over literature in jolting us out of print culture and/or logocentrism, it remained an essentially *modernist* formulation, locked in a set of cultural values and categories which are in full postmodernism demonstrably antiquated and 'historical.' That film has today become postmodernist, or at least that certain films have, is obvious enough; but so have some forms of literary production. The argument turned, however, on the priority of these forms, that is, their capacity to serve as some supreme and privileged, symptomatic, index of the zeitgeist; to stand, using a more contemporary language, as the cultural *dominant* of a new social and economic conjuncture; to stand – now finally putting the most philosophically adequate face on the matter – as the richest allegorical and hermeneutic vehicles for some new description of the system itself. Film and literature no longer do that, although I will not belabor the largely circumstantial evidence of the increasing dependency of each on materials, forms, technology, and even thematics borrowed from the other art or medium I have in mind as the most likely candidate for cultural hegemony today.

The identity of that candidate is certainly no secret: it is clearly video, in its twin manifestations as commercial television and experimental video, or 'video art.' This is not a proposition one proves; rather, one seeks, as I will in the remainder of this chapter, to demonstrate the interest of presupposing it, and in particular the variety of new consequences that flow from assigning some new and more central priority to video processes.

One very significant feature of this presupposition must, however, be underscored at the outset, for it logically involves the radical and virtually a priori differentiation of film theory from whatever is to be proposed in the nature of a theory or even a description of video itself. The very richness of film theory today makes this decision and this warning unavoidable. If the experience of the movie screen and its mesmerizing images is distinct, and fundamentally different, from the experience of the television monitor – something that might be scientifically inferred by technical differences in their respective modes of encoding visual information but which could also be phenomenologically argued – then the very maturity and sophistication of film conceptualities will necessarily obscure the originality of its cousin, whose specific features demand to be reconstructed afresh and empty-handed, without imported and extrapolated categories. A parable can indeed be adduced here to support this methodological decision: discussing the hesitation Central European Jewish writers faced between writing in German and writing in Yiddish, Kafka once observed that these languages were too close to each other for any satisfactory translation from one into the other to be possible. Something like this, then, is what one would want to affirm about the relationship of the language of film theory to that of video theory, if indeed anything like this last exists in the first place.

Doubts on that score have frequently been raised, nowhere more dramatically than at an ambitious conference on the subject sponsored by *The Kitchen* in October 1980, at which a long line of dignitaries trooped to the podium only to complain that they couldn't understand why they had been invited, since they had no particular thoughts about television (which some of them admitted they watched), many then adding, as in afterthought, that only one halfway viable concept 'produced' about television occurred to them, and that was Raymond Williams's idea of 'whole flow.'[1]

Perhaps these two remarks go together more intimately than we imagine: the blockage of fresh thinking before this solid little window against which we strike our heads being not unrelated to precisely that whole or total flow we observe through it.

For it seems plausible that in a situation of total flow, the contents of the screen streaming before us all day long without interruption (or where the interruptions – called *commercials* – are less intermissions than they are fleeting opportunities to visit the bathroom or throw a sandwich together), what used to be called 'critical distance' seems to have become obsolete. Turning the television set off has little in common either with the intermission of a play or an opera or with the grand finale of a feature film, when the lights slowly come back on and memory begins its mysterious work. Indeed, if anything like critical distance is still possible in film, it is surely bound up with memory itself. But memory seems to play no role in television, commercial or otherwise (or, I am tempted to say, in postmodernism generally): nothing here haunts the mind or leaves its afterimages in the manner of the great moments of film (which do not necessarily happen, of course, in the 'great' films.) A description of the structural exclusion of memory, then, and of critical distance, might well lead on into the impossible, namely, a theory of video itself – how the thing blocks its own theorization becoming a theory in its own right.

My experience, however, is that you can't manage to think about things simply by deciding to, and that the mind's deeper currents often need to be surprised by indirection, sometimes, indeed, by treachery and ruse, as when you steer away from a goal in order to reach it more directly or look away from an object to register it more exactly. In that sense, thinking anything about something else; in this instance, experimental video (or alternatively, that new form or genre called MTV, which I cannot deal with here). This is less a matter of mass versus elite culture than it is of controlled laboratory situations: what is so highly specialized as to seem aberrant and uncharacteristic in the world of daily life – hermetic poetry, for example – can often yield crucial information about the properties of an object of study (language, in that case), whose familiar everyday forms obscure it. Released from all conventional constraints, experimental video allows us to witness the full range of possibilities and potentialities of the medium in a way which illuminates its various more restricted uses, the latter being subsets and special cases of the former.

Even this approach to television via experimental video, however, needs to be estranged and displaced if the language of formal innovation and enlarged possibility leads us to expect a flowering and a multiplicity of new forms and visual languages: they exist, of course, and to a degree so bewildering in the short history of video art (sometimes dated from Nam June Paik's first experiments in 1963) that one is tempted to wonder whether any description or theory could ever encompass their variety. I have found it enlightening to come at this issue from a different direction, however, by raising the question of *boredom* as an aesthetic response and a phenomenological problem. In both the Freudian and the Marxist traditions (for the second, Lukács, but also Sartre's discussion of 'stupidity' in Sartre's *Journal of the Phony War*), 'boredom' is taken not so much as an objective property of things and works but rather as a response to the blockage of energies (whether those be grasped in terms of desire or of praxis). Boredom then becomes interesting as a reaction to situation of paralysis and also, no doubt, as defense mechanism or avoidance behavior. Even taken in the narrower realm of cultural reception, boredom with a particular kind of work or style or content can always be used productively as a precious symptom of our own existential, ideological, and cultural limits, an index of what has to be refused in the way of other people's cultural practices and their threat to our own rationalizations about the nature and value of art. Meanwhile, it is no great secret that in some of the most significant works of high modernism, what is boring can often be very interesting indeed, and vice versa: a combination which the reading of any hundred sentences by Raymond Roussel, say, will at once dramatize. We must therefore initially try to strip the concept of the *boring* (and its experience) of any axiological overtones and bracket the whole question of aesthetic value. It is a paradox one can get used to: if a boring text can also be good (or interesting, as we now put it), exciting texts, which incorporate diversion, distraction, temporal commodification, can also perhaps sometimes be 'bad' (or 'degraded,' to use Frankfurt School language).

Imagine at any event a face on your television screen accompanied by an incomprehensible and never-ending stream of keenings and mutterings: the face remaining utterly without expression, unchanging throughout the course of the 'work,' and coming at length to seem some icon or floating immobile timeless mask. It is an experience to which you might be willing to submit out of curiosity for a few minutes. When, however, you begin to leaf through your program in distraction, only to discover that this particular videotext is twenty-one minutes long, then panic overcomes the mind and almost anything else seems preferable. But twenty-one minutes is not terribly long in other contexts (the immobility of the adept or religious mystic might offer some point of reference), and the nature of this particularly form of aesthetic boredom becomes an interesting problem, particularly when we recall the difference between the viewing situation of video art and analogous experiences in experimental film (we can always shut the first one off, without sitting politely through a social and institutional ritual). As I have already suggested, however, we must avoid the easy conclusion that this tape or text is simply bad; one wants immediately to add, to forestall misconceptions, that there are many, many diverting and captivating videotexts of all kinds – but then one would also want to avoid the conclusion that those are simply better (or 'good' in the axiological sense).

[...] As for total flow, meanwhile, it has significant methodological consequences for the analysis of experimental video, and in particular for the constitution of the object or unity of study such a medium presents. It is, of course, no accident that today, in full postmodernism, the older language of the 'work' – the work of art, the masterwork – has everywhere largely been displaced by the rather different language of the 'text', of texts and textuality – a language from which the achievement of organic or monumental form is strategically excluded. Everything can now be a text in that sense (daily life, the body, political representations), while objects that were formerly 'works' can now be reread as immense ensembles or systems of texts of various kinds, superimposed on each other by way of the various intertextualities, successions of fragments, or, yet again, sheer process (henceforth called textual production or textualization). The autonomous work of art thereby – along with the old autonomous subject or ego – seems to have vanished, to have been volatilized.

Nowhere is this more materially demonstrable than with the 'texts' of experimental video – a situation which, however, now confronts the analyst with some new and unusual problems characteristic in one way or another of all the postmodernisms, but even more acute here. If the old modernizing and monumental forms – the Book of the World, the 'magic mountains' of the architectural modernisms, the central mythic opera cycle of a Bayreuth, the Museum itself as the center of all the possibilities of painting – if such totalizing ensembles are no longer the fundamental organizing frames for analysis and interpretation; if, in other words, there are no more masterpieces, let alone their canon, no more 'great' books (and if even the concept of *good* books has become problematic) – if we find ourselves confronted henceforth with 'texts,' that is, with the ephemeral, with disposable works that wish to fold back immediately into the accumulating detritus of historical time – then it becomes difficult and even contradictory to organize an analysis and an interpretation around any single one of these fragments in flight. To select – even as an 'example' – a single videotext, and to discuss it in isolation, is fatally to regenerate the illusion of the masterpiece or the canonical text and to reify the experience of total flow from which it was momentarily extracted. Video viewing indeed involves immersion in the total flow of the thing itself, preferably a kind of random succession of three or four hours of tapes at regular intervals. Indeed, video is in this sense (and owing to the commercialization of public television and cable) an urban phenomenon demanding video banks or museums in your neighborhood which can thus be visited with something of the institutional habits and relaxed informality with which we used to visit the theater or the opera house (or even the movie palace). What is quite out of the question is to look at a single 'video work' all by itself; in that sense, one would want to say, there are no video masterpieces, there can never be a video canon, and even an auteur theory of video (where signatures are still evidently present) becomes very problematical indeed. The 'interesting' text now has to stand out of an undifferentiated and random flow of other texts. Something like a Heisenberg principle of video analysis thereby emerges: analysts and readers are shackled to the examination of specific and individual texts, one after the other; or, if you prefer, they are condemned to a kind of linear *Darstellung* in which they have to talk about individual texts one at a time. But this very form of perception and criticism at once interferes with the reality of the thing perceived and intercepts it in mid-lightstream, distorting all the findings beyond recognition. The discussion, the indispensable preliminary selection and isolation, of a single 'text' then automatically transforms it back into a 'work,' turns the anonymous video-maker[2] back into a named artist or auteur, and opens the way for the return of all those features of an older modernist aesthetic which it was in the revolutionary nature of the newer medium to have precisely effaced and dispelled.

In spite of these qualifications and reservations, it does not seem possible to go further in this exploration of the possibilities of video without interrogating a concrete text. We will consider a twenty-nine-minute 'work' called *AlienNATION*, produced at the School of the Art Institute of Chicago by Edward Rankus, John Manning, and Barbara Latham in 1979. For the reader this will evidently remain an imaginary text; but the reader need not 'imagine' that the spectator is in an altogether different situation. To describe,

afterward, this stream of images of all kinds is necessarily to violate the perpetual present of the image and to reorganize the few fragments that
remain in the memory according to schemes which probably reveal more
about the reading mind than the text itself: do we try to turn it back into a
story of some kind? (A very interesting book by Jacques Leenhardt and
Pierre Józsa [*Lire la lecture* (Paris: Le Sycamore, 1982)] shows this process at
work even in the reading of 'plotless novels' – the reader's memory creates
'protagonists' out of whole cloth, violates the reading experience in order to
reassemble it into recognizable scenes and narrative sequences, and so
forth.) Or, at some more critically sophisticated level, do we at least try to
sort the material out into thematic blocks and rhythms and repunctuate it
with beginnings and endings with graphs of rising and falling emotivity, cli-
maxes, dead passages, transitions, recapitulations, and the like? No doubt;
only the reconstruction of these overall formal movements turns out differently every time we watch the tape. For one thing, twenty-nine minutes in
video is much longer than the equivalent temporal segment of any feature
film; nor is it excessive to speak of a genuine and a very acute *contradiction*
between the virtually druglike experience of the present of the image in the
videotape and any kind of textual memory into which the successive presents might be inserted (even the return and recognition of older images is,
as it were, seized on the run, laterally and virtually too late for it to do us
any good). If the contrast here with the memory structures of Hollywood-
type fiction films is stark and obvious, one has the feeling – more difficult to
document or to argue – that the gap between this temporal experience and
that of *experimental* film is no less great. These op art tricks and elaborate
visual montages in particular recall the classics of yesteryear such as *Ballet
mechanique*; but I have the impression that, above and beyond the difference
in our institutional situation (art movie theater here, television monitor
either at home or in a museum for the videotext), these experiences are very
different ones, and in particular that the blocks of material in film are larger
and more grossly and tangibly perceptible (even when they pass by rapidly), determining a more leisurely sense of combinations than can be the case
with these attenuated visual data on the television screen.

One is therefore reduced to enumerating a few of these video materials,
which are not themes (since for the most part they are material quotations
from a quasi-commercial storehouse somewhere), but which certainly have
none of the density of Bazinian mise-en-scène either, since even the segments which are not lifted from already existing sequences, but which have
obviously been filmed explicitly for use in this tape, have a kind of shabbi-
ness of low-grade color stock which marks them somehow as 'fictional' and
staged, as opposed to the manifest reality of the other images-in-the-world,
the image objects. There is therefore a sense in which the word *collage* could
still obtain for this juxtaposition of what one is tempted to call 'natural'
materials (the newly or directly filmed sequences) and artificial ones (the
precooked image materials which have been 'mixed' by the machine itself).
What would be misleading is the ontological hierarchy of the older painter-
ly collage: in this videotape the 'natural' is worse and more degraded than
the artificial, which itself no longer connotes the secure daily life of a new
humanly constructed society (as in the objects of cubism) but rather the

noise and jumbled signals, the unimaginable informational garbage, of the new media society.

First, a little existential joke about a 'spot' of time, which is excised from a temporal 'culture' that looks a little like a crepe; then experimental mice, voice-overed by various pseudoscientific reports and therapeutic programs (how to deal with stress, beauty care, hypnosis for weight loss, etc.); then science fiction footage (including monster music and camp dialogue), mostly drawn from a Japanese film, *Monster Zero* (1965). At this point the rush of image materials becomes too dense to enumerate: optical effects, children's blocks and erector sets, reproductions of classical paintings, as well as mannequins, advertising images, computer printouts, textbook illustrations of all kinds, cartoon figures rising and falling (including a wonderful Margritte hat slowly sinking into Lake Michigan); sheet lightning: a woman lying down and possibly under hypnosis (unless, as in a Robbe-Grillet novel, this is merely the photograph of a woman lying down and possibly under hypnosis); ultra-modern hotel or office building lobbies with escalators rising in all directions and at various angles; shots of a street corner with sparse traffic, a child on a big wheel and a few pedestrians carrying groceries; a haunting closeup of detritus and children's blocks on the lakeshore (in one of which the Magritte hat reappears, in real life: poised on stick in the sand); Beethoven sonatas, Holst's *Planets*, disco music, funeral parlor organs, outer space sound effects, the *Lawrence of Arabia* theme accompanying the arrival of flying saucers over the Chicago skyline; a grotesque sequence as well in which friable orange oblongs (that resemble Hostess Twinkies) are dissected with scalpels, squeezed by vises, and shattered by fists; a leaky container of milk; the disco dancers in their habitat; shots of alien planets; closeups of various kinds of brushstrokes; ads for 1950s kitchens; and many more. Sometimes these seem to be combined in longer sequences, as when the sheet lightning is overcharged with a whole series of opticals, advertisements, cartoon figures, movie music, and unrelated radio dialogue. Sometimes, as in the transition from a relatively pensive 'classical music' accompaniment to the stridence of a mass-cultural beat, the principle of variation seems obvious and heavy-handed. Sometimes the accelerated flow of mixed images strikes one as modeling a certain unified temporal urgency, the tempo of delirium, let's say, or of direct experimental assault on the viewer-subject; while the whole is randomly punctuated with formal signals – the 'prepare to disconnect' which is presumably designed to warn the viewer of impending closure, and the final shot of the beach, which borrows a more recognizably filmic connotative language – dispersal of an object world into fragments, but also the touching of a kind of limit or ultimate edge (as in the closing sequence of Fellini's *La Dolce Vita*). It is all, no doubt, an elaborate visual joke or hoax (if you were expecting something more 'serious'): a student's training exercise, if you like; while such is the tempo of the history of experimental video that insiders or connoisseurs are capable of watching this 1979 production with a certain nostalgia and remembering that people did that kind of thing in those days but are now busy doing something else.

The most interesting questions posed by a videotext of this kind – and I hope it will be clear that the text *works*, whatever its value or its meaning: it can be seen again and again (at least partly on account of its informational overload, which the viewer will never be able to master) – remain questions of value and of interpretation, provided it is understood that it may be the absence of any possible response to those questions which is the historically interesting matter. But my attempt to tell or summarize this text makes it clear that even before we reach the interpretative question – 'what does it mean?' or, to use its petit bourgeois version, 'what is it supposed to represent?' – we have to confront the preliminary matters of form and reading. It is not evident that a spectator will ever reach a moment of knowledge and saturated memory from which a formal reading of this text in time slowly disengages itself: beginnings and thematic emergences, combinations and developments, resistances and struggles for dominance, partial resolutions, forms of closure leading on to one or another full stop. Could one establish such an overall chart of the work's formal time, even in a very crude and general way, our description would necessarily remain as empty and as abstract as the terminology of musical form, whose problems today, in aleatory and post-twelve-tone music, are analogous, even though the mathematical dimensions of sound and musical notation provide what look like more tangible solutions. My sense is, however, that even the few formal markers we have been able to isolate – the lakeshore, the building blocks, the 'sense of an ending' – are deceptive; they are now no longer features or elements of a form but signs and traces of older forms. We must remember that those older forms are still included within the bits and pieces, the bricolated material, of this text: Beethoven's sonata is but one component of this bricolage, like a broken pipe retrieved and inserted in a sculpture or a torn piece of newspaper pasted onto a canvas. Yet within the musical segment of the older Beethoven work, 'form' in the traditional sense persists and can be named – the 'falling cadence', say, or the 'reappearance of the first theme.' The same can be said of the film clips of the Japanese monster movie: they include quotations of the SF form itself: 'discovery,' 'menace,' 'attempted flight,' and so forth (here the available formal terminology – in analogy to the musical nomenclature – would probably be restricted to Aristotle or to Propp and his successors, or to Eisenstein, virtually the only sources of a neutral language of the movement of narrative form). The question that suggests itself, then, is whether the formal properties within these quoted segments and pieces are anywhere transferred to the videotext itself, to the bricolage of which they are parts and components. But this is a question that must first be raised on the microlevel of individual episodes and moments. As for the larger formal properties of the text considered as a 'work' and as temporal organization, the lakeshore image suggests that the strong form of an older temporal or musical closure is here present merely as a formal residue: whatever in Fellini's ending still bore the traces of a mythic residue – the sea as some primordial element, as the place at which the human and the social confront the otherness of nature – is here already long since effaced and forgotten. That content has disappeared, leaving but a faint aftertrace of its original formal connotation, that is, of its syntactical function as closure. At this most attenuated point in the sign system the signifier has become little more than a dim memory of a former sign, and indeed, of the formal function of that now extinct sign.

The language of connotation which began to impose itself in the preceding paragraph would seem to impose a reexamination of the central elaboration of this concept, which we owe to Roland Barthes, who elaborated it, following Hjemslev, in his *Mythologies*, only in his later 'textual' work to repudiate its implicit differentiation of first- and second-degree languages (denotation and connotation), which must have come to strike him as a replication of the old divisions between aesthetic and social, artistic free play and historical referentiality – divisions which essays like *Le Plaisir du texte* were concerned to evade or escape. No matter that the earlier theory (still enormously influential in media studies) ingeniously reversed the priorities of this opposition, assigning authenticity (and thereby aesthetic value) to the denotative value of the photographic image, and a guilty social or ideological functionality to its more 'artificial' prolongation in advertising texts that take the original denotative text as their own new content, pressing already existent images into the service of some heightened play of degraded thoughts and commercial messages. Whatever the stakes and implications of this debate, it seems clear that Barthes's earlier, classical conception of how connotation functions can be suggestive for us here only if it is appropriately complicated, perhaps beyond all recognition. For the situation here is rather the inverse of the advertising one, where 'purer' and somehow more material signs were appropriated and readapted to serve as vehicles for a whole range of ideological signals. Here, on the contrary, the ideological signals are already deeply embedded in the primary texts, which are already profoundly cultural and ideological: the Beethoven music already includes the connotator of 'classical music' in general, the science fiction film already includes multiple political messages and anxieties (an American Cold War form readapted to Japanese antinuclear politics, and both then folding into the new cultural connotator of 'camp'). But connotation is here – in a cultural sphere whose 'products' have functions that largely transcend the narrowly commercial ones of advertising images (while no doubt still including some of those and surely replicating their structures in other ways) – a polysemic process in which a number of 'messages' coexist. Thus the alternation of Beethoven and disco no doubt emits a class message – high versus popular or mass culture, privilege and education versus more popular and bodily forms of diversion – but it also continues to vehiculate the older content of some tragic gravity, the formal time sense of the sonata form itself, the 'high seriousness' of the most rigorous bourgeois aesthetic in its grappling with time, contradiction, and death; which now finds itself opposed to the relentless temporal distraction of the big city commercial music of the postmodern age that fills time and space implacably to the point where the older 'tragic' questions seem irrelevant. All these connotations are in play simultaneously. To the degree to which they appear easily reducible to some of the binary oppositions just mentioned (high and low culture), and to that degree alone, we are in the presence of a kind of 'theme,' which might at the outside limit be the occasion for an interpretive act and allow us to suggest that the videotext is 'about' this particular opposition. We will return to such interpretive possibilities or options later on.

What must be excluded, however, is anything like a process of demystification at work in this particular videotext: all its materials are degraded in that sense, Beethoven no less than disco. And although, as we will shortly make clear, there is a very complex interaction at work here between various levels and components of the text, or various languages (image versus sound, music versus dialogue), the political use of one of these levels against another (as in Godard), the attempt somehow to purify the image by setting it off against the written or spoken, is here no longer on the agenda, if it is even still conceivable. This is something that can be clarified, I believe, if we think of the various quoted elements and components – the broken pieces of a whole range of primary texts in the contemporary cultural sphere – as so many logos, that is to say, as a new form of advertising language which is structurally and historically a good deal more advanced and complicated than any of the advertising images with which Barthes's earlier theories had to deal. A logo is something like the synthesis of an advertising image and a brand name; better still, it is a brand name which has been transformed into an image, a sign or emblem which carries the memory of a whole tradition of earlier advertisements within itself in a well-nigh intertextual way. Such logos can be visual or auditory and musical (as in the Pepsi theme): an enlargement which allows us to include the materials of the sound track under this category, along with the more immediately identifiable logo segments of the office escalators, the fashion mannequins, the psychological counseling clips, the street corner, the lakefront, *Monster Zero*, and so forth. 'Logo' then signifies the transformation of each of these fragments into a kind of sign in its own right; yet it is not yet clear what such new signs might be signs of, since no product seems identifiable, nor even the range of generic products strictly designated by the logo in its original sense, as the badge of a diversified multinational corporation. Still, the term *generic* is itself suggestive if we conceive of its literary implications a little more broadly than the older, more static, tables of 'genres,' or fixed kinds. The generic cultural consumption projected by these fragments is more dynamic and demands some association with narrative (itself now grasped in the wider sense of a type of textual consumption). In that sense, the scientific experiments are narratives fully as much as *Lawrence of Arabia*; the vision of white-collar workers and bureaucrats mounting flights of escalators is no less a narrative vision than the science fiction film clips (or horror music); even the still photograph of sheet lightning suggests a multiple set of narrative frames (Ansel Adams, or the terror of the great storm, or the 'logo' of the Remington-type western landscape, or the eighteenth-century sublime, or the answer of God to the rainmaking ceremony, or the beginning of the end of the world).

The matter grows more complicated, however, when we realize that none of these elements or new cultural signs or logos exists in isolation; the videotext itself is at virtually all moments a process of ceaseless, apparently random, interaction between them. This is clearly the structure which demands description and analysis, but it is a relationship between signs for which we have only the most approximate theoretical models. It is indeed a matter of apprehending a constant stream, or 'total flow,' of multiple materials, each of which can be seen as something like a shorthand signal for a distinct type of narrative or a specific narrative process. But our immediate questions will be synchronic rather than diachronic: how do these various narrative signals or logos intersect? Is one to imagine a mental compartmentalization in which each is received in isolation, or does the mind somehow establish connections of some kind; and in that case, how can we describe those connections? How are these materials wired into one another, if at all? Or do we merely confront a simultaneity of distinct streams of elements which the senses grasp all together like a kaleidoscope? The measure of our conceptual weakness here is that we are tempted to begin with the most unsatisfactory methodological decision – the Cartesian point of departure – in which we begin by reducing the phenomenon to its simplest form, namely, the interaction of two such elements or signals (whereas dialectical thinking asks us to begin with the most complex form, of which the simpler ones are considered derivatives).

[...] The interpretive question – 'what is the text or work *about*?' – generally encourages a thematic answer, as indeed in the obliging title of the present tape, *AlienNATION*. There it is and now we know: it is the alienation of a whole nation, or perhaps a new kind of nation organized around alienation itself. The concept of alienation had rigor when specifically used to articulate the various concrete privations of workingclass life (as in Marx's Paris manuscripts): and it also had a specific function at a specific historical moment (the Khrushchev opening), which radicals in the East (Poland, Yugoslavia) and the West (Sartre) believed could inaugurate a new tradition in Marxist thinking and practice. It surely does not amount to much, however, as a general designation for (bourgeois) spiritual malaise. But this is not the only reason for the discontent one feels when, in the midst of splendid postmodernist performances like Laurie Anderson's *USA*, the repetition of the word *alienation* (as it were, whispered in passing to the public) made it difficult to avoid the conclusion that this was indeed what that also was supposed to be 'about.' Two virtually identical responses then follow: so that's what it was supposed to mean; so that's all it was supposed to mean. The problem is twofold: alienation is, first of all, not merely a *modernist* concept but also a modernist *experience* (something I cannot argue further here, except to say that 'psychic fragmentation' is a better term for what ails us today, if we need a term for it). But the problem's second ramification is the decisive one: whatever such a meaning and its adequacy (qua meaning), one has the deeper feeling that 'texts' like *USA* or *AlienNATION* ought not to have any 'meaning' at all in that thematic sense. This is something everyone is free to verify, by self-observation and a little closer attention to precisely those moments in which we briefly feel that disillusionment I have described experiencing at the thematically explicit moments in *USA*. In effect, the points at which one can feel something similar during the Rankus-Manning-Latham videotape have already been enumerated in another context. They are very precisely those points at which the intersection of sign and interpretant seems to produce a fleeting message: high versus low culture, in the modern world we're all programmed like laboratory mice, nature versus culture, and so forth. The wisdom of the vernacular tells us that these 'themes' are corny, as corny as alienation itself (but not old-fashioned enough to be camp). Yet it would be a mistake to simplify this interesting situation and reduce it to a question of the nature and quality, the intellectual substance, of the themes themselves; indeed, our preceding analysis has the makings of a much better explanation of such lapses.

We tried to show, indeed, that what characterizes this particular video process (or 'experimental' total flow) is a ceaseless rotation of elements such that they change place at every moment, with the result that no single element can occupy the position of 'interpretant' (or that of primary sign) for any length of time but must be dislodged in turn in the following instant (the filmic terminology of 'frames' and 'shots' does not seem appropriate for this kind of succession), falling to the subordinate position in its turn, where it will then be 'interpreted' or narrativized by a radically different kind of logo or image content altogether. If this is an accurate account of the process, however, then it follows logically that anything which arrests or interrupts it will be sensed as an aesthetic flaw. The thematic moments we have complained about above are just such moments of interruption, of a kind of blockage in this process: at such points a provisional 'narrativization' – the provisional dominance of one sign or logo over another, which it interprets and rewrites according to its own narrative logic – quickly spreads out over the sequence like a burn spot on the film, at that point 'held' long enough to generate and emit a thematic message quite inconsistent with the textual logic of the thing itself. Such moments involve a peculiar form of reification, which we might characterize equally well as a *thematization* – a word the late Paul DeMan was fond of, using it to characterize the misreading of Derrida as a 'philosopher' whose 'philosophical system' was somehow 'about' writing. Thematization is then the moment in which an element, a component, of a text is promoted to the status of official theme, at which point it becomes a candidate for that even higher honor, the work's 'meaning.' But such thematic reification is not necessarily a function of the philosophical or intellectual quality of the 'theme' itself: whatever the philosophical interest and viability of the notion of the alienation of contemporary bureaucratic life, its emergence here as a 'theme' is registered as a flaw for what are essentially formal reasons. The proposition might be argued the other way around by identifying another possible lapse in our text as the excessive dependence on the 'estrangement effects' of the Japanese SF film clips (repeated viewings, however, make it clear that they were not so frequent as one remembered). If so, we have here to do with a thematization of a narrative or generic type rather than a degradation via pop philosophy and stereotypical doxa.

We can now draw some unexpected consequences from this analysis, consequences that bear not only on the vexed question of interpretation in postmodernism but also on another matter, that of aesthetic value, which had been provisionally tabled at the outset of this discussion. If interpretation is understood, in the thematic way, as the disengagement of a fundamental theme or meaning, then it seems clear that the postmodernist text – of which we have taken the videotape in question to be a privileged exemplar – is from that perspective defined as a structure or sign flow which resists meaning, whose fundamental inner logic is the exclusion of the emergence of themes as such in that sense, and which therefore systematically sets out to short-circuit traditional interpretive temptations (something Susan Sontag prophetically intuited in the appropriately titled *Against Interpretation*, at the very dawn of what was not yet called the postmodern age). New criteria of aesthetic value then unexpectedly emerge from this proposition: whatever a good, let alone a great, videotext might be, it will be bad or flawed whenever such interpretation proves possible, whenever the text slackly opens up just such places and areas of thematization itself.

Thematic interpretation, however – the search for the 'meaning' of the work – is not the only conceivable hermeneutic operation to which texts, including this one, can be subjected, and I want to describe two other interpretive options before concluding. The first returns us to the question of the referent in an unexpected fashion, by way of that other set of component materials to which we have so far paid less attention than to the quoted inscribed and recorded spools of canned cultural junk which are here interwoven: those (characterized as 'natural' materials) were the segments of directly shot footage, which, above and beyond the lakeshore sequence, essentially fell into three groups. The urban street crossing, to begin with, is a kind of degraded space, which – distant, poor cousin in that to the astonishing concluding sequence of Antonioni's *Eclipse* – begins faintly to project the abstraction of an empty stage, a place of the Event, a bounded space in which something may happen and before which one waits in formal expectation. In *Eclipse*, of course, when the event fails to materialize and neither of the lovers appears at the rendezvous, place – now forgotten – slowly finds itself degraded back into space again, the reified space of the modern city, quantified and measurable, in which land and earth are parceled out into so many commodities and lots for sale. Here also nothing happens; only the very sense of the possibility of something happening and of the faint emergence of the very category of the Event itself is unusual in this particular tape (the menaced events and anxieties of the science fiction clips are merely 'images' of events or, if you prefer, spectacle events without any temporality of their own).

The second sequence is that of the perforated milk carton, a sequence which perpetuates and confirms the peculiar logic of the first one, since here we have in some sense the pure event itself, about which there's no point crying, the irrevocable. The finger must give up stopping the breach, the milk must pour out across the table and over the edge, with all the visual fascination of this starkly white substance. If this quite wonderful image seems to me to revert even distantly to a more properly filmic status, my own aberrant and strictly personal association of it with a famous scene in *The Manchurian Candidate* is no doubt also partially responsible.

As for the third segment, the wackiest and more pointless, I have already described the absurdity of a laboratory experiment conducted with hardware store tools on orange objects of indeterminate size which have something of the consistency of a Hostess Twinkie. What is scandalous and vaguely disturbing about this homemade bit of dada is its apparent lack of motivation: one tries, without any great satisfaction, to see it as an Ernie Kovacs parody of the laboratory animal sequence; in any case, nothing else in the tape echoes this particular mode or zaniness of 'voice.' All three groups of images, but in particular this autopsy of a Twinkie, reminds one vaguely of a strand of organic material which has been woven in among an organic texture, like the whale blubber in Joseph Beuys's sculpture.

Nonetheless, a first approach suggested itself to me on the level of unconscious anxiety, where the hole in the milk carton – following the assassination scene in *The Manchurian Candidate*, where the victim is surprised at a midnight snack in front of the open refrigerator door – is now explicitly read as a bullet hole. I have meanwhile neglected to supply another clue, namely, the computer-generated X that moves across the empty street crossing like the sights of a long-range rifle. It remained for an astute listener (at an earlier version of this paper) to make the connection and point out the henceforth obvious and unassailable: for the American media public, the combination of the two elements – milk and Twinkie – is too peculiar to be unmotivated. In fact, on November 27, 1978 (the year preceding the composition of this particular videotape), San Francisco Mayor George Moscone and City Supervisor Harvey Milk were shot to death by a former supervisor, who entered the unforgettable plea of not guilty by reason of insanity owing to the excessive consumption of Hostess Twinkies.

Here, then, at last, the referent itself is disclosed: the brute fact, the historical event, the real load in this particular imaginary garden. To track such a reference down is surely to perform an act of interpretation or hermeneutic disclosure of a very different kind from that previously discussed: for if *AlienNATION* is 'about' this, then such an expression can only have a sense quite distinct from its use in the proposition that the text was 'about' alienation itself.

The problem of reference has been singularly displaced and stigmatized in the hegemony of the various poststructuralist discourses which characterizes the current moment (and along with it, anything that smacks of 'reality,' 'representation,' 'realism,' and the like – even the word *history* has an *r* in it); only Lacan has shamelessly continued to talk about 'the Real' (defined, however, as an absence). The respectable philosophical solutions to the problem of an external real world independent of consciousness are all traditional ones, which means that however logically satisfying they may be (and none of them were ever really very satisfactory from a logical standpoint), they are not suitable candidates for participation in contemporary polemics. The hegemony of theories of textuality and textualization means, among other things, that your entry ticket to the public sphere in which these matters are debated is an agreement, tacit or otherwise, with the basic presuppositions of a general problem field, something traditional positions on these matters refuse in advance. My own feeling has been that historicism offers a peculiarly unexpected escape from this vicious circle or double bind.

To raise the issue, for example, of the fate of the 'referent' in contemporary culture and thought is not the same thing as to assert some older theory of reference or to repudiate all the new theoretical problems in advance. On the contrary, such problems are retained and endorsed, with the proviso that they are not only interesting problems in their own right but also, at the same time, symptoms of a historical transformation.

In the immediate instance that concerns us here, I have argued for the presence and existence of what seems to me a palpable referent – namely, death and historical fact, which are ultimately not textualizable and tear through the tissues of textual elaboration, of combination and free play ('the Real,' Lacan tells us, 'is what resists symbolization absolutely'). I want to add at once that this is no particularly triumphant philosophical victory for some putative realism or other over the various textualizing worldviews. For the assertion of a buried referent – as in the present example – is a two-way street whose antithetical directions might emblematically be named 'repression' and *Aufhebung*, or 'sublation': the picture has no way of telling us whether we are looking at a rising or a setting sun. Does our discovery document the persistence and stubborn, all-informing gravitational charge of reference, or, on the contrary, does it show the tendential historical process whereby reference is systematically processed, dismantled, textualized, and volatilized, leaving little more than some indigestible remnant?

However this ambiguity is handled, there remains the matter of the structural logic of the tape itself, of which this particular directly filmed sequence is only a single strand among many, and a particularly minor one at that (although its properties attract a certain attention). Even if its referential value could be satisfactorily demonstrated, the logic of rotating conjunction and disjunction that has been described above clearly works to dissolve such a value, which cannot be tolerated any more than the emergence of individual themes. Nor is it clear how an axiological system could be developed in the name of which we might then affirm that these strange sequences are somehow better than the random and aimless 'irresponsibility' of the collages of media stereotypes.

Yet another way of interpreting such a tape is conceivable, however – an interpretation that would seek to foreground the process of production itself rather than its putative messages, meanings, or content. On this reading some distant consonance might be invoked between the fantasies and anxieties aroused by the idea of assassination and the global system of media and reproductive technology. The structural analogy between the two seemingly unrelated spheres is secured in the collective unconscious by notions of conspiracy, while the historical juncture between the two was burned into historical memory by the Kennedy assassination itself, which can no longer be separated from its media coverage. The problem posed by such interpretation in terms of autoreferentiality is not its plausibility: one would want to defend the proposition that the deepest 'subject' of all video art, and even of all postmodernism, is very precisely reproductive technology itself. The methodological difficulty lies rather in the way in which such a global 'meaning' – even of some type and status newer than the interpretive meanings we have touched on above – once again dissolves the individual text into an even more disastrous indistinction than the total flow–individual work antinomy evoked above: if all videotexts simply designate the process of production/reproduction, then presumably they all turn out to be 'the same' in a peculiarly unhelpful way.

I will not try to solve any of these problems: instead I will restage the approaches and perspectives of the historicism I have called for by way of a kind of myth I have found useful in characterizing the nature of contemporary (postmodernist) cultural production and also in positioning its various theoretical projections.

Once upon a time at the dawn of capitalism and middle-class society, there emerged something called the sign, which seemed to entertain unproblematical relations with its referent. This initial heyday of the sign – the moment of literal or referential language or of the unproblematic claims of so-called scientific discourse – came into being because of the corrosive dissolution of older forms of magical language by a force which I will call that of reification, a force whose logic is one of ruthless separation and disjunction, of specialization and rationalization, of a Taylorizing division of labor in all realms. Unfortunately, that force – which brought traditional reference into being – continued unremittingly, being the very logic of capital itself. Thus this first moment of decoding or of realism cannot long endure; by a dialectical reversal it then itself in turn becomes the object of the corrosive force of reification, which enters the realm of language to disjoin the sign from the referent. Such a disjunction does not completely abolish the referent, or the objective world, or reality, which still continue to entertain a feeble existence on the horizon like a shrunken star or red dwarf. But its great distance from the sign now allows the latter to enter a moment of autonomy, of a relatively free-floating Utopian existence, as over against its former objects. This autonomy of culture, this semiautonomy of language, is the moment of modernism, and of a realm of the aesthetic which redoubles the world without being altogether of it, thereby winning a certain negative or critical power, but also a certain otherworldly futility. Yet the force of reification, which was responsible for this new moment, does not stop there either: in another stage, heightened, a kind of reversal of quantity into quality, reification penetrates the sign itself and disjoins the signifier from the signified. Now reference and reality disappear altogether, and even meaning – the signified – is problematized. We are left with that pure and random play of signifiers that we call postmodernism, which no longer produces monumental works of the modernist type but ceaselessly reshuffles the fragments of preexistent texts, the building blocks of older cultural and social production, in some new and heightened bricolage: metabooks which cannibalize other books, metatexts which collate bits of other texts – such is the logic of postmodernism in general, which finds one of its strongest and most original, authentic[1] forms in the new art of experimental video.

## Notes

1. Raymond Williams, *Television* (New York, 1975), p. 92. Readers of collections like E. Ann Kaplan's *Regarding Television* (Los Angeles, American Film Institute, 1983), and John Hanhardt's *Video Culture. A Critical Investigation* (New York, 1986), may find such assertions astonishing. A frequent theme of these articles remains, however, the absence, tardiness, repression, or impossibility of video theory proper.
2. I mean here essentially the *good* anonymity of handicraft work of the medieval kind, as opposed to the supreme demiurgic subjectivity or 'genius' of the modern Master.

# 22

## Uncanny feminism

*Patricia Mellencamp*

From *Indiscretions. Avant-garde film, video and feminism* (Indiana University Press 1990)

> The traces of the storyteller cling to the story the way the handprints of the potter cling to the clay vessel.
> Walter Benjamin[1]

> The princess may very well have had an uncanny feeling, indeed she very probably fell into a swoon; but we have no such sensations, for we put ourselves in the thief's place, not in hers.
> Sigmund Freud[2]

Before analyzing Cecilia Condit's videotapes *Beneath the Skin* (1981) and *Possibly in Michigan* (1983), marvelous tales told from the princess' point of view, I will wander through the metaphorical, treacherous forests of other stories, discovering 'invisible adversaries' along the path. The first is a handsome prince in a cautionary fable, 'The Twelve Dancing Princesses':[3] 'Once upon a time there was a king who had twelve daughters, each more beautiful than the other. They slept together in a hall where their beds stood close to one another. At night when they had gone to bed, the king locked the door and bolted it. But when he unlocked it in the morning, he noticed that their shoes had been danced to pieces, and nobody could explain how it happened.' Although imprisoned by patriarchy, these dancing daughters gleefully and confidently escaped the king's gaze of surveillance and power; together 'they danced, every night, on the opposite shore, in a splendid light, till three in the morning, when their shoes were danced into holes and they were obliged to stop.'

In this celebration of female adolescence and adventure, however – as in most of the 'once upon a time' of fiction – something is wrong, and the youngest sister is suspicious: 'I don't know what it is. You may rejoice, but I feel so strange. A misfortune is certainly hanging over us.' For women, on a par with being scrutinized and contained by vision, the end is the dire, dreaded misfortune – in this fairy tale, marriage to a prince, a quick and unhappy conclusion which separates the sisters and censures their nightly escapades. Anne Sexton's rewriting: 'Now the runaways would run no more and never / again would their hair be tangled into diamonds, / never again their shoes worn down to a laugh, / He had won.'[4] A fellow had been given a cloak of invisibility by an old woman and had secretly spied on their nightly pleasures and reported to the king. For his voyeurism (and successful surveillance), he was given the kingdom and a princess of his choice. The peril of being the visible, private object of desire and the safe power of being the invisible, desiring, public subject are two morals of this and contemporary theory's story. The undisciplined sisters had transgressed the patrolled frontier between private and public – that demarcation line of power – and their passionate, dancing bodies were duly arrested.

Although the prince inadvertently revealed his presence through touch and sound, eleven of the princesses paid no attention: 'And, as he broke off a twig, a sharp crack came from the tree. The youngest cried out, "All is not well! Did you hear that sound?"' No one else listened to these sounds, which made 'the youngest princess start with terror.' While many feminists are proudly standing on opposite shores, watching the 'splendid light' of independent films and videotapes and being invited to the intellectual dance of postmodernism by scholars and the art world,[5] we might heed the alarm of the youngest sister, for there are warnings in the academic air of godly wrath and signs of virulent condescension, brazenly heralding a resurgence of reactionary, antifeminist positions – signaled by arguments for women's return to private space, the home. 'New traditionalists,' we are told in magazine ads, are women garbed in tailored, professional fashion; rather than being in the office, they are photographed with children, in domesticity, preferring to remain at home.

Lawrence Stone, Dodge professor of history at Princeton, another prince of a fellow and the second adversary of this essay, caused me to 'start with terror' and conclude with furor at his patronizing, biblical admonishments in the *New York Review of Books* – at best a naked emperor when the topic rarely turns to feminism; at worst, which is usually the case, a wolf without the guise of sheep's clothing. In the first paragraph of 'Only Women,' a foreboding title, King Stone speaks to the princesses: 'I must first set out the ten commandments which should, in my opinion, govern the writing of women's history at any time and in any place' – certainly a specious claim when discussing the writing of history. (Ruminous sounds, awkwardly famous movie stars, and unearthly special effects restage this spectacle in the film version of *Only Women*, co-directed by Lizzie Borden and Cecil B. De Mille, in which Stone plays himself and is duly disemboweled in the film/theory remake of the beginning of Michel Foucault's *Discipline and Punish*.) Having claimed truth and the world for all times and all places, the Stone tablets are thus writ by this Moses impersonator: 'I. Thou shalt not write about women except in relation to men and children. [The wife/mother plea suppresses the very reality of women's lives, forgetting both women's relationships with other women and the exhausting fact that most women always have at least two full-time jobs – taking care of children and men.] Women are not a distinct caste, and their history is a story of complex interactions; 2. Thou shalt strive not to distort the evidence and the conclusions to support modern feminist ideology . . . 4. Thou shalt not confuse prescriptive norms with social reality . . . 9. Thou shalt be clear about what constitutes real change in the experience and treatment of women.'[6] Because Stone is male and thus omnipotent, he, like his godly predecessors, knows 'what constitutes real change' in the experience of women or 'thou.'

This catalogue of imperative 'shalts' is an intellectual aberration – a paranoid delusion of divine intervention into feminist scholarship and history. I 'start with terror' when I imagine the collective, knowing laughter of educated readers at his chastisement of women writers and feminism. For Prince Stone, women (not just feminists) have broken the bonds of propriety and chastity by entering priestly male domains of 'history'; he marshals his defensive attack on women under the disguise or banner of research. Like the prince's cloak, scholarship and prestigious chairs (a veritable star system of academia reminiscent of the Hollywood studio era, replete with gossip and credits, is operative in this magazine) provide various screens, briefly concealing, like the prince's invisible presence, the argument.

*American Film* joins the *New York Review of Books* in mockery through the terrain of 'with-it' popular culture in a breezy piece by Raymond Durgnat on Grace Jones – an essay and a female subject made strangely respectable (as if Jones were not) by dropping sundry names, e.g., Visconti, Renoir, and Vertov, in a swaggering display of his superior knowledge of and desire for her 'phallic-narcissistic swagger and strut.' (This lurid psychoanalysis suggests Lee Marvin's black-leathered Liberty Valence in John Ford's film and describes Durgnat's argument and style.) After glorifying Jones and her traversals of boundaries, Durgnat suddenly turns on feminism, on women as the objects of his contempt, the real reason for his essay. He smugly writes with scorn: 'Jones disturbs the Brand X forms of feminism. She's too frivolous for its schoolmarms, too sexual for its puritans, too strong for its sensitive plants, too competitive for its pacifists, too capitalist for its radicals, too effective for its neurotics, too hetero for its separatists, too responsibly independent to put the blame on pop for everything (war, the weather, old age).'[7]

Durgnat's dismissive compendium, modeled on Linnaeus rather than the Bible, reiterates the nauseating typologies used to assault feminism and employs biological arguments used to contain women, e.g., frivolous, sensitive, pacifists, puritans, schoolmarms, and, of course, neurotic and dependent. It is not insignificant that *American Film* would publish, without notation, words of undisguised racism and sexism, setting women in opposition under the cover of praising a black woman – the imperialist tactic of divide and conquer, the king's move against the sisters, a gambit of subjection rather than subjectivity.

These all-knowing enunciators protest too much, however; perhaps they are afraid of something, including the assertive, stylish representations of Grace Jones. Perhaps women, white and of color, are upping the ante, redirecting the terms of vision and spectacle in stories and theories which dance on opposite shores without the fatal end of patriarchy. In vastly different ways, Condit and other feminist artists 'play with our curiosity and finally refuse to submit to our gaze. *They turn being looked at into an aggressive act* [my emphasis] . . . they are playing with the only power at their disposal – the power to discomfit, the power, that is, to pose . . . to pose a threat . . . They must exceed definitions of the proper and the permissible . . . And there is pleasure in transgression.'[8] (As a qualification or addition to this acute remark by Dick Hebdige, women also have language 'at their disposal' – for some, a troubling incursion into grammars of power as women interrupt the masculine ecology of speech *and* dispose of, or trash, kingly discourses – which Condit does in the garbage sequence which concludes *Possibly in Michigan*.) Along lines similar to Hebdige, Mary Russo writes about masquerade: 'To put on femininity with a vengeance suggests the power of taking it off.'[9] Condit does 'pose a threat' by putting on femininity with a visual and narrative vengeance; her disconcerting irony and sweetly gruesome stories also put on and undo societal prescriptions and taboos regarding women's options to subjugation by violence or the gaze, letting us see and hear what often remains hidden, behaving with impropriety. Feminist films and video are telling stories differently *and* looking at difference differently – the latter, a key to feminist influences on current debates on postmodernism, particularly the issues focused on notions of the Other. Women are posited as the schizophrenic subject of postmodern culture, just as television is its latent object – the embodiment of every emblematic feature. Yet rarely are either subject or object acknowledged other than for feminism as Other – as a 'great divide'[10] or bipolarity (containing, in order of historical fashion, vestiges of Lacan's endless division of the subject in language, the split between 'I' of enunciation and 'I' of enounced, the separation of the inner world of the 'self' from the outside 'world' of reality and facticity which can be mastered and owned, the division of subject from object, men from women, women from women, word from image, and soul from body[11]).

I want briefly to elaborate on this strange situation of feminism's acclaimed marginality and unstated centrality through a selective reading of an *October* essay, 'The "Primitive" Unconscious of Modern Art,' by a leading figure in the debate, Hal Foster. Among complex, political issues, he explicates *bricolage*: 'Myth is a one-way appropriation, an act of power; *bricolage* is a process of textual play, of loss and gain: whereas myth abstracts and pretends to the natural, bricolage cuts up, makes concrete, delights in the artificial.' (Condit's work literally 'cuts up' and 'delights in the artificial.') Up to this point, drawing on Levi-Strauss and Barthes, Foster's definition of the 'primitive style' is uncannily similar to feminist art and argument – against biology, which for women emerges as the 'eternal,' the goddess whore myth. Foster provocatively asserts that 'the rupture of the primitive, managed by the moderns, becomes our postmodern event'; he concludes by invoking feminists for whom 'there are other ways to narrate this history.'[12] Thus, by extension and in/direct elision, feminism becomes the repressed, managed rupture of postmodernism – posited, like 'primitivism' earlier, *outside* the debate as the estranged, unknowable other, along with other races and cultures. I repeat: in postmodern discourses, 'woman' is not fascinating as she was to modernism; 'feminism' is.

If feminism is going to be invoked as a desirable dialogue or a discourse of salvation, it is time to realize that at least white, intellectual, middle-class feminism is not Other in the sense of being outside a shared history and politics of class and race; white women are Other for psychoanalysis' male subjects and analysts for whom 'woman' *is* the problem; 'she' is a paradoxical dilemma which grants male identity and exists as an inscrutable mystery, in both myths serving as the object of male desire/fear rather than as a subject. Indeed, an exceedingly primitive unconscious is posited by the modernists Freud and Lacan. Within this European, historical account of male sexuality/subjectivity, yes, 'woman' is other and lacking, truly a problem – with an essay by Freud 'On Femininity' but no comparable piece on masculinity. But for political and fashionable U.S. writers on postmodernism? The blind yet concerned visage of Oedipus, now miserable as Colonus, again misreads women or feminism which is alluded to rather than translated and which servilely works, without recognition, as source of the argument and/or the condemnation of postmodern culture.

The task for feminists involved 're-vising the old apprehension of sexual difference and making it possible to multiply differences, to move away from homogeneity,'[13] a notion picked up, then amplified by de Lauretis to include 'differences among women' and 'differences within women': 'differences which are not purely sexual or merely racial, economic, or (sub)cultural, but all of these together and often enough in conflict with one another.'[14] These delineations of hetereogenity, together *and* in conflict, of historical women are resolutely against the notions of 'purely' and 'merely' usually applied to eternal 'woman' and veer from princely mastery through colonization, bipolarity, hierarchy and otherness. These gambits which divide and conquer rely on a central, defining term or superior reality (usually white and/or male) rather than a series of equivalent or nonhierarchical options.

Several strategies of 'heterogeneity' are apparent in recent feminist cinema and video: (1) the emphasis on enunciation and address to women *as subjects* (including multiple voices in personal dialogues and the use of private speech), a reciprocity between author, text, and audience involving collective/contradictory identifications and shared 'situations'; (2) the telling of 'stories' rather than 'novels' or grand master narratives as Walter Benjamin distinguished these two forms; (3) the inextricable bricolage of personal and theoretical knowledge; (4) the performance of parody or the telling of jokes, with irony and wit as women's allies rather than enemies; no wonder women in the audience laugh with such bursts of mutual delight; neither tale nor laughter are at their expense; (5) an implicit or explicit critique and refashioning of theories of subjectivity constructed by vision; and (6) a transgression of the boundaries between private and public spaces and experiences, entering with intimacy the 'public sphere' and unsettling these metaphorical and real spaces of power through confinement by looking and talking back. I will scatter these intersecting issues throughout the discussion of Condit's sassy video work.

*Beneath the Skin* (1981) and *Possibly in Michigan* (1983) are unnerving and funny retellings of Oedipus as tabloid sensationalism. Imagine Freud's essay on the uncanny as either a feminist fairy tale or a murderous scandal, excerpted in the *National Inquirer* and *Art Forum*, illustrated by photographs of masquerade women or mutilated corpses, and accompanied by bold headlines of first person quotations. This lucid critique/lurid exposé would return – collapsing criticism's bipolarity of art versus popular culture, fiction opposed to fact, simulation against the real, canny against the uncanny – as a performance staged by Cindy Sherman with voices by Lily Tomlin. Scholarly explications via 'theoretical' postmodernism would be published in *October* while personal stories of the artists would appear in *People*; clips from the piece would be shown on CBS on Sunday morning in the sacred art slot near the end of the program. Condit, Sherman, Tomlin, and Annette Michelson would intimately/polemically chat/assert on 'The Phil Donahue Show' before a female audience of nonfeminists. Or as real life would have it, Condit's work would be broadcast on 'The 700 Club' – without its sound track – and dubbed over with a poet reading his work about homosexuality. We would be held in a disconcerting uncertainty concerning origins, originals, mastery, truth, art, popular culture and 'the real' (all of which are complex processes, dispersed discourses which, like mass culture, most criticism posits as monoliths or 'things' which are locatable, almost tangible) – currently labeled 'pastiche' and 'schizophrenia' as the emblematic condition of the postmodern object and its confused subject.[15] Or, as Barthes argued earlier, 'Taken aslant by language, the world is written through and through; signs, endlessly deferring their foundations . . . infinitely citing one another, nowhere come to a halt . . . .'[16]

Or, in another interpretation of this crazy return, we would be as ambivalently delighted and unwarily off-centered as we are by watching Condit's videotapes. Their status as hyperreal – the mesmerizing, fibrillating images of masquerade and the grotesque – is undercut by the irony of the smiling voice speaking of violence and death with the amazed, homey incredulity of backyard gossip or doubly displaced by innocent, sing-song exchanges and girlish operettas. Grizzly scandal collides with female adolescence, just as sound intercepts image, derailing spectators and interpretation alike; the real violence in women's lives coincides with fairy tales and princesses. Teresa de Lauretis concluded *Alice Doesn't* with a marvelous, riddling question: 'it is the signifier who plays and wins before Alice does, even when she's aware of it. But to what end, if Alice doesn't?'[17] Cecilia doesn't and Condit's work unravels the sentence's paradox while imaging blackly ironic, startling 'endings' to de Lauretis's question.

Condit's tapes unequivocally position us in the princess' place, Sleeping Beauty's swoon, that nightmare of Anne Sexton's poem in which the awakened princess 'married the prince':

> and all went well
> except for the fear –
> the fear of sleep.
> Briar Rose
> was an insomniac . . .
> I must not sleep
> for while asleep I'm ninety
> and think I'm dying.
> Death rattles in my throat.[18]

Unlike Freud and Sexton, Condit has no interest in either marriages to princes or thieves' viewpoints, however fascinated she is, as they are, by sleep and dream, violence and death. Her strategy, however unaware of either source, is a combination of Freud and Sexton, rewriting the 'uncanny' as a fairy tale (a form which Freud absolutely and repeatedly denied was an instance of uncanny experiences) and taking Sexton's feminist revisions to different, less lonely and suicidal ends. Condit's translucent, artificial, video bodies are interrupted by recreations and documentary footage of epileptic seizures and still photographs of mummies' heads; the 'classical' body is disrupted by the 'grotesque' body; the private, controlled, sleeping beauty is transformed into the public, uncontrollable epileptic or the decaying body of a murderous scandal; all are instances of violent spectacle, exquisite corpses. No longer effaced or held in private spaces by 'proper' discourse and decorous words, these are 'undisciplined,' speaking bodies – on the frontier between the modern body and the carnival body before the seventeenth century incarceration in asylums, prisons, and homes, before the ascendancy of the word over the carnal, guilty flesh and other great divides of power – adolescent rather than grown up bodies which suggest that another interpretation of masquerade as a possibility for feminism rather than a disguise, lure, or mark of envious lack is necessary.

Via Bakhtin's work on carnival and Rabelais, Mary Russo writes in 'Female Grotesques: Carnival and Theory': 'The grotesque body is the open, protruding, extended, secreting body, the body of becoming, process, and change. The grotesque body is opposed to the classical body, which is monumental, static, closed, and sleek . . . .' Condit's work alternates and merges the 'classical' body with the grotesque body – the latter the uncontrollable, erupting body as spectacle on public display. Russo writes of historical, female performers: 'They used their bodies in public, in extravagant ways that could have only provoked wonder and ambivalence in the female viewer . . . .'[19] This image of the body and the ambivalent spectator is applicable to the 'style' of Condit's work: 'a body in the act of becoming. It is never finished, never completed; it is continually built, created, and builds and creates another body . . . a double body in which one link joins the other, in which the life of one body is born from the death of the preceding, older one . . . the body can merge with various natural phenomena . . . .'[20] The carnival body is an indivisible body without inner/outer, self/other polarities in which the exterior is inauthentic, merely a cover-up; it is a body of doubled surfaces rather than inner recesses which are analyzed, explained. Video is well suited to this transforming, seamless emergence of one surface from another, a fluid editing/processing capacity which Condit utilizes with skill.

'[T]his hyperbolic style, this "overacting" can be read as double representations . . . .'[21] 'Double representation' (both Bakhtin's 'double body' and the 'double-directed discourse' of parody) – extended to include the critique of the schizophrenic subject and the intersection of sound and image tracks – aptly describes Condit's tapes, which also demonstrate a tactic suggested by Luce Irigaray and endorsed by Russo: 'to play with mimesis is thus, for a woman, to try to recover the place of her exploitation by discourse, without allowing herself simply to be reduced to it. It means to resubmit herself . . . to ideas . . . that are elaborated in/by masculine logic, but so as to make "visible" what was supposed to remain invisible.'[22] (In certain ways, this reads like a summary of Foucault's and perhaps Bakhtin's projects, which, however, were mainly about and for men.) Among the seemingly contradictory yet comparable exploitations to which Condit 'resubmits' are masquerade and epilepsy, which she restages as extravagant, hyperbolic spectacle, challenging the divisions of vision and the body while escaping the confines of 'discourse.'

*Beneath the Skin* (1981) opens with Condit's conversationally intimate, incredulous voice narrating: 'Let me tell you what a nightmare that *that* was. Most of the time it just feels like the news extravaganza that it was.'[23] Benjamin argued that storytellers speak of the 'circumstances' they have directly learned or 'simply pass it off as their own experience.'[24] Eliding story with the teller (raising issues of authorship), Condit's rehearsed, naive voice scales Midwest verbal registers of astonishment, stressing and elongating words like 'body,' and relates a lurid, first person account of her boyfriend's murder of his previous lover, whom he dismembered, 'mummified, decapitated, and wrapped in plastic' and stored in his apartment during his affair with her, the storyteller 'I.' The film is about 'this guy I had been seeing for the last four years, the police just found a body in his apartment . . . .' The passions of the body are rumors, gossip, and scandal; perhaps they are real, or not: 'I'd never know if he killed her or not . . . a helluva way to continue a relationship . . . .' The audience is caught off guard by off-handed comments and laughs – *The Star* as standup comedy *and* everyday life. The details of decapitation and odorous decay on the ironic sound track – 'But one of the funniest things about it . . . it came out that her head was missing' – parallels rapidly edited images of the fragmented female body, which decays in video as the corpse in the story rots. The tape goes 'beneath the skin' by traversing the 'inside/outside' of the body (a sack, a container) to reveal skeletons, aging, death; beneath surfaces to uncover horror or the 'unconscious'; beneath the romance of relationships – of the lyrics of Frank Sinatra dreamily singing 'I've got you under my skin' – to reveal beatings and murder. Perhaps these are separate but equal terrains; or they are equivalent planes of representation; or, perhaps, this is not a modern body at all which can be present only through the distance of representation but an archaic, violent, repressed body. Recurring closeups of red lips and white teeth are juxtaposed with the verbal description of the corpse's dental records. ('But the most important of all human features for the grotesque is the mouth. It dominates all else. The grotesque face is actually reduced to the gaping mouth . . . a bodily abyss': Bakhtin.[25]) Life and death, the pin-up and the coroner's report, the fetish and the fact, the beautiful and the grotesque, and the word and the image are of equal representational value.

The collision, or (in)vertical montage, of a lurid tabloid story akin to *Rear Window, Psycho,* and *Frenzy* of murder, dismemberment, and investigation (including Hitchcock's perversely comic, cannibalistic dinner-table scenes conjoined with scenes of crimes) with images of young, masquerading girls and glimpses of death, illness, and age, resembles a gyrating Möbius strip in which sound and image tracks never meet but are indissolubly connected by us in the process of enunciation – a reciprocity between author, text, and audience. As Linda Hutcheon writes in *A Theory of Parody,* parody, like Bakhtin's medieval carnival, 'exists in the self-conscious borderline between art and life, making little formal distinction between actor and spectator, between author and co-creating reader.'[26] For her, parody 'enlists the audience in contradiction' and activates 'collective participation.'[27] Depending on one's gendered experiences, the collective contradictions elicited by Condit's disarming, eye-catching work are more extreme, less appetizing, hard to swallow and even harder to digest for some viewers (mainly men) than others.

Her distinctive style involves an intricate montage which spirals and loops back, intersecting the lurid narration. Studio footage alternates with processed location shots; found black and white footage is mixed by/with video in an uncanny enunciation, placing the enounced of murder in a precarious irony. Visual delicacy, like the images of the sweet young woman, disguises *and* underscores the sensational story – is this real, is this possible, is this a fable, is this serious – or not? 'This' exemplifies contradiction – of response, of the structure of irony, of women's lives, crossing the 'self-conscious borderline between art and life.' This emphasis on process and experience in a reciprocity between speaker/listener is also central to Benjamin's valorization of the story as opposed to the novel which 'neither comes from oral tradition nor goes into it. This distinguishes it from storytelling in particular. The storyteller takes what [she] tells from experience – [her] own or that reported by others. And [she] in turn makes it the experience of those who are listening to [her] tale. The novelist has isolated himself.'[28] In this, the storyteller ('The first true storyteller is, and will continue to be, the teller of fairy tales'[29]) resembles the chronicler (rather than the contemporary historian) who is interested in interpretation rather than explanation, the terrain of the novel's narrative which has been divorced from 'the realm of living speech.' Thus, the listener has a stake not only in hearing but in remembering the story – a shared experience, a process. 'A [woman] listening to a story is in the company of the storyteller; even a [woman] reading [watching] one shares this companionship.'[30] It is this realm of interpretation via 'living speech' forged in shared experience which is intriguing for feminism and what distinguishes the work of Condit – a telling as much as a watching.

The initial and recurring visual image is an overhead, 'glamor' close-up of a young woman's face – sleeping, artifically made up and lighted. This shot is overlaid with another female face, a visual trace outlining a divided, schizophrenic subject – a complex dialogue imbricated in much feminist work. 'Call them femininity and feminism, the one is made representable by the critical work of the other; the one is kept at a distance, constructed, "framed," to be sure, and yet "respected," "loved," "given space" by the other.'[31] (In this writing, women are 'other' with/for each other rather than another, a man, and thus, a very different story.) The teller begins to identify with the murdered woman: 'I always thought that she was epileptic and I, diabetic, and I identified with her.' (Because Condit is epileptic, the status of 'I' is complicated, biographically elided with 'she.') As the tape returns to the opening shot, the dreamer/teller, self/other, voice-over/'other woman,' the dead and the living merge, taking up the question of the real and fiction, the possible and the impossible, in a double denial that, like de Lauretis's Alice riddle, reaffirms women and the story's reality: 'But it was never real, it was just a bizarre story . . . but I had this dream that it was so real. I dreamed that it was me, not her, that he killed two years ago.'

'It is characteristic that not only a man's knowledge or wisdom, but above all his real life – and this is the stuff that stories are made of – first assumes transmissable form at the moment of his death . . . . Death is the sanction of everything that the storyteller can tell. He has borrowed his authority from death.'[32] (Benjamin and Bakhtin analyze the 'modern' concealment of death with arguments remarkably similar, again, to Foucault's theses.) Like the 'he' of Benjamin's remarks, Condit takes her authority from death and goes public as few women storytellers do, speaking about violence through the forbidden terrain of femininity, with sacrilegious moments of gallows humor. This rewriting of Freudian bedtime stories as sensationalism concludes with 'And that's another story.' Like Scheherazade, Condit continues the tale two years later, this time radically revising Freud's interpretations and conclusions with a sweet-tasting vengeance and without his proper cover of 'scientific discourse' which explains and contains the hysterical, spectacular body.

*Possibly in Michigan* (1983) is a feminist musical in which the couple doesn't, continuing the deathly, stifling scenario of *Beneath the Skin* which foreshadowed the musical style of musical voices in a chanting, childlike operetta, 'gee i jo': 'Talk to us about Barbie and Ken, Barbie and Men, Ken and Men . . . . Never ends.' Both tapes reverse the classical text's heterosexual inevitability of Barbie and Ken, marriage or murder – both resolutions or 'endings' functioning as containments of the male fear of castration posed by the 'lacking' spectacle of the female body. On the contrary, Condit gleefully realizes Freud's imaginary, anxious scenario; cannibalism, an extreme extension of dismemberment, castration, and other Freudian metaphors and/or fairy tales, is the 'happy' ending.

Unlike the mainly singular storyteller of the first tape, three styles of voice alternate in this gruesomely enchanting fairy tale of female adolescence: the a cappella chorus; the sing-song dialogue/conversation between the two girl/women 'stars'; and the voice-over of Condit speaking about her characters, Sharon, Janice, and Arthur, in a conspiratorial, editorial voice no longer an 'I' but dispersed throughout the telling. This postmodern 'once upon a time' opens in a shopping mall of diffused pastels where two young women are pursued by surreal men wearing business suits and grotesque animal heads. ('The head, ears, and nose also acquire a grotesque character when they adopt the animal form . . . the eyes have no part in these comic images; they express an individual . . . not essential to the grotesque': Bakhtin.[33]) The opening lyrics of the chorus cheerily prophesy: 'I bite at the hand that feeds me, slap at the face that eats me. Some kind of animal, cannibal . . . . Animal? Cannibal?' Music sweetens the scenario which equates men with animals as the frog/prince is made literal and visible. While the mundane of shopping malls and everyday life is transformed into fantasy, the second use of the voice, a sing-song dialogue, exemplifies Condit's disarming wit: 'He has the head and it's the size of a wolf.' A deep, echoing, male voice says: 'The better to eat you with, my dear . . . . You have two choices . . . . I will cut your arms and legs off and eat them, one by one, slowly.' The female chorus intones 'Why?' He: 'For Love.' Chorus: 'Why?' He: 'For Love.' Chorus: 'But love shouldn't cost an arm and a leg.'

As Sharon, the dreamer/actant, rides down the escalator, the third style of voice, Condit's voice, discusses women and violence, the complex concern beneath the veneer of fairy tales, of her work, and of women's 'private' lives: 'Sharon attracted violent men. She had a way of making the violence seem as if it was their idea. Her friend, Janice, was cut from the same mold.' This frank, disconcerting analysis reiterates a line from *Beneath the Skin*: 'I realize that if I courted violence more, I might get myself seriously hurt.' In that tape she laughs, reminding me of the opening laugh of Sally Potter's 1979 film, *Thriller*, a laugh which occurs in blackness before the white of the first image, a laugh in concert with an aria of death. As Herbert Blau writes: 'that seeming remembrance of/in laughter which is a mnemonic stoppage of breath. It is the mystery of the interruption which preserves something tragic in comedy, since it seems a synopsis of death . . . . Which is to say that *meaning stops for that moment*, as if in homage to more than meaning . . . .' Violence is always more or less than meaning, Condit's art and laughter are 'synopses of death,' stopped, as if gasping, by laughter; 'when laughter comes the meaning is deadly, or there's just no meaning at all.'[34]

The posing, giggling girls/women are from *Beneath the Skin*, including the raven-haired, sleeping/decaying beauty surrounded by red roses. Unlike the earlier tape, this story's violence exists more on the image track with sound as an ironic chorus or commentator: 'Arthur longed for that sexual scent that smelled like home . . . he had used so many masks to disguise himself that he had forgotten who he was. He imagined himself a frog transformed into a Prince Charming. He felt the moment he kissed her, he would become the man she wanted him to be.' This frog/prince inversion of Lacan's female masquerade as carnival follows the imaginary intrusion of domestic life, reality amid the colors of fantasy. Janice, her friend, races to Sharon's house, rescues her, and shoots Arthur. These gossamer girls, together again, cook, eat, and toss Arthur's remains into the garbage after sharing Arthur with their dog, a girl's best friend. Hacking the body into stew meat is a comic parody, a shared act of intimacy, and grotesque equation of the body with food. This grizzly meal concludes with the innocent, satisfied 'girls,' presumably naked, made up, smoking cigarettes, and coughing in a delightfully perverse, soft-focus rendering of adolescent friendship and misbehavior. The tape concludes with the 'real' garbage man and truck picking up the garbage or prince, accompanied by 'natural' sound as the credits roll in this 'reality.'

This sensational remake of Freud, which fragments and fetishizes the female body while dismantling oedipal narratives, does indeed have conflicting effects on audiences, inverting Freud's analysis of the uncanny as an experience, a frightening effect which hinges on two figures – loss of the eyes and dismemberment – and which involves a discrepancy between the 'incredible' and the 'possible.'[35] (It is important to 'remember' that this essay depicts the dismembered, spectacular body – that 'animistic' body of yore which is not fully contained by Freud's discourse, dependent as his argument is on uncertainty.) Epilepsy and the beautiful female automaton create 'doubts whether an apparently animate being is really alive; or conversely, whether a lifeless object might not be in fact animate.' Freud's fear of confusing the biological with the technological, the real with its simulation (a model and an essay which fits Fritz Lang's *Metropolis* like a historical glove) suggests that the 'uncanny' is the precursor (or the repressed) of Baudrillard's simulacrum which, unlike Freud, skirts the castration it fears with the loss of the real, referents, and mastery. This notion of the 'double' becomes, for Freud and Condit, 'a harbinger of death.'[36] Condit's beautiful faces decay, dissolving into eyeless skulls; her narratives detail the dismemberment which Freud feared and analyzed: 'the substitutive relation between the eye and the male organ which is seen to exist in dreams and myths and phantasies . . . the threat of being castrated is what first gives the idea of losing other organs its intense colouring.'[37] Cannibalism, not only the losing but the devouring of 'other organs,' is an 'intense colouring' of Freud's book. *Possibly in Michigan* is a serious and amusing challenge to the 'relation between the eye and the male organ,' a personal, historical, and recent equation certainly not 'substitutive' in 'women's dreams and myths and phantasies.'

The fear of/defense against castration is also elicited by what Freud labels 'the Medusa effect,' a tactic which produces the very image which is feared for protection – yet another Freudian trope literalized in *Possibly in Michigan* in a shot of the masked man picking up a rock revealing a skull crawling with snakes which he throws through Sharon's window; it lands on her bed. The Medusa effect is reiterated in a close-up of worms/snakes crawling over a photograph of Sharon. These special effects 'serve actually as a mitigation of the horror, for they replace the penis, the absence of which is the cause of the horror.' Freud seriously goes on to say: 'This is a confirmation of the technical rule according to which a multiplication of penis symbols signifies castration.'[38] (No wonder Hélène Cixous's Medusa is laughing! This reads as if Freud were writing directions for a Milton & Bradley board game, or better, a television game show. I can hear the referee's admonition: 'You lose ten points on a technical rule: no multiplication of penis symbols.' With the elevation of the phallus as the dominant signifier, Lacan was the big winner on 'Jeopardy.')

Condit's Medusa scene, like the images of epilepsy and the automated doll-like women, takes Freud at his word; however, her Medusa effect portends violence to women and rape rather than or before castration. Because of this, she breaks Freud's crucial rule by not symbolizing disavowal but joyously 'performing' dismemberment, turning the imaginary scenario of the Oedipus complex into the conclusion of cannibalism and female friendship – uniting women in an ending and relationship that classical texts have avoided and contained. It's as if the two women of *Beneath the Skin*, like Mimi and Musetta of Puccini's *La Bohème*, then Potter's *Thriller*, joined forces and refused their murder by seemingly but perversely playing by, then inverting or rewriting the rules and kicking Oedipus out of the narrative. As Benjamin suggests, 'The wisest thing – so the fairytale taught mankind . . . is to meet the forces of the mythological world with cunning and high spirits.' The mythological world of Freud is met by Sharon, Janice, and Cecelia, a creative trio – 'with high spirits and cunning,' living 'happily ever after' so that Scheherazade, speaking to/with women, will continue this trilogy in *Not a Jealous Bone* concerning an old woman, another fairy-tale figure which Condit imagines in her off-center way.

'In every case the storyteller is a [woman] who has counsel for [her] readers. But if today "having counsel" is beginning to have an old-fashioned ring, this is because the communicability of experience is decreasing . . . . After all, counsel is less an answer to a question than a proposal concerning the continuation of a story which is just unfolding.'[39] Unlike all the recent declarations of the death of feminism because completed, old-hat, a failure, or a mistake, the public, artistic formulation of female subjects, desires, pleasures, and peculiarities continues to 'unfold' fifty years after Benjamin's words; the 'communicability' of women's private experiences is going massively, transgressively public. Cecilia Condit, just an 'old-fashioned girl' but what a wickedly clever one, is giving us counsel, making outrageous proposals, with laughter from the audience signaling possibilities. After all, without his cloak of invisibility, the prince doesn't stand a chance.

*Could you imagine a world of women only,*
the interviewer asked. *Can you imagine*

*a world where women are absent.* (He believed
he was joking.) Yet I have to imagine

at one and the same moment, both. Because
I live in both. *Can you imagine,*

the interviewer asked, *a world of men?*
(He thought he was joking.) *If so, then,*

*a world where men are absent?*

Adrienne Rich[40]

## Notes

1. Walter Benjamin, 'The Storyteller. Reflections on the Works of Nikolai Leskov', *Illuminations* (New York, Collins Fontann, 1973), p. 92.
2. Sigmund Freud. 'The "Uncanny"', *Standard Edition*, **18**, p. 252.
3. Brothers Grimm, *Grimms' Fairy Tales*, trans. Mrs E. V. Lucas, Lucy Crane and Marian Edwards (New York, Grosset & Dunlap, 1945), pp. 1–6.
4. Anne Sexton, 'The Twelve Dancing Princesses.' from *Transformations* (1971); collected in *The Complete Poems* (Boston, MA, Houghton Mifflin, 1981), p. 281.
5. I am referring to the essays by, for example, Hal Foster and Andreas Huyssen in *New German Critique* and Craig Owens in *The Anti-Aesthetic*, ed. H. Foster (Port Townsend, WA, Bay Press, 1983).
6. Lawrence Stone, 'Only Women', *New York Review of Books*, 32:6 (11 April 1985), p. 21.
7. Raymond Durgnat, 'Amazing Grace', *American Film*, **11**: (January–February 1986), p. 35.
8. Dick, Hebdige, 'Posing . . . Threats, Striking . . . Poses. Youth, Surveillance, and Display', *Substance*, 37/38 (1983), pp. 85, 86. I have collapsed remarks from several paragraphs in this very interesting essay concerning youth subcultures – a topic which overlaps to a vague degree Condit's concern with adolescence or moments of passage, and an area or approach which can be applied fruitfully to the 'subcultures' of the art scene, including avant-garde, independent filmmaking.
9. Mary Russo, 'Female Grotesques'. 'Carnival and Theory', from her manuscript for Teresa de Lauretis, ed., *Feminist Studies/Critical Studies*, IN, (Bloomington Indiana University Press, 1986).
10. Perhaps more than other divides, for example, between art and mass culture, the gap between men and women is the one that needs to be acknowledged, a division enhanced by sexual difference as the kingpin difference. As de Lauretis

wrote in *Alice Doesn't* (Bloomington, IN, Indiana University Press, 1984) 'It may well be, however, that the story has to be told differently. Take Oedipus, for instance.' I love the timing of the last sentence, p. 156.

11. My essay 'Postmodern TV: Wegmar and Smith' (*Afterimage* [US], Dec. 1985) details a model of postmodernism as it relates to video and feminism.

12. Hal Foster, 'The "Primitive" Unconscious of Modern Art', *October*, 34 (1985), pp. 64, 65, 69. This last reference is comparable to other marginal allusions to feminism – for 'feminists', for 'minorities,' for 'tribal peoples.' Taxonomy is not innocent, no matter how qualified by quotations.

13. Mary Ann Doane, Patricia Mellencamp and Linda Williams, 'Feminist Film Criticism. An Introduction'; *Re-Vision. Essays in Feminist Film Criticism* (Los Angeles: The American Film Institute; Frederick, Maryland: University Publications of America, 1984), p. 15.

14. Teresa de Lauretis, 'Aesthetic and Feminist Theory. Rethinking Women's Cinema', *New German Critique*, 34 (Winter 1985), pp. 164, 168.

15. Fredric Jameson, 'Postmodernism and Consumer Society', in Foster, *The Anti-Aesthetic*, p. 125.

16. Roland Barthes, 'Change the Object Itself. Mythology Today', *Image-Music-Text* (London: Fontana, 1977), pp. 167–168. This short, five-page essay is an update of Barthes's earlier work on mythology – the latter, cited by Foster.

17. De Lauretis, *Alice Doesn't*, p. 186. The end of this book, like that of the classical Hollywood film, circles back to the beginning: 'In the heart of Looking-Glass country, between her fifth and sixth moves across the chessboard, Alice comes to the centre of the labyrinth of language,' p. 1.

18. Anne Sexton, 'Briar Rose (Sleeping Beauty)'; *The Complete Poems*, p. 293.

19. Russo, 'Female Grotesques.'

20. Mikhail Bakhtin, *Rabelais and His World*, trans. Helene Iswolksy (Bloomington: Indiana University Press, 1984), pp. 317–318.

21. Mary Russo, 'Female Grotesques',

22. Quoted from Russo, 'Female Grotesques'.

23. I transcribed the videotapes and hope the quotations are accurate.

24. Benjamin, 'The Storyteller', p. 92.

25. M. L Bakhtin, '*Rabelais and His World*', p. 317.

26. Linda Hutcheon, *A Theory of Parody* (New York, Methuen, 1985); p. 72. Her chapter 'The Paradox of Parody', pp. 69–83, discusses Bakhtin's writings, taking issue with his negative regard toward modern parody, what she calls 'his rejection of the contemporary.' Thus Hutcheon argues (p. 71) that 'we should look to what the theories suggest, rather than what the practice denies . . . .'

27. Hutcheon, *A Theory of Parody*, pp. 92, 99.

28. Benjamin 'The Storyteller', p. 87.

29. Benjamin, 'The Storyteller'. p. 102.

30. Benjamin, 'The Storyteller', p. 100.

31. De Lauretis, 'Aesthetic and Feminist Theory', p. 160.

32. Benjamin, 'The Storyteller', p. 94.

33. Bakhtin, *Rabelais and His World*, p. 316.

34. Herbert Blau, ('Comedy since the Absurd', *Modern Drama*, 25(4): (December 1982), pp. 555, 556.

35. Freud, 'The "Uncanny"', p. 250.

36. Freud, 'The "Uncanny"', p. 235.

37. Freud, 'The "Uncanny"', p. 231.

38. Sigmund Freud, 'Medusa's Head', *Standard Edition*, 18, p. 273.

39. Benjamin, 'The Storyteller', p. 86.

40. Adrienne Rich, 'Natural Resources', *The Dream of a Common Language* (New York, Norton, 1978), p. 61.

# 23

## That moment of emergence

*Pratibha Parmar*

From M. Gever, P. Parmar and J. Greyson (eds), *Queer looks. Perspectives on lesbian and gay film and video* (Routledge 1993)

> To be a lesbian means engaging in a complex, often treacherous, system of cultural identities, representations and institutions, and a history of sexual regulation . . . . Being a lesbian tests the meanings of sexual identity in ways that evoke intense, sometimes violent, social disapproval, while being straight is taken for granted as a neutral position from which gay folks deviate.
> Martha Gever[1]

> For me being a lesbian is not only a fight against homophobia and the kind of homophobia we face everyday, but it's also a fight against the system that creates that ... a class system as well as a system that is imperialist. It's a system that's responsible for the incidences of racism that all of my family and all of the people I know of Asian and African descent have had to go through in all of the Western countries, and I think it's critical that we come together and bring all these experiences together and actually reach beyond ourselves . . . .
> Punam Khosla[2]

To be an artist, a lesbian and a woman of color engaged in mapping out our visual imaginations is both exciting and exhausting. The creative upsurge in black women and women of color's cultural production in Britain has not been given the spotlight and visibility that it deserves. Women of color have been organizing and creating communities which have inspired a new sense of collective identity, and it is only through our own efforts that we have ensured against our erasure as artists and cultural producers.

I don't think that this is because of a mere oversight or even deliberate conspiracy. I think it is much more to do with the persistence of a fantasy of what constitutes an authentic national culture, a fantasy which posits what and who is English. The dominance of the ideology of English ethnicity, although deeply ingrained in the cultural canons of British society and arts institutions, is and has been challenged by black artists and cultural producers through our work. We have been changing the very heart of what constitutes Englishness by recoding it with our diasporan sensibilities. Our ancestral as well as personal experiences of migration, dispersal, and dislocation give us an acute sense of the limitations of national identities. Some of us claim an English as well as a British identity, and in so doing transform the very terrain of Englishness and expose the ruptures in the discourses of white supremacy. The fact that British national culture is heterogeneous and ethnically differentiated is something that still needs hammering home to those who are persistent in their view that to be black and British is an anachronism. Our visual outpourings are our referents for our 'imagined communities' and utopian visions, which we seek to articulate and live and work towards.

By reflecting on my own working practices as a filmmaker and video artist, and in unfolding my personal and historical context, I hope to be able to contribute to the ongoing development of a general theoretical framework for discussing the cultural and political significance of black arts in postcolonial Britain.[3] It is a framework which differs from previous forms of cultural critiques because of the ways in which it seeks to centralize the black subjectivity and our experiences of difference. The more we assert our own identities as historically marginalized groups, the more we expose the tyranny of a so-called center.

I came into making videos and films from a background in political activism and cultural practice, and not from film school or art school. As an Asian woman I have never considered myself as somebody's 'other,' nor have I seen myself as 'marginal' to an ubiquitous, unchanging, monolithic 'center.' But since my arrival in England in the mid-sixties, it has been a constant challenge and struggle to defy those institutions and cultural canons which seek repeatedly to make me believe that because of my visible difference as an Asian woman I am an 'other' and therefore 'marginal.'

There is a particular history that informs the thematic concerns of my work as much as my aesthetic sensibilities. That history is about a forced migration to an England that is intensely xenophobic and insular, an England that is so infused with outdated notions of itself as the Mother Country for its ex-colonial subjects that it refuses to look at the ashes of its own images as a decaying nation, let alone a long-dead empire.

When my family, like many other Indian families, arrived in Britain in the mid-sixties, anti-black feelings were running high and 'Paki-bashing' was a popular sport amongst white youths. It was in the school playground that I first encountered myself as an undesirable alien, objectified in the frame of 'otherness.' All those of us perceived as 'marginal,' 'peripheral,' and the 'other' know what it is like to be defined by someone else's reality and often someone else's psychosis.

> We can read ourselves against another people's pattern, but since it is not ours . . . we emerge as its effects, its errata, its counternarratives. Whenever we try to narrate ourselves, we appear as dislocations in their discourse.
>
> Edward Said[4]

I do not speak from a position of marginalization but more crucially from the resistance to that marginalization. As a filmmaker, it is important for me to reflect upon the process through which I constantly negotiate the borderlines between shifting territories . . . between the margin and the center . . . between inclusion and exclusion . . . between visibility and invisibility. For example, as lesbians and gays of color, we have had to constantly negotiate and challenge the racism of the white gay community, and at the same time confront the homophobia of communities of color.

What we have been seeing in recent years is the development of a new politics of difference which states that we are not interested in defining ourselves in relation to someone else or something else, nor are we simply articulating our cultural and sexual differences. This is not a unique position, but one that is shared by many cultural activists and critics on both sides of the Atlantic. We are creating a sense of ourselves and our place within different and sometimes contradictory communities, not simply in relation to . . . not in opposition to . . . nor in reversal to . . . nor as a corrective to . . . but in and for ourselves. Precisely because of our lived experiences of racism and homophobia, we locate ourselves not within any one community but in the spaces between these different communities.

Toni Morrison was once asked why she wrote the books that she did, and she replied that these were the books she wanted to read. In some ways, the reason why I make the films and videos that I do is also because they are the kinds of films and videos I would like to see: films and videos that engage with the creation of images of ourselves as women, as people of color and as lesbians and gays; images that evoke passionate stirrings and that enable us to construct ourselves in our complexities. I am also interested in making work that documents our stories and celebrates and validates our existence to ourselves and our communities. As a lesbian I have searched in vain for images of lesbians of color on the screen but I very quickly realized that they exist only in my own imagination, so one of my aims as a filmmaker is to begin to compile that repertoire of images of ourselves. The joy, the passion and desire embodied in our lives is as important to highlight and nourish as are the struggles against racism and homophobia. Desire for me is expressed sexually, but also in a need to recreate communities which are affirming and strengthening.

Experiences of migration and displacement, and the need to make organic links between race and sexuality, guide my desire to create works that throw up the contradictions of being 'queer' and Asian. Images of Asian women in the British media have their root in the heyday of the British empire. The commonsense racist ideas about Asian women's sexuality have been determined by racist patriarchal ideologies. On the one hand we are seen as sexually erotic and exotic creatures full of oriental promise, and on the other as sari-clad women who are dominated by their men, as oppressed wives or mothers breeding prolifically and colorizing the British landscape.

The idea that many of us have our own self-defined sexuality is seen as subversive and threatening by the dominant white society in which we live, as well as by the majority of the Asian community. Within our communities our existence as lesbians and gays continues to be denied or is dismissed as a by-product of corrupting Western influences. In fact many of us are internal exiles within our own communities. This is despite the fact that there is an ancient history of homosexuality in India predating the Western history of homosexuality. This history is only now being uncovered by Indian lesbian and gay historians.

Unique to the British context has been the use of the word 'black,' which was mobilized as a political definition for peoples of African, Asian, and Afro-Caribbean descent. As different ethnic groups use 'people of color' in

North America, so in Britain a political alliance was formed using the word black. This united us in a fragile alliance against racism, since we experienced British institutional racism in very similar ways. However, in recent years this strategic use has lost its currency as questions of ethnic difference and national identities begin to take primacy.

The mid-1980s have seen a new generation of video artists and filmmakers emerging from the different black communities in Britain. This growth of independent film and video cultures has shown that there are many of us working not only to challenge harmful images but also to construct a whole new language of visual representation. Instead of allowing our marginality to impose a silence on us, we are actively engaged in making videos and films that have begun to redefine and recast notions of 'mainstream,' 'difference,' and 'otherness.'

It is important to create and proclaim assertive and empowering images which question and unsettle the dominant discourses of representation of people who are not white, male, and heterosexual, but it is equally important to move beyond the merely oppositional. Interrupting the discourses of dominant media with a strong counterdiscourse or corrective is sometimes necessary and has been an effective strategy used by some black filmmakers in Britain, particularly in the early 1970s. But one of the dangers with this has been the way in which perceptions of the black communities as a homogeneous group have been reinforced. Differences of class, culture, ethnicity, sexuality, and gender became subjugated, and the black communities were represented as an undifferentiated mass. Diversity, the multiplicity of our histories, experiences, and identities were reduced to 'typical' and 'representative' stereotypes.

My personal and political history of involvement in the antiracist movement in the mid-seventies, in feminism, and in lesbian and gay initiatives has given me the grounding for my work in film and video in many fundamental ways.

The development of cultural studies in the mid-eighties has been an important theoretical influence on my work as a filmmaker, and on the work of many other black filmmakers. As a postgraduate student at the Centre for Contemporary Cultural Studies at the University of Birmingham in the early eighties, I was involved with a group of students in writing and publishing the book, *The Empire Strikes Back: Race and Racism in 70s Britain*.[5] Our project was to examine the everyday lived experiences of black British people as culture. We developed critiques of the paradigms of race relations which had consistently pathologized black cultures and communities. We also critiqued white feminist theory and practice which did not acknowledge or grapple with the power dynamics around race and class. We rejected their Eurocentric bias and put forward our own analysis. We were the new generation that saw ourselves as both black and British, and, unlike the dominant communities, we did not see a contradiction between these two terms. Our alternative discourse around issues of race, gender, national identity, sexual identity, and culture marked a turning point. We, the children of postcolonial migrant citizens, were indeed striking back with no punches pulled.

As one of the founding members of the first black lesbian group in Britain in 1984, it was invigorating finally to find a community of lesbians of color where we could talk about our common experiences of racism and isolation within the white lesbian and feminist community, as well as share cultural similarities and a sense of integration. The collective empowerment that came as a result of this coming together was also crucial for our political visibility. The key point here was that my experiences as a woman, as a lesbian, and as an Asian person were not compartmentalized or seen as mutually exclusive; instead it was the ways in which I/we located ourselves within and between these differing subjectivities that gave us a sense of integration. This was against the duality that was constantly being either self-imposed or externally imposed upon us, so that the much-asked question of whether we were going to prioritize our race over our sexuality was made redundant. This claim to an integrated identity was a strategic claim inasmuch as many of us found political empowerment in a collective group identity and a heightening of our consciousness. Of course, in due course many of us also realized that 'there is no real me to return to, no whole self that synthesizes the woman, the woman of color, and the (writer or the artist or the lesbian). There are, instead, diverse recognitions of self through difference, and unfinished, contingent, arbitrary closures that make possible both politics and identity.'[6]

It was only in the late eighties that a rigorous critique of an 'identity politics' was initiated, attempting to prioritize or create hierarchies of oppression. This revealed some extremely useful and positive insights, namely, that it is the constant negotiating between these identities that provides the framework for our cultural and political practice. Secondly, identities are not fixed in time and space, but what is valuable is the multiplicity of our experiences as lesbians of color, as women and as black people. June Jordan, the black American poet, writer, and political activist, has said, 'We should try to measure each other on the basis of what we do for each other rather than on the basis of who we are.'[7]

Indeed, some of the insights about the fluctuating nature of identities and a critique of identity politics have been pioneered and initiated by black feminists and feminists of color, and subsequently incorporated into writings on black cultural production.[8]

The choices I have made about what themes or issues to highlight in my work have also been about timing, funding, and how particular political moments have thrown up urgent issues. For example, I made the video *ReFraming AIDS* in the summer of 1987, when there were concerted and massive attacks both at the local and national level against lesbian and gay rights in Britain. This was at a time when the first government media campaign on AIDS fuelled existing antigay prejudices by representing AIDS as a gay plague. The antigay blacklash was vehement, and through the video I wanted to create a space where different lesbians and gays could talk about the content of that backlash, for instance showing how black lesbians and gay men were being affected specifically around immigration and policing, and how AIDS was being used to further restrict the entry of black people into the country. By intercutting the government media ads with images and voices from the lesbian and gay communities, I also attempted to subvert the dominant images of the disease by linking ideas about racial difference, social difference, and sexuality in an historical context. The filmmaker Stuart

Marshall was instrumental in allowing me to make these historical connections within the video.

One of the responses to my making *ReFraming AIDS* was that of surprise. What was I, an Asian lesbian, doing making a video about AIDS that did not have just black women's voices, but also the voices of black and white men? Why had I dared to cross the boundaries of race and gender? Underlying this criticism was the idea that, as an Asian lesbian filmmaker, my territory should be proscribed and limited to my very specific identities, and to my 'own' communities.

It is such experiences that have reinforced my criticism of an essentialist identity politics as being divisive, exclusionary, and retrogressive. I would assert that our territories should be as broad as we choose. Without doubt we still need categories of self-enunciation, but we need them in a political and theoretical discourse on identity which gives us the space for the diversity of our imaginations and visions.

While it is crucial to acknowledge Stuart Hall's valuable insight that 'it is important to recognize that we all speak from a particular place, out of particular experiences, histories and cultures,' for me it is equally important that we are not constrained and contained by those positions . . . by fixed identity tags . . . that we do not get caught up in an essentialist 'bantustan'[9] that decrees that you do not cross boundaries of your experiences. Such prescriptive thinking can be both creatively and politically stultifying.

One of my concerns as a filmmaker is to challenge the normalizing and universalizing tendencies within the predominantly white lesbian and gay communities – to assert the diversity of cultural and racial identities within the umbrella category of gay and lesbian. There is a need also to redefine 'community,' and just as there isn't a homogeneous black community, similarly there isn't a monolithic lesbian and gay community.

In my video *Memory Pictures*, and my films *Flesh and Paper* and *Khush*, I interrogate Asian gay and lesbian identities in ways which point to the complexities that we occupy as lesbians and gays of color. I explore our histories of diaspora, the memories of migration and upheaval, the search for an integration of our many selves, and the celebration of 'us,' our differences, and our eroticisms.

It is a condition of these postmodernist times that we all live heterogeneous realities, constructing our sense of selves through the hybridity of cultural practices, and this is inevitably reflected in the aesthetic form employed in my work. The form itself needs to be interrogated as much as the content, and by using a combination of styles and narratives – for instance, documentary realism, poetry, dramatic reconstructions, experimental, autobiographical – I attempt to enunciate the nuances of our subjectivities in my work. Furthermore, the influences of the mass media and popular culture inevitably find their way into the work in a self-conscious way. The four-minute video, *Bhangra Jig*, commissioned by Channel Four as a 'television intervention' piece to celebrate Glasgow as the cultural capital of Europe for 1991, borrows unashamedly from advertising codes and pop promos.

In the film *Khush*, which I made for Channel Four's lesbian and gay series *Out on Tuesday*, one of my strategies was to use a diverse range of visual modes. So, for instance, my reworking of a classical dance sequence from an old Indian popular film utilizes the strategy of disrupting the given heterosexual codes. In the original film, the female dancer's act is intercut with a male gaze, but for *Khush* I reedited this sequence and took out the male gaze. I reused this sequence with scenarios of two Asian women watching and enjoying this dance. The gaze and the spectator became inverted. Clearly, postmodernist interest in reworking available material gives us an opportunity to use strategies of appropriation as an assault on racism, sexism, and homophobia. It is these politicized appropriations of dominant codes and signifying systems which give us powerful weapons in the struggle for empowerment.

This hybrid aesthetic, as it has come to be known, works with and against the 'tools of the master' because these are tools which we, as cultural activists and artists, have appropriated and reformulated with our diasporic imaginations. In *Bhangra Jig* this was precisely my aim: to allude to Glasgow's history as the second biggest city of the British empire, as reflected in the city's architectural signs and symbols. At the same time I juxtapose against these memories of colonial carnage the vibrancy of our cultures of resistance: Bhangra music and dance as signifying practices of Asian youth culture, crossovers of reggae, soul, and traditional agrarian Indian music and dance. For *Bhangra Jig* to be shown several times within one week on British TV (known for its history of stereotyping and the invisibility of self-determined imagery of Asian people) not only disrupts dominant ideas of European culture but also offers new meanings of what constitute national cultures and identities.

Just as much as I distance myself from any notion of an essentialist lesbian or black aesthetic, so, too, do I reject the idea that I am forever relegated to the confines of an outsider looking in. Lesbians of color around the world are asserting our visions through film and video, and our creative efforts can only but grow in the twenty-first century as the map continues to be redrawn with our imaginations.

## Notes

1. Martha Gever, 'The Names We Give Ourselves', in Russell Ferguson et al., eds, *Out There Marginalization and Contemporary Cultures* (Cambridge/New York, MIT Press and the New Museum of Contemporary Art, 1990), p. 191.
2. Punam Khosla, speaking in the film *Khush*, by Pratibha Parmar, made for Channel Four's lesbian and gay series *Out on Tuesday*, 1991.
3. See the writings of Stuart Hall, Paul Gilroy, Kobena Mercer, Lubaina Himid, and the journal *Third Text*.
4. Edward Said, *After the Last. Sky Palestinian Lives* (New York, Pantheon, 1986).
5. Centre for Contemporary Cultural Studies, *The Empire Strikes Back Race and Racism in 70s Britain* (London, Hutchinson, 1982).
6. 'Woman, Native, Other Pratibha Parmar Interviews Trinh T. Minh-ha', *Feminist Review*, **36** (Autumn 1990), p. 73.
7. Pratibha Parmar, 'Other Kinds of Dreams An Interview with June Jordan', *Feminist Review*, **31** (Spring 1989), p. 63.
8. See Barbara Christian, 'The Race for Theory', *Feminist Studies*, 4: 1 (1988), S. Grewal et al., eds, *Charting the Journey Writings by Black and Third World Women*

(London, Sheba Feminist Publishers, 1987); Pratibha Parmar, 'Black Feminism The Politics of Articulation', in Jonathan Rutherford, ed., *Identity Community, Culture, Difference* (London, Lawrence & Wishart, 1990), pp. 101–26.
9. I thank Trinh T. Minh-ha for voicing this very apt analogy.

# About the contributors

**Jean Baudrillard** was Professor of Sociology at the University of Paris, X, Nanterre between 1966 and 1988. His writings, in translation, include *The Mirror of Production* (1975), *Symbolic Exchange and Death* (1993) and *The Illusion of the End* (1994). A volume of *Selected Writings*, ed. Mark Poster, was published in 1988.

**Scott Bukatman** is the author of articles on cyberculture and virtual textuality and of *Terminal Identity. The Virtual Subject in Postmodern Science Fiction* (1993).

**Jim Collins** is Associate Professor of Communication and English and Director of Film and Television Studies at the University of Notre Dame. He is the author of *Uncommon Cultures. Popular Culture and Postmodernism* (1989), *Architectures of Excess. Cultural Life in the Information Age* (1995) and co-editor of *Film Theory Goes to the Movies* (1993).

**Barbara Creed** teaches Cinema Studies in the Department of Fine Arts, Melbourne University. She has lectured and published widely in the areas of cinema, cultural studies and feminism and is author of *The Monstrous Feminine. Film, Feminism and Psychoanalysis* (1993).

**Umberto Eco** is Professor of Semiotics at the University of Bologna and contributes a regular newspaper column to *L'Espresso*. His writings include *Travels in Hyperreality* (1987), *Limits of Interpretation* (1990) and *Apocalypse Postponed* (1994) as well as the novels *The Name of the Rose* (1980) and *Islands of the Day Before* (1995).

**Marie Gillespie** is a lecturer in the Department of Sociology and Anthropology at the University of Wales, Swansea. She is the author of *Television Ethnicity and Cultural Change* (1995) and of numerous articles on issues of media and ethnicity. She is currently researching in diasporic media, cross-cultural consumption and appropriation.

**David Harvey** is the Halford Mackfinder Professor of Geography at Oxford University. He is the author of *The Urban Experience* (1985) and *Social Justice and the City* (1988) and *The Condition of Postmodernity* (1989).

**Linda Hutcheon** is Professor of English and Comparative Literature at the University of Toronto and the author of a number of studies on postmodernism including *The Politics of Postmodernism* (1989). Her latest work is *Irony's Edge. The Theory and Politics of Irony* (1994).

**Fredric Jameson** is Distinguished Professor of Comparative Literature at Duke University where he is Director of the Graduate Program in Literature and the Center for Cultural Theory. His works include *The Political Unconscious* (1981), *Late Marxism* (1990), *Postmodernism, or, the Cultural Logic of Late Capitalism* (1991) and *The Seeds of Time* (1994).

**Lynne Joyrich** is Associate Professor and Co-ordinator of English and Comparative Literature at the University of Wisconsin-Milwaukee, and is the author of a number of recent journal articles on feminism, postmodernism, TV and film.

**E. Ann Kaplan** is Professor of English and Comparative Studies and Director of the Humanities Institute at the State University of New York at Stony Brook. She is the author of *Women and Film* (1983) and editor of *Regarding Televison. Critical Approaches* (1983) and *Pyschoanalysis and Cinema* (1990). A volume called *Motherhood and Representation. Maternity Discourse in Popular Culture* is forthcoming.

**Douglas Kellner** is Professor of Philosophy at the University of Texas at Austin. He is the author of a number of works on social theory and the media, including *From Marxism to Postmodernism and Beyond. Critical Studies of Jean Baudrillard* (1989) and *Television and the Crisis of Democracy* (1990), and is co-editor (with Michael Ryan) of *Camera Politica. The Politics and Ideology of Hollywood Films* (1988).

**Marshall McLuhan** taught at the Centre for Culture and Technology at the University of Toronto and at various other Canadian and American universities. His studies of the human and cultural effects of the media of communication include *The Gutenberg Galaxy* (1962), *Understanding Media* (1964) and, with Quentin Fiore, *The Medium is the Massage* (1967) and *War and Peace in the Global Village* (1968).

**Patricia Mellencamp** is Associate Professor of Art History at the University of Wisconsin-Milwaukee. She is editor of *Logics of Television* (1990) and author of *Indiscretions. Avant-Garde Film Video and Television* (1990).

**Kobena Mercer** teaches in the Art History and History of Consciousness Departments, University of California, Santa Cruz. He is the author of *Welcome to the Jungle. New Positions in Black Cultural Studies* (1994).

**Christopher Norris** is Professor of English at University College, Cardiff. He is the author of several works on deconstruction and postmodernism, including *Jacques Derrida* (1987) and *What's Wrong with Postmodernism?* (1990).

**Pratibha Parmar** is a writer and independent film- and video-maker. Her films include *Khush, Sari Red, A Place of Rage* and *Double the Trouble, Twice the Fun*.

**Vivian Sobchack** is Assistant Dean in the School of Theatre, Film and Televsion at the University of California, Los Angeles. She is author of *Screening Space. The American Science Fiction Film* (1993) and editor of *The Persistence of History. Cinema, Television and the Modern Event* (1996).

**Peter Wollen** is Professor of Film at the University of California, Los Angeles. He is an independent film-maker as well as author. His writings include *Signs and Meanings in the Cinema* (1972), *Readings and Writings* (1982) and *Raiding the Ice Box. Reflections on Twentieth-Century Culture* (1993).

## The Editors

**Peter Brooker** is Professor of Modern Literature and Culture at Nene College, Northampton. He is the editor of *Modernism/Postmodernism* (1992) and author of *New York Fictions* (1995).

**Will Brooker** is researching and teaching at the Tom Hopkinson Centre for Cultural Studies at the University of Wales at Cardiff.

# Index: of names and titles